# Issues
# for a
# Catholic Bioethic

Proceedings of the International Conference
to celebrate the Twentieth Anniversary
of the foundation of The Linacre Centre
28–31 July 1997

Edited by

## Luke Gormally

London – The Linacre Centre

Published by The Linacre Centre
60 Grove End Road, London NW8 9NH

*British Library Cataloguing in Publication Data*

A catalogue record for this book is available from
the British Library

ISBN 0 906561 09 4

Typeset by Academic and Technical, Bristol
Printed and bound by Redwood Books, Trowbridge, Wiltshire

In memory of
David Williams CBE MA
Founder Director of The Linacre Centre (1977–1980)
and subsequently a member of its Governing Body (1983–1988)
and of
John Utting MA MB ChB FRCA
Emeritus Professor of Anaesthesia, University of Liverpool,
Governor of the Centre (1984–1996) and
Chairman of its Governing Body (1989–1994):
two generous servants and friends of the Centre
and
two good friends of the Editor

# Contents

# I

# Introduction

LUKE GORMALLY

THIS VOLUME contains all the invited papers and a small selection of submitted papers given at the International Conference held at Queens' College, Cambridge, in July 1997 to celebrate the twentieth anniversary of the foundation of The Linacre Centre. The Centre was established in the summer of 1977 by a Trust of which the Trustees were (and are) the five Roman Catholic Metropolitan Arch-bishops of England and Wales. The general purpose of the Trust is to help, both directly and indirectly, Catholics working in the fields of healthcare and biomedi-cal research to confront the ethical issues which arise in their professional work in the light of the Church's teaching of moral truth. The help required is in part that of elucidating moral truths which may be obscured by the dominant moral culture of our society, in part that of exploring the implications of those truths for practical reflection and choice in face of new ethical issues arising from developments in clinical practice and biomedical research. Hence, the Centre established by the Trust is committed to programmes of study, research and publication, of teaching, and of service to and collaboration with other bodies with similar aims. Given the Catholic character of the Centre, it seemed appropriate to celebrate its first twenty years of existence by inviting a distinguished international group of speakers to address some of the issues which a specifically Catholic engagement with the field of bioethics must confront.

Cardinal Winning's Opening Address to the Conference observes that The Linacre Centre has sought to contribute both to ethical reflection within the Church and to public policy debates within society. In both kinds of undertaking our work has been informed by the Church's teaching of moral truth. The Gospel of salvation which the Church has been commissioned to proclaim is the 'good news' of our being enabled through God's mercy to live in accordance with the truth which makes us free (*John* 8:32). Christianity is in the business of helping us to 'Choose life' in face of the choice between life and death (*Deuteron-omy* 30:19). Hence, teaching about the kinds of choice which make for human flourishing and the kinds which undermine and can ultimately destroy our abil-ity to flourish is an integral part of the evangelical teaching ministry of the Church. Much of this moral teaching consists of truths which are in principle available to rational inquiry, understanding and judgement. And that is why the Church's substantive moral teaching can properly inform participation in public policy debates in which one aims to secure agreement on the basis of reason rather than on the basis of an authority, the warrant for which is accepted in faith.

The range of the Centre's work, and the understanding which informs our engagement in that range of work, should help explain why in turn the invited papers in this volume range from those concerned with the ecclesial context of a Catholic bioethic to those concerned with the issues raised by participation in public policy debates. It is not the purpose of this Introduction to provide an abstract of the book's varied contents[1], but some indication of what they are may help readers to find their way around the volume. I have not resisted the temptation to comment on some contributions when they have seemed to invite further reflection on the significance of the Centre's work.

The three papers in the first main section on **The ecclesial context of Catholic bioethics** when considered together do tend to suggest what is most significant in the work of an institute like the Linacre Centre. The first paper by Cardinal Cahal Daly identifies the essence of the moral crisis of our times as consisting in the abandonment of universal moral norms and the growth of moral relativism and subjectivism. What replaces the discourse characteristic of the tradition of common morality, which had practical truth as its subject, is a discourse aimed at manipulation and at the rationalization of the exercise of dominative power by the powerful over the powerless. As Cardinal Daly remarks,

> "The Catholic response to the crisis has been weakened by the acceptance in too many sectors of Catholic moral theology of a theory of consequentialism, which bases moral judgement on a subjective calculation of the overall consequences of an action, rather than on its intrinsic and objective moral nature."

Pope John Paul II has responded to this moral crisis in both Church and society, particularly in his encyclicals *Veritatis Splendor* and *Evangelium Vitae*, by reaffirming the existence of universal and objective moral norms and of types of action which are *per se* evil and, as such, can never be rightly chosen. In solemnly confirming in *Evangelium Vitae* that three particular absolute negative norms (the more general one against killing the innocent, the two more particular ones against abortion and euthanasia) are infallibly taught by the Ordinary Magisterium of the Church, the Pope says that the truth about these norms "man, in the light of reason, finds in his own heart" *(Evangelium Vitae, 57)*; in other words, they are truths of the natural law. In saying these moral truths are disclosable in the light of reason, Pope John Paul II has in mind the basis on which those who are neither Catholics, nor Christians who recognise the witness of our common tradition, might cooperate in reversing the oppressive tyranny of the culture of death by working for a culture of life.

Professor Michael Banner, in the second paper in this section ('Catholics and Anglicans and contemporary bioethics: divided or united?'), finds precisely this claim for the independent exercise of reason to be one which must divide Anglicans from Catholics in the field of bioethics in so far as Catholics are

---

[1] I was taken to task by a reviewer of an earlier volume I edited for not providing a resumé of its contents in my introduction. But it was not my purpose then, and it is not my purpose here, to relieve reviewers of the task of reading what they purport to review.

committed to upholding it and Anglicans are committed to maintaining Article 18 of the Thirtynine Articles. Professor Banner is an Anglican for whom the Thirty-nine Articles are normative and who accepts something close to Catholic teaching on the substantive norms of morality. He has proved to be someone with whom cooperation in defence of human life has been fruitful, and someone, therefore, with whom dialogue about the grounds of cooperation is important. At the heart of his complex paper is the contention that there can be no adequate knowledge of the content of morality apart from revelation, and what he sees as *Evangelium Vitae*'s failure to follow through the logic of this claim explains, in his view, the Encyclical's inadequate comprehension of the powerful purchase the culture of death has on many minds as well as impeding a clear understanding of the fact that it is only the proclamation of the Resurrection of Jesus which can provide a basis for an authentic culture of life. It is a pity that the programme of the Conference did not allow for detailed discussion of Professor Banner's paper, for there are many claims in it which a predominantly Catholic audience would surely have wanted to qualify or contest.[2] One distinction which is surely crucial, but which does not appear to play a role in Professor Banner's reflections, is that between adequate and partial moral knowledge. Catholic interest in moral dialogue with those who do not accept revelation clearly looks for limited (and inevitably incomplete) shared understanding from which to advance by reasoning to a less incomplete recognition of moral truth. If one denies the existence of any such partial knowledge of moral truth on the part of those who are unbelievers it is difficult to explain what it is in their understanding of their lives which could make

---

[2] To illustrate, by reference to directly relevant texts: contrary to what Professor Banner seems to imply, not all contemporary theories of rights are offspring of the Lockean tradition of 'possessive individualism'. (According to Professor Banner, contemporary rights theories are vitiated by their antecedents in this tradition, so that John Paul II is mistaken in articulating any moral claims in terms of rights. The root of this mistake is alleged to be the pervasive error of thinking that there is any validity to moral reasoning carried out independently of revelation.) John Finnis in chapter 8 of his *Natural Law and Natural Rights* (Oxford: Clarendon Press 1980) has shown how the language of rights may be used as a way of expressing most of the claims of practical reasonableness in our relations with others, but such rights language is given sense by more fundamental principles and norms which may be expressed without reference to the concept of 'rights'. And this particular theory of rights, as Robert George has remarked, is committed to a denial of the characteristic theses of 'possessive individualism', in particular the dualistic understanding of human beings and its non-cognitivist understanding of human motivation and practical understanding. See Robert George, 'A Response' [to Joan Lockwood O'Donovan, 'The Concept of Rights in Christian Moral Discourse'] in Michael Cromartie (ed), A *Preserving Grace. Protestants, Catholics and Natural Law*, Washington, DC: The Ethics and Public Policy Center and Grand Rapid, Mich: Eerdmans 1997, pp. 157–161, at 159. Professor Banner's criticism of Pope John Paul II on this point draws directly from Joan Lockwood O'Donovan. He has recently dismissed Robert George's 'Response' to her on the grounds that even if it is possible to cleanse 'rights talk' of its false presuppositions "in our present context such rights talk can hardly fail to be misunderstood". Since Professor Banner does not choose to challenge Robert George's case that one may talk about rights without making any false presuppositions, his own case against talking about rights may be no more than the belief that one cannot dislodge the false presuppositions from contemporary minds. See his review of the Cromartie volume in 12/1 (1999) *Studies in Christian Ethics* 96–101.

them capable of being addressed by (I do not say 'capable of accepting') the Word of God as a word which can even *seem* possibly relevant to their lives.

To claim that some degree of moral knowledge, the content of which may be arrived at independently of revelation, is the condition of hearing revelation, and to claim that this knowledge may develop in rational dialogue independently of revelation, neither commits one to any distinct claim that one could be saved by such knowledge, nor does it commit one to an optimistic view of the prospects for dialogue in our present society. It was a strong sense that those prospects were not good which prompted the invitation to Professor Michael Waldstein to speak about 'Medicine, Moral Crisis and the Need for Evangelization', a paper which, though it now appears in the first major division of this volume, was originally the closing address of the Conference.

Professor Waldstein shows no inclination to think that a greater degree of rational consensus about some of the moral issues which characterise bioethics would even begin to address the depth of the problem manifested in the culture of death. Evangelization – the effective communication of the truth of the Gospel – is alone adequate to meeting that problem. For reason in modernity has been characteristically confined to the role of "a mere instrument of power", giving rise to a complex fabric of practice and ideology which sustain a false sense of self-asserting independence of God and prevent awareness of the truth that we are creatures of God called to be his children. In this alienated condition human relations are violently oppressive and the language of morality itself is deployed manipulatively. What is needed in this cultural environment is a radically new awareness of our true relationship to God which would inform the way we perceive, know, feel and act. That relationship is grounded in the inner Trinitarian life, which is manifested in the death and resurrection of Jesus (Jesus's "hour" in St John's Gospel) as a life of giving and grateful receiving. We become witnesses to the "glory" of God manifested in Jesus's "hour" in experiencing the power of the Risen Lord to bring about a communion between brothers which overcomes our addiction to manipulative violence, thereby creating the reality of community within the local Church. So what the deeply alienated condition of human beings in our society needs is the renewal of Christian community at the local level within which people could begin to discover the true freedom of the children of God.

There is nothing in Professor Waldstein's paper to suggest that he thinks some measure of rational dialogue is neither possible nor – at least in some circumstances – desirable. But like Professor Banner he does think that the characteristic rationalizations of abortion, euthanasia and other manifestations of the culture of death have a powerful purchase on many minds, and their having that purchase is evidence of a deep-lying alienation from God which can only be ended by the grace of religious conversion. This seems to me to be true. And if it is, it suggests that the work of an institution such as The Linacre Centre is likely to be rather more significant in helping to maintain the integrity of the Church's concrete witness to moral truth in the lives of faithful Catholics than it is in any contributions it may have to make in the public policy forum. For both purposes, however, a number of substantive issues call for renewed reflection.

The remainder of the volume is devoted to a selection of these issues. None of the papers pretends to be a definitive treatment of any one issue but the range of the papers suggests something of the intellectual challenge represented by an adequate engagement in Catholic bioethics.

The next section, entitled **Anthropology**, is concerned with the basic understanding of human life. Evidently human beings are bodily beings, and it seems uncontroversial that medicine is concerned with living human bodies. Many who want to say that medicine's primary focus should be human *persons* are unclear about the relation of the human body to the human person. Much modern medicine seems to take a mechanistic view of human life in taking a mechanistic view of human bodies. Professor John Haldane's paper on 'Bioethics and the philosophy of the body' indicates the basic intellectual framework for an adequate philosophy of the body and suggests that this framework provides the basis for an understanding of objective moral values necessary to overcome the subjectivism characteristic of our culture.

He surveys the history of reflection on the nature of the human body and the human person in the Western philosophical tradition and identifies the failure of contemporary versions of materialism and dualism to give a satisfactory account of what it is about the nature of human beings which explains their manifest capacities as features of a unified life. Professor Haldane suggests that the way out of the contemporary impasse in philosophical anthropology is a retrieval of an Aristotelian understanding of human beings as rational animals. What explains the human body as an organism with the unified life characteristic of human persons is the human soul. For Haldane an adequate philosophical anthropology provides the basis for an adequate ethic: "Our activities may be judged good or bad depending on their relationship to a norm of human flourishing whose content is given by our nature." Thus: "... the human body is the locus of value inasmuch as it is the location of human life".

A dualistic anthropology is often implicit in many objectionable developments in medicine, from embryo experimentation to euthanasia on the basis of 'quality of life' considerations. Dr Gregory Glazov, a biblical scholar with some prior training in the biological sciences, makes reflection on such dualism a central theme of his paper on 'Biblical anthropology and medical ethics'. He shows that the purchase dualism has on the modern imagination (as exemplified in the recrudescence of gnosticism in the New Age Movement) is often associated with a sense of what is horrible about its practical implications, in face of which however the characteristic response is denial or evasion. By contrast the biblical understanding of man as "the image of God", repudiating dualism as it does, holds out a prospect for human beings which is the antithesis of the horrible. The perfect realization of this image is the Risen Body of the Crucified Lord. Resurrection is the Father's response to the obedient self-giving (kenosis) of the Son. Glazov explores what the realization of the image of God through faithful obedience and self-giving (made possible through our union with the Risen Lord) means in different dimensions of our lives. It means, for example, acceptance of marriage and the family as the God-given environment for nurturing and supporting the realisation of the image of God in human beings. On this account a biblical anthropology is to be seen as providing grounds for opposing, *inter alia*, much that goes under the name of reproductive technology in modern medicine.

The notions of 'sexual health' and 'reproductive health' as they are used in contemporary medical discourse betray radically distorting understandings of human sexuality. The section on **Sexual ethics** contains two papers, one devoted to the anthropological foundations of a sexual ethic, the other devoted to what is required for the development of chastity. The first paper, 'The nuptial meaning of the body and sexual ethics' by Professor Jorge Vincente Arregui, elucidates the anthropological underpinnings of Pope John Paul II's teaching on the self-giving love of marriage as the proper fulfilment of human sexuality. If human beings are to honour the good of marriage in their lives (as all of us need to), and if we are to authentically share in that good, then we need the distinctive virtue of chastity, the disposition to choose and act rightly in regard to sex. In the second paper in this section, 'Formation in chastity: the need and the requirements', Professor Bartholomew Kiely SJ first explains some of the obstacles to an understanding of chastity created by theological dissent, and more broadly by dominant features of our society and individualist culture. At the centre of his paper is a clarification of chastity as an essential ingredient in the integral good of the human person. For chastity is the condition of one's sexuality being integrated into that self-giving which is the necessary characteristic of every form of Christian vocation; it is the condition of respect for the body as integral to one's personal life (and therefore not to be treated as merely instrumental to ends such as pleasure); and it is part of that discipline of hope for a fulfilment which transcends immediate gratification. The paper concludes with a review of some of the particular requirements for formation in chastity beginning with willingness to learn from the tradition of the Church. We need to pass on that tradition on love and chastity if future generations are to "enjoy trust between the sexes, committed and stable and loving marriages, dedication of parents to children, and the joy of making a total gift of oneself in marriage or in the consecrated life".

The next section on **Situating health care** contains three papers. The first, by Professor Germain Grisez, on 'Health care as part of a Christian's vocation' was one of the opening keynote papers of the Conference. Professor Grisez begins by pointing out that it does not make sense to reflect on vocation as Christians understand vocation if one does not have a lively interest in heaven, and there is no reason to have a lively interest in heaven (of the kind that makes a difference to one's choices) if hell does not seem a real possibility. Every member of the Church has a unique personal vocation which requires him or her to discern God's plan for his or her life. That plan is part of the divine plan which "directs everything toward creation's eventual consummation in [God's] heavenly kingdom". In faithfully following our personal vocation we "effectively seek the kingdom and prepare material for it." Against this general understanding of the significance of vocation Professor Grisez analyses first the nature and limits of the obligation to care for one's own health, which is an integral part of everyone's vocation, and of the obligation to care for the health of children and other dependents which may form part of anyone's vocation. He then analyses the

implications of saying that the vocation to healthcare of the healthcare professional is a vocation to dedicated service.

The second paper in this section is by Fr David Albert Jones OP on 'The encounter with suffering in the practice of medicine in the light of Christian revelation'. It
begins by elucidating an orthodox Christian understanding of the evils which
cause suffering and what it is that makes suffering redemptive: not suffering
itself but the power of God whose love for us we may acknowledge in faith in
face of the mystery of his permissive will. The paper argues that it is crucial to
the care offered by doctors and nurses that they should be able to recognise
when they cannot relieve suffering or certain types of suffering and why the
aspiration nevertheless to do so (a characteristic temptation in our culture) is
misguided hubris. What they need above all in their work is the virtue of
mercy, together with those of prudence and justice.

The final paper in this section is on 'Medicine as a profession and the meaning
of health as its goal' by the present writer. It seeks to define the purpose of medicine
by reference to a delimited concept of health ('somatic health'). Such a concept, it
is argued, is essential to sustaining an understanding of medicine as a profession
with an ethic internal to it; has the advantage of depriving misuses of medicine of
those ideological justifications which rely on an overextended concept of health;
and gives clear content to the notion of 'medical treatment', a notion of critical
importance in contemporary debates about withdrawing and withholding
'treatment'.

The following section comprises two papers on **Integrity in health care**. The
first, 'Collaboration and integrity: how to think clearly about moral problems of
cooperation', is by Professor Joseph Boyle. It is principally concerned with issues
of integrity as they present themselves to the individual practitioner who is
expected, in more or less constraining (sometimes coercive) circumstances, to
play "a subordinate role in carrying out or facilitating [a] primary agent's evil
action". Boyle, by a careful elucidation of the ideas of formal and material cooperation, distinguishes those cases in which constraints "can change one's
ordinary obligations, most importantly the obligation not to contribute to
wrongdoing", from those cases in which it would remain the case that one
acted wrongly in contributing to wrongdoing even though one was subject to
constraints, including duress.

The second paper in this section is by Fr Anthony Fisher OP on the question "Is
there a distinctive role for the Catholic hospital in a pluralist society?" The paper is
concerned with the *institutional* integrity of Catholic hospitals. Fr Fisher's answer
to the question posed by his title is that Catholic hospitals have no good reason to
continue in existence unless they are distinctively Catholic, and he is inclined to
think that retention of a niche in the contemporary healthcare 'market' will
depend on remaining unashamedly Catholic. He does not underestimate the problems of remaining viable in the changing economic environment, but points out
that too frequently the response to economic pressures has driven hospitals into
mergers and collaborative arrangements many of which involve cooperation in
wrongdoing and loss of Catholic identity. Catholic hospitals lose their *raison*

*d'être*, he explains, if they cease to share in the sacramentality of the Church – its being "a sign and instrument of our union with God". The Catholic hospital is this through the character of its service of the sick (particularly the poor who are sick and dying), through the witness it gives to Gospel truth (particularly in its exemplary conformity to the moral demands of the Gospel), and through the worship offered in it in prayer and pastoral care. He concludes with six recommendations to those responsible for Catholic hospitals about what requires to be done if they are to retain or recover their identity as Catholic hospitals sharing in the mission of the Church.

The penultimate section of the book contains four papers related to **Law, public policy and the prolife cause**. The first, by Dr John Keown, is on 'The legal revolution: from "sanctity of life" to "quality of life" and "autonomy".' The paper argues that legislatures and more particularly the judiciary across the Western world have seriously eroded respect for the sanctity of life in recent decades. Increasingly judgements in cases coming before the courts have been governed by a 'Quality of life' ethic and by allowing an indefensibly wide scope to considerations of autonomy. He illustrates this thesis from the House of Lords judgement in the *Bland* case which, as one of the Law Lords involved observed, has left the law of homicide in a "morally and intellectually misshapen state". The only way of restoring it to a sound condition, Keown argues, is by retrieving an accurate understanding both of the principle of the sanctity of life (avoiding as it does the opposed extremes of vitalism and a 'Quality of life' ethic) and of the limits to which one can reasonably invoke considerations of autonomy.

The second paper in this section is by Professor John Finnis on 'The Catholic Church and public policy debates in Western liberal societies: the basis and limits of intellectual engagement'. The paper first offers some reflections on the faith which can shape our choices to participate in public debate. Finnis distinguishes among the truths taught by the Church those propositions which can be known only through revelation from those propositions which are knowable through natural reason. Evidently we can participate in public debate on the basis of the latter. But we can also do so on the basis of the former truths because the grounds for accepting revelation are publicly accessible and creditworthy. Since "the centre of human history is the life and teachings of Jesus Christ" there is every reason to seek to make available for public deliberation "the truths which the Church conveys" since they "are the true centre of the culture which can and should direct political deliberation in Western liberal as much as any other kind of political society". In the second part of his paper Professor Finnis discusses issues of cooperation with wrongdoing, covering similar ground to Professor Boyle but with particular reference to the choices facing legislators. And in the final part of his paper he considers the role of the Church acting precisely as Church, i.e. through her pastors, in public policy debates. The principal responsibility of bishops in this regard is to announce and confirm the faith. The challenge facing them is considerable because of the pervasive influence of that practical atheism called secularism. Among many Christians this takes the form of thinking that God is vaguely benevolent and indifferent to how they behave, so that there are no specific requirements rejection of which by us would entail radical and potentially final alienation from Him. Bishops have the crucial responsibility of confronting the inroads of secularism by making clear that heaven is the true object of our hope, that we can live in expectation of that hope only if we choose to do the will of God, and what kinds of choice are compatible and what incompatible with doing God's will. It is not the job of bishops, Professor Finnis argues, to assess the complex contingent circumstances (economic, medical, military and so on) which condition the making of specific choices on specific occasions.

Professor Robert George's paper ('Bioethics and public policy: Catholic participation in the American debate') serves to illustrate the practical importance of John Finnis's contention. George, while acknowledging the importance of many of the initiatives taken by the US Bishops and while admiring in particular the outstanding work of the Committee for Pro-Life Activities of the United States Catholic Conference, is principally concerned with the factors which have been obstacles to the influence of Church teaching on public policy in the field of bioethics. Among these factors he lays considerable stress on the consequences of the Bishops appearing to put on a par the Church's teaching on abortion with teaching about, say, what is required in the way of positive programmes for care of the poor. Whereas the former teaching does translate straightforwardly into a specific public policy ("abortion is to be generally prohibited and never publicly promoted") the Church's teaching on care for the poor does not: it requires for translation into public policy contestable factual and prudential judgements on which faithful Catholics and others reasonably differ. One effect of appearing to make the two kinds of teaching similar in character has been that Catholic politicians who wished to align themselves with elite opinion in favour of abortion rationalised their position with the claim that public policy on abortion also involved factual and prudential judgements about which Catholics could legitimately differ. That move would hardly have been possible if the bishops had confined themselves to saying "what they can say as a matter of moral principle consistent with their authority to preach the Gospel".

Among other major factors identified by Professor George as undermining the influence on public policy of the Church's teaching on abortion are the failure over a quarter of a century to put a stop to the scandalous pro-choice advocacy of Fr Robert Drinan SJ (culminating in his support for partial-birth abortions) and the seriously debilitating influence on Catholic belief and practice of the rejection of the Church's teaching authority by a substantial body of dissenting theologians.

Professor Scarisbrick's paper on 'The prolife cause in Great Britain' concludes the final topic-based section of the volume. Against a picture of the pioneering and sanctioning of many anti-life practices in Great Britain, he brings out the feebleness of the intellectual case for these practices. One pro-choice argument after another has been shown to be indefensible. It remains, however, as Professor Scarisbrick remarks, that "we have not yet won back the hearts and minds of many of our fellow citizens". In face of this situation what is required is "heroic prophecy". And that demands the witness of action and of words: both that caring activity which makes perspicuous what a pro-life commitment means, and an unswerving dedication to bringing home to people that the authentic values they confusedly invoke in pro-choice advocacy – such as respect for the dignity of women – are realisable only in a polity which affords protection to the weakest and most vulnerable human beings. Catholics, as Professor Scarisbrick concludes, are in principle singularly well-placed to rise to the task of "heroic prophecy": for they can both "discern the enormity of the man-made catastrophe which surrounds them" and in face of it they have a Gospel of Life to proclaim. Professor Scarisbrick would agree with Professor George that lay Catholics (among whom are to be counted leaders of the pro-life cause in the UK) are best helped by their pastors in advancing the pro-life cause when those pastors recognise their responsibility to proclaim the fundamental moral truths which should govern public policy but in doing so confine themselves to saying "what they can say as a matter of moral principle consistent with their authority to preach the Gospel".

The final section of this volume prints some of the contributions to the **Disputed questions** which were discussed and debated during a number of parallel sessions at the Conference. Two of those sessions were conducted between invited disputants: Professor Richard Frackowiak and Professor Alan Shewmon (on the question: Is it reasonable to use as a basis for diagnosing death the UK protocol for the clinical diagnosis of 'brain stem death'?) and Dr Mary Geach and Dr Helen Watt (on the question: Are there any circumstances in which it would be morally admirable for a woman to seek to have an orphan embryo implanted in her womb?). The contributions of Professor Shewmon[3], Dr Geach and Dr Watt are published here. In addition to invited speakers a number of people submitted papers on specified topics. From among those presented at the Conference three are published in this section of the Proceedings[4]. There is a paper by Dr Bernadette Tobin on the question 'Can a patient's refusal of life-prolonging treatment be morally upright when it is motivated neither by the belief that the treatment would be clearly futile nor by the belief that the consequences of treatment would be unduly burdensome?' Finally, a pair of papers from Professor Christopher Kaczor and the Rev Dr Gerald Gleeson dispute what is the correct answer to the question 'Is the medical management of ectopic pregnancy by the administration of methotrexate morally acceptable?'

$$* \quad * \quad *$$

[3] See editorial note appended to Professor Shewmon's paper at p. 315.
[4] The presentations of Dr Teresa Iglesias, on the one side, and of Fr Kevin O'Rourke OP and his colleague Fr Patrick Norris OP, on the other, on the question 'Can it be morally acceptable to withdraw tubefeeding from a patient in PVS who had not previously made clear his own wishes?', though attracting considerable interest at the Conference, restated lines of argument which are already very familiar in the literature. The paper by the Rev Dr George Woodall on the question 'Are there any circumstances in which it may be morally acceptable to advise the use of condoms to prevent transmission of HIV?' was subsequently published in 48 (1998) *Medicina e Morale* 545–579.

In concluding this Introduction it remains for me to acknowledge a number of substantial debts to colleagues and friends who helped to make possible both the Conference and this subsequent volume. Both projects had the active support of the Governing Body of The Linacre Centre which established from its membership a small Advisory Committee to help in planning the Conference: Professor John Finnis, Dr John Keown and Mr Stratford Caldecott. In addition to chairing the occasional consultations I had with this group, giving sage advice as well as a paper at the Conference, John Finnis also generously undertook the duty of presiding at the Conference Banquet. John Keown, as a Fellow of Queens' College, Cambridge, at which the Conference was held, did much through his contacts with the College administration to ensure the smooth running of a very enjoyable Conference, to which he also contributed a paper.

The major work of organising publicity, registration and other material arrangements for the Conference was undertaken by the Administrator of the Linacre Centre, Mrs Clarissa Fleischer. Almost everyone who took part in the Conference must have been aware of how much its success was owing to the efficiency and unfailing good humour she displayed. During the course of the Conference she was generously assisted by her husband, Mr Patrick Fleischer, as well as by the Centre's Librarian, Mr Donald Smith, and Research Fellow, Dr Helen Watt (who also contributed a paper). I am also indebted to Dr Watt for undertaking the tedious task of compiling the Index to this volume.

There were 240 participants at the Conference from mainland European countries, from North and South America, from Africa and from Australia, as well as from Great Britain and Ireland. The attendance of some was made possible by the generosity of others. One particularly generous benefactor who contributed significantly to the success of the Conference was Mr Joseph Santamaria QC for whose support I am very grateful.

Gratitude is evidently owing to all those who gave papers, but no one I am sure will resent my singling out for special mention Cardinal Winning and Cardinal Daly who not only presented papers to the Conference but graced the entire occasion with their presence. We also enjoyed the presence at the Conference of Bishop Elio Sgreccia in his capacity as Vice-President of the Pontifical Academy for Life.

In the initial stages of preparing the Proceedings for publication I was assisted by work done by Dr F J Fitzpatrick in getting most of the contributions into something approximating a uniform format. I have not, however, aimed at rigid uniformity. To have done so would have had more disadvantages than advantages. Some variation in the layout of chapters should not disturb readers. Furthermore, while it is good to have footnotes providing the information or comment they are intended to provide on the main text at the foot of that text, an exception had to be made to this ideal in the case of Professor Shewmon's text: a full detailing of his references on the same page as his text would have had the effect in places of almost swamping that text!

The published Proceedings are dedicated to the memory of two fine and generous servants and friends of the Centre who were also good personal friends of the editor. Others have made distinguished and generous contributions to the development and life of the Centre who are still happily with us. I hope the opportunity will arise in due course to honour them. But the memory of David Williams and John Utting who are now dead evokes a strong sense of how blessed the Centre was in their leadership as well as how blessed I was by their friendship.

# 2

# Opening address

CARDINAL THOMAS J. WINNING

MY DEAR FRIENDS,

It is for me a great privilege and an immense pleasure to open this International Conference, and to welcome all of you to what, we may hope, will be an occasion for learning, for fruitful exchanges, for deepening old bonds of friendship and collaboration, and for creating new ones.

My prayer for this Conference is that we will all keep our minds and hearts focused on the human person, remembering that whatever we as individual Christians or as Church have to offer will be for the benefit of our brothers and sisters whoever and wherever they are.

We need to live in the real world and not in the world of make-believe. The Church does not choose the kind of world she is called to live in.

This was brought home to me very forcibly a couple of nights ago. During our diocesan Lourdes pilgrimage I had a fax from a Catholic family asking me to visit their second son, a youngster of 12 in the Intensive Care Unit of our Children's Hospital in Glasgow. I called there on Friday evening when I got home from Lourdes to find David on an oscillator. He had had a collapse after an operation on the lower end of his gullet.

The doctors don't hold out any hope, but his father and mother are looking for something, for a cure; they are people of faith.

After praying for David and with his parents I felt the need to bring God's blessing on all the children in the Intensive Care Unit: a four-year-old girl who had been facing life on a ventilator for the past 3 years; a youngster on a ventilator as a result of a muscular disease; an 11-year-old girl on a ventilator with lung and kidney failure; an infant of 6 months recovering from a heart operation; and a young boy of 5 or 6 in a similar condition, the last two with good life prospects.

Technological advances have presented us with complex issues to do with the meaning of life and death. It occurred to me that the Lord has opened the secrets of His world for our benefit. Yet at the same time the dark side of life will not be eliminated by technology and the Church can address suffering and death as no other institution in this world can.

Engaging the world is part of the Church's vocation. She has to be courageous and meet the challenges of today.

This Conference, as you know, has been organised to celebrate the twentieth anniversary of the foundation of The Linacre Centre in the summer of 1977.

It is good for us to reflect both on the kind of institution the Linacre Centre is, and on some of the challenges which have been facing it since its establishment.

As Chairman of the Catholic Bishops' Joint Bioethics Committee for almost 15 years, I have had many opportunities to observe the work of the Centre and I have come to value it immensely.

Typically, a Centre is a place at which particular objectives are pursued, principally through the activities of those who work there, but also through the contributions of individuals and organisations who from time to time are drawn into its activities.

The Linacre Centre was opened in 1977 as a result of an initiative which had been supported by the late Cardinal Heenan, Archbishop of Westminster, and through the work of a group of Catholics distinguished principally in the fields of medicine and nursing. The main purpose of the Centre in the eyes of its founders was:

1. To help Catholics engaged in health care and biomedical research to understand the relevance of Catholic teaching in resolving the moral questions which arise in the course of their work, and
2. to aid them in carrying out their work as professionals.

As an organisation committed to these objectives, the Centre has a mission within the church and to society at large.

The mission within the Church has been that of helping in the exposition and development of a Catholic bioethic.

Social, cultural and political changes have given fresh urgency to long-standing issues such as abortion and euthanasia. Developments in applied biology and in medicine have raised new questions such as those prompted by the so-called reproductive technologies, by genetic screening and genetic therapy, by care of the handicapped new-born and care of those who are permanently comatose, and by developments in transplantation.

Catholic teaching about what is required if we are to respect human life and human dignity is both clear and rich. It provides the authority for the work and values promoted by the Linacre Centre. This teaching has been splendidly articulated by the present Holy Father, particularly in his encyclicals *Veritatis Splendor* and *Evangelium Vitae.* It is part of the mission of an organisation such as the Linacre Centre to help in the proper understanding and interpretation of these documents.

There are fundamental moral truths which must not be doubted. They should enlighten Catholic practical reflection on many ethical issues which arise in clinical practice and biomedical research. The implications of these truths are clear for a good many issues. Their implications are not entirely clear for other issues, among which one should number the "disputed questions" which are to be discussed at this Conference. And there are issues raised, for example, by developments in genetics, about which we do not have a clear view of the truths relevant to their resolution. What, for example, should we think about proposals to modify a person's genetic constitution, not in order to overcome the effects of some genetic disorder, but simply to enhance normal ability? All the elements of a wholly satisfactory response to this question have yet to be brought together.

14

At the same time new questions have already led to a deepening of moral understanding in some areas. Take, for example, questions posed by developments in *in vitro* fertilisation. They have already prompted a deepening and development of Catholic moral thought which have enabled the Church's Magisterium to take a decisive position on IVF and related technologies. The teaching about the inseparability of the unitive and procreative meanings[1] of the marital act is the key to what the church has to say about what is wrong with such techniques (as well as what is wrong with contraception). It is inconsistent with the dignity of a human being to be generated in ways analogous to product manufacture. A human being is properly begotten through that act in which husband and wife are united as "one flesh". When so begotten, a child's conception has as its human cause precisely that act which is apt for the expression of the parents' mutual self-giving. The child can therefore enter their lives as the fruit of their embodied self-giving, which is open to the child to the degree that the self-giving is unreserved. For the openness which characterises the unreserved self-giving of parents (as that finds expression in the marital act) is the disposition required for acceptance of the child *just as he or she is*. Such a disposition of openness contrasts with that manipulative attitude which would devise the child to fit the specifications we desire.

The understanding that, if we are to respect human dignity in the conception of children, they should be begotten by their parents, not made by technicians, underlies the teaching of *Donum Vitae* (1987) on the wrongness of IVF, artificial insemination and similar techniques. I think it is worthy of mention that this understanding and its implications had already been worked out in the document *In Vitro Fertilisation: Morality and Public Policy* which the Catholic Bishops' Joint Committee on Bioethical Issues submitted as their evidence to the Warnock Committee in 1983.

As another part of its mission within the Church, the Linacre Centre has been very much part of collaborative undertakings aimed at developing thinking consistent with Catholic tradition in response to some of the new moral issues raised by biomedical developments. Despite the fact that staff have always been few in numbers, they have produced over the years a large number of advisory papers for bishops, Bishops' Conferences, and dicasteries of the Holy See. More especially, they have provided since 1984 very substantial support for the work of the Catholic Bishops' Joint Bioethics Committee. All the publications of that Committee since 1984 have borne the imprint of the Centre's work, and a number of them have been substantially drafted by members of the Centre.

In addition to its collaborative activities such as those just referred to, the Centre has always had its own programme. This involves study and writing and has resulted in a number of publications by the Centre. Some of them are available at this Conference. The Centre has also organised and directed, particularly throughout the 1980s, courses, seminars and study days for hospital chaplains, nurse educationalists, junior doctors and nurses, and medical and

---

[1] "*sensus*"; cf. *Humanae Vitae*, para. 12.

nursing students. This teaching activity was organised in different parts of England and Scotland, and over the years the Centre established an impressive network of collaborators, particularly from the disciplines of medicine and the law, who have contributed to the teaching. The collaboration of many generous Catholic professionals in the work of the Centre has been essential to many of its achievements, and the Centre is now recognised generally as a precious resource for the Church's involvement in bioethics.

I should like to reflect on the mission of the Centre within society. You might say that the founding purpose of the Centre was to aid Catholic professionals to make health care "part of a Christian's vocation" – to quote the title of Professor Grisez's paper. If we are serious in our profession of Christian belief then we allow it to shape every part of our life. But the cultural, institutional and political obstacles to making contemporary health care "part of a Christian's vocation" are formidable. This is particularly so in the United Kingdom where most health care is carried out within the National Health Service. The National Health Service is in many ways the finest achievement of the post-war welfare state, most parts of which are now being drastically modified. But the dominance of health care provision by the National Health Service has also had malign consequences. For example, the NHS has created institutional arrangements which render practically impossible the pursuit of a career in obstetrics and gynaecology for anyone who accepts the Church's teaching relevant to that area of clinical practice. There is a real danger of similar difficulties arising in other specialities: if, for example, euthanasia were to be legalised, we would doubtless see a quite rapid revolution in the ethos of geriatric medicine, and hospice care, as we now know it, could be marginalised. In both these areas of clinical practice Catholics are today leading members of the profession, just as thirty years ago there were a good number of Catholics who were leading figures in obstetrics and gynaecology. But that generation has retired and has not been succeeded by a comparable generation of Catholics. In other words it is clear to us that what the Holy Father calls "the culture of death" has made major inroads into the practice of health care in Britain.

What can one do in face of this? The work of the Linacre Centre has been most conspicuous in relation to proposals to legalise euthanasia. It is fairly well known that the substantial submission which the Centre made in 1993 to the House of Lords' Select Committee on Medical Ethics had a significant influence on the deliberations of that Committee. For it is, indeed, remarkable that a Committee which at the outset seemed to have a built-in bias favouring legalisation should have been unanimous in their Report in opposing the legalisation of active euthanasia. The Committee did fail to make recommendations it should have made, notably a recommendation to reverse the ruling of the majority of the Law Lords in the Bland case that it is lawful to aim to end a patient's life by a course of planned omissions if, following 'responsible medical opinion', one thinks that the patient would be better off dead. But despite this failure, the effect of the Report on many advocates of euthanasia was to persuade them that there was no immediate prospect of a legislative accommodation of euthanasia.

More recently, the Centre has been credited with some influence in helping to secure the narrow but decisive majority for the Andrews Bill in the Senate of the Australian Federal Parliament, which deprived the Northern Territory (and the other two Territories) of the power to legalise euthanasia and assisting in suicide.

We may be winning battles but the war continues. Advocates of euthanasia have rethought their strategies. In so far as the preferred route to accommodating euthanasia remains legislative there has been a semantic shift to advocating the legalisation of *assisted suicide*. But since the draft bills currently circulating in the UK require the doctor to ensure that the suicide is successful, they aim in effect to legalise euthanasia. Those who are less optimistic about the legislative route look to the judiciary for some creative decision-making which will progressively accommodate the practice of euthanasia. In this regard they may be thought to have a favourable beginning in the judgements in the *Bland* case.

The persistent pressure to accommodate the practice of euthanasia, which receives strong support in the media, is symptomatic of attitudes to human life which also find expression in the widespread practice of abortion.

Here we find ourselves confronted with a philosophy of our common life which is gravely flawed and which goes a long way to explain the malaise of contemporary society.

Why is it thought justifiable to kill unborn children, the handicapped newborn and the debilitated elderly? The radical justification which is now a commonplace of the bioethical literature rests on the claim that certain human beings do not have a serious right to life. For to have a serious right to life, on the view asserted, one must have developed abilities for understanding, reflection and choice, since without such abilities one cannot value one's life; and it is only in so far as people value their lives that those lives have value.

One striking feature of such views is that the transition point in the life of a human being to acquiring or losing basic rights is determined in an essentially arbitrary way. For arbitrariness is unavoidable in determining how developed the abilities for understanding, reflection and choice must be before someone can value his or her life.

A philosophy of fundamental human rights which adopts an arbitrary basis for recognising their presence is not a philosophy of justice in social relationships. Justice of its nature excludes arbitrariness in determining who are entitled to be treated justly, and who therefore possess basic human rights. The only non-arbitrary title to just treatment is the one which has been upheld throughout the Christian tradition: our common humanity. Human beings possess basic human rights simply because they are human beings.

It seems clear that our secularised society has abandoned this tenet of traditional morality. The abandonment is embodied in the protection the law in practice offers to abortion on demand. And people, sensing the logic of this abandonment, are unashamed in their defence of non-voluntary euthanasia, whether of the handicapped newborn or of the dependent elderly.

The abandonment in practice of the belief that human beings enjoy basic human rights simply because they are human beings, and its replacement by an arbitrary way of determining who possess rights, has implications reaching well beyond the practice of medicine. What medicine makes plain is that the exercise of raw power to kill the innocent is protected in our society. But if raw power enjoys a sort of pseudo-legitimacy under the law in medicine, what reason of principle is there for confining its exercise within medicine?

Even if the exercise of raw power to kill does not reach beyond medicine, its exercise there is sufficient to alienate many good citizens from the State. For what is the most fundamental duty of the State if not to protect the innocent? The State's claim to legitimacy and to our allegiance rests largely on its honest commitment to fulfil that duty. That is why the questions of abortion and euthanasia are not marginal but at the heart of politics. No political party which condones our present abortion law has any right to expect us to take seriously its rhetoric about social justice; that rhetoric will remain hollow just so long as the foundation of justice is denied.

I would appeal in particular to the present Government to recognise that a public philosophy of our common life in society requires the affirmation of the inalienable worth of every human being. And *that* affirmation, in turn, requires a radically different legal settlement of the abortion issue from one which allows the practically unfettered killing of the innocent.

These brief reflections on the political significance of abortion and euthanasia for our society also serve to bring out the political context of the Centre's mission to society at large. Like all who are seeking to contribute from within the Catholic tradition to public policy debates, the Centre is confronted with formidable difficulties. One is that the dominant voices shaping policy simply do not share our assumptions. What in theory can be done, and what in practice has been done, in face of radically opposed outlooks, will be the topic of papers and discussions at this Conference on Wednesday.

It is in the nature of the Centre that its own contributions have been in the presentation of argument and the analysis of counter-arguments. That work has been undertaken as a contribution to the much larger witness of the work of education, practical caring and political activism of the pro-life movement. It is a great pleasure to see some of the distinguished stalwarts of that movement at this celebratory Conference.

We should not underestimate the appeal of truth to the human mind – particularly the truth about human worth and human dignity. Nor should we underestimate the ideological resistance to this truth which has taken hold of many minds. This means that perhaps more than ever before, the defence of human life is inseparable from the proclamation of the Good News of our salvation from sin – and from the blindness, fear and death which are the wages of sin. For people need that Good News to make possible a radical conversion of mind and heart which are necessary for a generous openness to human life in its weakest and most dependent forms.

Pro-life witness, and the scholarly contribution the Linacre Centre makes to it, are best seen, then, as part of the prophetic witness of the Church to the world. All of us who are baptised are called to be prophets. Since we are called, we are given the grace of that calling. So let us not lose courage in face of the difficulties which confront us. We may not see the immediate successes we hope for. But if we give ourselves with a good heart to the work to which we are called, we will surely be surprised to discover, when the Lord of History comes into His Kingdom, what fruits of our labours belong there: hearts changed, minds brought to the truth, human lives cherished.

Going back to my experience last Friday amongst our sick children, I had a very strong sense of the presence of Jesus Christ: the children and their pain and suffering; the parents and their patience; the smiling, caring nurses; the doctors fighting to save lives. I saw there the values of the Kingdom in practice. I saw life on earth changing to life in God at the flick of a switch. I felt the preciousness of a human life. I knew that the Lord of History was not abandoning his people.

We should thank God for the first twenty years of the Linacre Centre and we should also pray that the little group who work there, and those who have generously collaborated with and supported them, should continue to accept the challenges of their mission within the Church and of the part they are called to play in the Church's mission to the world.

# The
# ecclesial context
# of
# Catholic bioethics

# 3

# The Church's Magisterium in face of the moral crisis of our time

## CARDINAL CAHAL B. DALY

THAT THERE is moral crisis in our time few would deny. A wide range of behaviours which, until comparatively recently, would have been regarded as morally wrong by majority public opinion and would have been officially condemned as sinful by virtually all the Christian Churches, and indeed by the great religious traditions of the world, are now widely regarded in public opinion as morally blameless and are indeed socially acceptable and in some cases legally sanctioned. There is no need to give examples, they are evident all around us, they exist in all social strata and pervade much of what we like to call "the developed world".

It is not only in practical behaviour that this moral change has come about; the actual moral principles and values by which people justify behaviour have themselves changed. The very concept of universally valid moral principles is today called in question, so that we can say that contemporary thinking about morality makes moral consensus in society virtually impossible, and indeed makes it in principle impossible to call any behaviour morally wrong in any absolute or universal sense. The principle of universality has, however, been accepted by the mainstream of Western tradition over many centuries as a defining characteristic of moral discourse.

From pre-Christian Rome, for example, we have the following declaration:

There is in fact a true law – namely right reason – which is in accordance with nature, applies to all men, and is unchangeable and eternal. By its commands this law summons men to the performance of their duties; by its prohibitions it restrains them from doing wrong.... To invalidate this law by human legislation is never morally right, nor is it permissible ever to restrict its operation, and to annul it wholly is impossible. Neither the Senate nor the people can absolve us from our obligations to obey this law, and it requires no [jurist] to expound and interpret it.

It will not lay down one rule at Rome and another at Athens, nor will it be one rule today and another tomorrow. But there will be one law, eternal and unchangeable, binding at all times upon all people; and there will be, as it were, one common master and ruler of men, namely God, who is the author of this law, its interpreter and its sponsor. The man who will not obey will abandon his better self, and, in denying the true nature of man, will thereby suffer the severest of penalties, though he has escaped all the other consequences which men call punishment.

This statement is from Marcus Tullius Cicero *(De Republica* III 33).

I pass to the beginning of the modern period, and to one of the leading thinkers of the 'Enlightenment', Immanuel Kant. Kant, as is well known, regarded the universalisability of moral principle as a defining quality of moral judgement, indeed as "the Type" of the moral law. Kant wrote:

> Act only on that maxim whereby thou canst at the same time will that [your maxim] should become universal law.

This is Kant's first formulation of the "categorical imperative". He goes on to give two other formulations. The second is:

> So act as to treat humanity, whether in thine own person or in that of any other, in every case as an end and never only as a means.

This is preceded by the statement that there is a being "whose existence has in itself an absolute worth, something which, being an end in itself, could be a source of definite laws". The human person is such a being, who "exists as an end in himself, not merely as a means to be arbitrarily used" by others. The third formulation of the categorical imperative is "the idea of the will of every rational being as a universal legislative will".

The categorical imperative, in each of its three formulations, enables Kant to pronounce certain specific types of behaviour as objectively and universally and absolutely wrong: for example, suicide, promise-breaking, failure to respect the rights of others; all of these are held by Kant to contradict the very nature of moral law and to be, therefore, intrinsically morally wrong. Furthermore, according to Kant, the human race is called and indeed obliged to aim at becoming a "kingdom of ends", namely "a union of different rational beings in a system of common laws". This latter comes close to a statement of the rationality and objectivity and universality of human rights, where every person is, as an end in himself or herself, morally entitled to be treated as such by others and is, reciprocally, morally obliged to treat others as each an end in himself or herself and never as a means to someone else's end.

Kant's *Critique of Practical Reason,* therefore, has many of the elements of the great Graeco-Roman and Judaeo-Christian moral tradition which is the basis of Western civilisation, even if Kant's formulation paradoxically carried within it the seeds of a philosophical overgrowth which later seriously damaged that tradition. The contemporary situation is in effect a reversal of both the Graeco-Roman and the Judaeo-Christian and of the Kantian insistence on the objectivity, the immutability and the universal validity of moral principles and, consequently, of human rights.

## Crisis of civilisation

The rejection by many, both in principle and in practice, of such moral principles, therefore, amounts to a real moral crisis, a crisis of immense magnitude and of potentially very serious implications for the future of humanity. Indeed this has to be called a crisis of civilisation; for it contains many of the elements of an abandonment in principle of universally binding moral law. The idea of a universally binding moral law has been associated historically with the concept of natural law. Natural law has been a foundation principle of Western civilisation since Graeco-Roman times, and it is the principle which still underlay both the French and the American revolutions, and which, to this day, underpins the efforts within the United Nations and otherwise to obtain international recognition and eventual enforcement of a universal charter of human rights, based on moral duties which are universal in time and in place, and from which no State and no individual can claim exemption.

This is the moral consensus on which freedom under truth and freedom under law depend, and consequently on which the future of civilisation depends. But this consensus is fatally undermined by the growing acceptance in our culture of moral relativism or moral subjectivism. The Catholic response to this crisis has been in some respects weakened by the acceptance in too many sectors of Catholic moral theology of a theory of consequentialism or proportionalism, which bases moral judgement on a subjective calculation of the overall consequences of an action, rather than on its intrinsic and objective moral nature. Pope John Paul II's concern about this situation is such that he has devoted to it two major encyclicals, *Veritatis Splendor* (1993) and *Evangelium Vitae* (1995).

## Conscience

I wish to look at one or two of the frightening lessons to be learned from the contemporary moral crisis. One lesson is that of the fragility of the moral conscience. Conscience is indeed, as the Second Vatican Council says, "the most secret core and sanctuary of man", where he is "alone with God, whose voice echoes in his depths" *(Gaudium et Spes,* 16). But, as Newman pointed out, the noble name of conscience can be debased into "a liberty of self-will". "What", Newman asked, a century and a quarter ago, "if a man's conscience embraces the duty of ... infanticide or free love?" This would, for Newman, be "of all conceivable absurdities ... the wildest and most stupid"[1]. Yet we are all too sadly aware how widespread, in contemporary society, is, precisely, "free love": sexual intercourse before marriage, cohabitation, relations outside marriage, have become commonplace. Sadly, even some Catholics have come to see such practices as acceptable. The media and certain participants in public debate sometimes go so far as to condone infanticide on grounds of compassion for a distressed mother; while "partial birth" abortions, which are impossible to distinguish

---

[1] John Henry Newman, *A Letter addressed to His Grace the Duke of Norfolk on occasion of Mr Gladstone's recent Expostulation* (London: Pickering 1875), reprinted in *Newman and Gladstone. The Vatican Decrees,* with an Introduction by Alvan Ryan (Notre Dame, IN: University of Notre Dame Press 1962), at p. 148.

from infanticide, are camouflaged as a necessary part of "reproductive health care", and are presently in danger of being explicitly legally sanctioned in the United States of America; and abortion, which is morally of the same genus as infanticide, has become common obstetric practice in most of the countries of Europe and North America.

The virtually universal moral consensus about the evil of abortion, which prevailed until comparatively recently, has been superseded with alarming speed in many countries by a social and cultural and legal acceptance of abortion, to the point where 'walk-in' abortions can calmly be advertised as a service to women's health. Sterilisation, which once was regarded with horror and was associated with the moral depravity and wickedness of Nazism, is now commonly presented as merely a simple and normal surgical procedure, and has even been hailed as "the most loving thing a man can do for a woman".

Nor is this debasing of conscience and of language found only in the realms of sex and reproduction; it is found also in politics, in business and finance, in the arms trade, in the practices of terrorism and in the conduct of war. In many of these areas, we find a casual acceptance of such principles as that "the end justifies the means", "it increases profits", "it increases employment", etc.

How much more shamefully true it is, therefore, in contemporary society than it was when Newman wrote his *Letter to the Duke of Norfolk*, that

> ... in this age, with a large portion of the public (conscience) is the very right and freedom of conscience to dispense with conscience, to ignore a Lawgiver and Judge... Conscience is a stern monitor, but, in this century, it has been superseded by a counterfeit, which the eighteen centuries prior to it never heard of and could not have mistaken for it if they had. It is the right of self-will.[2]

The speed and apparent ease with which conscience itself can be conditioned and corrupted raises very serious pastoral questions for the Church in a pluralist society.

### The power of words

A second lesson of the contemporary moral and cultural crisis is that of the power of words to alter moral perceptions and to persuade people that what once was sin is now morally licit. We need not look far for examples. It has become 'politically incorrect' to use moral language about behaviour, particularly in the area of so-called 'private morality', because this is 'judgmental' and 'discriminatory', and causes 'unhealthy guilt feelings' in others. Moral judgement is often casually assumed to be a private matter for oneself only; and no individual is allowed any right to judge others by his or her own moral standards, or to impose her or his moral values on others. Instead, people have come to use morally neutral

[2] Newman, *op. cit.*, at p. 130.

terms, or terms of psychological categorisation, or even terms of commendation of the agent, but very rarely moral condemnation of another's actions.

Moral attitudes are subtly conditioned by changes in the use of words. Moral distinctions are blurred, for example, by interchanging the terms 'husband' and 'partner', or 'marriage' and 'relationship'. Efforts are made to alter the definition of 'family'. Moral terms are gradually excluded from large areas of behaviour. Thus the word 'fornication' is banished from public discourse and is replaced by such terms as 'being in a relationship'; adultery is 'being in a second relationship' or 'having an affair'; contraception or even sterilisation is 'responsible sex'. The moral reality of abortion is obscured when it is subsumed into the persuasive term 'reproductive health care'. In other areas of behaviour similar linguistic shifts have become common. Civilian caualties in war are spoken of as 'collateral damage'; area bombing becomes 'precision bombing'; low-wage economies or those which employ child labour are called economies which have "highly competitive labour costs" or which "follow the laws of the marketplace". Deliberately ending the life of a senile or incurably ill person is called "letting him or her die with dignity". The abuse of language in these cases is subtle but potent. Pope John Paul, in *Evangelium Vitae*, has referred in this connection to St. Paul's description of the pagans of his time as people who "become futile in their thinking", whose "senseless minds are darkened"[3].

That there is widespread moral confusion in our time is illustrated by the fact that rigorous moral standards are quite rightly applied to matters in the political and civic and public domain, while permissive attitudes are shown towards matters of personal behaviour, particularly in the area of sexual morality. Michael Polanyi contrasted the moral absolutism and authoritarianism adopted by Marxists in reference to the political domain, with their moral relativism in respect of the so-called 'private' domain. He called it "moral inversion".


**Emotive use of language**

A further abuse of language which is relevant to the present moral debate is the use of words, not to communicate about a moral issue, but to discredit the opponent and disqualify him or her from being even listened to. In recent debates in Ireland about abortion and about divorce, for example, no terms were more often used in the media and in public discussion about pro-life and anti-divorce spokespersons or groups than terms like "fundamentalists", "extremists", or, horror of horrors, "extremist fundamentalists", or "right-wing Catholics", "conservative Catholics", "old-style Catholics", "sectarian bigots", etc. The issues as such are not debated, but the protagonists for life and for family are labelled in such a way as to exclude them from 'modem', 'progressive', and 'civilised' society and consequently to classify them as people whose views could by definition have no validity. We know how often the teaching of Pope John Paul is similarly

---

[3] *Evangelium Vitae*, 24.

dismissed by derogatory remarks about his so-called 'conservative' background in 'pre-Vatican II Polish Catholicism', or about his alleged attempts to 'roll back' the Second Vatican Council, etc.

The persuasive power of ethical terms, which Charles L. Stevenson developed into a comprehensive theory of ethics, has certainly played a part in to-day's moral crisis. Ian Robinson, in a book on *The Survival of English*, has spoken of "linguistic magic"[4]. Pope John Paul again calls attention to this seductive danger and urges us

> now more than ever to have the courage to look the truth in the eye and to call things by their proper names without yielding to convenient compromises or to the temptation of self-deception.... No words have the power to change the intrinsic reality of things.[5]

## Religion and morality

Another conclusion to be drawn from the contemporary crisis is that religious faith and morality are very closely connected. It has long been a dogma of secular humanists that ethics is completely independent of religion and carries within itself its own self-validating power. Indeed, following Kant, many, if not most, moral philosophers have held that decisions and choices made for religious motives are not truly moral; it is said that moral choices have to be "autonomous", whereas choices made on religious grounds are "heteronomous", and therefore morally inauthentic. Surely, however, it would be implausible to deny that the crisis in contemporary morals has been, not just accompanied by, but in large part caused by, decline in religious faith and practice. Pope John Paul is surely right when he calls, in both of his great moral encyclicals, for a deep conversion of consciences and an individual and collective response to the Christian call to contemplative prayer and to holiness. Nothing less will equip us to resist the modern "culture of death" and to create a new "culture of life".

The decline in moral thinking and in moral standards in contemporary society, however, does not justify a blanket condemnation of modem society. Critics of this decline are not to be dismissed as nostalgic, backward-looking, *laudatores temporis acti*. There was immorality in every society throughout history, and there is much in modern society which represents genuine moral progress. We must as Christians embrace all that is true and good in modern culture; and indeed it is those who have a deep understanding and a genuine appreciation of what is true and good in modem society who can most credibly criticise what is erroneous and evil. This is precisely how Pope John Paul views modern culture, with full appreciation of "the positive signs at work in humanity's present situation". He

[4] Ian Robinson, *The Survival of English. Essays in Criticism of Language* (Cambridge: Cambridge University Press 1973).
[5] *Evangelium Vitae*, 58.

warns against "sterile discouragement", and enumerates many "signs of hope" which give us courage.[6]

## Role of magisterium

The modern crisis of morality unfortunately coincided with something of a crisis in Catholic moral theology. The profound renewal of dogmatic theology which climaxed in the Second Vatican Council was preceded by many decades of previous preparation. A number of distinguished Catholic exegetes and theologians were laying the foundations long before the Council, particularly in the post World War II period. Great names like those of Bea, Benoit, Feuillet, Dupont, in Scripture, and von Balthasar, Rahner, de Lubac and Congar, in theology, come immediately to mind. Sadly, there were no comparable great names in moral theology, although Pope Pius XII had made very significant contributions to Catholic teaching on the great moral issues of his time. The Council itself did not formally address the area of moral theology, although its documents, especially *Gaudium et Spes*, have important paragraphs on moral themes, especially in the area of marriage and family and of social justice. The Council did, however, issue a call to scholars to undertake a renewal of moral theology, based on the teaching of Scripture and responding to the problems and aspirations of modern culture (Decree on Priestly Formation, *Optatam Totius* 16 and *Gaudium et Spes* 62). Bernard Häring made a valiant effort to outline a new approach to moral theology, based on Christ's new commandment of love, but faithful to the great tradition of the Church. Unfortunately, however, like many others, Häring got caught up in the *Humanae Vitae* controversy and increasingly took the line of dissent.

The negative reaction of some to *Humanae Vitae* both exposed the existing weaknesses in the teaching of modern theology and created new weaknesses. Those in the first wave of dissent seemed sincerely to believe that the Church's traditional ruling on contraception could be changed without any effect on the rest of Catholic moral teaching. They quickly found, however, that the logic of their position on contraception went very much further than they had originally intended; indeed it obliged them to adopt positions which lead logically to the unravelling of the whole of the Church's sexual morality, and, not only that, but also involved a drastic rewriting of large areas of traditional Catholic moral teaching. Helped by an enthusiastically compliant media, dissent spread rather widely among the Catholic moral theological community and spread from there to considerable sections of the wider Catholic family. This undoubtedly weakened the Church's stand in face of the many grave evils confronting her in modern society.

[6] *Evangelium Vitae*, 26–27.

*In Veritatis Splendor* Pope John Paul, in firm language, declares that

> within the context of the theological debates which have followed the Council there have developed certain interpretations of Christian morality which are not consistent with "sound teaching"... The Magisterium has the duty to state that some trends of theological thinking and certain philosophical affirmations are incompatible with revealed truth.[7]

The Pope affirms that conscience is not the origin of moral values, but is itself subject to moral values, obliged by the "inescapable claims" of moral truth.[8] He strongly emphasises the truth that there are moral laws which bind universally and there are behaviours which are objectively and intrinsically evil in themselves.[9] Three times in *Evangelium Vitae* Pope John Paul invokes Holy Scripture and the Tradition of the Church and the universal magisterium of the Bishops united with the Pope, and his own Petrine authority, as well as the natural law, to declare certain specific acts to be intrinsically morally wrong:

> ... by the authority which Christ conferred upon Peter and his Successors, and in communion with the Bishops of the Catholic Church, *I confirm that the direct and voluntary killing of an innocent human being is always gravely immoral.* This doctrine, based upon that unwritten law which man, in the light of reason, finds in his own heart (cf. *Rom* 2:14–15), is reaffirmed by Sacred Scripture, transmitted by the Tradition of the Church and taught by the ordinary and universal Magisterium.[10]

> ... by the authority which Christ conferred upon Peter and his Successors, in communion with the Bishops... *I declare that direct abortion, that is, abortion willed as an end or as a means, always constitutes a grave moral disorder,* since it is the deliberate killing of an innocent human being. This doctrine is based upon the natural law and upon the written Word of God, is transmitted by the Church's Tradition and taught by the ordinary and universal Magisterium.[11]

> ... in harmony with the Magisterium of my Predecessors and in communion with the Bishops of the Catholic Church, *I confirm that euthanasia is a grave violation of the law of God,* since it is the deliberate and morally unacceptable killing of a human person. This doctrine is based upon the natural law and upon the written word of God, is transmitted by the Church's Tradition and taught by the ordinary and universal Magisterium.[12]

*Veritatis Splendor* is addressed directly to Bishops. The Pope speaks to them as "brothers who share with me the responsibility of safeguarding sound teaching".

[7] *Veritatis Splendor*, 29.
[8] *Veritatis Splendor*, 32.
[9] *Veritatis Splendor*, 51–53.
[10] *Evangelium Vitae*, 57. [Italics in original]
[11] *Evangelium Vitae*, 62. [Italics in original]
[12] *Evangelium Vitae*, 65. [Italics in original]

He speaks of himself and the Bishops together as "we Pastors". Obviously, this document is intended as a statement of the moral principles upheld by the Church's ordinary and universal magisterium. Published in 1995, *Evangelium Vitae* was prepared for by a specially convened Consistory of Cardinals in 1991, and by a questionnaire sent to every Bishop in the Church. This encyclical is also, therefore, clearly an exercise of the ordinary and universal Magisterium. Taken together, these two documents lay down firm principles for Catholic moral teaching and clear parameters for the still incomplete renewal of Catholic moral theology.

## Challenge to Church and Society

These documents constitute a challenge to Church and to society. The Pope is, as always, conscious that the Church is engaged in a mighty spiritual combat, and that only a real struggle for holiness of life on the part of all Catholics will arm us for that combat. He calls for a renewal of the sense of mystery, of wonder and of reverence before God and before God's gift of human life. He calls for the fostering of a contemplative outlook[13], and a renewed sense of the sacredness of human life. He outlines what can be called a comprehensive and consistent pro-life ethic, indeed a "culture of life" which will confront the growing "culture of death" in modern society. He asks all Catholics to become "people of life", so that "a new culture of love and solidarity may develop for the true good of the whole of human society"[14].

The pressures against the Church's teaching in virtually all areas of morality might seem irresistible. A remark attributed to the American judge, Mr Justice Brandeis, is worth recalling: "The irresistible is often only that which is not resisted".[15]

I wish to quote some remarkable words from a most unlikely witness, Bertrand Russell. In his celebrated book *Marriage and Morals*, Russell accurately foresaw, as many Catholic moral theologians later failed to foresee, that the acceptance of contraception implied what he called an entirely new ethics of sexuality. In *The Scientific Attitude* (1931, 1954) he outlines some of the probable outcomes of the application of science to human problems, including the question of sex and reproduction. His predictions at the time had something of the character of science fiction, but they are now everyday matters of fact. He granted that his predictions were "not to be taken altogether as serious prophecy"; they are "visions of Cassandra". Russell himself was clearly disturbed by these possibilities; he saw them as possibilities "in a world governed by knowledge without love and power without delight". He deplores the cult of "power for its own sake"; he

---

[13] *Evangelium Vitae*, 83.

[14] *Evangelium Vitae*, 101.

[15] Cited by Isaiah Berlin in his lecture on 'Historical Inevitability', reprinted in his *Four Essays on Liberty*, London: Oxford University Press 1969, p. 116, footnote 2.

fears those for whom "the fact that they can do something that no-one previously thought it possible to do is a sufficient reason for doing it".

They represent, he said, the world "which would result if scientific technique were to rule unchecked". Russell saw, though without much hope, possible alternatives in a rediscovery of contemplation. He speaks of "the ecstasy of contemplation". He quotes: "In knowledge of God standeth our eternal life". (*The Scientific Attitude*, esp. Ch. XVII, 'Science and Values'.) Sadly, for Russell ecstasy can come only from human love, chiefly sexual love; but this does not provide the "peace that passes all understanding" which the human heart seeks, and which only God can give.

Pope John Paul, contemplative as well as pastor and teacher, brings us back in the end of *Evangelium Vitae* to Christ, who alone has the words of eternal life, and to Mary, who kept all his words and pondered them in her heart. It is here that we find courage for the immense tasks which confront us as Catholics facing the moral crisis of our time. Like St. Paul:

> We are in difficulties on all sides, but never cornered; we see no answer to our problems, but never despair; we have been persecuted but never deserted; knocked down but never killed .... So we have no eyes for things that are visible, but only for the things that are invisible; for visible things last only for a time, and the invisible things are eternal. (2 *Corinthians* 4: 8–9, 18)

### Reflections in Holocaust Museum

While in Washington last month for a lecture, I visited the United States Holocaust Memorial Museum there. I am still haunted by the awful images of the "culture of death" which surround one as one goes from gallery to gallery of that Museum. The question that kept coming to me was this: "How could this happen in a modern, advanced, technologically highly developed European country in the middle of the 20th century? How could so many of the professional elites in such a country have tolerated this or even colluded in it? Could it happen here?" Our instinct is to reply immediately: "Impossible. Unthinkable"; but we need to pause and reflect. When sterilisation, euthanasia, the elimination of the mentally or physically handicapped and of eugenically inferior breeds, were introduced by the Nazis in 1935, shock waves of moral revulsion spread across the Western world. Moral sensitivities have profoundly deteriorated since then. There is no universal moral revulsion now when euthanasia, sterilisation, abortion, eugenic "breeding", are discussed.

Professor Leibbrand, expert witness for the prosecution at the Nuremberg Trial of German doctors who conducted experiments on human beings in the Nazi regime, declared that the Nazis substituted the "biological idea" for the "metaphysical idea", and that it was this that mentally conditioned doctors for their systematic medical experimentation on human beings, particularly prisoners, internees and others. There are disturbing signs of a similar substitution of the biological view of the human being for the metaphysical view, and much more for the Christian view, in some medical circles today. Some proposed re-writings of the Hippocratic Oath would scarcely have been possible without such a shift of meanings and of values. The inscription on a pillar in the Chapel area in the Holocaust Museum reads:

For the dead and the living we must bear witness.

Much more must we bear witness to the Lord of life, who came and dwelt amongst us in order that we might have life and might have it to the full.

# 4

# Catholics and Anglicans and contemporary bioethics: divided or united?[1]

MICHAEL BANNER

I

IN HIS REFLECTIONS on the bidding, "Hallowed be thy name", Karl Barth connects this prayer with the knowledge and ignorance of God which, so he maintains, is manifest in the life of the world, the church and the individual Christian. Each of these in their different ways, he contends, dwells in that impossible and intolerable twilight in which God's name is not only honoured "but also desecrated, disputed, and slandered".[2] Thus when we pray as we may and must, "hallowed be thy name", we pray that this known and unknown God will finally overcome the darkness in which humans would live, bringing each and all into the kingdom of Jesus Christ, in whom, unambiguously and unequivocally, God knows humankind and humankind God.

Now for all that it is paradoxical, since it belongs to "the very nature, constitution, and structure of the church"[3] that it exists in the knowledge of God, this knowing and not knowing of God is indeed manifest in the church and manifest, says Barth, in two particular forms. In the one form we have what he calls the "church in excess", in the other "the church in defect". In both we have a church which, contrary to its true nature, lives as in ignorance of the living Lord whose church it truly is.

The church in excess "is the church exceeding the limit within which alone it can be the church of Jesus Christ: the limit of the basic determination that the living one to whom it owes the origin and constitution of its life, who in relation to it – and to it specifically – is the freely acting and speaking *Lord*, that this one is its sovereign".[4] This church, the church in excess, is in danger of forgetting that the church is a creature of the word of God:

> Appealing to its institution and empowering through him, it wants to be the
> church that reigns in his name. He must act only on and with and through
> it. As to the world, so also to itself, he must speak only in the form of its

[1] I am grateful to Ben Quash, Francis Watson and Oliver O'Donovan for comments on a draft of this paper and to Germain Grisez for conversations concerning its themes.
[2] K. Barth, *The Christian Life*, trans. G.W. Bromiley, Edinburgh: T & T Clark 1981, p. 116.
[3] Barth, *The Christian Life*, p. 134.
[4] Barth, *The Christian Life*, p. 136.

own speech and action. It integrates his priestly, kingly, and prophetic office with its own. *It* speaks his truth; *it* extends or denies his grace; *it* proclaims his law. With his staff, sceptre, and sword in its own hand, exercising his authority in the power of its own, *it* reigns: only in his place, it will assert again and again, yet still in his place, as his full representative. *It* has his Spirit. *It* expounds the Scripture that bears witness to him. In dealing thus with him, in leaping over the barrier between it and him, the church makes it hard to see how far he is over it, how far he is its Lord, as it does not cease to profess, how far he is the Lord whom it must hear and obey and to whom it is answerable, how far it has not exalted itself as his lord, how far it has not made the Word the creature of the church. Can it still be the church in this form?[5]

If the "church in excess" needs to learn again that it is the church of a living *Lord*, the "church in defect", on the other hand, needs to learn that it really is the church of a *living* Lord. The "church in defect" is "the church which does not take itself seriously enough because it is only half sure of its cause, which takes up this cause only hesitantly and with reservations and compromises, which only in a timid and uncommitted way ventures to give itself to its task".[6] In effect it does not know "the Lord who by his resurrection from the dead is in his death superior to death, and therefore to the world as the world that is marked and ruled by death; the Lord who overcomes the world, since God reconciled it to himself in him, so that his people need fear no one and nothing in this world".

The church in defect is not comforted as it may and should be in view of this victory. To be sure, it knows and recites the words: "The third day he rose again from the dead; he ascended into heaven and sitteth on the right hand of God the Father Almighty." But it does not say this with total confidence, only with half confidence. It does not stand defiantly on it. Only occasionally and not fundamentally and consistently does it think and speak and act in the light of it. It is at any moment ready and able to think and speak and act apart from this presupposition.[7]

Of course, as may be already apparent and as Barth points out, these two forms of the church, the "church in excess" and the "church in defect", are, as described, the stuff of the typical suspicions between Roman Catholics and Protestants. In the church of Rome, Protestants have seen a church which claims too much for itself and thereby denies that Jesus Christ is the church's living *Lord*, while in the Protestant churches, Roman Catholics have found "a painfully small trust in the authority and power of him who has called, gathered and sent out the church as his community" and thus a denial that Jesus Christ is the church's *living* Lord. To put it in other words, Roman Catholicism has seen

[5] Barth, *The Christian Life*, pp. 136–7.
[6] Barth, *The Christian Life*, p. 137.
[7] Barth, *The Christian Life*, p. 138.

in the Protestant churches the "church in defect" which tends to secularisation, while Protestants have seen in the Church of Rome that inclination to sacralisation which is the temptation of the "church in excess".

If these characterisations (or caricatures) are not without some purchase on reality, in relation to Roman Catholic bioethics they lead us badly astray, so I shall maintain. It would be easy enough for Protestants in search of the "church in excess" – that is, a church which is in danger of making so much of itself as to make the word of God its creature – to be struck by, let us say, *Evangelium Vitae*'s solemn formulations of the condemnations of direct and voluntary killing of the innocent, of direct abortion and of euthanasia, appealing as they variously do to the "authority Christ conferred upon Peter and his Successors" and to the "Church's Tradition".[8] But to find such significance in these formulations is, in actual fact, to miss what is going on since, contrary to what may seem to be at first sight likely, the proper question to put to the Roman Church in the matter of its bioethics, on the basis of this Encyclical at least, is whether it tends more to being the "church in defect" than the "church in excess". The Roman Church, that is to say, is not so much in danger here of making the word of God a creature of the church, but, so it turns out, of forgetting the particular authority which belongs to the church as itself the creature of the word of God.

This thought is forced upon us, as we shall see, by a more careful study of *Evangelium Vitae* and by reflection upon its presuppositions, and it is to the consideration and interpretation of that Encyclical to which we now turn. It is only as we have explored these questions that we can come to this paper's particular concern with the relationship between Anglican and Roman Catholic bioethics.

## II

The interpretation of *Evangelium Vitae* is a matter of some difficulty just because the Encyclical develops three strands of argument or themes without finally resolving the tensions between them. As is well known, the Encyclical treats of threats to human life affecting particularly its earliest and its final stages. Within this treatment one theme concerns the so-called "culture of death", of which the Encyclical proposes, at least in outline, a description and a genealogy. A second theme is found in the explication of the nature and grounds of a Christian commitment to the sanctity and protection of human life. A third theme has to do with the basis for the protection of life in secular thinking, and here the Encyclical refers to conscience, to rights and to the proper relationship between the moral and civil law. Whatever may be the merit of the handling of these individual themes, the Encyclical, so I shall argue, pays insufficient attention to the fact that the three sit rather uneasily together, something which begins to

[8] John Paul II, *Evangelium Vitae*, English translation (London, 1995), para. 57, 62 and 65. (All subsequent references will be to numbered paragraphs.)

emerge even in the introduction which announces and prefigures the document's chief concerns.

In that introduction the Encyclical draws attention to the development of "a new cultural climate... which gives crimes against life a new and – if possible – even more sinister character".[9] This character, as the Encyclical will explain, comes from the fact that "choices once unanimously considered criminal and rejected by the common moral sense are gradually becoming socially acceptable".[10] Indeed the attacks upon life at its beginning and end with which the Encyclical is principally concerned "tend no longer to be considered as 'crimes'" but "paradoxically... assume the nature of 'rights' to the point that the State is called upon to give them legal recognition and to make them available through the free services of health-care personnel".[11] And what makes this the more striking is that these attacks are most often "carried out in the heart of and with the complicity of the family – the family which by its nature is called to be the 'sanctuary of life'".[12] What is important for the Encyclical however, is that the social acceptance of these attacks on life, wherever they may occur, points to a "problem which exists at the cultural, social and political level".[13] Thus when the Encyclical comes to speak of "a war of the powerful against the weak" and "a conspiracy against life", it means to refer to a movement which is more than simply a matter of individual and independent bad choices, and amounts to "a veritable structure of sin" or "a veritable 'culture of death'", "fostered by powerful cultural, economic and political currents which encourage an idea of society excessively concerned with efficiency".[14] It is a question, then, "in a certain sense, of the 'moral conscience' of society", which as a result of the "eclipse of the sense of God and of man", "not only... tolerates or fosters behaviour contrary to life, but also... encourages the 'culture of death', creating and consolidating actual 'structures of sin' which go against life".[15] Such is the character of this culture of death, that the church which opposes it is engaged in "a dramatic struggle" which, in the conclusion to the Encyclical, will be evoked in the highly charged imagery of chapter 12 of the Book of Revelation.[16]

The introduction to the Encyclical also makes reference to a second theme, this one concerning the nature and basis of a Christian commitment to human life and its protection. According to that introduction, "Christmas... reveals the full meaning of every human birth, and the joy which accompanies the Birth of the Messiah is thus seen to be the foundation and fulfilment of joy at every child born into the world."[17] Joy at a human birth is related to the joy at the birth of

---

[9] *Evangelium Vitae*, 4.

[10] *Evangelium Vitae*, 4.

[11] *Evangelium Vitae*, 11.

[12] *Evangelium Vitae*, 11.

[13] *Evangelium Vitae*, 18.

[14] *Evangelium Vitae*, 12.

[15] *Evangelium Vitae*, 24.

[16] *Evangelium Vitae*, 104.

[17] *Evangelium Vitae*, 1.

the messiah through the gift of eternal life, the communion of the Son with the Father, "to which every person is freely called in the Son by the power of the Sanctifying Spirit" and in which "all aspects and stages of human life achieve their full significance."[18] Now this "supernatural calling . . . highlights the relative character of each individual's earthly life", but is also the ground for the particular vocation which belongs to Christians as those "aware . . . of the wonderful truth recalled by the Second Vatican Council: 'By his incarnation the Son of God has united himself in some fashion with every human being'."[19] This truth reveals both God's love and also "the incomparable value of every human person".[20] Thus:

> The Church, faithfully contemplating the mystery of the Redemption, acknowledges this value with ever new wonder. She feels called to proclaim to the people of all times this "Gospel", the source of invincible hope and true joy for every period of history. The Gospel of God's love for man, the Gospel of the dignity of the person and the Gospel of life are a single and indivisible Gospel.[21]

In maintaining this theme, however – namely, the indivisibility of the Gospel of redemption and the Gospel of the dignity of human life which provides the document with its title – the Encyclical means to stress only, it seems, that the first necessarily implies the second, not that the second necessarily presupposes the first. Or at least, to put it more strictly, it allows that the dignity of human life can be known independently of the Gospel of redemption, even if it is not then known as Gospel:

> The Church knows that this Gospel of life, which she has received from her Lord, has a profound and persuasive echo in the heart of every person – believer and non-believer alike – because it marvellously fulfils all the heart's expectations while infinitely surpassing them. Even in the midst of difficulties and uncertainties, every person sincerely open to truth and goodness can, by the light of reason and the hidden action of grace, come to recognise in the natural law written in the heart (cf Rom 2:14–15) the sacred value of human life from its very beginning until its end, and can affirm the right of every human being to have this primary good respected to the highest degree. Upon the recognition of this right, every human community and the political community itself are founded.[22]

This, then, announces the main elements of a third and seemingly independent theme which will recur throughout the Encyclical and especially in Chapter III which deals with the command, "You shall not kill". According to this theme,

---

[18] *Ibid.*
[19] *Evangelium Vitae*, 2.
[20] *Ibid.*
[21] *Ibid.*
[22] *Ibid.*

the acknowledgement of and respect for those essential values epitomised for the Encyclical in the notion of the rights of the person – "among which in the first place is the inviolable right of every innocent human being to life"[23] – is in principle, so it seems, independent of the knowledge of the Gospel with which it was previously associated. Whereas previously, that is to say, it had been stressed that "the dignity of... life is linked not only to its beginning, to the fact that it comes from God, but also to its final end, to its destiny of fellowship with God in knowledge and love of him"[24] and thus that the loss of man is connected with the loss of God and vice versa[25], now this dignity is simply known in the moral law to which the conscience witnesses. Furthermore, according to the Encyclical, the "basic elements of a vision of the relationship between the civil law and the moral law...are...part of the patrimony of the great juridical traditions of humanity" as well as being forwarded by the Church.[26] Fundamental to this vision, so it is said, is the protection of the right to life; thus if it is held that "abortion and euthanasia are... crimes which no human law can claim to legitimize"[27], this is a principle which a purely human jurisprudence will itself affirm.

According to the development of this theme, then, the rise of the culture of death makes it "urgently necessary, for the future of society and development of a sound democracy, to rediscover those essential and innate human and moral values which flow from the very truth of the human being and express and safeguard the dignity of the person: values which no individual, no majority and no State can ever create, modify or destroy, but must only acknowledge, respect and promote".[28] Thus, as the Encyclical sees it, "what is urgently called for is a general mobilization of consciences"[29], for it is the conscience which bears witness to the value of life, a "value... which every human being can grasp by the light of reason".[30]

The problem in relating these three themes one to another ought to be plain enough. The themes concern, let us recall, the culture of death, the nature and grounds of the Christian commitment to life and its protection in the Gospel of creation, incarnation and redemption, and the basis of the protection of life in the moral law known to the conscience, mediated through the concept of rights, and properly related to the civil law. The chief difficulty is this: insofar as the existence, character and operation of the culture of death is portrayed in the lurid colours of battle borrowed from the Book of Revelation, the plausibility or truth of certain of the claims found in the treatment of the third theme looks highly doubtful – or put it the other way round: if it really is the case that "all the conditioning and efforts to enforce silence fail to stifle the voice of the Lord echoing in the conscience of every

---

[23] *Evangelium Vitae*, 60, quoting directly *Donum Vitae*, I, 1.
[24] *Evangelium Vitae*, 38.
[25] *Evangelium Vitae*, 21.
[26] *Evangelium Vitae*, 71.
[27] *Evangelium Vitae*, 73.
[28] *Evangelium Vitae*, 71.
[29] *Evangelium Vitae*, 95.
[30] *Evangelium Vitae*, 101.

individual"[31], the very existence of the culture of death – as a culture in which what is reckoned manifestly contrary to the moral law is socially acceptable – becomes highly mysterious. If the "Gospel of life ... has a profound and persuasive echo in the heart of every person – believer and non-believer alike"[32], how has the culture of death arisen? How is it, if there is this "profound and persuasive echo", that "Humanity today offers us a truly alarming spectacle, if we consider not only how extensively attacks on life are spreading but also their unheard-of numerical proportion, and the fact that they receive widespread and powerful support from a broad consensus on the part of society, from widespread legal approval and the involvement of certain sectors of health-care personnel"[33]?

If the treatment of the third theme – that is, the basis for the protection of life in the moral law known to conscience – sits awkwardly with the first theme concerning the culture of death, that first theme is altogether more happily placed in company with the second theme as we have identified it, concerning the nature and grounds of the Christian commitment to life and its protection in the Gospel of creation, incarnation and redemption. If, as the Encyclical holds, Christianity provides a particular and specific basis for a belief in the sanctity of life, even if not the only conceivable basis, the rise of the culture of death alongside a decline in Christian belief is not in the least surprising. If "by living 'as if God did not exist', man not only loses sight of the mystery of God, but also of the mystery of the world and mystery of his own being";[34] if, moreover, the

---

[31] *Evangelium Vitae*, 24.

[32] *Evangelium Vitae*, 2.

[33] *Evangelium Vitae*, 17. In comments on this section of my paper, Oliver O'Donovan notes that there is, strictly, no problem of consistency in *Evangelium Vitae* claiming a certain validity for what I am terming "general moral enquiry" while also asserting the general or total purchase of the "culture of death" – *Evangelium Vitae* could hold that the actual consensus of society was corrupt and anti-life, while retaining the view that it is open to moral reasoning at any point to break through the imprisonment of this cultural deception since there is nothing necessary about moral error, however pervasive. On this reading, the appeal to conscience is not to a source of demonstration, but is precisely an appeal, asking that we attend to the question in hand in the hope that this attention might be the occasion of the insight of which the conscience is capable under the direction of the Holy Spirit. While Professor O'Donovan is right to avert to the possibility of reading the encyclical thus, and so of saving it from any charge of inconsistency, he is also right to ask "whether EV really observes the theological discipline that this interpretation attributes to it". My reading of the encyclical is that it does not; as we shall see in the next section, it is inclined to treat the moral knowledge which should enable us to escape our cultural imprisonment as an actuality and thus, so to say, as an initial condition in contemporary debate and not as a possibility which may be realised through the specific action of the Holy Spirit. To put it in other words, the encyclical is all too inclined to speak as if the appeal to conscience must work, not as if it may, the latter thesis being one which, unlike the former, there is no reason to deny. Indeed, since medical practice, for example, is not wholly corrupt, but is still dependent in all sorts of ways on traditions of Christian life and thought, that appeal will doubtless have a certain utility. But the effectiveness of the appeal cannot be taken for granted, and in particular it can be expected to decline in so far as the church fails to enunciate the specifically Christian understanding of reality which informed that earlier medical self-understanding and practice.

[34] *Evangelium Vitae*, 22.

preaching of the Gospel is "the presentation of human life as a relationship, a gift of God" and "the proclamation that Jesus has a unique relationship with every person"; and if the claims that "human life, as a gift of God, is sacred and inviolable" and that "procured abortion and euthanasia are absolutely unacceptable", are "consequences of this Gospel"[35], it will be readily understandable that the repudiation of the Christian message, as a repudiation of the Gospel of life, should be accompanied by the rise of a culture of death in which such convictions are increasingly marginalised.

The problem of the interpretation of the Encyclical is, then, a problem about the relationship between, and reconciliation of, these three themes. The possibility which the Encyclical seems to entertain, of answering the culture of death by appeal to a moral law mediated by conscience, is seemingly belied both by its own understanding of the very nature or character of the culture of death, and also by its articulation of belief in the sacredness and inviolability of human life as arising out of the central tenets of Christian doctrine. By its own lights, that is to say, the possibility of answering the culture of death from the supposedly metaphysics-free realm of conscience and rights appears somewhat remote, but it does, so it seems, wish to maintain this possibility.

## III

It is in maintaining this possibility, so we shall contend, that the Encyclical invites the church to be "the church in defect". We shall argue, that is to say, that the Encyclical's presupposition as to the validity of general moral enquiry is implicitly a denial of the authority which belongs to the church in virtue of its being a creature of the word of God. We shall further argue that this invitation to be the "church in defect" is one which the church has every reason to decline, not only because of this fundamental objection to it, but also because, as well as creating a tension within the Encyclical, the presumption which constitutes the invitation is the cause of quite definite difficulties in the Encyclical's argument.

Although it is in tension with the other themes it develops, the Encyclical seems ready to allow to general moral enquiry a certain autonomy and validity. Now to grant such validity to general moral enquiry is, so it can be maintained, necessarily to cast doubt upon the authority of the moral understanding, interpretation and judgement which the church possesses, practises and exercises in virtue of its standing under the word of God. How is this so? The allowance of autonomy and validity to general moral enquiry casts doubt upon the authority of Christian ethics by supposing, in effect, that Christian ethics and general ethics rule jointly over the same sphere. But once it is allowed that there is such a "co-regency", so to say, it follows that Christian ethics must always be ready and able to prove itself to general moral enquiry – the allowance of the validity of general moral enquiry would mean nothing if it did not follow that Christian ethics must submit to questioning by, and seek a mandate from, such moral

---

[35] *Evangelium Vitae*, 81.

enquiry. *Evangelium Vitae*, so it can be claimed, admits this very "co-regency" and allows a validity to general moral enquiry just by entertaining a belief in the possibility of apologetics in relation to bioethics; in believing that Christian bioethics can and should vindicate itself before general moral enquiry it presupposes the validity of the latter, for if the latter possessed no such validity such vindication would be neither probable nor particularly desirable. But, as we have said, to presuppose this validity is to think it appropriate, and if appropriate then necessary, for Christian ethics to prove itself before this court – "necessary" for the reason that the admission of the validity of general moral enquiry immediately poses a question as to the status of any other ethics, including Christian ethics. Hence *Evangelium Vitae* invites the church to be the "church in defect", just by inviting it to believe in the validity of general moral enquiry and thus to doubt the authority of the church's moral understanding, interpretation and judgement, an authority which belongs to that understanding as it is a faithful reflection on the meaning of the grace of God shown in Jesus Christ. This invitation asks the church to treat the Lordship of Christ as if it must itself be vindicated before other lordships and authorities, and thus to doubt its own authority as the subject of this Lord. It invites the church, that is to say, to set up general ethics as judge over itself, or more particularly, over the word it has from this Lord.[36]

*Evangelium Vitae*'s belief in the validity of general moral enquiry and the possibility of apologetics is, however, as we have seen, a belief with which the Encyclical shows itself to be far from comfortable, at least insofar as we take seriously the other themes in the Encyclical which are in distinct tension with it. We must now note that this belief is not only a source of tension (which might, after all, simply be termed "fruitful" or "creative" and thus disregarded), but of quite definite difficulties in the Encyclical's argument and engagement. Our point here will be, then, that the temptation to which the "church in defect" succumbs leads it seriously astray in a number of respects: I shall indicate, rather than fully explore, four particular problems in the development of the Encyclical's arguments and concerns, created or at least encouraged by its commitment to the general possibility of apologetics.

(i) Although one of the most notable and important features of *Evangelium Vitae* is its willingness to understand the "culture of death" as the creation of diverse historical circumstances and social forces, its inclination to maintain a residual commitment to the possibility of a general apologetic leads to a certain equivocation even in the description and portrayal of the modern crisis represented by the culture of death – and indeed also, as I shall maintain in the next point, a certain wrong emphasis at the very least, in the presentation of the specifically Christian basis for the valuation and protection of human life.

---

[36] I am here relying on Karl Barth's treatment of ethics, in particular in *The Church Dogmatics*, II/2, section 36, "Ethics as a Task of the Doctrine of God"; I have discussed his argument and its implications in an inaugural lecture, *Turning the World Upside Down (and Some Other Tasks for Dogmatic Christian Ethics)* (King's College, London, 1996), reprinted in *Christian Ethics and Contemporary Moral Problems* (Cambridge, 1999).

I have already noted that *Evangelium Vitae* deploys the highly charged imagery of the Book of Revelation in its description of "sinister" modern developments and of the conflict between the culture of life and the culture of death. But perhaps because of the persistence of the apologetic theme it cannot allow itself to believe that the culture of death is, finally, quite as set in its opposition to the culture of life as that imagery would lead one to suppose; after all, according to the Encyclical the culture of death can still be expected to be moved by the appeal of the moral law and of conscience. So it is that the Encyclical hesitates before the "linguistic phenomenon" of the "widespread use of ambiguous terminology, such as 'interruption of pregnancy'" and wonders whether this phenomenon "is itself a symptom of an uneasiness of conscience."[37]

Such a thought, however, is one which the Encyclical's own lively sense of the radical nature of the conflict between the culture of life and the culture of death should cause it to reject if it is conceived as providing not just a possible and occasional, but a generally serviceable account of the phenomenon in question. What this sense of the radicality of the conflict really requires is the recognition that even if such terminology was once used, at its genesis perhaps, euphemistically for the sake of a slightly delicate conscience and on occasions is still so used, in contemporary usage it is just as often employed as a morally neutral description of a morally neutral act. The termination of a pregnancy really is, for this way of thought, a termination of a pregnancy and not the killing of a child; the latter description is not held to be accurate though somewhat vulgar or in bad taste as being rather too explicit, but is thought to be quite simply inappropriate or wrong – this latter fact the Encyclical knows only too well or it would find no place for the repeated insistence that from the moment of conception there is a human being deserving of protection. What we have in this modern usage, is not only, then, a case of people calling things they know to be bad by names which consciously serve to conceal that fact, but also of people using morally neutral terms to refer to what is genuinely thought to be so. The culture of death, that is to say, is not a culture with a bad conscience which must always be carefully guarded from reminders of what it secretly knows, but a culture which has come quite genuinely to regard as outside the sphere of moral critique what is, in actuality and from the Encyclical's perspective, contrary to the moral law.

If the Encyclical had held to its identification of this aspect of the modern situation (and not only the modern situation) with greater firmness, the contemporary situation might have been more properly described and analysed. However, the lurking conviction as to the general possibility of apologetics vitiates even the handling of this of the Encyclical's themes, since the description which the Encyclical offers is, in effect, crucially qualified by the assumption that "We shall find important points of contact and dialogue also with non-believers, in our common commitment to the establishment of a new culture of life."[38] Of

---

[37] *Evangelium Vitae*, 58.
[38] *Evangelium Vitae*, 82.

course, contingently and for a variety of reasons, such points of contact may emerge – medical practice, for example, is not wholly and consistently in the grip of the culture of death, and this because its self-understanding is still partly owing to the influence which the Christian tradition has had on its development. Thus the church will properly make use of these and any other "points of contact" in *ad hoc, ad hominem* and eclectic arguments in support of its moral claims.[39] But if the Church, which "well knows that it is difficult to mount an effective legal defence of life in pluralistic democracies, because of the presence of strong cultural currents with differing outlooks", "at the same time... encourages political leaders, starting with those who are Christians, not to give in, but to make those choices which, taking into account what is realistically attainable, will lead to the re-establishment of a just order in the defence and promotion of the value of life", it need not do so on the basis of the conviction that – to replace the words omitted from the quotation – it is "certain that moral truth cannot fail to make its presence deeply felt in every conscience".[40] It may follow this path out of a simple realism which tells it not that this strategy must work, but that it might, so that it follows this strategy without qualifying or moderating in any way its critical appraisal of the culture of death. That appraisal, however, will be framed with the rigour and clarity it deserves only when moral theology's description, and indeed perception, of how things are, is not conditioned and constrained by the extraneous demands of a prior epistemological commitment of the sort which is found in *Evangelium Vitae*.

(ii) The second point is that a commitment to the general possibility of an apologetic bioethic threatens to distort the Encyclical's understanding and treatment of the relationship between law and Gospel which, like the identification and characterisation of the existence of the culture of death, is potentially one of the Encyclical's most important contributions.

In the course of his discussion of abortion, Barth claims that the Protestant Church:

> neither could nor can range itself with the Roman Catholic Church and its hard preaching of the Law. It must proclaim its own message in this matter, namely the Gospel. In so doing, however, it must not underbid the severity of the Roman Catholic No. It must overbid its abstract and negative: "Thou shalt not", by the force of its positive: "Thou mayest", in which, of course, the corresponding: "Thou mayest not", is included, the No having the force not merely of the word of man but of the Word of God.[41]

---

[39] I have discussed this point somewhat more fully in *Turning the World Upside Down (and Some Other Tasks for Dogmatic Christian Ethics)*. My purpose there was to maintain that Christian ethics which is "fully aware of its own particularity, and possessed of no *a priori* faith in the possibility of finding a realm of autonomous values with which it can make common cause" may be as fully engaged in public debate and discussion as a supposedly traditional natural law ethic which typically charges the former conception of Christian ethics with being sectarian.
[40] *Evangelium Vitae*, 90.
[41] Barth, *Church Dogmatics*, III/iv, trans. A.T. Mackay et al (Edinburgh, 1961), 418.

As he puts it again: "the Church knows and has the Word of the free mercy of God which also ascribes and grants freedom to man. It could and can tell and show humanity which is tormented by life because it thinks it must live it, that it may do so."[42]

The sensitivities of *Evangelium Vitae* to the relationship between, and proper ordering of, Gospel and law are such that Barth's sharp contrast between Protestant and Roman Catholic ethics cannot, in relation to this Encyclical (nor in relation to much Protestant thought), readily be sustained – we have already noted, for example, the affirmation with which the Encyclical begins, that "the joy which accompanies the Birth of the Messiah is...the foundation and fulfilment of joy at every child born into the world".[43] And we might also note the insistence that:

> God's commandment is never detached from his love: it is always a gift meant for man's growth and joy. As such, it represents an essential and indispensable aspect of the Gospel, actually becoming "gospel" itself: joyful good news. The Gospel of life is both a great gift of God and an exacting task for humanity. It gives rise to amazement and gratitude in the person graced with freedom, and it asks to be welcomed, preserved and esteemed, with a deep sense of responsibility. In giving life to man, God demands that he love, respect and promote life. The gift thus becomes a commandment, and the commandment is itself a gift.[44]

According to the Encyclical, then, the church is the bearer of a Gospel of life: not first or only a bearer of a word of law which threatens condemnation, but first of all a bearer of good tidings which make regard for human life an appropriate expression of the simple celebration of those good tidings. But for all that this is well said, *Evangelium Vitae*, as with its initial insight concerning the existence of a culture of death, cannot quite maintain this perspective, but feels obliged in fact to neglect it, just because, so it seems, it is concerned to maintain that the commandment can be known as a commandment independently of the Gospel.

Perhaps the most striking aspect of this neglect is that the resurrection of Christ from the dead, on which, as O'Donovan puts it, "Paul based his Gospel of life", receives here "astonishingly, almost no mention". "John Paul", writes O'Donovan, "bases his on creation, Incarnation and the sacrifice of the cross, in which Jesus poured out his life for the whole world to share. It is almost as if he fears that the resurrection may offer a kind of legitimacy to death." But what the Pope overlooks, argues O'Donovan, is just that "the root of the culture of death *is* a certain culture of life".

> Precisely because it seems that our brief span must carry all the meaning of existence and offer all the reconciliation we can hope to find, we become greedy

---

[42] *Ibid.*

[43] *Evangelium Vitae*, 1.

[44] *Evangelium Vitae*, 52.

of life and demand to live it every moment to the full, snatching away from others opportunities to live that could enhance our own, making calculated sacrifices of 'worthless' lives to enrich the 'worthwhile'.[45]

It is the sense, that is to say, that this life is all we have which is the basis for its avid preservation through attacks on whatever may seem to threaten it, even if that "whatever" includes other human lives. The irony is that by turning away from the resurrection, and hence "with only the categories of life-enhancement at his disposal, [John Paul] ends up reinforcing certain vitalist perceptions which are fuelling the cultural conflagration"[46] which he actually intends to oppose. Had he developed his teaching at this point out of reflection on the resurrection, he might have better maintained that dialectic between the preservation of life and the readiness to relinquish it which is central to the teaching of the early fathers in relation to suicide and martyrdom, and which is so obviously lacking in contemporary perspectives.[47]

To put the point in the terms previously used, the Encyclical, while at times acknowledging the priority of the Gospel, neglects its explication at the very point where the contemporary crisis demands it; and it does so, I suggest, for the reason that its commitment to the possibility of apologetics encourages it to rely on the law since the law, unlike the Gospel, may conceivably make an appeal to the conscience and the moral sense. Here again then, the tension created in the Encyclical by its faith in the general possibility of apologetics is far from being fruitful, but actually inhibits the resolute development of a bioethic based on the authentic "may" of the Gospel. Thus the Encyclical's attempts to co-ordinate law and Gospel, for all the good intentions which it displays, finally founder in the way that all such attempts founder where the priority of the latter over the former is not rigorously maintained. Jüngel's comment on Lutheran treatments of the law is to the point:

> The alleged, general revelation of God in the Law becomes therefore, in an underhand way, a concrete norm from which the Gospel also is supposed to acquire its concreteness from the very first. The knowledge of God as lawgiver (*cognitio Dei legalis*) understood as 'general revelation' (*revelatio generalis*) becomes, *de facto*, *revelatio specialissima*, through which the Gospel undergoes 'concretion' for the first time.[48]

(iii) The third point is that a conviction as to the possibility of apologetics renders *Evangelium Vitae* rather uncritical of the company it keeps; specifically,

[45] Oliver O'Donovan, review of *Evangelium Vitae*, 9 (1996) *Studies in Christian Ethics* 94.
[46] O'Donovan, review of *Evangelium Vitae*, 94.
[47] On this point see further my 'Christian Anthropology at the Beginning and End of Life', 51 (1998) *Scottish Journal of Theology* 1–39.
[48] E. Jüngel, *Christ, Justice and Peace*, trans. D.B. Hamill and A.J. Torrance (Edinburgh: T & T Clark 1992), p. 31. Jüngel notes that Ernst Wolf has "strikingly emphasised this paradox of the [Lutheran] teaching about *revelatio generalis*". Wolf comments: "Again and again the *revelatio generalis* becomes thus a ... *revelatio specialis*, which normalises itself *today*, and *today* is placed decisively next to the revelation of Christ."

it leads the Pope into a seeming endorsement of a theory of rights, albeit a theory shorn of those developments which have led to what he terms "a surprising contradiction": "precisely in an age when the inviolable rights of the person are solemnly proclaimed and the value of life is publicly affirmed, the very right to life is being denied and trampled upon, especially at the more significant moments of existence: the moment of birth and death."[49]

This "surprising contradiction" is arguably, however, neither a contradiction nor, hence, surprising. If, as for example Joan Lockwood O'Donovan has importantly argued, the "three dominant conceptual elements of the Western tradition of rights theory" are "property right, contract, and freedom of choice"[50], the denial of rights to the unborn and the dying is to be expected, since they are only with the greatest of difficulty regarded as the self-possessing and freely contracting individuals who are, within this tradition, paradigmatically the legitimate claimants of rights. Of course, as *Evangelium Vitae* seeks to cleanse the doctrine of human rights from its unwelcome associations it stresses, for example, freedom's proper and "essential link with the truth"[51], echoing a strain of *Veritatis Splendor*. But surely the Encyclical would have been well-advised to wonder whether this is to offer to the modern theory of rights a cure – viz. "the truth" – which in the eyes of its original advocates is the very disease from which the theory was free, and on which freedom its claims to health depended! However that may be, and to change the imagery, the Encyclical's attempts to rectify the difficulties in contemporary theories of rights by some hasty additions or subtractions arguably promises a construction neither coherent nor stable and seems more likely to prop up a building which deserves demolition as itself the cause of its inhabitants' parlous state. It is again, so one suspects, the *a priori* conviction as to the possibility of apologetics which is responsible for this lack of discrimination in the identification of reliable allies and prevents what one might have expected, namely a critical and reserved handling of modern rights talk, with all its incoherencies and rationalisations.

(iv) A fourth point, relating closely to the first is also, as it were, the other side of the third. Just as the commitment to the general possibility of an apologetic causes Christian bioethics to be uncritical of certain of the company it keeps, so it encourages it to shun other company from which, as a matter of fact, it has much to gain. To put the point less allusively: a commitment to the general possibility of apologetics disposes Christianity to treat much modern thought exclusively, not inclusively – that is to say, to rule it out as wrong, rather than to learn from it where and what it may, and thus, in both senses, to comprehend it. This is true, in particular, in relation to those we might think of as the "genealogists", to use the term favoured by MacIntyre, including under that label the likes of Marx, Darwin, Nietzsche, Freud and Foucault. For just because these thinkers have found no explanatory value in their various cultural and

[49] *Evangelium Vitae*, 18.
[50] Joan Lockwood O'Donovan, "Historical Prolegomena to a Theological Review of 'Human Rights'", 9 (1996) *Studies in Christian Ethics*, p. 64.
[51] *Evangelium Vitae*, 19.

social genealogies for a general knowledge of the moral law, they are bound to be treated with a high degree of suspicion by the would-be apologist. And yet the overcoming of this suspicion through a rejection of a dogmatic belief in the general possibility of apologetics would, so it can be argued, bear much fruit for Christian thought and not least in its engagement with modern medicine. To take a single example, a critique of the treatment of infertility would gain in scope and power insofar as it was willing to locate medical practice in a richer cultural, economic and political context than traditional casuistry typically allows, and was in particular ready to examine, for example, a Marxist analysis of the social general-isation of the "commodity form" in late Western capitalism.[52] But Christian bioethics will only go in this direction as it relinquishes the thought which renders it in general hostile to, or suspicious of, the genealogists, namely that modern medicine must, in actual fact, already be disciplined by the moral law to which human conscience gives it access. To return to the point from which this section began – *Evangelium Vitae* would have developed a more adequate genealogy had it overcome the inhibitions in relation to such a project which commitment to the general possibility of apologetics necessarily fosters.


## IV

My point in the previous two sections of this paper has been that attention to *Evangelium Vitae* reveals tensions within it which are the cause of certain diffi-culties in the articulation and defence of its principal themes. I have claimed in particular that these difficulties are created by an underlying commitment to the general possibility of an apologetic bioethic which, on other grounds, I have held to be problematic as constituting an invitation to the church to be the "church in defect". In the next section I shall turn directly to the issue of the relationship between Anglican and Roman Catholic bioethics, but for reasons which will emerge, it is important to ask first of all whether the underlying commitment which causes the tensions within the Encyclical does not also cause difficulties between this Encyclical and the Roman Catholic tradition itself – or at least, with other recent magisterial teaching.

Of course it is the question of the compatibility of the Encyclical on this point with the wider tradition which is of most interest, but to answer that particular question within the constraints imposed by a paper of this sort is hardly feasible – we would be seriously delayed by enquiries as to what is meant by the tradition, enquiries which would in turn depend upon answers to such vexed questions as those concerning the nature and authority of the magisterium, the interpretation of Thomas Aquinas, and so on. Lacking space and expertise for such refinements, it seems better to begin to answer the less interesting and more modest, but

---

[52] I have made some limited and tentative remarks on this issue in " 'Who Are my Mother and my Brothers?': Marx, Bonhoeffer and Benedict and the Redemption of the Family", 9 (1996) *Studies in Christian Ethics* 1–22.

nonetheless relevant question as to the compatibility on the matter which concerns us between the Encyclical and recent magisterial teaching, even if that question cannot itself receive fully adequate treatment. All I can do is to give some grounds for the suspicion of a lack of fit between *Evangelium Vitae* and other magisterial teaching by noting in the first place that certain readings of *Veritatis Splendor*, for example, distance that Encyclical from any supposed faith in substantive non-theological knowledge of the moral law, and further, that both *Donum Vitae* and the *Catechism*, to take two important documents, while pointing in a number of different directions, seem, in practice, to reckon with the distinctly theological character of right belief in relation to matters of life and death. My claim will be, then, that recent Roman teaching implicitly recognises the problematic character of that very commitment to the general possibility of an apologetic bioethic which creates the tensions within *Evangelium Vitae* itself and, as we will have cause to note in the next section, would cause profound difficulties for Anglican bioethics.

In a recent essay Russell Hittinger maintains that "as for the use of natural law within moral theology, *Veritatis Splendor* reintegrates natural law into the dogmatic theology of revelation and Christology."[53] What does he mean by this claim? According to Hittinger, the question as to what a theory of natural law is a theory *of*, can be approached in three ways:

> In the first place, natural law can be regarded as a matter of propositions or precepts that are first in the order of practical cognition.... In the second place, natural law can be regarded as an issue of nature or human nature, in which case it is a problem not only of epistemology and logic but also of how practical reason is situated in a broader order of causality. Third, natural law can be approached not only as order in the mind or order in nature but also as the ordinance of a divine lawgiver.[54]

It is, so he alleges, the integration of these three foci in terms of what the Pope calls "participated theonomy"[55] which is characteristic of *Veritatis Splendor* and indeed, of the moral theology of Thomas Aquinas. Now this integration makes clear that what has been attempted in certain secular uses of natural law, and in what Hittinger would regard as an impoverished moral theology – namely the construction of a natural law on the basis of the first or second of these three foci in independence from the other two – is far from being what *Veritatis Splendor* proposes. In fact *Veritatis Splendor* is aware that the secular attempts at natural law thinking which proceed in this manner have highly ambiguous results, a point to which *Evangelium Vitae* is itself sensitive, so Hittinger alleges, in noting the service being done by appeal to rights in the advocacy of abortion and euthanasia. Thus, in relation to the "modern experiment in constitutional democracy

[53] R. Hittinger, 'Natural Law and Catholic Moral Theology' in M. Cromartie (ed.), *A Preserving Grace: Protestants, Catholics and the Natural Law*, Grand Rapids: Eerdmans 1997, p. 30.
[54] Hittinger, 'Natural Law and Catholic Moral Theology', p. 2.
[55] *Veritatis Splendor*, 41.

and human rights" which, as Hittinger observes, the Pope supports, it is none-theless the case according to *Evangelium Vitae* that, as Hittinger puts it, "The gentiles need and deserve the whole truth, even in order to preserve the rationality embedded in their own 'secular' experiment."[56]

Such a reading of *Veritatis Splendor* is by no means the only possible reading, but it is certainly one which has a claim to be taken seriously. It is moreover, a reading which seems to bring *Veritatis Splendor* into line, as we shall see, with the discussion of these matters in the *Catechism* and in *Donum Vitae*.

At the very beginning of its treatment of the commandment "You shall not kill", the *Catechism* quotes the following statement from *Donum Vitae*:

> Human life is sacred because from its beginning it involves the creative action of God and it remains for ever in a special relationship with the Creator, who is its sole end. God alone is the Lord of life from its beginning until its end: no one can under any circumstances claim for himself the right directly to destroy an innocent human life.[57]

That this commandment has a specifically theological basis is something of which the *Catechism* does not lose sight as it treats more specific issues in regard to life and death. Thus although in relation to abortion it is asserted that "Human life must be respected and protected absolutely from the moment of conception" and that "from the first moment of his existence, a human being must be recognized as having the rights of a person – among which is the inviolable right of every innocent being to life"[58], no attempt is made to ground these assertions independently of the general theological rationale already provided, making reference as it does to the provenance of human life in the "creative action of God" and of that life's "special relationship with the Creator". And when the *Catechism* further asserts that "The inalienable right to life of every innocent human individual is a constitutive element of a civil society and its legislation"[59], its explication of this claim relies once again on that foundational theological rationale with another quotation from *Donum Vitae*:

> The inalienable rights of the person must be recognised and respected by civil society and the political authority. These human rights depend neither on single individuals nor on parents; nor do they represent a concession made by society and the state; they belong to human nature and are inherent in the person *by virtue of the creative act from which the person took his origin.*[60]

---

[56] Hittinger, 'Natural Law and Catholic Moral Theology', p. 30. It will be clear, of course, that in relation to *Evangelium Vitae* I regard this as an interpretation based more on what should be, rather than what is, said.

[57] *The Catechism of the Catholic Church*, English translation (London: Chapman 1994), para. 2258, quoting *Donum Vitae*, introduction, section 5, which itself refers to previous papal and conciliar teaching.

[58] *Catechism*, 2270.

[59] *Catechism*, 2273.

[60] *Catechism*, 2273, quoting *Donum Vitae*, III. Italics added.

Just as in its discussion of abortion the *Catechism* maintains the theological perspective from which it begins its treatment of matters of life and death, so too in relation to euthanasia and suicide it relies on quite explicitly theological premises of which civil society as such will, naturally enough, know nothing. As regards euthanasia the *Catechism* asserts that "an act or omission which, of itself or by intention, causes death in order to eliminate suffering constitutes a murder gravely contrary to the dignity of the human person and to the respect due to the living God, his Creator."[61] Now since the notion of the dignity of the human person is surely to be related to the "creative act" from mention of which the whole reflection on the fifth commandment sets out, the dignity of the human person and the respect due to the Creator are plainly not to be regarded as independent or alternative accounts of the wrongness of euthanasia – in both cases the *Catechism* relies on argument of a theological character. Of its discussion of suicide the very same point can be made. According to the *Catechism*:

> Everyone is responsible for his life before God who has given it to him. It is God who remains the sovereign Master of life. We are obliged to accept life gratefully and preserve it for his honour and the salvation of our souls. We are stewards, not owners, of the life God has entrusted to us. It is not ours to dispose of.[62]

Yet again the appeal is to a theological principle – to the stewardship which is owed to a life which is the gift of God, and thus to a duty which, in these terms, must be unknown to secular thought.

In its discussion of matters of life and death then, the *Catechism* shows no enthusiasm for the construction of a non-theological ethic, relying instead on the theological rationales for the protection of life which are offered by *Donum Vitae*. We may regret that the *Catechism* should use so freely the current language of rights in discussing these issues, fraught as the concept of rights is with a variety of problems as we have had cause to note; but attention to the nature of its arguments does not obviously suggest that the *Catechism* is committed to the adequacy of what we might term a self-contained theory of human rights. Rather, given the arguments it offers, it seems better to conclude that for the *Catechism* talk of rights is favoured merely pragmatically as a convenient means of expressing the implications of strictly and consciously theological argument.

Of course, in construing the *Catechism's* understanding of the status of a theory of rights, we cannot overlook the claim in its treatment of sin that "no one is deemed to be ignorant of the principles of the moral law, which are written in the conscience of every man"[63], and further, that though sin may tend "to reproduce itself and reinforce itself, . . . it cannot destroy the moral sense at its root."[64] Similarly we have to reckon with the fact that in that discussion of sin

[61] *Catechism*, 2277.
[62] *Catechism*, 2280.
[63] *Catechism*, 1860.
[64] *Catechism*, 1865.

it seems inclined to read the social situation in a slightly less stark way than does *Evangelium Vitae* with its notion of a culture of death, even though the *Catechism* notes that "Sins give rise to social situations and institutions that are contrary to the divine goodness" and refers to "structures of sin" which "lead their victims to do evil in their turn".[65] But whatever we make of these aspects of the *Catechism*'s argument, we are left with the surely rather telling point that when it comes to practical ethical questions, it relies openly and crucially on specifically theological arguments.

The fact that the *Catechism* constructs its argument on the basis of statements drawn from *Donum Vitae* which give a theological justification for the valuing and protecting of human life does not show in itself that *Donum Vitae* approaches these matters in quite the same way. Perhaps, in spite of what can be borrowed from it, *Donum Vitae* is sympathetic to the notion of there being other bases for maintaining such valuing and protecting. A full treatment of the argument of *Donum Vitae* would require more attention than is possible or appropriate here and it must suffice to note that in its account of "the criteria of moral judgement as regards the applications of scientific research and technology" it reveals what may arguably be held to be characteristic of its approach:

> These criteria are the respect, defence and promotion of man, his "primary and fundamental right" to life, his dignity as a person who is endowed with a spiritual soul and with moral responsibility and who is called to beatific communion with God.[66]

What is characteristic is the placing of these criteria together in such a way as to suggest that none is finally independent of the theological anthropology which is presupposed in the mention of "a spiritual soul" and "beatific communion". *Donum Vitae*, no less than the *Catechism* and *Veritatis Splendor*, uses what might appear to be secular moral notions only whilst relating them to the altogether wider and more adequate context of theological teaching. Like them, that is to say, it implicitly recognises the problematic character of that commitment to the general possibility of an apologetic bioethic which creates tensions and difficulties within *Evangelium Vitae* itself.

## V

According to Barth, the "church in defect . . . knows and recites the words: 'The third day he rose again from the dead; he ascended into heaven and sitteth on the right hand of God the Father Almighty.' But it does not say this with total confidence, only with half confidence. It does not stand defiantly on it. Only

[65] *Catechism*, 1869.
[66] Congregation for the Doctrine of the Faith, *Instruction on Respect for Human Life in its Origin and on the Dignity of Procreation, "Donum Vitae"*, English translation (London: Catholic Truth Society 1987), Introduction, section 1.

occasionally and not fundamentally and consistently does it think and speak and act in the light of it. It is at any moment ready and able to think and speak and act apart from this presupposition."[67] He continues:

> One might also call the church in defect the extroverted church. It is the church that certainly looks to Jesus Christ but not without the subsidiary thought that perhaps he is only an idea or *mythologoumenon* to whom it might be dangerous to cling. It wants to go to him, to celebrate Christmas, Easter, and Pentecost seriously, to be the Christian church, but it finds and feels itself burdened by the fact that it is also powerfully impressed and frightened by the world around it, by the autonomy and despotism of the world's doings, by its politics, economics and science, and by what is called "real life". The church in defect is the church which looks anxiously to its Lord but even more anxiously to everything else; which painfully compares itself to the world; which for this reason seeks possible points of contact from or to it; which is intent on bridges from one place to the other. The favourite word of this church is the little word "and", not in the forceful sense of the New Testament *kai*, but in the weak sense of a mere hyphen, in such expressions as "revelation and reason", "church and culture", "gospel and state", "Bible and science", "theology and philosophy". The anxious purpose always is to give the first element in these expressions a small but guaranteed place alongside the second, or at best to achieve security for it in the protective sphere of the second. The church in defect – in what one might call its defective faith, its little faith – is the church which, in order to have a joyful certainty of the reality of what it believes, thinks it has first to ask concerning the possibility of its faith.[68]

That element in the argument of *Evangelium Vitae* which I have been particularly concerned to examine betrays, so I would argue, an anxiety of the sort Barth here diagnoses. The inclination of the Encyclical, at this one point, to grant a relative validity and adequacy to the understanding, interpretation and judgement of the world to be found in secular moral thought, not only sits ill with its other themes and indeed with other recent magisterial teaching, but suggests a concern to vindicate this viewpoint so that in turn this viewpoint might offer back to the church an assurance of the possibility of its faith and consequent understanding, interpretation and judgement. Thus far from exalting the church, the Encyclical seems to doubt the particular authority which belongs to the church in virtue of its vocation to understand, interpret and judge the world from the one adequate locus of interpretation, namely the gospel of Christ.

If we ask about the division or unity of Catholics and Anglicans in the matter of bioethics, the epistemological presuppositions of *Evangelium Vitae* – those presuppositions which belong to the "church in defect" – seem to present us with a difficulty. What precludes Anglican acceptance of these presuppositions is not

---

[67] Barth, *The Christian Life*, p. 138.
[68] Barth, *Ibid.*, p. 139.

only the, so to say, *a posteriori* problems in this approach which I have tried to indicate, but more fundamentally the *a priori* refusal of anything but a theological moral epistemology in the Thirty Nine Articles.

According to Article 18:

> They are also to be had accursed that presume to say, that every man shall be saved by the law or sect which he professeth, so that he be diligent to frame his life according to that law, and the light of nature. For holy scripture doth set out unto us only the name of Jesus Christ, whereby men must be saved.

It is vital to understand that this claim, as it is explicated in modern Anglican thought which maintains this tradition, is not simply a formal but a material claim. That is to say, that when we read in O'Donovan's *Resurrection and Moral Order* that "Christian ethics must arise from the gospel of Jesus Christ. Otherwise it could not be *Christian* ethics", we have also to read alongside it the assertion that "Christian ethics depends upon the resurrection of Christ from the dead."[69] The first claim, after all, might be carelessly read as signifying that Jesus Christ is the source of Christian ethics in the sense which is conveyed by the notion found in certain strains of natural law thinking, that the divine law constitutes chiefly a "republishing" of what is known by "the light of nature". To this way of thinking, Jesus tells us things which our cloudy, because sinful, perceptions have concealed from us. But this is not what is meant by the Article nor by O'Donovan, or at least not only what is meant – the dependence of Christian ethics on Jesus Christ is not formal in this way, but material. The point is clear enough when O'Donovan maintains that:

> Eschatological transformation [achieved in Jesus Christ] resolves the unanswered question of creation, the question of what its temporal extension means. This question would be unanswered even in an unfallen world and to an unfallen mind; the sealed scroll of history is painfully inscrutable even to one who has gazed devoutly and joyfully on the order of creation in all its wholeness.[70]

If eschatology resolves the question of the meaning of creation, it does so by determining the path which the history of this creation will take. Thus Adam and Eve in the garden of Eden before the fall, to put it figuratively, would not have fully understood themselves and the created order, unless they had understood themselves and this order prophetically, so to speak, in the light of the history of salvation which would unfold in Jesus Christ. Hence the dependence of Christian ethics on Christ is material, not formal, for the very reason that the "shape of things" which determines Christian ethics is a shape which takes its character from the fact of the resurrection of Christ from the dead.[71]

[69] O.M.T. O'Donovan, *Resurrection and Moral Order*, Leicester: IVP 1986, pp. 11 and 13.
[70] *Ibid.*, p. 55.
[71] My thought about this problem has been assisted greatly by reading Rufus Black's very fine doctoral dissertation, *Towards an Ecumenical Ethic* (Oxford, 1996), which compares the work of Grisez, Hauerwas and O'Donovan, but on this point fails, I believe, to capture what is really at stake between O'Donovan and Grisez.

It is the nature of this dependence which explains why a certain reply which might be made on behalf of the Encyclical, or more generally on behalf of a pre-supposition as to the general possibility of apologetics, fails to meet the difficulty.

The reply might go along the following lines. The Encyclical, so it might be said, certainly does believe in the general possibility of apologetics, but to do so does not render it guilty as charged of setting up general moral enquiry as judge over Christian ethics and thus of inviting the church to be the "church in defect". And it does not do so for the reason that belief in the general possibility of apologetics is perfectly compatible with proceeding in the following way. The moral theologian will, to be sure, compare and contrast the deliverances of reason against what is taught by the word of God (and it does not matter at this point whether that phrase covers the Bible only, or in addition the Church, the magisterium, tradition, or some combination of these or other authorities). Furthermore, if there is a conflict, the moral theologian may even wonder whether what is taught by the word of God has been properly construed and understood. But once that question is settled, assent will be given to the word of God even if a conflict remains. Thus there is no question of autonomous moral enquiry being granted a validity which threatens the authority of theological ethics, nor is there a need to believe in "autonomous moral enquiry" as such in any case. Where there is right moral belief and action, so it can be said, this will always be a matter of divine grace, as the Council of Trent seems to have taught.[72] (And as Thomas certainly taught: "With regard to the gentiles mentioned in Romans 2:14, those "who having not the Law, did naturally [*naturaliter... faciunt*] things of the Law", St. Thomas points out that the words *naturaliter* and *faciunt* indicate that St. Paul was referring to gentiles whose "nature had been reformed by grace [*per naturam gratia reformatam*]." Any other interpretation, Thomas warns, would be Pelagian[73] – a point which *Evangelium Vitae* might itself have noted at para. 2.) Hence the concern for a theological moral epistemology which finds expression in Article 18 and provides the ground of complaint against *Evangelium Vitae* is a concern which that document can properly share while still maintaining the general possibility of apologetics.

Now this reply certainly goes some way towards meeting the difficulties which have concerned us. Of course we may wonder whether the tradition of moral theology, and whether *Evangelium Vitae* in particular, has really allowed the use of reason to be disciplined by doctrine in quite this manner, or whether in fact there has been a tendency to allow to reason a superiority and independence which is here denied. But that would be a quibble unrelated to the substance of the defence. It is better to reiterate the point we have made in spelling out what we have called the material dependence of Christian ethics on Jesus Christ – a dependence which, so we believe, would explain the distinctiveness of Christian ethics in relation to problems of bioethics as to other problems in applied ethics

---

[72] See the "Decree on Justification".
[73] Hittinger, 'Natural Law and Catholic Moral Theology', p. 7, citing Thomas's lectures on Romans.

– since this dependence shows that the conviction that "scripture doth set out unto us only the name of Jesus Christ, whereby men must be saved" cannot be expressed by procedural or formal moves of the sort we have mentioned. To put it another way, the defence of the Encyclical in the terms we have imagined is achieved only by overlooking the material dependence of Christian ethics on Jesus Christ. And to overlook this systematically is, as it were, to allow for the autonomy and authority of general moral enquiry in principle even if this autonomy and authority is then concealed in practice.

It could hardly be considered uncharitable were readers of this essay, Anglican or otherwise, to observe that to have an article of religion is not thereby to live by it; certainly the story of the recent contribution of certain Anglicans to ethical and bioethical debate would probably not allow one to infer the existence of this article (or for that matter many of the others) amongst the church's formulae of belief. Indeed, were we to use the word "Anglican" simply descriptively as naming every-thing Anglicans have said or written in relation to bioethics over the last thirty years, we would have to admit that much of what would thus be termed "Angli-can" is no more committed to the material dependence of Christian ethics on Jesus Christ than is *Evangelium Vitae* – and, if we had a choice, we would have to prefer *Evangelium Vitae* since its fault is, so to say, a knowing one, and is in any case mitigated by the development of what we termed the Encyclical's second and third themes. However that may be, the descriptive is not as such prescriptive (even if uncritically minded defenders of the "Anglican way of doing things" cannot grasp that distinction and think that error long observed thereby becomes normative) and one is entitled to hope that the possibility of repentance may yet lead the Anglican church to rediscover its proper voice in this matter and thus contribute to the formulation of a fully Christian bioethic on the basis of its credal principles. If it were to do so, then between such a bioethic and the bioethic envisaged by *Evangelium Vitae* in its commitment to the general possibility of an apologetic, there lies a division of principle.

We have, however, already implicitly noted the further irony of the situation which lies before us: for if the Anglican Church is to rediscover its proper voice in this matter, it could hardly do better than to learn from the practice of Roman Catholic bioethics in the *Catechism* or *Donum Vitae* say, and even more from the works of John Paul II in general. In these writings Anglicans will discover not only the seriousness, vigour and sophistication which is traditionally credited to Roman Catholic casuistry, but also, so I would maintain, a concern for a properly theological epistemology which the false note of *Evangelium Vitae* and perhaps of other elements in the tradition, does not obliterate. *Veritatis Splendor, Christifideles Laici, Familiaris Consortio* and even more that impressive body of more informal catechesis which includes such works at the *Original Unity of Man and Woman*[74],

---

[74] I am extremely grateful to Agneta Sutton for drawing my attention to the *Original Unity of Man and Woman* and to the subsequent exegetical works in that series. They are now available in a single volume: John Paul II, *The Theology of the Body. Human Love in the Divine Plan*, Boston: Pauline Books and Media 1997.

indicate a willingness to interpret the world from the scriptures which is unknown to much Anglican thought (using the adjective descriptively and the noun loosely). From this Pope, that is to say, Anglicans may yet learn what it is to live and think under the word of God, even if they may not learn it from certain elements in the teaching of *Evangelium Vitae*.

Putting that irony to one side, the point and purpose of the previous section was to suggest that *Evangelium Vitae*'s seeming commitment to the adequacy of general moral enquiry creates difficulties in relation to other recent magisterial teaching which on this issue, at least in practice, takes the view to which the Anglican church is committed but which it may still need to learn, that Christian bioethics can understand itself and its relationship to secular bioethics only as it understands the particular authority which belongs to the church in virtue of its interpreting the world through the word of God. Thus it can be seen that the answer to the question posed in the title of this paper finally turns on how the Roman Church will itself resolve the problems raised for Catholic bioethics by that particular element in the teaching of *Evangelium Vitae* to which we have given particular attention. Unity between Anglicans and Roman Catholics on these matters will come only as both learn again, and learn more thoroughly, to interrogate medical practice with the authority and insight which belongs only to that body which has received and believed the Gospel, namely the body of Christ.

# 5

# Medicine, moral crisis and the need for evangelization: the challenge to Christians in Western liberal societies

MICHAEL WALDSTEIN

A NUMBER OF papers at this conference have sketched the difficult situation we find ourselves in as Christians. A Christian ethic of medical practice is in retreat in the field of clinical practice and is being overturned in the law courts and the legislatures. There are formidable obstacles to reversing these trends within the cultural and intellectual confines of public policy debates in our societies. In the face of these realities, what is the positive vision to which we ought to hold? The character of the contemporary moral crisis – clearly shown in the practice of medicine – makes evident the need for evangelization. For without the good news of our salvation and the grace of conversion, moral conversion is hardly possible, and without moral conversion our addiction to violent and rationalizing ideologies can hardly be broken.

There is an image that has been particularly effective in evangelization, strangely and surprisingly effective. What is it that moves millions to tune in and stay tuned to the station that carries Pope John Paul's pastoral visits? No rock star, no politician, perhaps only a few sport events, can rival the papal TV ratings. Yet the scenario is an unlikely one for consumption on television. An old man, increasingly broken by his wounds and diseases, with a hip operation that seems not to work well any more, hands trembling and face partially paralyzed, sluggish in expression and slurred in speech. Every step seems to be painful. The merciless close-up of the television camera shows him signed by death, inexorably slipping closer to death's grip. The power of medicine is defeated in him.

If one compares this image with the usual image of film stars and politicians, one realizes how extraordinary it is. In political life, old age, disease and death are banished and hidden under a screen euphemistically called retirement, made invisible by the lie of a peaceful and happy evening of life. The image of Pope John Paul II is an impossible one for a politician. And yet there is an inexorable fascination that draws people to it. It is not easy to analyze the roots of this fascination. They have perhaps something to do with a longing for truthfulness. The close-ups seen in millions of living-rooms show that this old sick Pope is not putting on an act, actor though he was in his youth. He is spending the last drops of his energy in an act of oblation to Christ. The variegated world of appearance created by television is suddenly pierced by a note of reality. The roots of fascination have perhaps also something to do with the greatness of the Papal office and the consequent impossibility of retirement from it. It is a greatness that corresponds to the greatness of the Christian hope in the face of sickness and death.

One thing is clear. The image of John Paul II is not an image simply of weakness and failure. It contains the power of the Gospel of life. Paul formulates the paradox sharply: "When I am weak, then I am powerful" (2 Cor 12,10). The very failure of medicine's power before the aging Pope heightens his mysterious power. The paradox is illumined most clearly in a passage of the Gospel of John. "The hour has come for the Son of man to be glorified. Amen, Amen, I say to you, unless a grain of wheat falls into the earth and dies, it remains alone; but if it dies, it bears much fruit. He who loves his life loses it, and he who hates his life in this world will keep it for eternal life. If any one serves me, he must follow me; and where I am, there will my servant be also; if any one serves me, the Father will honour him. Now my soul is troubled. And what should I say? – Father, save me from this hour? No, it is for this reason that I have come to this hour. Father, glorify your name. Then a voice came from heaven, I have glorified and I will again glorify" (John 12,23–28). We stand here at the very roots of the Christian paradox of power in weakness, of the brightness of glory in the very hour of suffering and death.

Allow me to bring this passage to bear on the topic before us in two steps, corresponding to two important concepts in the topic assigned to me: *need* and *evangelization.*

## 1. Power in modernity

According to the penetrating analysis of Hans Urs von Balthasar, the cultural situation of Modernity is shaped by two principal spiritual movements: *liberation*, particularly in the form of emancipation, and *power*, particularly in the form of technical power over nature.[1] The two movements, though in some ways apparently opposed, are intimately linked with each other, like two sides of a coin. In what follows I will focus primarily on the second.

I should emphasize right away that both movements contain much that is good. No period of history is utterly godforsaken. Achievements and dangers are often inextricably linked. The reason why the following discussion focuses primarily on negative aspects is that we need to understand some of the central problems of our time if we want to advance in understanding the challenge of evangelization.

[1] See Hans Urs von Balthasar, *Theodramatik* III, Einsiedeln: Johannes 1980, pp. 125–186.

## *1.1. Balthasar's analysis of power in modernity*

### *1.1.1. The paradoxes of human freedom*

Balthasar develops his cultural analysis on the basis of an account of human free-dom before God[2] to which I turn first. Our self-possession as human beings through reason and will has a paradoxical structure. On the one hand I grasp myself as existing as this and no other incommunicable and unique person. On the other hand I grasp being as supremely communicable and common. "I can only be this unique one in leaving to countless others free room to be likewise unique."[3] In this context Balthasar cites Thomas Aquinas, who argues that the part, as part, naturally loves the whole more than itself and that we in particular naturally know and love ourselves as parts of a universe of beings and as taking part in the creator's being.[4] One can see in this perspective that solidarity is not a mere call from the outside. Rather, it corresponds to the very nature of human personhood as uniqueness in communicability.

One can formulate the paradox from a slightly different angle as follows: On the one hand I grasp myself as having the power of self-movement, the power which the Greek Fathers of the Church, following the Stoics, call the aut'exousion, or self-power (from *autos*, "self" and *exousia*, "power"). On the other hand I do not have power over my origin and goal, but in both directions I depend upon others and, in a most comprehensive way, upon God, my beginning and end, who gives me being and is my fulfilment. Both on the level of human relations, as in marriage, and in relation to God I depend upon others who freely open themselves up to me. Here lies the paradox of nature and grace: contrary to the received teaching of Neo-Thomism, one cannot stake off a sphere of pure human nature distinct from the order of grace since our nature is ordered to what can be received only as a freely given gift, particularly grace. "It is precisely here that we find the deepest paradox of man which was recognized and formulated most clearly by Thomas Aquinas and brought to light again [against Neo-Thomism] by Henri de Lubac (*Surnaturel*, 1946)."[5]

Accordingly, the nucleus of an authentically human life consists of an aware-ness that we are creatures of God (God as Alpha), called to be children of God (God as Omega), gratefully owing ourselves to the gift of being (Alpha), in need of and asking for the gift of supernatural fulfilment (Omega). Here lies the reason why Balthasar insists so strongly that the nucleus of an authentically human life is *feminine*. It consists of an inseparably active and receptive activity of which Mary is the supreme instance, "Behold, I am the handmaid of the Lord; let it be with me according to your word" (Luke 1,38).[6]

[2] See Hans Urs von Balthasar, *Theodramatik* II.1, Einsiedeln: Johannes 1976, pp. 186–219; *Theodramatik* III, pp. 125–135.
[3] Balthasar, *Theodramatik* II.1, p. 188.
[4] Balthasar, *Theodramatik* II.1, p. 191 with footnote 6.
[5] Balthasar, *Theodramatik* III, p. 130.
[6] Balthasar, *Theodramatik* II.2, 'Die Personen in Christus', Einsiedeln: Johannes 1978, pp. 260–330.

### 1.1.2. *Power and Evil*

Balthasar's cultural analysis of Modernity is built upon this account of freedom which I have sketched only in its barest outlines. Here is the central thesis connecting the account of freedom and the analysis of Modernity: "Every form in which the self attempts to detach itself from its groundedness in God and gain a standing in itself is an attempt at empowering itself over its freedom; it is a grasping after power."[7] This is not to say that all forms of power are evil. On the contrary, as the Greek theological tradition has it, the *aut'exousion* or self-power is an essential aspect of human freedom. It is to say, however, that "Power is in a particular way the occasion and the field for decision – more particularly for the final decision between God and the demonic."[8] Augustine, for example, sees the lust for power, *libido dominandi,* as the central characteristic of the earthly city in contrast to the City of God.[9] A further point is implied in this analysis of sin as detachment from groundedness in God, a point already mentioned above. Self-empowerment, i.e., liberation as emancipation, and grasping for power belong together like sides of a single coin.

Power in the sense just discussed includes the whole range of human power from the use of things or of oneself for pleasure all the way to political power. Power in this broad sense is as old as humanity. And again, such power is in itself not necessarily evil, but it becomes a privileged arena and expression of evil.

Modernity, Balthasar argues, is characterized by a particular form of power. It is characterized by "...the emergence of an hegemony of instrumental reason which seeks above all manipulative power over nature and which, since it reduces nature to mere facticity, can do without the personal pole of gratitude and goodness, thus understanding itself and employing itself as a mere instrument of power... In this light the history of modernity and the manifold ways of its self-liberation become understandable."[10]

### 1.2. *Francis Bacon*

A brief look at one of Modernity's seminal thinkers, a student for at least two years at this illustrious University of Cambridge, can help to illustrate Balthasar's thesis. Francis Bacon is surely not one of the primary protagonists of the scientific revolution. His instructions for elaborate experiments are for the most part quite vacuous, as are many of his physical theories. Nevertheless, it is uncanny how clearly and vigorously his "Great Instauration" (1620) articulates the fundamental philosophical principles that in fact came to inform the overall shape of scientific reason.[11]

---

[7] Balthasar, *Theodramatik* III, p. 134.

[8] Balthasar, *Theodramatik* III, p. 136.

[9] Augustine, *The City of God,* 13.14; 15.4; 18.49; see Balthasar, *Theodramatik* III, p. 140, note 11.

[10] Balthasar, *Theodramatik* III, pp. 142–143.

[11] See the discussion of Bacon in Hans Urs von Balthasar, *Herrlichkeit: Eine theologische Ästhetik,* Vol. III,1,1: *Im Raum der Metaphysik, Neuzeit,* Einsiedeln: Johannes 1965, p. 634; *Theodramatik* III, pp. 82–83.

What makes Bacon particularly interesting is that he formulates these principles in contact with the Christian intellectual tradition before him, so that the distinctive features of the new project stand out clearly against their background. Seventeen years later (1637), Descartes was to present to the public a project remarkably similar to Bacon's both in its basic principles and in its relation to the Christian intellectual tradition.

### 1.2.1. Power as the goal of knowledge

Bacon sets forth his ambition in the Preface to his *Instauratio Magna*, a title probably chosen to reflect Eph 1,10 which speaks of God's action "in the fullness of time to gather everything under Christ as head" (Vulgate: *instaurare omnia in Christo*):

> [T]he state of knowledge is not prosperous nor greatly advancing; and... a way must be opened for the human understanding entirely different from any hitherto known, and other helps provided, in order that the mind may exercise over the nature of things the authority which properly belongs to it.[12]

Authority over nature belonged to the human race before the fall, and it is to this primeval condition that Bacon intends to return, undoing the consequences of the fall (such as sickness) as far as possible. God's own economy of salvation after the fall, the cross and resurrection of Jesus, does not play any architectonic role in Bacon's project of technological salvation.

The knowledge attained in the Greek, Roman and Christian tradition, Bacon asserts, is immature. "[F]or its value and utility it must be plainly avowed that that wisdom which we have derived principally from the Greeks is but like the boyhood of knowledge, and has the characteristic property of boys: it can talk, but it cannot generate, for it is fruitful of controversies but barren of works."[13] Human knowledge becomes mature and manly, able to beget, only if it is directed to its true end, namely, power over nature in order to minister to the needs of life.[14]

There is a passage on the great mathematician Archimedes in Plutarch's life of Marcellus which helps to throw into relief the truly revolutionary character of Bacon's central thesis. Plutarch describes the powerful machines by which Archimedes was able to hold off the Roman army during the siege of Syracuse. He extols Archimedes's mechanical power, but even more so his refusal to make such power a primary pursuit.

---

[12] Francis Bacon, *The New Organon and Related Writings*, Indianapolis: Bobbs-Merrill 1960, pp. 3–4.

[13] Bacon, *New Organon*, pp. 7–8.

[14] "[N]ow their understanding is emancipated and come as it were of age; whence there cannot but follow an improvement in man's estate and an enlargement of his power over nature. For man by the fall fell at the same time from his state of innocency and from his dominion over creation. Both of these losses however can even in this life be in some part repaired, the former by religion and faith, the latter by arts and sciences. For creation was not by the curse made altogether and forever a rebel, but in virtue of that charter 'In the sweat of thy face shalt thou eat bread', it is now by various labours (not certainly by disputations or idle magical ceremonies, but by various labours) at length and in some measure subdued to the supplying of man with bread, that is, to the uses of human life." (Bacon, *New Organon*, pp. 267–268)

For in reality, all the rest of the Syracusans were but a body for the designs of Archimedes, and his the one soul moving and managing everything; for all other weapons lay idle, and his alone were then employed by the city both in offence and defence.... And yet Archimedes possessed such a lofty spirit, so profound a soul, and such a wealth of scientific theory, that although his inventions had won for him a name and fame for superhuman wisdom, he would not consent to leave behind him any treatise on this subject, but regarding the work of an engineer and every art that ministers to the needs of life as ignoble and vulgar, he devoted his earnest efforts only to those studies the beauty and excellence of which are unmixed with necessity.[15]

From the vantage-point of a modern sensibility shaped by principles akin to Bacon's one is likely to criticize Archimedes as an elitist and, from a Christian vantage-point that uncritically adopts this sensibility, as fundamentally pagan, hardly compatible with the claims of Christian charity that urge us to do good to our neighbour. Both criticisms are in my judgment quite incorrect. Archimedes and the Christian tradition before Bacon are closer to each other than they are to Bacon.

### 1.2.2. *The goal shapes knowledge*

Bacon himself is sceptical of the value of the final cause or goal for understanding nature. Yet if one wishes to grasp the overall shape of the knowledge he proposes, it is very useful to consider the final cause or goal he proposes. The goal of power deeply determines what is and what is not a proper subject of knowledge and therefore what belongs and what does not belong in a true representation of nature. Of the four causes investigated by the Aristotelian philosophy of nature before Bacon's day, the two considered most important, namely final and formal cause, are dismissed. "[T]he final cause rather corrupts than advances the sciences."[16] This is quite reasonable. If one intends to use sheep to produce serum against certain diseases, the final cause of the sheep, the goal for which they live and act, is not of interest. In fact, worrying about that final cause hinders the concerns of power since power is concerned with subjecting something as material to a superimposed purpose. A similar point applies to the formal cause, understood as the nature of a thing. "Matter rather than forms should be the object of our attention, its configurations and changes of configuration, and simple action, and laws of action or motion, for forms are figments of the human mind, unless you call those laws of action forms."[17] In the Twentieth Century we are still predominantly living with the same selective image of nature, different as it may be in many points of detail.

The point can be illustrated by the growth of the modern concept of physical reality or "matter" or "body" which several speakers discussed earlier in this

[15] Plutarch, 'Life of Marcellus', 307, 2–4; Loeb, *Lives* V, pp. 479–480.
[16] Bacon, *New Organon*, p. 121.
[17] Bacon, *New Organon*, p. 53.

conference. Descartes was perhaps more formative than Bacon in this area, but his driving motives are quite similar. Matter, or *res extensa* is defined almost exclusively in geometric terms so that it can become a perfect object for the science/technology of mechanics. Once all qualitative features and all natures, especially living natures with their inner orientation toward certain activities, have been removed from "body", the relation between mind and body becomes a dead-end riddle.

The point can be illustrated by a most alarming development in medicine of which Luke Gormally speaks in his paper. Health is generally taken to be the goal that defines medicine. And it seems to be a goal that is relatively easy to identify. Some years ago the American government made it obligatory for food stores to carry a sign on their door: "Attention: this store sells products containing saccharine. The Surgeon General has determined that saccharine is dangerous to your health." It would be surprising to find a sign that says: "Attention: this store sells magazines containing pornography. The Surgeon General has determined that pornography is dangerous to your family life and your soul." Yet, self-evident as the concept of physical health may seem, it is increasingly disappearing from medicine. This development is quite logical, given the overall shape of contemporary natural science. Kateryna Fedoryka shows how the concept of health is being squeezed into non-existence between two residual concepts: a value-free or mechanistic concept of health as statistical norm in a given species; and a purely subjective value concept as whatever a particular person happens to feel is a state of equilibrium or well-being.[18] It is not surprising, for example, that homosexuality has been dropped from the list of diseases by the medical establishment. As far as statistical norm is concerned, homosexual inclination is reasonably common; and as far as feeling well is concerned, many people feel quite well with it.

### 1.2.3. *The morality of power*

Bacon does give some thought to the question of the morality of the power he proposes. He urges men

> that they consider what are the true ends of knowledge, and that they seek it not either for pleasure of the mind, or for contention, or for superiority to others, or for profit, or fame, or power, or any of these inferior things, but for the benefit and use of life; and that they perfect and govern it in charity. For it was from lust of power that the angels fell, from lust of knowledge that man fell; but of charity there can be no excess, neither did angel or man ever come in danger by it.[19]

---

[18] See Kateryna Fedoryka, *Understanding Health: The Foundations of its Normativity and its Foundational Normativity for Medicine* (Ph.D. dissertation, International Academy of Philosophy in Liechtenstein, 1996), pp. 25–44.
[19] Bacon, *New Organon*, pp. 15–16.

It seems quite in keeping with the Christian tradition to posit charity as the highest end of knowledge. Yet, in fact, the immediate and formative end of the science proposed by Bacon is that of technical power. His purpose is to "lay more firmly the foundations, and extend more widely the limits of the power and greatness of man".[20] It is a science of means which can be, but need not be, employed for charitable ends. If charity were truly a formative end, one would expect Bacon to give an account of the human good which we intend for ourselves and our neighbour in charity, the sort of account one finds in Augustine or Thomas Aquinas. Yet, nowhere does Bacon attempt to give such an account. He is aware of the possible problem of an abuse of technical power, but dismisses it in a remarkable feat of thoughtlessness.

> [I]f the debasement of arts and sciences to purposes of wickedness, luxury and the like, be made a ground of objection, let no one be moved thereby. For the same may be said of all earthly goods: of wit, courage, strength, beauty, wealth, light and the rest. Only let the human race recover that right over nature which belongs to it by divine bequest, and let power be given it: the exercise thereof *will be governed by sound reason and true religion.*[21]

It is chilling to read this thoughtless statement about the automatically self-governing goodness of human power next to a statement about human ambition found only a few sentences earlier:

> [I]t will not be amiss to distinguish the three kinds and, as it were, grades of ambition in mankind. The first is of those who desire to extend their own power in their native country, a vulgar and degenerate kind. The second is of those who labour to extend the power of their country and its dominion among men. This certainly has more dignity, though not less covetousness. But if a man endeavour to establish and extend the power and dominion of the human race itself over the universe, his ambition (if ambition it can be called) is without doubt both a more wholesome and a more noble thing than the other two. Now the empire of man over things depends wholly on the arts and sciences. For we cannot command nature except by obeying her.[22]

Is it likely, one must ask, that human ambition, which wreaks such havoc in the first two grades of ambition, will do anything else in the third, which is truly apocalyptic in its proportions? Is it not much more likely that such ambition will transform the knowledge it pursues into a kind of knowledge that, true as it may be at many points, contains the deadly poison of making everything we see appear as mere raw-material for the exercise of power? If knowledge is sought to establish "the empire of man over things" is it likely to further good or evil? Does it remain indifferent or does it become a structure of sin?

---

[20] Bacon, *New Organon*, p. 106.
[21] Bacon, *New Organon*, p. 119; emphasis added.
[22] Bacon, *New Organon*, p. 118.

Bacon can perhaps be forgiven for crude thoughtlessness on these questions. The same thoughtlessness is unforgivable in the Twentieth Century. Richard Dawkins, for example, attempts to put the questions to sleep with a stridently superficial bromide.

> People certainly blame science for nuclear weapons and similar horrors. It's been said before but needs to be said again: if you want to do evil, science provides the most powerful weapons to do evil; but equally, if you want to do good, science puts into your hands the most powerful tools to do so. The trick is to want the right things, then science will provide you with the most effective methods of achieving them.[23]

### 1.3. Conclusion

The purpose of these remarks on one of the main cultural forces of our day, natural science, is to indicate the seriousness of the challenge with which Christians are faced. A similar cultural analysis applies to other cultural forces of modernity such as the predominant understanding of human rights, in which rights increasingly become the project of those who can claim them, i.e., the powerful. It would be a disastrous error to think that the situation of *need* in which Western liberal societies find themselves is a situation of simple *moral need* in Dawkins's sense of "The trick is to want the right things". "Good people will want the right things. One simply has to address their conscience, explain the matter, and all will be well."

The reason why this error is disastrous is that it hides our true need. The error makes invisible the structures of sin that imprison us in violent rationalizing ideologies. The very roots of how we look at the world are affected by these structures of sin. The world as shaped by human beings to their purposes, the world filled with human projects, this is the world in which the dominant mentality lives. The creator of nature becomes invisible in that mentality as does the order he placed in nature, including human nature. In the famous words of Cornelio Fabro, for the dominant mentality, even if God exists, it makes no difference. The situation of need which Christians face is that of an anti-Christian culture, a comprehensive and intricate fabric of seeing, intending and acting that dominates the life of entire *peoples* within which the life of individual persons takes place.

Here, then, is the conclusion of this first part of my paper. The need for evangelization reaches to the very roots of humanity. The consequent challenge to Christians in Western liberal societies is to live and proclaim the Christian message in such a way that it generates a new culture. It is to reach the very roots of humanity and to transform the habitual awareness we have of ourselves and of the world, our entire way of being, seeing, knowing, feeling and acting.

---

[23] Richard Dawkins, Richard Dimbleby Lecture on BBC 1 Television, November 12th, 1996.

## 2. The Glory of God according to John, focal point of evangelization

The conclusion reached above suggests that reflection on evangelization must penetrate deep down into the cultural roots of humanity. The reflection which follows proceeds in three steps. The first deals with some of the fundamental patterns of being, seeing, knowing, feeling and acting that inform a culture shaped by the Christian faith according to the Gospel of John. The second turns to that which, according to the Gospel of John, constitutes the primary motive and the primary content of faith, namely, the glory of God. The third addresses the question where and how, concretely and practically, we find entry into a life of faith.

### 2.1. He Gave them Power to Become Children of God (John 1,12)

The Prologue to the Gospel of John expresses in marvellous simplicity and depth the most important elements of a Christian logic of life and thought.

> He came to what was his own, and his own did not accept him.
> But to all who received him, who believed in his name, he gave power to become children of God,
> who were born, not of blood or of the will of the flesh or of the will of man, but of God.
> And the Word became flesh and lived among us, and we have seen his glory, the glory as of the Father's only-begotten Son, full of grace and truth.
> (John 1,11–14)

Several elements in this text are present also in the text quoted at the beginning, "The hour has come for the Son of man to be glorified. Amen, Amen, I say to you, unless a grain of wheat falls into the earth and dies..." Just as glory and the grain of wheat falling into the earth are linked, so are glory and the word becoming flesh. The immediately following section of this paper turns to this linkage. Against the backdrop of the grasping for power in the knowledge sought by the scientific tradition one cannot but be struck particularly by one phrase, "He gave them power to become children of God." What is striking in the first place is the conjunction of power and being a child. If one thing is characteristic of children, it is their lack of power. And so it seems incongruous to speak of the power to become a child. There is another point, even more important for our topic. The text does not say, "He gave them power *(exousia)* to BE children of God," though that may be true as well, but it says, "He gave them power *(exousia)* to BECOME children of God." In his commentary on John, Thomas Aquinas notes the striking emphasis on freedom contained in the claim that we BECOME children of God by our own power, *exousia.* Our entire entry into the life of being children of God is a free entry, an entry in which our *aut'exousion,* our self-power, plays an active role, not the role of a spectator.[24]

[24] See Thomas Aquinas, *Super Evangelium S. Ioannis Lectura*, Turin: Marietti 1952, n. 150–153.

Equally important is another part of the phrase. "He GAVE them power to become children of God." Our power and its exercise in activity do not arise from ourselves. Both the will as a power and its exercise in particular acts of willing and loving are caused in us by God; they are gifts of the creator.[25] In thinking about free will we easily fall into reserving at least a very small final chamber in the fortress of our being to human power alone without God, a point where we act in a manner uncaused by God, at least in accepting or refusing his grace. This is the heresy dubbed Semipelagianism. In his sermon at the beginning of this conference Cardinal Daly spoke about the spiritual principle, "Act as if everything depended upon you and pray as if everything depended on God." The reason why this is a good spiritual principle is that it corresponds to the facts.

This point is very important in our time which has such a great sensitivity for problems of freedom and power. The trouble is that our understanding of cause and effect is shaped in fundamental ways by the causes and effects we experience. It is only with difficulty that we rise to consider the causality of the creator. The causes we experience in this world for the most part compete with each other. If I am arrested drunk by the police I either walk with them to the police station by my own power, or they carry me by their power. To the degree that I am carried by their power, I don't walk by my own power; and to the degree that I walk by my own power I am not carried by their power. This is not what the relation between the creator and his creatures can be like. The creator does not compete with the creature. On the contrary, to create is to give to the creature its own being and agency. This paradoxical relation is possible only if God is not one among other beings next to me or outside me, but the fullness of being in which I participate. Augustine expresses the point in the paradoxical formulation that God is *interior intimo meo*, more interior than my innermost.[26] God is not outside me pushing me this way or that, but the source of all my being and activity.

It is not accidental that the period of scientific rationalism after Bacon and Descartes, which saw the explosion of knowledge for the sake of power, was also the period of a deistic understanding of God as one particularly powerful being among others. To view God in this way is not only false; it is a structure of sin which leads to untold damage including the phenomena which Freud analyzes in his discussion of the Oedipus complex. In this structure of sin I do not see myself in my entirety as grounded in God, as a gift of his love, but I see myself as standing first of all in myself and only secondarily related in various ways to an infinite spirit who, as I discover at a certain point in my life, happens to be ruling the universe. "The human tendency of relapse into sinful alienation remains so strong that Christian evangelization must continually combat the stubbornly recurring idea of God as one being among others, of his revelation as one fact among others, and of the light proceeding from him as one law among others."[27]

---

[25] See Thomas, *Super Ioannem*, n. 154–156.
[26] Augustine, *Confessions*, Book III, chapter 6.
[27] Hans Urs von Balthasar, *Theodramatik* II,1: *Der Mensch in Gott*, Einsiedeln: Johannes 1976, p. 208.

The meaning of the Johannine phrase, ''He gave them power to become children of God'' becomes more understandable if one examines it in the light of Johannine statements about the Trinity. ''For just as the Father has life in himself, so has he given to the Son also to have life in himself' (John 5,26). ''To have life in oneself' is the divine prerogative not shared by those who have life, not in themselves, but ''in his name'' (John 20,31). And yet this is precisely what is given by the Father to the Son. Already in God himself there is an exchange of life, there is gift and obedient grateful receiving. Since the Trinity is the creative origin of all, its logic of gift and of love is the fundamental logic of everything in creation.[28]

What is the point of all this? The point is that the challenge of evangelization in our time is at root the challenge to make such a logic of love visible and understandable, so that it can truly generate a culture, a fundamental pattern of being, seeing, knowing, feeling and acting.

## 2.2. And we Have Seen his Glory (John 1,14)

The logically next question is: Where does the love of God become visible to us in its inner logic, where does it come to light persuasively and convincingly? The Gospel of John answers this question in its reflection on the ''glory'' of God. In doing so, it brings to completion a theme that runs through the entire Bible. One can sketch some of the dimensions of this theme in seven points:[29]

- God is glorious because he is light, not darkness. ''In the middle of the living creatures there was something that looked like burning coals of fire; . . . the fire was bright, and lightning issued from the fire . . . and seated above the likeness of a throne was something that seemed like a human form. Upward from what appeared like the loins I saw something like gleaming amber, something that looked like fire enclosed all around; and downward from what looked like the loins I saw something that looked like fire, and there was a splendour all around. Like the bow in a cloud on a rainy day, such was the appearance of the splendour all around. This was the appearance of the likeness of the glory of the LORD'' (Ezekiel 1,13−14;26−28).
- This light is not self-enclosed; it shines and is present everywhere: ''The sun looks down on everything with its light, and the work of the Lord is full of his glory.'' (Sirach 42,16)
- It is not an impersonal light, but the light of God's face: ''For it is the God who said, 'Let light shine out of darkness,' who has shone in our hearts to give the light of the knowledge of the glory of God in the face of Jesus Christ.'' (2 Corinthians 4,6)
- It is not merely a cognitive light, but transforms what it strikes: ''And all of us, with unveiled faces, seeing the glory of the Lord as though reflected in a mirror,

---

[28] This principle, fundamental for John, was elaborated by Thomas Aquinas and Bonaventure; see Hans Urs von Balthasar, *Theodramatik* IV: *Das Endspiel*, Einsiedeln: Johannes 1983, pp. 53−57.

are being transformed into the same image from one degree of glory to another; for this comes from the Lord, the Spirit." (2 Corinthians 3,18)

- It is closely related to God's beauty. "In that day the LORD of hosts will be a garland of glory, and a diadem of beauty, to the remnant of his people." (Isaiah 28,5)
- It does not compel by power from the outside, but its beauty persuades from within by giving joy. "In the latter time he will make glorious the way of the sea, the land beyond the Jordan, Galilee of the nations. The people who walked in darkness have seen a great light; those who lived in a land of deep darkness – on them light has shined. You have multiplied the nation, you have increased its joy." (Isaiah 9,1–3)
- It is inexhaustible. "I pray that, according to the riches of his glory, he may grant that you... may have the power to comprehend, with all the saints, what is the breadth and length and height and depth, and to know the love of Christ that surpasses all knowledge..." (Ephesians 3,16–19)

In the text from John quoted at the beginning of this paper, the link between glory and Jesus' suffering is clear. "The hour has come for the Son of man to be glorified. Amen, Amen, I say to you, unless a grain of wheat falls into the earth and dies, it remains alone; but if it dies, it bears much fruit." (John 12,23–24) The falling of the grain into the earth and its dying to bring much fruit, this is where God's glory becomes manifest. The connection is most fully explored at the beginning of chapter 17, Jesus' high-priestly prayer to the Father. The first five verses are carefully put together in a symmetrical structure:[30]

(1) **Father**, the **HOUR** has come: *GLORIFY your Son*

so that your *Son* may *GLORIFY you*;
(2) so that (as you have given *him* power over all flesh) he may give eternal life to all **you** have given *him*.

(3) And eternal life is this: to know you, the only true God, and Jesus Christ whom you have sent.

(4) *I* have *GLORIFIED* you on earth by completing the work that **you** gave *me* to do.

(5) **NOW, Father**, *GLORIFY me* in **your** presence with the glory *I* had with **you** before the world existed.

[29] See Karl Barth, *Kirchliche Dogmatik*, Vol. 2/1, Zollikon: Evangelischer Verlag 1958, pp. 722–739.
[30] See Edward Malatesta, 'The Literary Structure of John 17', 52 (1971) *Biblica* 190–214; here pp. 195–198.

17,1 and 17,5 correspond to each other as petitions for the Son's glorification: "Father... glorify your Son" (17,1); "and now, glorify me, Father..." (17,5). In addition, "the hour" (17,1) corresponds to "now" (17,5). 17,1b-2 and 17,4 are likewise closely related as references to the Father's glorification by the Son: "so that the Son may glorify you" (17,1b); "I glorified you on earth" (17,4).

The two parts set against each other by this symmetrical structure interpret the hour of Jesus' suffering and death in two opposite directions: the first part (17,1–2) focuses on its effect, the gift of eternal life; the second (17,4–5) on its theological root and goal, the pre-existent glory of the Son.

"Father, glorify your Son" is not a petition for an isolated personal glorification. It is ordered to the glorification of the Father ("so that the Son may glorify you") which is identified, in turn, with the gift of eternal life to those the Father gave him ("so that... he may give them eternal life"). The second final clause probably picks up and explains the first: "so that the Son may glorify you... i.e., so that he may give eternal life to all..." Cf. from the perspective of the continuation of Jesus' fruitfulness, "In this is my Father glorified that you bring much fruit and become my disciples" (15,8).

The parenthetical clause ("as you have given him power over all flesh") specifies the extent of the power given to the Son in the hour through which he achieves the glorification of the Father. Cf. "When I am lifted up from the earth I will draw all to myself. He said this to signify the kind of death he was to die" (12,32–33). The same point is made from a slightly different angle in the grain of wheat text quoted at the beginning of this paper.

> The hour has come for the Son of Man to be glorified. Amen, Amen, I say to you,
> Unless the grain of wheat falls into the ground and dies, it remains alone.
> But if it dies, it brings much fruit (12,23–24; cf. 12,27–28).

The image of the grain of wheat that falls into the ground and dies to bring much fruit interprets the glorification of the Son of Man. As the grain of wheat becomes fruitful through its death, so also the Son of Man: through his death, he no longer remains alone, but constructs the community of his own. His glory appears in the effects of his work, in the construction of a new community.

The second part of the symmetrical unit 17,1–5 interprets Jesus' hour in the opposite direction: not in terms of its effectiveness in giving life, but in terms of its root and goal, namely, Jesus' pre-existent glory. "I have glorified you on earth by completing the work you gave me to do. And now, Father, glorify me in your presence with the glory I had with you before the world existed" (17,4–5). The nature of this pre-existent glory is clarified in the third part of Jesus' prayer:

> I have given them the glory you gave me,
> so that they may be one as we are one.
> I in them and you in me,
> that they may be completed toward one,

so that the world may know that you sent me,
and that you loved them as you loved me. (17,22–23).

This text suggests that the glory of the Son consists in his unity with the Father or in the Father's being "in" the Son. This unity, perceived as it is communicated to human beings, is not an end-point; the true end-point is the Father's love:

... my glory which you have given me
because you loved me
before the foundation of the world. (17,24).

An even closer link between "glory" and the Father's love is suggested by the parallel between 17,22 ("I have given them the glory you have given me, so that they may be one as we are one") and 17,26 ("I have made your name known to them ... so that the love with which you loved me may be in them"). The parallel suggests that Jesus' glory is the presence of the Father's love in him. Jesus' pre-existent glory is thus not only based on the love of the Father, it is determined by this love not only causally, but in its very contents or nature. One can under-stand the "glory" of 17,5;24 as the Son's being filled with the fire and light of the Father's love.

17,5 can be understood on this basis: "Now, Father, glorify me in your presence with the glory I had with you before the world existed." The Son's pre-existent glory consists in his unity with the Father, in the presence of the Father's love in him. The glory spoken of in 17,1–2 is nothing but a continuation or effective projection of this glory. In this way, 17,5 interprets Jesus' death, not merely as a passage through to his pre-existent glory, but as the break-through of that glory. The Father's eternal love of the Son becomes effectively present in Jesus' death; it is, as it were, transferred and continued into the economy of salva-tion: " ... so that the world may understand ... that you loved them as you loved me" (17,23; cf. 15,9).

The great Johannine scholar C. H. Dodd formulates the point with great precision:

The human career of Jesus is, as it were, a projection of this eternal relation (which is the divine agape) upon the field of time. It is such, not as a mere reflection or representation of the reality, but in the sense that the love which the Father bore the Son "before the foundation of the world", and which he perpetually returns, is actively at work in the historical life of Jesus.[31]

### 2.3 Come and See (John 1,39)

If the centre of evangelization, according to the Gospel of John, lies in the glory of God, because this glory is the main motive and content of faith, the logically next

---

[31] C.H. Dodd, *The Interpretation of the Fourth Gospel*, Cambridge: Cambridge University Press 1953, p. 262.

question is, Where and how can one come into contact with this glory in a way that is pedagogically persuasive and effective?

The Gospel of John is full of paradigmatic scenes. If one searches for a scene that contains the principal elements of the divine pedagogy, one will notice the very first encounter between Jesus and his disciples.

- "The next day John again was standing with two of his disciples, and as he watched Jesus walk by, he exclaimed, 'Look, here is the Lamb of God!' The two disciples heard him say this, and they followed Jesus.
- When Jesus turned and saw them following, he said to them, 'What are you looking for?' They said to him, 'Rabbi' (which translated means Teacher), 'where are you staying?'
- He said to them, 'Come and see.' They came and saw where he was staying, and they remained with him that day. It was about four o'clock in the afternoon."

Three elements are particularly important for understanding the divine pedagogy in this paradigmatic scene. The first is that the disciples, after hearing a statement which is difficult for them to understand, do not in the first place turn to their Master John for an explanation of what a "lamb of God" might be. Their inquiry does not take the form of thought or speech, but the form of following behind the person of Jesus.

Second, Jesus' first words to his disciples focus, not on a doctrine about himself, but on a desire or question that is being awakened in them, "What are you looking for?" This attention to desire and question is of great pedagogic importance. Pedagogically there is nothing quite as useless as the answer to a question one has not asked. If I cry out, "Two!" in a classroom, my fellow students will be perplexed. But if my teacher asks me, "How much is one and one?" and I answer, "Two!" the cry can be understood. The desire or question of the disciples is not in the first place a desire for explanation or a question about the meaning of certain words, but a desire to discover the place where Jesus "remains". The point here is similar to the very beginning of the story: the fundamental thing is not an explanation, important as explanations may be. The fundamental thing is a communion of life, a communion that "takes place" in the place where one "remains" or "lives". When the disciples and Jesus remain in the same place, he becomes their Rabbi, their teacher. Simon Peter articulates the same desire when a number of disciples leave Jesus after his Eucharistic discourse: "Lord, to whom shall we go? You have the words of everlasting life" (John 6,68). What Simon Peter points to here is what many biblical texts call "the heart", the central point in the person from which a culture is generated.

Third, Jesus responds to the desire or question of the heart by inviting the disciples to remain or live with him, "Come and see." This invitation further highlights the importance of communion of life as the basic pedagogic step. It is the most important step, solemnly fixed in memory by the precise hour in which it began. "They remained with him that day. It was about four o'clock in the afternoon."

How can those who live many years after these events participate in them? The First Letter of John gives an emphatic answer. "What was from the beginning, what we have heard, what we have seen with our eyes, what we have looked at and touched with our hands, concerning the word of life – this life was revealed, and we have seen it and testify to it, and declare to you the eternal life that was with the Father and was revealed to us – we declare to you what we have seen and heard so that you also may have communion with us and so that our communion may be truly with the Father and with his Son Jesus Christ." The community of disciples plays the key mediating role, continuing in some way the incarnation of the Word. "What matters at this stage is the construction of local forms of community. We are waiting not for a Godot, but for another – doubtless very different – St. Benedict."[32]


### 3. Conclusion

The contemporary crisis – clearly shown in the practice of medicine – has deep roots in the exaltation of human power as the normative and formative goal of human knowledge. These roots affect the habitual awareness we have of ourselves and of the world, our entire way of being, seeing, knowing, feeling and acting. If evangelization is to address this situation, it must reach deeply into the roots of Christian life so as to generate a new culture. Questions of morality can only play a subordinate role in this context. Primary importance belongs to ontology and not to ethics. The Gospel of John suggests three important aspects of evangelization. First, the decisive ontology is to be sought in the doctrine of the Trinity, in the doctrine which suggests that a logic of gift and of love is the fundamental logic of everything. Second, this logic of love becomes persuasively visible to us as the "glory" of God's love manifested in Christ's "hour". This glory is both the motivating cause and the primary content of faith. Third, the pedagogically effective place of such perception is the Christian community, tangible not only in its overarching structures, but as a local community. Evangelization involves at root an appeal to the deepest desires of the human heart and an invitation for all to "come and see" and to "remain" in the place where the testimony of communion and its glory is to be found.

---

[32] Alasdair MacIntyre, *After Virtue: A Study in Moral Theory* (2nd edition), Notre Dame, Indiana: Notre Dame University Press 1984, p. 263.

# Anthropology

# 6

## Bioethics and the Philosophy of the Human Body

### JOHN HALDANE

I

AS MEDICAL SCIENCE develops, more and more possibilities are put before us. Some of these are versions of familiar circumstances, but others are genuinely novel. Such developments often bring benefits; but not infrequently they raise ethical problems, concerning, for example, the distribution of goods, and the legitimacy of transgressing boundaries hitherto uncrossed. In trying to deal with these problems we need to have a sure grasp of relevant values and principles. Yet it is one of the pronounced features of the modern era that as ethical problems have multiplied, our common ethical resources have also diminished. Oddly we seem able to recognise that human embryo research, gene manipulation, and xeno-transplantation all raise difficult questions, but we are at sea when it comes to finding an agreed basis for answering them, let alone to agreeing particular answers.

Several factors underlie the inability to achieve consensus. Some are attributable to cultural pluralism. Modern societies are made up of different ethnic, religious, and ideological groupings, and while each may hold to a definite set of principles (though it is an idealisation to suppose so), there is no significant set adhered to by all. There is, however, a more general problem which is the lack of confidence in the very existence of any secure basis for ethical deliberation. For obvious reasons appeals to the will of God are held to be problematic, and the idea that a special faculty of moral intuition or the exercise of pure practical reason might yield incontestable values and principles is difficult to take seriously given the failure of either to do so.

There is, however, one approach that seems to have flourished notwithstanding that philosophers have generally been critical of it. This is utilitarianism, or the 'maximisation of happiness' principle. Its success is due, I think, to the following. First, it is easy to confuse the particular and restricted utilitarian doctrine that one has a duty to promote the greatest happiness of the greatest number, with a general principle of beneficence common to most moral systems, namely, where it is appropriate and where one can, and other things being equal, one should act so as to produce good. The fact that the latter is not equivalent to utilitarianism emerges when one notices the *ceteris paribus* clause and the non-identification of goodness and happiness. Unlike the utilitarian the advocate of beneficence may say that in a given circumstance it is not permitted to bring about some good because the only way of doing so would be by doing something which was unjust, say. Nevertheless, utilitarianism may seem unexceptionable for being confused with beneficence.

Second, and following from what was said above, those who argue that happiness is not everything and that some values and principles may be more important, generally have difficulty justifying those other ethical features. Third, when it comes to practical ethics utilitarianism enjoys the apparent advantage of ease of application. While it may be difficult to gauge the likely utilities of conflicting options, this problem is taken to be of a quite different and more tractable sort than faces the application of distinct and often incommensurable values, such as justice, liberty and the protection of the innocent.

Philosophers' qualms about utilitarianism have generally been ineffective in halting its adoption, in part because of its apparent advantages, in part because of the failure of critics to provide a compelling alternative, and in part because the philosophical criticisms of it tend to be rather abstract. For example, it is sometimes said that utilitarianism aggregates happiness and thereby fails to respect the distinctness of persons.[1] It is also objected that it undermines agency by denying moral actors any legitimate motive other than the maximisation of happiness.[2] Again it is argued that the very idea of double comparatives such as 'the greatest happiness of the greatest number' fails to specify any unique state of affairs to be aimed at. While one situation may involve *the greater happiness of the people* than another situation, the second may involve *more people being happy;* and for any given combination of people and happiness it is possible to imagine acting in a way that results in either more people or more happiness, with neither option uniquely satisfying the description 'the greatest happiness of the greatest number'.

Here I shall assume that for these or other reasons readers are disposed to reject utilitarianism, and I will direct my efforts to the task of providing a better philosophical basis for thinking about ethical issues concerning the care and treatment of human beings. As will emerge, the approach I favour is a version of what is sometime referred to as 'naturalism'. However, since this term is used in different and contrasting ways a word of clarification is appropriate. As it refers to positions of the sort I wish to defend, 'naturalism' indicates that claims of value, virtue, or requirement, are to be justified by appeal to what befits the nature of human beings. On this account, an action is right if, other things being equal, it promotes or contributes to human well being as this is implied by human nature. So conceived, 'naturalism' is a form of moral objectivism and is related to 'natural law theory'.

The other main use, by contrast, associates 'naturalism' with forms of subjectivism. The most prominent example is David Hume's view according to which ethical claims are to be understood not as describing states of affairs independent

---

[1] This is John Rawls's main objection to utilitarianism in *A Theory of Justice* (Oxford: Oxford University Press, 1971).

[2] This line of objection originates in Bernard Williams, 'A Critique of Utilitarianism' in J.J.C. Smart and B. Williams, *Utilitarianism: For and Against* (Cambridge: Cambridge University Press, 1973), pp. 108–18.

of the state of mind of the claimant but precisely as reporting or expressing his or her sentiments of approval or disapproval. Why this second view is also termed 'naturalism' is that it reduces the ethical to something that might be the subject of natural study namely the psychological states of human beings. I shall not attempt to refute the second kind of naturalism beyond making and emphasising the point that it is one thing to ask if something is good and quite another to ask if it is approved of. The first concerns the thing itself, the second does not. This difference also comes out in the fact that we can ask of the sentiments of approval whether they are themselves good. For the subjectivist this question will be analysed as asking whether those sentiments should be the subject of second order sentiments of approbation. Yet we can ask the same question of these: is it good to approve of (approving of) such and such? At each turn the subjectivist can appeal to yet higher order sentiments or social norms, but the question of *their* value awaits an answer, and reference to what is felt is an answer of the wrong logical sort. Either common morality has an objective foundation or it rests on a mistake. The reason most commonly advanced for drawing the second conclusion is the belief that no objective foundation is available. I think this itself is a mistake and I will try to show that it is.


## II


Since the naturalism I aim to expound roots ethical value in human nature it is necessary that I develop a philosophical account of human beings, and this involves understanding the relationship between a person and his or her body – hence my title. Although this is an ancient topic of philosophical reflection the work of one of the greatest philosophers of this century, namely Wittgenstein, casts doubt upon the assumption that there is a philosophical issue to be resolved. Wittgenstein was much exercised by the fact that the central problems of philosophy involve matters with which we are, in an everyday sense, quite familiar. We are perfectly at ease with words, know how to use them and are generally understood in our use by others. Yet when we ask such questions as 'what is language?' or 'what does reference consist in?', the whole thing spins out of focus and we feel lost for answers. This is not new, of course. In the *Confessions* Augustine asks 'what is time?' and observes 'if no one asks me I know; if I want to explain it to a questioner I do not know' (Book Eleven, chapter XIV). One diagnosis of this gap between everyday competence and philosophical understanding is that offered by Wittgenstein himself. This involves the remarkable suggestion that philosophical perplexity is a kind of psychic illness induced by the misuse of thought. His claim is that we take ideas out of their natural setting and then ask questions about them which really do not make any sense.

By way of analogy consider driving along in a car and asking a companion-cum-navigator questions about directions and likely times of arrival; and contrast this with a situation in which the car is sitting in the garage and one asks similar questions: where should it be going? when should it turn off? how far is there still to go? what time will it get there? These were perfectly sensible things to ask in the first context; in the second they make no sense. Going one step beyond this, imagine someone asking where cars as such are going and how long that journey will take. Madness has descended. Wittgenstein's treatment for the parallel condition that constitutes philosophical perplexity is a form of intellectual therapy involving repeated reminders of how language works in its proper use. The intended effect is that the patient will stop asking the misplaced questions and all will then be well. He or she, like the car, will be back on the road.

The relevance of this in the present context is that it may seem that there is something peculiar about the idea of the need for philosophical reflection on the human body. After all, there would be something peculiar in the suggestion that there is a philosophical problem about 'the snake body', say. There are snakes. They have bodies. Indeed, they *are* − living − bodies. What is puzzling about this? If the answer is 'nothing' that invites the thought that either the same response is appropriate so far as the human body is concerned, or else there is a significant disanalogy between the cases. The latter, of course, is what many suppose. One kind of disanalogy is expressed by saying humans have souls, snakes do not. Consequently, while the whole truth about snakes may be exhausted by telling the appropriate biological story about their bodies the same is not the case so far as human beings are concerned: 'John Brown's *body* lies a mouldering in the grave, but his *soul* goes marching on'.

Wittgenstein was not averse to talk of the human soul, in fact he uses the term approvingly; but he thought that this should be understood as expressively characterising aspects of living human beings (bodies), not immaterial spirits that inhabit them in life and depart them at death. Brilliant as he was, however, I think that Wittgenstein had too restricted a sense of the range of possible views of human beings, and underestimated the need for philosophical justification of one or other of them − including his own preferred 'ordinary' account. He thought that there was *materialism* (including *behaviourism*) which holds that everything true about human beings is reducible to descriptions of their bodies; *dualism* which supposes that the most important things about human persons are attributable to something other than their bodies (their immaterial souls); and his own view, let me just term it *Wittgensteineanism*, which is that while human persons *are* their (living) bodies, not everything that is true and important about them is reducible to descriptions of matter in motion. 'She was sad and cried' is not the same as 'her body was in such and such a state and a saline solution flowed from her eyes'. In addition to (living) human bodies, says Wittgenstein, there is the human form of life and this is affective, cognitive, artistic, and so on; it is of the nature of human beings that they have feelings, that they think and that they engage in creative practices.

The last is, of course, a philosophical view but it differs from the others in denying that in order to understand the human one has to see it in terms of something more fundamental: the material or the immaterial. What Wittgenstein missed out, I believe, was the possibility suggested by Aristotle and developed by Aquinas, which is that human beings are not immaterial selves plus material bodies but irreducibly psychophysical substances, that is to say beings to whose essence belong activities some of which are evidently physical (such as motion) and some of which are demonstrably non-physical (such as thought). The irreducibility of the human person to the human body is not due to the ineliminability of social modes of description but to the fact that what makes human social life possible is that human beings transcend the mechanico-physical powers of their bodies. In disagreeing with Wittgenstein, however, I think it remains the case that much of what he says fits very well with the metaphysical view I will be defending. His error, if I may presume to put it that way, was to confuse bad metaphysics with metaphysics as such. Everyday competence may not require a theoretical underpinning but there remains the question of what must be the case if what we ordinarily suppose to be so is as we suppose it to be. Identifying and answering such questions is the proper task of philosophy.

## III

Western thinking about the human body has various sources of inspiration and influence. The first centuries of the Christian era were shaped by two important forces: one an understanding of the religion of Holy Scripture, bequeathed by Judaism; the other, the progressive incorporation of Graeco-Roman thought and the development of Christian philosophies. Figures such as St Augustine and Boethius are tremendously important in this connection, because they convey the influence of Neoplatonic thought into the developing Western tradition. Each was concerned with the nature and identity of persons; and each offers a relevant definition. According to Augustine a soul is "a rational substance suited to ruling a body";[3] and for Boethius a person is "an individual substance of rational nature".[4] From the viewpoint of historical interpretation Boethius's definition is in the tradition of the dualism espoused by Augustine. For while a divine or an angelic person need not be thought suited to ruling a body, human persons, conceived of as Augustinian souls, would be such. Happily, however, the words of Boethius are more generally adaptable. That is to say one may accept the definition without thereby endorsing dualism; for one need not suppose that the rational substance that is the person is related to a living body as a driver is to a vehicle. Instead, for example, one might consider that the individual substance of rational nature is nothing other than a living human being, a rational animal.

In antiquity, Aristotle had already turned away from dualism of the Platonic sort, and something of his movement was to be re-enacted in the later medieval period. The thirteenth century saw the translation for the first time into Latin of

---

[3] Augustine *De Quantitatae Animae*, 13, translated by J.J. McMahon, *Fathers of the Church*, Vol. 4 (Washington: Catholic University of America Press, 1947).
[4] Boethius, *Contra Eutychen*, 13, in H.F. Stewart, E.K. Rand and S.J. Tester (eds. and trans.) *Theological Tractates* (Cambridge, MA: Harvard University Press, 1973).

most of the works of Aristotle including his great text on the nature of living substances, the *De Anima*. This corpus had been preserved in the Arab world where it had also been the subject of a number of significant commentaries among the most influential of which were those in the Averroistic tradition. Averroes himself and those who followed him were very interested in Aristotelian natural philosophy, and they had much to say about human nature and the sense in which we are 'besouled bodies'.[5]

Unsurprisingly, the reception of Arabic-cum-Greek philosophy into the medieval Latin West raised questions about its compatibility with traditional Christian teachings, and for a significant period the new philosophy met with more opposition than support. Among those who saw merit in it, however, was the greatest figure of the period, viz. Thomas Aquinas, and in his commentary on the *De Anima* of Aristotle, and in his own writings on the soul, Aquinas goes as far as anyone yet has to reconcile the anti-Platonic character of Aristotle's view with the anti-materialist and spiritual teachings of Christianity.[6] I shall say more about the prospects for this project in due course, but for the present let me just extract two elements from it. First, on this account a human being is to be thought of as an animated substance and as a single unified entity. This draws from general Aristotelian natural philosophy according to which substances (things) are to be understood in terms of their organisation and powers. Accordingly, if you wish to know what a thing is, look at what it does; and if you want to understand what a human being is, look at what a human being does and consider what is distinctive of its activities as a being of that sort. A second Aristotelian element is the idea that natural bodies can be analysed in terms of two aspects: their *form* (or organisation) and their *matter* (that in which the organisation is realised). In the case of animate bodies, living things, the principle of organisation (form) is the soul.

In the century and a half following the death of St Thomas Aquinas there was a strong revival of the more dualistically and Platonistically inclined Augustinian tradition which thought of a human being as, in effect, a conjunction of two substances: a natural, material substance, the human *body*, and a transcendent, immaterial substance, the human *soul*. At the same time, however, another more 'naturalistic' trend was developing particularly among empirically-minded renaissance humanists. This movement might be termed 'Averroes's revenge' because it reasserted the interpretation of Aristotle with which he was associated, and because some of its advocates looked back upon the Averroistic tradition with approval.[7]

[5] For a scholarly treatment of aspects of the Arabic tradition see Herbert Davidson, *Alfarabi, Avicenna and Averroes on Intellect* (Oxford: Oxford University Press, 1992).

[6] See *Aristotle's De Anima in the version of William of Moerbeke and the Commentary of St Thomas Aquinas* translated by K. Foster and S. Humphries (London: Routledge and Kegan Paul, 1951); *The Soul: A Translation of St Thomas Aquinas' De Anima* by John Patrick Rowan (London: Herder, 1949); and *Summa Theologiae* Ia, 75–83 translated by Timothy Suttor (London: Eyre & S. ottiswoode, 1970).

[7] For an outline of the history of this period see John Haldane, 'Medieval and Renaissance Philosophy of Mind' in S. Guttenplan (ed.) *A Companion to Philosophy of Mind* (Oxford: Blackwell, 1994).

In the Seventeenth Century, two great figures came upon the stage, Descartes and Hobbes. Descartes famously gives expression to a view very like Augustine's, in which he separates out mind and body. Hobbes, by contrast, looks to be, and is often characterised as, the first materialist of the modern age. It is a tribute to the power of these thinkers, and evidence of a tendency of opinion on the metaphysics of human nature to polarise along immaterialist/materialist lines, that Hobbes in one way and Descartes in another really defined the terms in which people currently think about human persons, human beings and human bodies. The inheritors of the Hobbesian tradition are ones who presume that thought and consciousness can be understood as 'motions in the brain' – to use a rather antique way of characterising materialism. Meanwhile the followers of Descartes think that there is something naturalistically inexplicable about human beings and that is their capacity for consciousness, thought and action.

Contemporary philosophical thinking about these matters is complex and extremely diverse at the level of detail. Those unfamiliar with it might suppose that there is now a consensus around reductive materialism. In fact, however, most philosophers are very unsure about how to characterise the nature of human persons, and it is far from being the case that they are deeply confident that the physicalist story is right.[8] They know that there are difficulties with materialism; on the other hand there is significant, and I think not inappropriate, hostility to the kind of dualism that is associated with Descartes.

Despairing of the possibility of reconciling the existence of ineliminably psycho-logical states with universal materialism some have gone so far as to try and elim-inate the mental descriptions in favour of neurophysiology. A different response to the same difficulty is to throw up one's hands and say that the whole thing is an unsolvable mystery; not only do we not have a clue as to how the personal could be explained in terms of the physical but we cannot even see what it would be to have a physical explanation. Somehow mind and body are conjoined, but we are never going to know what the nature of that connection is. Interestingly there are Cartesian and Augustinian echoes in this. At one point Descartes writes "It does not seem to me that the human mind is capable of conceiving, quite distinctly and at the same time, both the distinction between mind and body and their union."[9] And Augustine gave voice to similar puzzlement some centuries earlier when he wrote that, "the manner in which spirits are united to bodies is altogether wonderful and transcends the understanding of men".[10]

Eliminativism and 'mysterianism' (as one might term it) are responses to the difficulty of trying to give a coherent and plausible account of human beings,

---

[8] For a representative sample of current opinion see the chapters in R. Warner and T. Szubka (eds.) *The Mind-Body Problem: A Guide to the Current Debate* (Oxford: Blackwell, 1994). The view advocated in the present essay is further described and defended in J. Haldane 'A Return to Form in the Philosophy of Mind' in D. Oderberg (ed.) *Form and Matter* (Oxford: Blackwell, 1999).

[9] See A. Kenny (ed. and trans.) *Descartes: Philosophical Letters* (Oxford: Clarendon Press, 1970) p. 142.

[10] Augustine, *De Civitate Dei*, XXI, 10.

one that recognises that they are bodily creatures but also that they are possessed of minds. These are, however, minority positions and most prominent Anglo-American philosophers retain the ambition of harmonising the two elements within a broadly naturalistic framework. The most brilliant attempt to do so is that associated with Donald Davidson whose influence has been such that the expression he coined to describe his own account, viz. *'anomalous monism'*, is often used as a general term to describe reconciliationist projects of the same broad sort.[11] It is worth taking a few lines to characterise Davidson's position, first of all because it has, without question, been the most influential approach in the philosophy of mind and philosophy of the person in the last twenty five years, second, because it is a fine example of philosophical ingenuity, but third because it is a solution that is itself dissolving.

Davidson starts off with the thought that there obviously are mental states. It clearly is the case that human beings are moved by their thoughts, and that their thoughts are often induced by the world. In other words there is some causal inter-play between persons and their environment. Yet Davidson accepts the claim of hermeneuticists, personalists, Wittgensteinians and other non-reductionists that there are no scientific or any other strict laws governing mental/physical inter-actions. However, since he also supposes that all interactions are law-like he concludes that any "mental-physical" interaction has in fact to be a physical-physical interaction. If there is interaction it has to be between two physical things or physical events.

Without denying mentality, therefore, we are forced to assert physicality. This amounts to the thesis that human beings are physical substances with physical attributes, but which also have mental attributes. The latter characteristics are not identical to the former ones but they do depend upon them. If you want to explain what human beings are doing, you have to bring together these two kinds of attributes. You have to see human action as involving both the physical and the mental attributes or characteristics of physical objects. Davidson's theory is physicalist for the obvious reason that it takes human beings to be purely physical objects; yet it is non-reductive since it rejects the possibility of explaining the mental attributes physicalistically.

Throughout the 1970s and into the 80s this had the appearance of a happy and harmonious resolution, but in the last decade it has come to be thought of as discordant. The problem is simple. Anybody who really thinks that bodily movement is something wholly physical, something that has a complete physical explanation, is going to be in difficulty if they also want to say that it has a mental explanation; for this conjunction implies causal over-determination. It is equivalent to saying that a deliberate movement of my arm has two fully sufficient causes, a phys(iologi)ical cause and also a mental cause. But two completely sufficient causes seem one cause too many, and it looks as if one must make a choice as to which is the 'real' cause. This is liable to provoke one of two reactions:

[11] For Davidson's influential writings on this subject see *Essays on Actions and Events* (Oxford: Clarendon Press, 1982) especially essays 11–13.

either a lapse back into some kind of dualism which holds that what *really* moved my arm were my thoughts, my mental states and so on; or a return to a version of materialism according to which what really moved my arm were motions in the brain. What seems impossible to fashion is an account that accords reality to both aspects.

This problem arises not just in respect of the mental and physical. It arises wherever there is an apparent rival to a purely physical explanation. Supposing we say that as well as the physical there is the chemical, that as well as the chemical there is the biological, as well as the biological there is the psychological, and that each of these makes its contribution to the activity of the relevant kind of substance – a human being, say. Then we are going to have multiple causal over-determination, because physics will completely explain the movement of the object at the level of the physical; chemistry ought to explain it at the level of the chemical, biology at the level of the biological, and psychology at the rational level. But now it seems as if we have four competing stories of why the object moved: a mechanico-physical one, a chemical one, a biological one, a psychological one; and these are now *three* stories too many.

The upshot is to force a single answer to the question of where the real causality lies. If one favours the physical, what you end up with is the idea that the psychological explanations are either merely a convenient way of speaking without realist implications, or else, if you think that the psychological has some reality it is reduced to an epiphenomenon. On the latter account his having a mind is not in any way responsible for a human being's movements; and since the idea of a rational substance is in part that of a substance whose activity is due to thought, this option leads to the denial that human beings really are rational substances or persons.

Perhaps it should have been clear from the outset that the attempt to combine physicalism with opposition to physical reductionism was an impossible one. At any rate there is now a growing consensus that anomalous monism has fallen apart. And as this consensus grows so there is a return to versions of the Cartesian or Hobbesian positions. If one thinks that Davidson was right about the non-reducibility of the mental, and about its ineliminability from the explanation of action, then dualism may seem attractive. On the other hand, if one judges that Davidson's true insight was his insistence upon the physicality of substances and of causation, then reductive materialism beckons. I wrote earlier of 'the revenge of Averroes'; one might speak now of 'the revenge of Descartes and Hobbes'. For all these centuries later we appear to have returned to the situation of trying, like Hobbes, to explain everything about human beings materialistically; or else like Descartes, of having to say that there are really two substances involved, and then confessing puzzlement as to their nature and that of the compositional and causal relations between them.

In light of this, Wittgenstein's rejection of any metaphysics of human persons is likely to have renewed appeal. In the *Philosophical Investigations* he writes that "the best picture of the human soul is the human body", and elsewhere he comments that, "the best picture of the human soul is the human being". Taken out of context these can seem somewhat puzzling aphorisms. It will be helpful, therefore, to quote at somewhat greater length. First from the *Philosophical Investigations* (Part I)

> It comes to this: only of a living human being and what resembles (behaves like) a living human being can one say: it has sensations; it sees; is blind; hears; is deaf; is conscious or unconscious . . . .
>
> Look at a stone and imagine it having sensation. One says to oneself, 'How could one so much as get the idea of ascribing a *sensation* to a *thing?*' One might as well try to ascribe it to a number. – And now look at a wriggling fly and at once these difficulties vanish and pain seems able to get a foothold here, where before everything was, so to speak, too smooth for it.
>
> And so, too, a corpse seems to us quite inaccessible to pain. Our attitude to what is alive and what is dead is not the same.[12]

Later (in Part II) we are given the following

> 'I believe that he is suffering'. Do I also believe that he isn't an automaton?
>
> It would go against the grain to use the word in both connections . . . .
>
> 'I believe that he's not an automaton', just like that, so far makes no sense.
>
> My attitude towards him is an attitude towards a soul. I am not of the *opinion* that he has a soul . . . .
>
> The human body is the best picture of the human soul.[13]

Part of Wittgenstein's aim in these passages is to remind the reader (as he often sought to do) of the unconcealed facts of the matter. We are so exhausted with the familiar that it is difficult for us to see things as they are, and theory rushes in where intuition has gone out the door. Wittgenstein is intent on trying to get us to see what lies before us, and in this case the most obvious thing is that human beings are animated human bodies. They are living things possessed of various sorts of characteristics, and these characteristics are regularly on display. When I see somebody talking, or watch them writing, or indeed just watch them walk across a room, I am in the presence of, and a witness to the activities of a rational animal. I see their rationality in action. I do not infer it, or conjecture it as part of a theoretical explanation.

The shared error of the dualist and the materialist is to assume that what I really see is only a physical object in movement, concerning which the question arises of what is making it move. That assumption leads immediately to a theory of the inner causes of observed effects. At which point one might either adopt a Cartesian theory: the inner causes are thoughts (in an immaterial medium) that somehow interact through some part of the brain so as to make muscles move; or a Hobbesian theory: the inner causes are motions in the brain that are communicated through the nerves, and so on. Wittgenstein's opposition

---

[12] L. Wittgenstein, *Philosophical Investigations* trans. G.E.M. Anscombe (Oxford: Blackwell, 1953) 281 and 284, pp. 96 and 98.

[13] *Philosophical Investigations*, Part II, Sec iv, p. 178.

is to any theory of the mind as something distinct from, and lying behind, the behaviour of living human bodies. He is certainly not denying that there is knowledge of human psychology to be had, but this comes from looking at what is happening. Watch somebody walk and you can see psychology in action. A human being is a rational animal whose nature is expressed in the activities that constitute its life. That is why Wittgenstein says that the human body is the 'best picture' of the human soul. He does not mean that the human body is something whose operations invite us to infer the existence of something else, a soul, that is the cause of its behaviour. Rather the soul is the very principle of organisation of the body and of its activities.

Returning to the problem faced by Davidson and others concerning non-reducibility and epiphenomenalism, the difficulty arises from assuming a notion of the physical as that of the universal underlying nature of things. In this way of thinking, reality is ultimately composed of micro-physical objects. In order to explain the diversity of things it is then assumed that aggregates of these have various additional characteristics layered upon them. The problem is then one of allowing these subsequent features to play any role without thereby abandoning the assumption of the complete sufficiency of the physical. The fact that this problem has arisen and appears unsolvable has encouraged many philosophers to revisit the assumptions of Davidson's position; but few have been willing to give up physicalism; hence the current revival of reductionist varieties of it.[14]

The adherence to physicalism in these circumstances suggests a form of intellectual prejudice, and once free of it other possibilities come into view. That which I am recommending is, in effect, a combination of Wittgensteinian common sense and neo-Aristotelian metaphysics. Observation tells us that there are very many different kinds of substances, of which human beings are one sort, cats are another, and sulphuric acid is a third. By looking at things of these sorts, watching their actions and their reactions, and thinking about the significance of these we build up a picture of their defining characteristics and thus of their natures. When we do this with regard to ourselves and our fellow human beings what we discover is that we are rational animals, and that our rationality is expressed in bodily activities such as drawing and talking, as well as in abstract thought. The human body is the medium of our personal existence. Aquinas recognises this when he says in his commentary on St Paul's first letter to the Corinthians that the hope for future life depends upon bodily resurrection. A pure intellect may survive death but a pure intellect is not a human person.[15] A person does not so much *have* a body as *be* one. On this account, however, the body should not be thought of in the terms favoured by philosophical physicalism. Certainly a human body has physical properties such as spatial location, mass and so on,

[14] In this connection see the essays in Jaegwon Kim, *Supervenience and Mind* (Cambridge: Cambridge University Press, 1993)

[15] See the extract from Aquinas's *Super Epistolam Pauli Apostoli* appearing under the title "My Soul is not Me" in T. McDertnott (ed. and trans.) *Thomas Aquinas: Selected Philosophical Writings* (Oxford: Oxford University Press, 1993).

but it also has chemical, biological and psychological properties and these are in no way secondary or tertiary to the physical. As the principle of organisation and activity of a human being, a human soul is responsible for the shape of the body and for the activities of sub-personal biological systems as much as it is for emotions and thoughts.

## IV

Finally I turn to the bearing of this conception of the person/body relationship upon the consideration of bioethical questions. Here I may be brief for I am only concerned with the general framework of bioethics and not with particular issues located within it. An implication of the neo-Aristotelian view is that in important respects human life is continuous with other forms of animate existence. Equally, however, there is a dimension of human life that distinguishes us from fellow animals, namely our capacity for abstract thought and practical deliberation. In its speculative form reason aims at truth, in its practical form it is directed towards goodness. Both modes of rationality find expression in bodily activities and this gives them a significance and a value that transcends the activities of other animals. Art-making and scientific experimentation are just two examples of this. Accordingly, while there are good reasons not to mistreat non-human animals the human body enjoys a privileged position by virtue of being the medium of rational life.

In order to understand any form of animal existence it is necessary to identify various activities whose occurrence serves the needs of the organism. The vital powers are ordered towards certain ends, and their exercise is subject to implied norms of efficiency and effectiveness. An anatomist who recognises a part of an animal's body as being a heart is well-placed to determine whether the organ is operating as it should. Likewise for other bodily parts and functions. So too, the activity of the organism as a whole is open to evaluation by reference to a notion of well-being appropriate to the species in question. As with plants and non-rational animals so with human kind. Our activities may be judged good or bad depending on their relationship to a norm of human flourishing whose content is given by our nature. There is goodness and badness in posture and in diet, as well as in language use and in economic activity. It is the work of the human sciences and of moral philosophy to say what the relevant standards are but the general question of their objectivity should not be in doubt. The human body is a locus of value inasmuch as it is the location of human life. This is the basis of the ethical naturalism that I characterised earlier as holding that claims of value, virtue or requirement are to be justified by appeal to what befits the nature of human beings.[16]

---

[16] For a theologically and philosophically informed presentation of this sort of naturalism see P.T. Geach, *The Virtues* (Cambridge: Cambridge University Press, 1977).

Goodness is not an occult property like a neo-Platonic emanation. It is a state or condition of natural fulfilment (and theologically speaking, of supernatural completion). However complex bioethical issues may be, the starting point for investigating them must be the recognition that human well-being is rooted in our nature as rational animals. Utilitarians regard preferences as the basis for requirement; Aristotelians focus instead on human needs and interests. Not only may these criteria fail to coincide; they may actually conflict. At that point the Aristotelian has the advantage of being able to show how value in rooted in the very nature of the human animal: in its body as well as in its mind.

# 7

# Biblical anthropology and medical ethics

GREGORY GLAZOV

## 1. The relevance of biblical anthropology

1.1.  ANTHROPOLOGY, THE study of human nature, is relevant to medical ethics because ethical decisions are shaped by images of their objects. I here use the word "images" rather than "understanding" because of the centrality which the word "image" plays in biblical discourse about human nature. One has to be careful about how one understands, represents and imagines a human being since, according to the Bible, the human being is "made in the image and likeness of God" and one has to exercise the greatest care in the way one understands, represents and imagines Him lest the representation become a graven and idolatrous "image". Analogously, the "image" which our understanding fashions of human beings will influence our judgments about ethical, including medical, practice affecting them. The relationship between images and action may be illustrated by the use of a term such as "pre-embryo" or "pre-zygote" and its association, via the concept of delayed hominization, with practices described by terms such as "over-production", "turnover", etc. But representation and perception is also a function of desire. How one sees and hears also determines what one sees and hears (Luke 8:18; 11:34–36). Given the stakes, one cannot trivialize the need for anthropological discussions at the earliest stages of dealing with medical-ethical dilemmas. One must be vigilant to observe how imagination and desire fuse into conceptions that become personally, socially and culturally dominant. Well-being at all these levels demands the capacity to intercept, and contracept, the fusion of false images and evil desires (Matt 13:25; Gen 2:15).

1.2.  Contemporary society also requires justification for *taking the Bible seriously*. This demands identifying and removing the factors that trivialize and relativize biblical contributions to ethical discussions. One must reckon on the one hand with the scandal of fundamentalism, and, on the other hand, with the desires, which include technological curiosity, that give relativism its politically dominant force.[1] Both, fundamentalism and scientific rationalism, in their own ways, capitulate to relativism.[2] The reason for this is not hard to find. Implicit in each is an uncritical, self-confident fideism. Fundamentalism rejects rationalising approaches

[1] P. Ramsey, 'The Issues Facing Mankind', 1:3 (1985) *Ethics and Medicine* 37–43.
[2] J. Barton, 'The Place of the Bible in Moral Debate', 88 (1985) *Theology* 204–209.

to the Bible and matters of Faith, but its opposition to reason is relativistic and subjective. On the other hand, its enemies, rationalism and scientism, refuse to ground reason metaphysically, and in doing so, relativize their own claims for real insight and true understanding of things.[3] The attendant problems point to contemporary cultural oppositions to the metaphysical grounds of reason and its selftranscendence. This opposition supplies an important clue regarding the nature of contemporary opposition to *taking the Bible seriously*:

> There is found in [the modern age] a secular life which no longer knows a dependence on the Christian religion, a . . . revolutionary humanity, an existential individualism to which the transcendence of itself in an older religion and philosophy is repugnant and unthinkable. It is impossible to depart farther than this revolution, which still prevails, from original Christianity, and yet the contemporary society of individuals, certain of their rights [and possessing an] unlimited confidence in a technological reason, can give no account of itself apart from its Christian origins.[4]

The fideism of rationalism and fundamentalism arises from *forgetfulness* of the *logos* through which one can say anything at all. Recognition of the *logos*, of what grounds the possibility of meaning, of the principle of identity and contradiction, of what makes it possible for us to understand each other, permits us to recognize our common humanity and appreciate the grounds for its dignity. In countless ways, the *logos* establishes a firmament against all relativistic attempts to swallow up and confuse these cherished human principles in theory and practice (John 1:4–6).[5]

In view of this, I would advance that the inspiration for *taking the Bible seriously* should come from cultural and personal *remembering*. This proposal is prompted by reflections on the importance of remembering the Judeo-Christian origins of cherished contemporary institutions[6] and modes of thinking and acting, e.g. science[7] and consequently medicine.[8] But this proposal is also founded upon the classical Greek understanding that *memory (mnemosyne)* is the mother of inspiration (the Muses)[9] and on the demonstration that *memory (anamnesis)* is central to the Christian-apostolic understanding of Christ.[10] This

---

[3] C. S. Lewis, *Miracles*, London: Geoffrey Bles 1947, Chapter 3.

[4] J. A. Doull, 'The Christian Origin of Contemporary Institutions', 6 (1982) *Dionysius* 111–165, at p. 112.

[5] M. Archer, 'The Threat of Postmodernism in Christian Theology'. In F. P. McHugh & M. Natale (eds.), *Things Old and New: Catholic Social Teaching Revisited*, Lanham 1993.

[6] J. A. Doull, 'The Christian Origin of Contemporary Institutions', 6 (1982) *Dionysius* 111–165; E. Voegelin, *Anamnesis*, Notre Dame: University of Notre Dame Press 1978.

[7] S. L. Jaki, *Science and Creation*, Edinburgh: Scottish Academic Press 1978.

[8] L. Kass, *Toward a More Natural Science: Biology and Human Affairs*, New York: The Free Press (Macmillan) 1985.

[9] cf. J. Pieper, *Only the Lover Sings*, San Francisco: Ignatius Press 1990.

[10] J. Ratzinger, *Principles of Catholic Theology: Building Stones for a Fundamental Theology*, translated by Sr. M. F. McCarthy, SND, San Francisco: Ignatius Press 1987, p. 24

is clearly seen in the eucharistic liturgy (Luke 22:19; 1 Cor. 11:24) and in the Gospel of John where inspiration is linked to the apostolic remembering and understanding of Jesus in a way that was impossible prior to His death but made possible by His death and resurrection (John 16:7–14, 14:26). Central among the impediments to this understanding were the scandal of death (John 13:37f.) or the *horror* of suffering (cf. Isa 52:13–53:3; Matt 16:22). Taking a cue from the Gospels, we could say that the renewal of our own cultural and personal histories also requires *re-membering*, fleshing out, reconstituting, and illuminating things that were dismembered, had atrophied or been hidden from view either because living with them was too frightening and/or required too much self-transcendence.

1.3.    Bringing *memory* to the forefront of the discussion about biblical exegesis helps to diffuse the problem of fundamentalist vs. rationalist or subjectivist vs. objectivist readings. Indeed, such a statement needs to be tightened up by clarifying how "apostolic" *memories* are to be judged, evaluated, canonized and interpreted and by whom. Nevertheless, the category *of scripture* as an expression of living, communal, apostolic *memory* and witness to Jesus Christ avoids the pitfalls of subjectivist vs. objectivist readings[11] and undermines irresponsible use of dismissive labels. For example, when exegesis is conducted in the service of a living, apostolic, communal tradition that clashes with worldly, bourgeois desire, it cannot be reduced and identified with fundamentalism if it is structured and informed by a critical and scholarly *remembering* of that tradition.[12] This approach also helps to address the autonomous "methodologically objective" repugnance against engaging with the text from within and in the service of a communal, living tradition by exposing this repugnance as deriving from a kind of *necrophiliac* approach to texts.[13]

1.4.    A suggestion has been made that the Bible may be taken more seriously when discussing ethical problems when it is read as great literature.[14] I would like to incorporate this suggestion by examining the distinctive biblical perspectives on medical-ethical themes which have been the focus of other writing in our culture. My first move will be to show how the biblical notion of man as made in the *image* of God exposes the dehumanizing effects of applying humanist anthropologies to medical ethics. This will then establish a context for commanding the application of biblical anthropology to ethical issues, especially those concerned with the beginning and end of human life and with the roles of reproduction and the family.

[11] J. Alison, *Knowing Jesus*, London: SPCK 1993, p. 4.

[12] J. M. Finnis, *Moral Absolutes: Tradition, Revision, and Truth*, Washington, DC: The Catholic University of America Press 1991, p. 7.

[13] J. Ratzinger, *Eschatology: Death and Eternal Life*, edited by A. Nichols, OP, translated by M. Waldstein, Washington: Catholic University of America Press 1988, p. 249 (citing L. Kolakowski, *Die Gegenwärtigkeit des Mythos*, Munich: 1973, pp. 95ff).

[14] J. Barton, 'The Place of the Bible in Moral Debate', 88 (1985) *Theology*, 204–209.

## 2. Dualism, horror and the need for biblical anthropology

2.1.   The enigmatic character of human existence may be expressed by noting that man perceives a tension between his consciousness of being a bodily creature ruled by natural, physical laws, and his consciousness of being a thinking and therefore a free agent.[15] The sense of freedom may arise from perceptions of duty or potentiality for anarchy. The Greeks knew that this double consciousness makes man a mystery, a sphinx whose riddle is himself. Part of the riddle concerns the extent to which man has a body or is a body. The ethical dimensions of the problem are revealed in the most extreme dualistic solutions: the gnostic, substantial, or Cartesian ones on the one hand, or the materialist, functional, Lockean one on the other hand.[16] The problems are well seen in the Enlightenment philosophies in so far as these attempt to acknowledge the consciousness of being both bodily and free-thinking but ultimately reduce the body to a machine and the person to a ghost. The consequences of representing people in such ways are exposed in the literary genre of *horror.* The identification of the person with a disembodied spirit is also characteristic of some *New Age* phenomenologies. A brief look at a few examples from both genres will help to identify some of the key medical-ethical issues associated with Cartesian dualism and also help to clarify the relevance of biblical anthropology to the discussion of these issues.

2.2.   *The Body as Machine – Modernity.* The problems of representing the body as a machine are tackled in Mary Shelley's *Frankenstein, the Modern Prometheus.* First, a summary: Victor Frankenstein lost his mother at birth. The tragic loss reveals the limitations of traditional medicine: the problem lies not so much in medicine as in nature itself. To conquer death, nature must be subdued and transformed – a Promethean task. But it is an enlightened age. Benjamin Franklin's discovery of electricity, followed by Galvani's biological experiments, raise hopes of succeeding through science. Victor Frankenstein becomes a doctor of medicine and secures a laboratory. Working in a frenzied stupor, in isolation from his fiancée and in secret from his colleagues and the public, he builds a humanoid creature from the limbs of human cadavers and galvanizes him into life. The result is a monster from whom all, creator and public, recoil in horror. Curiously, he takes on the name of his creator: Frankenstein. Frankenstein's loneliness drives him to ask his creator to make him a mate, his Eve. Victor refuses. In anguish and fury, the monster vows to make Victor share his life and kills Victor's bride, thereafter escaping to the icy North to forever abandon humanity. Victor Frankenstein pursues his creature and somewhere beyond the icy reaches of Archangel he meets an English sea-captain, hell-bent on reaching the North Pole to discover the secret of magnetism at that centre of stillness for the good of humanity but without much regard for the life of his crew. Victor Frankenstein recognizes

---

[15] Solovyov, V., *Krisis Zapadnoy Philosofii* ('Crisis of Western Philosophy'), Paris: Sobranie Sochineniy V. S. Solovyeva, Foyer Oriental Chrétien, 1874 (1966); Rom 7; *Gaudium et spes* 10.
[16] Luke Gormally, 'Definitions of Personhood: Implications for the Care of PVS Patients', 9/3 (1993) *Ethics and Medicine* 44–48.

himself in the captain and narrates to him his story to cure him of his madness and, implicitly, to take heed of natural boundaries.

2.3.    In this novel, scientific, classical and biblical allusions combine to produce a prophetic critique of western scientific and romantic culture in so far as it follows the trajectory of Descartes' implicitly gnostic "flight from woman".[17] Stern faults modernity for turning the Cartesian method into a mentality by means of which the scientific view of nature and truth comes to exclude the poetic and thereby fails to give value to *mater and materia*, mother and matter:

> The sense of mystery which the poet and the contemplative have towards nature; the sense of imbeddedness, of a personal relationship of protectiveness or cruelty, of the familiar or the awe-ful – all this is not a matter of animism or of a vague sentiment which will eventually be repealed by scientific elucidation. Quite the contrary; if a kind of Cartesian ideal were ever completely fulfilled, i.e. if the whole of nature were only what can be explained in terms of mathematical relationships then we would look at the world with that fearful sense of alienation, with that utter loss of reality with which a future schizophrenic child looks at its mother. A machine cannot give birth.[18]

In Mary Shelley's conception, Frankenstein blasphemes against nature, science and theology.[19] In her conception, biology involves the studious analysis, classification, respect for and stewardship of animated beings. The same beings are understood to be the creations of evolution operating over countless millennia, meaning that human understanding may marvel at the immeasurable wisdom behind their ways and formations, but not measure or improve on it (cf. Job 38f). Medicine knows the good of health and vitality and applies human knowledge, of biology, to the healing and care of physiological life.[20] From this angle, Dr. Frankenstein's attempt to supersede and improve, with one rational leap, what nature took millennia to craft, is revealed as the negation of science and medicine. By galvanizing a homunculus assembled from dead men's limbs into life, Dr. Frankenstein betrays his own belief that man is basically a bio-chemical-electrical mechanism. Dr. Frankenstein thus makes Frankenstein after his own impoverished, Cartesian image of himself. That sex and love arise as a pressing afterthought reveals the alienation from the feminine and the social in which he conceived his grand idea. Now, in a face to face relationship, the plan is shattered. Whereas the Creator in the biblical garden showered his creature with care and love, Dr. Frankenstein recoils in horror from his Adam.[21] The monster, being lonely, demands his Eve. In the biblical narrative, Eve is given as a gift, a grace, and not as a merited right. As we shall note later, all of this is implicit in the description of their innocent

[17] K. Stern, *The Flight from Woman*, New York: Farrar, Straus and Giroux 1965.
[18] K. Stern, *The Flight from Woman*, pp. 78–79.
[19] A. Mellor, 'A Feminist Critique of Science'. In A. Mellor, *Mary Shelley: Her Life, Her Fiction, Her Monsters*, London: Methuen 1988, pp. 95ff.
[20] L. Kass, *Toward a More Natural Science: Biology and Human Affairs.*
[21] L. J. Kreitzer, 'Frankenstein: Male and Female *She* Created them', in L. J. Kreitzer, *The Old Testament in Fiction and Film*, Sheffield: Sheffield Academic Press, 1984, Chapter 4.

94

nakedness. The monster, on the other hand, demands an Eve. Does Frankenstein have a duty to make one for him? Does the monster have rights? And if it is not a question of rights, but of hope and expectation and sympathy, how much sympathy can a motherless and fatherless creature hope for and expect in life? Visceral love is hardly countable and measurable since it is beyond price (Song 8:7).

2.4.   The fury unleashed upon Victor Frankenstein has its inner logic in that it is a child of his own self-representation, conceived in the womanless, restless work-ethic of his laboratory, and, ultimately, in the circumstances of his own motherless, orphaned childhood. He learns the folly of replacing the garden with the laboratory and understands his own deeper human realities only by reflecting on the monstrosity of his self-representation. One may only hope that the same lesson will be drawn by Victor Frankenstein's real instantiations in modern laboratories when they aspire to fabricate man, in the name of science, medicine and health, with little forethought for the human feelings and fates of their subjects.[22]

2.5.   *The Person as a Ghost – The New Age.* The dualistic, gnostic or Cartesian identification of the person or self with an incorporeal spirit is the subject of another *horror* motif: that of disembodied spirits, e.g. ghosts. Albeit anathema to materialist humanism and the scientific establishment which supports a more holistic view,[23] some sort of substantial (body/soul rather than functional body/mind) dualism finds support amongst scientists, philosophers,[24] philosophers of religion[25] and medical doctors.[26]

2.6.   Currently the West is witnessing a rising tide of so-called New Age phenomenology which in some forms may be defined as a "popular occultism" or a "mysticism gone mainstream" in so far as it is interested in evidence for the "astral sphere", e.g. in the Near Death Experience or in data suggestive of reincarnation, and in establishing contact with this sphere through states on the borders of death and various "Out of Body Experiences", including those induced by psychedelic drugs.[27] Various cases adduced as evidence for the NDE and reincarnation are certainly explicable by reference to psychological categories but many resist this reductionism and expose the prejudice of rationalist

---

[22] P. Ramsey, *Fabricated Man: The Ethics of Genetic Control*, New Haven: Yale University Press 1970; O. O'Donovan, *Begotten or Made?*, Oxford: OUP 1984; L. Kass, 'The Wisdom of Repugnance: Why we should ban the cloning of humans', *The New Republic* June 2 1997: 17–26.

[23] A. Damasio, *Descartes' Error: Emotion, Reason and the Human Brain*, Basingstoke and New York: Macmillan 1994.

[24] K. R. Popper and J. C. Eccles, *The Self and its Brain. An Argument for Interactionism*, London: Routledge and Kegan Paul 1984 (first edition 1977).

[25] R. Swinburne, *The Evolution of the Soul*, Oxford: Clarendon Press 1997 (first edition 1986); cf. J. W. Cooper, *Body, Soul, and Life Everlasting: Biblical Anthropology and the Monism-Dualism Debate*, Grand Rapids: Eerdmans 1990.

[26] I. Stevenson, *Twenty Cases Suggestive of Reincarnation*, New York: American Society of Psychical Research 1966.

[27] W. N. Perry, 'Reincarnation: New Flesh on Old Bones', 14/3–4 (1980) *Studies in Comparative Religion*, 149–158, at p. 154.

objections.[28] Consequently, the advocates of the "New Age" may propose that science may now put rationalism in its place by corroborating the existence of an astral sphere believed in by many ancient sages, philosophers and mystics.[29] The New Age *Zeitgeist*, however, differs from the classical philosophical and eastern religious traditions in this: that whereas those traditions stamped their dualist doctrines, such as reincarnation, with a moral vision of a universe ruled by retributive justice *(karma)*, and emphasized the need of an angelic guide at the "hour of death", and of an intercessor at the Moment of Judgment,[30] the New Age reformulation of the same doctrines espouses the dictum that there is no need to be afraid of death, complacently asserting that what awaits us is unconditional happiness and that the question of a personal God is "an optional matter".[31] The repudiation of judgement and of the relevance of ethical categories for the transition into the hereafter, in effect, entails an anthropology which severs all links between one's earthly deeds and one's (posthumous) destiny. By means of this repudiation, this phenomenology exposes its own western individualist (modernist and post-modernist) allegiance (cf. 1.2 above) which is actually as primitive as sin (John 16:8).

2.7. As the anthropology of this *Zeitgeist* is thus shown to be rooted in the same western post-Enlightenment paradigm which it seeks to critique, it also requires critique. Christianity too knows the horrors of hell. But rather than addressing the problem by denying judgement and personal responsibility, it denies the principle of *karma* (understood as mechanical retributive justice) by espousing the doctrine of the *forgiveness of sin* by a *personal God*. My interest in highlighting these points stems from the need to identify aspects of biblical anthropology which are repugnant for moderns and post-moderns (cf. 1.1 and 1.2 above), and to dissolve this repugnance by showing how the biblical notion of man as an *image of God* is (a) the very antithesis of the *horrible* and (b) how its realization (i.e. our destiny) must be a matter of graceful righteous deeds.

2.8. I will confine this section to a discussion of documented evidence suggestive of reincarnation.[32] The pressure to countenance reincarnation claims greatly depends upon making memory-claims serve as the criteria for determining sameness of personal identity. However, memory-claims, however honest, can be false. Furthermore, ascertaining the truth of a memory claim that "it was I who did X in the past" assumes that one has a criterion independent of memory for

---

[28] I. Stevenson, *Twenty Cases Suggestive of Reincarnation*; W. N. Perry, 'Reincarnation: New Flesh on Old Bones'; W. Smith, 'The Near Death Experience: What does it mean?', 88 (July 1988) *Homiletic and Pastoral Review*, 52–59; cf. C. S. Lewis, *Miracles*, p. 7.

[29] cf. Ch. Schönborn, *From Death to Life: The Christian Journey*, San Francisco: Ignatius Press 1995 (first edition 1988); G. Scholem, *On The Mystical Shape of the Godhead: Basic Concepts in the Kabbalah*, New York: Schocken 1962 (1991).

[30] W. Smith, 'The Near Death Experience: What does it mean?'; Ch. Schönborn, *From Death to Life: The Christian Journey*, pp. 181 ff.

[31] E. Kübler-Ross, *Death: The Final Stage of Growth*, Englewood Cliffs: Prentice Hall 1975, pp. 155–163; Smith, 'The Near Death Experience: What does it mean?', p. 54.

[32] Stevenson, *Twenty Cases Suggestive of Reincarnation*.

ascertaining sameness in the identity of agents or persons. Bodily continuity could be such a criterion. For example, it is generally assumed that Anna Anderson's memory-claim to be the Grand Duchess Alexandra was undermined by DNA testing.[33] In so far as she claimed bodily continuity with Alexandra, her claim was undermined by the DNA testing; but bodily continuity is by definition ruled out as a criterion in the dualist reincarnationist perspective and so the identification of a criterion for determining identity becomes more difficult.[34] The questions raised are huge[35] and cannot be tackled here. In passing, however, I would like to set up some parameters for a more involved discussion at some other point with a number of examples from the New Testament and from Homer. In the New Testament, bodily continuity is a criterion in identifying the risen Christ, as is evident from the empty-tomb narratives (Matt 28:6, Mark 16:6–8, Luke 24:3,24; John 20:1–11), and from the "doubting Thomas" episode (John 20:20–27) although it is possible that the scars here may serve an anti-docetic purpose in attesting to Jesus' corporeality rather than identity. But the New Testament also presents memories of *shared* experiences as a criterion as well (Luke 24:31). The same with Homer's presentation of the recognition of Odysseus: Eurekleia recognizes him by the scar on his leg (*Odyssey*, XIX: 392, 475), while Penelope's ultimate test involves the shared memory of the construction of their bed around an olive tree, a secret that no other mortal man could possibly know (XXIII: 181–229).

2.9.   As bodily continuity cannot serve as a criterion for discussing reincarnationist claims, the more impressive cases for it are therefore those that appeal to shared memories. Here is one such example:

> Jasbir, the son of Sri Girdhari Lal Jat of Rasulpur, died of smallpox at 3.5 years in spring, 1954. At the funeral procession, his corpse stirred and returned to life and when his speech returned he claimed to be the son of Shankar of Vehedi village and refused food insisting he was of Brahmin caste. He related that in his former life he joined a wedding procession where he was poisoned, fell from a chariot, and died. Later, Jasbir meets a Brahmin lady from Vehedi whom he recognizes as his aunt. She relates his story to her family learning that a young Brahmin of 22, Sobha Ram, had died in a similar accident in May 1954. Jasbir goes to Vehedi, recognizes the Tyagi family, etc...[36]

An interesting detail in this case is that Sobha Ram and Jasbir were at one time simultaneously alive and were therefore two distinct personalities. What we have then is not necessarily a case of reincarnation but possibly some kind of haunting or possession. Thus, assuming that natural explanations for Jasbir's memory claims are wanting, the need to transcend such explanations should

---

[33] R. K. Massie, *The Romanovs: The Final Chapter*, New York: Random House 1995.

[34] B. Davies, *An Introduction to the Philosophy of Religion*, Oxford: OUP 1982, p. 123.

[35] cf. R. Swinburne, *The Evolution of the Soul*.

[36] Abridged from I. Stevenson, *Twenty Cases Suggestive of Reincarnation*, via W. N. Perry, 'Reincarnation: New Flesh on Old Bones'.

also open the discussion to alternative metaphysical explanations. Given the frequency with which subject B, like Jasbir, emerges in these accounts with a morbid discontentment saying: "this present life is not my real one", Jasbir's case is only superficially idiosyncratic. Even when subjects A and B are never simultaneously alive, it is still possible that B is a victim of something in the category of possession, haunting or curse. This still, however, does not necessitate any identification of the haunting factor with the self of A. One may, for example, propose an anthropological model which distinguishes the haunting factors from the personality as such by comparing and contrasting them to analogous beneficent spiritual influences.[37] Just as the spiritual traces of saints and the prayers of the faithful *associated with* places, relics, and people are not to be *identified with* their persons (cf. Num 11:16f.; 2 Kgs 2:9–15; 13:21, Sir 48:13; Mat 16:14–15, Mar 8:28, Luke 9:19), so the factors associated with the haunting of places and the possession of people may be residues of a personality whose guilt persists on earth, i.e., in history, and brings pain to other people.[38]

2.10.   To sum up: taken on their own, the data 'suggestive' of reincarnation, and to that extent of substantial dualist anthropology, are inconclusive and require independent criteria or revelation for more definitive assessment. For Christians, the Jewish doctrine of creation and Christ's resurrection become focal points of anthropological reflection and consequent opposition to the dualism implicit in reincarnation beliefs. The reasons for this opposition are at least three:

2.10.1.   The doctrine of the resurrection implies that the soul is incomplete without the body. Incarnation is not punishment but blessing. The biblical tradition affirmed the goodness of earthly life and forbade occult fixation with posthumous existence even though such existence is recognized (1 Sam 28:7–20). Gradually, biblical reflection on Yahweh's commitment to creation in history led it to formulate its own eschatological vision in the Jewish doctrine of the resurrection. Christianity witnesses to the concrete expression and realization of this expectation in the resurrection of Christ.

2.10.2.   If something personal survives bodily corruption, let us call it the soul, it should be regarded as a mutilated being. If Christians who are accustomed to the idea of "souls in heaven" find this last concept difficult, they only have to consider the example of the soul of a murdered individual to accept it more easily. This illustrates that traditional Christian ethics is another starting point for anthropological discussion. One could ground the affirmation of the integral nature of body and soul on the proscription against murder and its pre-suppositions. Here, however, the question is whether an entity such as the soul does survive bodily death.

2.10.3.   It seems that it does since the doctrine of the resurrection demands a principle which ensures the identity of the resurrected individual with the one who has lived and died. Since the body is and returns to dust (and ashes), nothing bears the burden of this demand better than the "soul", whatever be

---

[37] Perry, 'Reincarnation: New Flesh on Old Bones', p. 154.
[38] J. Ratzinger, *Eschatology: Death and Eternal Life*, p. 187.

its posthumous shape, guise, clothing and reason for survival (the biblical reason for the last seems to have less to do with the soul's substantial nature and more with the fact that it is known by the "God of Abraham, Isaac and Jacob").

2.11.   The preceding discussion is aimed at undermining the intrusion of dualistic anthropologies into medical-ethical discussions. The anthropological questions relate particularly to debates about abortion and euthanasia. Functional dualism weakens concern for physical human life in cases where an individual's rational faculties are not being exercised, e.g. where they are not developed, as in an embryo, or where they have been terminally suspended, as in a PVS victim. In such cases, the termination of the body is not regarded as killing since killing has the personal self as its object. The meaning of "undeveloped rational faculties" leaves wide scope for legal termination. The same is true of substantial dualism as shown by frequent religious support for abortion during the hypothetical "pre-ensoulment" period of the embryo,[39] or for euthanasia in cases where the soul is believed to have already departed, as was frequently said of Tony Bland[40], or to be in need of a liberating push. But with this anthropology, it may be rather difficult to understand how one can speak of killing at all when the killing refers to the body while the person is identified with the soul. Killing should have the self as its object. If the body is not identifiable with the self in any way, killing is not an issue if the body is destroyed. Ethics presupposes and contributes to anthropology. If traditional biblical and natural-legal prohibitions of murder and killing mean anything, they mean that the "self" must be constituted of the body as well, so that the destruction of the body entails a mutilation, if not the destruction, of the self.

2.12.   The debate may be broadened. Why not follow the ancient Epicureans and Stoics and commit suicide in all situations where life is judged to be of "no benefit"?[41] The reason why suicide should be eschewed is actually terribly striking but it is hard to discern on the basis of functional or substantial dualistic perspectives. This brings us back to the importance of anthropology for ethics:

> Descartes' error obscures the . . . tragedy implicit in the knowledge of (human) fragility, finiteness, and uniqueness. . . . Where humans fail to see [this] . . . , they feel far less called upon to do something about minimizing it, and may have less respect for the value of life . . . Cartesian dualism obscures the problem of mental suffering caused by physical pain and its converse: the physical ailments resulting from psychological conflict. Consequently, it has modified Western medical research and practice by driving a wedge between the study and healing of the physical and the mental diseases.[42]

[39] N. Ford, *When Did I Begin? Conception of the human individual in history, philosophy and science*, Cambridge: CUP 1988, Chapter 2.
[40] See references in Section II.3(11) of Dr Keown's paper (Chapter 15 below).
[41] A. H. Armstrong, *An Introduction to Ancient Philosophy*, London: Methuen 1947, p. 127.
[42] A. Damasio, *Descartes' Error: Emotion, Reason and the Human Brain*, p. 251.

Pain bears witness to the ontological reality of both body and mind/soul and to the goodness or desire for health of both. Reflection on the anthropological significance of the horror of pain thus demands that one abandon as untrue all the stoic and dualistic anthropologies which seek to resolve the problem of pain and suffering through *apatheia* and abandonment of the world. In essence, the latter entail the *anaesthetization* of consciousness and reflect the growing trend towards making ours an anaesthetic society.[43] Instead of turning away from the horror which afflicts people, one must, in the name of all that is human (Ps 31:11), look it in the face (Isa 53:3) and hear its cry (Job 31:35), even if this means embracing people on the cross and going through hell to save them.

### 3. From horror to blessing: the theology of creation, resurrection and the meaning of pain

3.1.   The principle that man learns through suffering is shared by biblical wisdom. But the lesson drawn, however, is neither a Buddhist despair with and escape from the body and the created order, nor a Marxist, Stalinist attempt to overhaul and re-engineer a "brave new world". To understand what biblical anthropology offers in place of the *horror* implied by the Cartesian image of man, one must consider the bases of biblical anthropology in its creation and resurrection narratives. The reason for emphasising the resurrection narratives is that they give meaning and content to the O.T. creation doctrine of man as made in the "image of God" in so far as the N.T. not only roots this idea in a theology of creation but also makes it an eschatological theme concerned with the destiny and future of humankind.[44]

3.2.   In reviewing these narratives, it will be instructive to contrast the "good" highlighted in them with the themes of *horror* noted above. Before proceeding, we may pause to ask what makes *horror* horrible. Etymologically, the Latin term means that which makes one "shaggy", i.e. what makes one's hair stand on end, turns one's skin into gooseflesh, and makes the body bristle and tremble. It is a painful emotion, either compounded of loathing, fear and shuddering with terror and repugnance, (Exod 1: 12, 15:12; Deut 1:29, 20:3, 28:67, Ps 31:11), or, a feeling of reverent fear and dread (Gen 15:12, Job 4:14f., Heb 10:31). Horror arises from defencelessness against the violation of personal intimate space, movement and autonomy whose ultimate boundaries are the body, soul, and senses – one's own and of those one loves. It is horrible to be blinded, choked, drowned, bound, confined, stripped naked, raped, dismembered, devoured, possessed, tortured, turned into a puppet by fear and drugs, forced to live a life that

---

[43] D. DeMarco, *The Anesthetic Society*, Front Royal, Virginia: Christendom College Press 1982.
[44] cf. J. Ratzinger, 'The Pastoral Constitution on the Church in the Modern World', in H. Vorgrimler (ed.), *Commentary on the Documents of Vatican II*, vol. 5, London: Burns & Oates 1969, p. 121, which critiques the omission of the N.T. perspective in Vatican II's discussion of "man as an image of God" in *Gaudium et Spes* 13.

is not one's own, become a puppet, a zombie, or a schizoid *legion*. It is all the more horrible to have this happen from the inside as it were, with an inability to guess whether the danger is inside or outside as in those horror-films where the murderer lives under one's roof masquerading as one's own doctor, spouse, sibling, parent, child (cf. Hitchcock's *Psycho*). Most horrible is it to have this state protracted in time and taken beyond the grave without hope of death so that one becomes something like a *walking or living dead*, like the Mummy, Frankenstein, or Dracula. It is interesting to contrast these images with the Bible's presentation of the created and the resurrected body.

3.3.　The doctrines of creation and resurrection are intimately linked. The Biblical account of creation speaks the language of myth but its word corrects myth in a threefold way. It distinguishes God from his creative work insisting that creation is not the blind result of *eros* and *eris* but is intelligently ordered towards reflecting God's goodness. Consequently, it distinguishes creation from the fall and finally, as a corollary, does not permit the resolution of the problem of evil and suffering through the hope of de-creation, i.e. it does not resolve the problem by seeking it in doctrines of other-worldly, disembodied existence.[45] Rather, the biblical reflection on the character of Yahweh and His intervention in history, articulates its solution in the notion of the resurrection. Let us now concentrate on some aspects of each.

Many patterns structure Genesis 1.[46] The sequence of the created works seems to follow Babylonian cosmological ideas: the deep, light, the separation of the waters by a firmament, the creation of the sun, stars and planets, the inhabitants of the earth and humankind. However, the biblical author demythologizes the created entities and imposes a 7-day structure which, with the correspondence between the works of days 1–3 (light, upper/lower waters, vegetation) with those of days 4–6 (stellar bodies, birds and fish, vegetation eating creatures) and the seventh-day sabbath, shows that creation is moved by divine forethought and by divine will that humankind share in divine blessing which includes work, fruitfulness and rest. The last point is stressed by the links between Gen. 1 and the Third Commandment (Exod. 20:8–10, esp. v. 11, Deut. 5:12–15). The goodness and blessing of being is repeatedly stressed in the chapter. What is essential for our purpose is to unpack the biblical concept of blessing and show how it bears upon the definition of man as made in the image and likeness of God and his vocation to work, be fruitful and rest. This can be made easier by contrasting the blessing to be found in this chapter with the motifs of horror surveyed above. A useful framework for this comparison is offered by a structure discerned in Genesis by Strauss and popularized by Kass. Strauss emphasizes that creation involves creation by separation:

> From the principle of separation, light [which allows discernment and distinction]; via something which separates, heaven; to something which is

---

[45] Job 14:7f., 19:25; Dan 12:2; cf. L. Bouyer, *The Christian Mystery: From Pagan Myth to Christian Mysticism*, Edinburgh: T. & T. Clark 1990.

[46] Wenham, G. J., *Genesis 1–15* (Word Biblical Commentary, Vol. 1), Waco, Texas: Word Books 1987, pp. 1–40.

separated, earth and sea; to things which are productive of separated things, trees, for example; then things which can separate themselves from their places, heavenly bodies; then things which can separate themselves from their courses, brutes; and finally a being which can separate it\-self from its way, the right way. The clue to the first chapter seems to be the fact that the account of creation consists of two main parts [days 1–3, days 4–6].

Leo Strauss' Creation By Division Schema[47]

| | |
|---|---|
| Lack place<br>    (light) | Have place |
| Lack definite place:<br>Regions needing to be<br>filled (heaven, sea, earth) | Have definite place;<br>fill place *within* a region |
| Lack local motion (plants) | Have local motion |
| Lack life<br>(sun, moon, stars) | Have life |
| Non-terrestrial (fish, birds) | Terrestrial |
| Not in God's Image<br>(land animals) | In God's Image<br>(man) |

This implies that the created world is conceived to be characterized by a fundamental dualism: things which are different from each other without having the capacity of local motion and things which in addition to being different from each other do have the capacity of local motion. This means the first chapter seems to be based on the assumption that the fundamental dualism is that of distinctness, otherness, as Plato would say, and of local motion.[48]

The dualism invoked here is the principle of distinction, and is not to be confused with the substantial dualism which opposes material to spiritual, intellectual substance. In commenting on Strauss' scheme, Kass notes that it also fits with the description of creation as proceeding through acts of intelligible speech inasmuch as speech presupposes capacity for distinction:

> To predicate or combine words in speech is to put together what mind has first seen as separate. Separation, otherness, distinction – or, if you prefer, the principle of contradiction, that A is other than not-A – is the very foundation of the possibility both of speech and of an articulated world.[49]

---

[47] L. Kass, *The Hungry Soul: Eating and the Perfecting of our Nature*, New York: The Free Press 1994, p. 203.

[48] L. Strauss, cited in L. Kass, *The Hungry Soul: Eating and the Perfecting of our Nature*, p. 202.

[49] Kass, *The Hungry Soul: Eating and the Perfecting of our Nature*, p. 203.

This reflection reveals a striking contrast with the confusion, emphasized above, of the relationship of "individual A and individual B" in *reincarnation* motifs. Adding to this the just noted themes of the violation of personal space, autonomy, and identity in *horror* motifs, one may clarify the preceding phenomenological descriptions of *horror* by emphasizing its violation of the principles of identity and contradiction in the sphere of the Self. *Horror* therefore has to do with the violation of personal identity. Conversely, *blessing* must deal with the bestowal of identity.

3.6.   Strauss's schema prompts still more fruitful contrasts between *horror* and the Priestly account of creation's *blessing* inasmuch as it reveals that the progressive bestowal of space, place, local motion, life, and terrestriality, is a progression towards the creation of the image of God. The "image" is realized in what is most concrete, definite, material, incarnate rather than in what is "spiritual" in the gnostic and substantial dualistic sense of mystical, ethereal, and heavenly. Hence, the "image of God" in man is not an immaterial soul but a spiritualized body. If man has an immaterial soul, it is a soul which attains self-realization in concreteness, i.e. in forms of embodiment. A possible good analogy is provided in the way that "words become flesh" when thoughts acquire definition and meaning in verbalized forms.

3.7.   But the progression evidenced by the scheme has an important emotive aspect which also helps to define the meaning of the "image of God". One may observe that whereas horror invades or confines personal space, the scheme shows God giving space. More contrasts can be drawn: whereas horror chokes or drowns or shakes one's foundations, God gives breath and a stable foothold; whereas horror binds, confines or turns one into an automaton, God gives autonomous movement and life. (In reference to the Yahwist account, one may add that whereas horror strips and shames, Yhwh clothes and dignifies.) It thus also follows that the image of God is fully realized not in what bears the deistic view of the divine, envisioned as a logical but emotionally cold, watchmaking power but rather in what stoops to give space, place, breath, movement, life, intelligence and choice, i.e. in what generously gives forethought for human personality, fate and feeling.

3.8.   The goodness of matter, the body and creation require the necessity of caring for it (Gen 1:26; 2:15). Should these fall away from their intended ends and fail to realize their forms, then disappointment, pain and suffering should be felt by both the creatures (Gen 3:7–19) and by their Creator (Gen 6:6–7, cf. *Dominum et Vivificantem* 39). In this state, concern for the body, the soul and creation, in spite of all painful alienation caused by sin, should be expressed in human and divine acts of forbearance, solicitude, grace and redemption. Thus, woman still clings to man in love despite the suffering of childbirth which this love entails (Gen 3:16), man works the earth despite the pain of toil (Gen 3:19), and the Creator is solicitous to restore man by clothing his shame (Gen 3:21) and rescuing him from perdition (8:1f.). In the context of the doctrine of creation and the affirmation of the Creator's redeeming love, pain becomes the basis for anti-dualist confessions of faith and expressions of eschatological hope. Physical pain troubles the soul, psychic pain troubles the body. The solution is not to separate the two but recognize their need to be integrally related. In Christian history, this anti-dualist stance frequently takes on the form of a Christological confession. Suffering is embraced, even unto death, because what is at stake is the belief that Christ was incarnate, died and rose again in the flesh.[50]

3.9.    These reflections on the meaning of pain allow one to develop the earlier statement about the enigmatic human consciousness of living under different laws – the physical and the spiritual. At this point one may add that this consciousness expresses itself in various forms of suffering, e.g. desires, hungers (Deut 8:3, Amo 8:11, Jer 15:16, Matt 4:4), and poverties (cf. Luke 6:20 and Matt 5:3). Consequently, it expresses itself in divided loyalties (Rom. 7; Matt 6:24, Luke 16:13). The fear of death, pain and privation of desire threaten the capacity to follow what is known to be true or good (Matt 13:21–22; John 13:36f.). In other words, the problem of being a rational animal means being prone to temptation on various levels (Matt. 4: 1f.; Matt. 26:41; Luke 4:1f.; Mark 14:38, Matt. 13, etc.).[51] As we have noted, the Christian solution to this problem takes its bearings from the Judeo-Christian doctrines of Creation and Resurrection. The latter provides the faith which is necessary for courageous attachment to the good and the true (4 Macc 5ff.) while the former demands that the choice of the good and the true must never harm created goods.

3.10.    Christianity's true "boast" lies in what Paul termed its folly and stumbling block: the horror of the Cross, which takes us to Jesus' doctrine of *the suffering Messiah* (1 Cor 23) and to his renunciation of the *Three Temptations* of the Jewish Messianic model.[52] The doctrine and renunciation explain His denunciation of Peter as "satan" for refusing to allow Jesus' passion predictions to shape his conception of Jesus as *messiah*. Peter, after all, like John the Baptist before him, maintained a more normative model of Jewish messianic expectation (cf. Matt. 16:23 and Mark 8:33 with Matt. 4:10 and Mark 1:13; Luke 12:50, Acts 1:6, etc.). The significance of Jesus' self-understanding was not grasped until after his resurrection for it was by means of his resurrection that Christ brought meaning and light where before there was nothing but a horrible bloody mess and a veiled refusal to see and repent of behaviour that ultimately creates or cooperates with the creation of horror.[53]

3.11.    The connotation of *horror* here both resembles and differs from the connotation given to the term above. Jesus endures the horrors of the most shameful bodily violation, death and descent into Hell. But the gospels show that he actively faced and confronted the "horror of the Cross" in order to overcome the alienation it symbolizes and therefore to redeem the created world from its enslavement to the fear of pain, death and horror.

---

[50] cf. Ignatius of Antioch, *The Epistle to the Romans*, in G. P. Goold (ed.), *The Apostolic Fathers*, Vol. 1, (Loeb Classical Library), London: Heinemann 1985.

[51] F. Dostoyevsky, *The Brothers Karamazov* (1880), chapters (Ivan's) "Mutiny" and "Grand Inquisitor".

[52] *Ibid.*

[53] cf. J. Alison, *Knowing Jesus*, p. 35.

3.12.   When we turn to the Christian biblical testimony to the state of Christ's risen body, we are not shown a body that had lived, died and then lived again as if the death was something cancelled by the Resurrection. The testimony is that His risen body lives on a different level than that which can be negated by death, for it not only bears the scars of death but preserves the meaning and actuality of His death. The image commemorated by the tradition is of a "lamb who lives forever slain", which is the literal meaning of the words *agnus qui vivit semper occisus*[54] by which the Roman Missal (Easter Preface no. III) recalls the image of Christ in Rev 5:6:

> If there is any phrase that comes near expressing this, it is the living dead. Not, obviously in the Hollywood sense of someone caught in a time warp between being dead and going to an eternal rest... but in the sense that the Resurrection life was the giving back of the whole human life, leading up to and including the death. It is this that is the sign that death has been conquered.... It is not as though the Resurrection cured him of being slaughtered – he was in a bad way but God bandaged him up. The gratuity of the Resurrection is what gives him back as the slaughtered one. It is here that the devotion to Christ Crucified has its place in the lives of some of the saints... [and] stigmatists like St. Francis or Padre Pio... The presence of Jesus as risen-slaughtered one is key to the sense in which the Resurrection is the presence of forgiveness, is the forgiveness of sin.[55]

## 4. The ethical implications of depicting the human person as an "image of God"

4.1.   Throughout the discussion, we have noted the importance that the image of man plays in determining how one should deal with the human body. We have illustrated in various ways how a Cartesian, dualistic or gnostic representation of the self results in a distorted approach to medical care for the body and impedes proper care for the whole man: body, mind and soul. More specifically, we have also emphasized, with the help of literary models, the dangers of fabricating man in the image of one's own limited, human preconceptions. The purpose of this section is to show how the biblical presentation of man as made "in the image of God" (Gen 1:26) anticipates, disparages and corrects these dangers.

4.2.   By stating that *'Adam* is made in God's "image", the Bible states that *'Adam*, meaning man and woman together, is intended to be the best picture of God in this world. The Hebrew word for "image" also means "idol" so that its usage here explains the Hebrew prohibition of "idolatry". It simply means that man's subservience to idols, i.e. to the fabrications of his hands and mind, subjects man, the creation of God's hands, made in God's image, to the fabrications of man's hands, made in man's image. To engage in such practices is to proceed

[54] Alison, *Knowing Jesus*, p. 21.
[55] Alison, *Knowing Jesus*, p. 20.

from blindness and deafness to the nature of things. It is to become as blind, deaf, and dumb as the things one makes. The ancient pagans sought to give their representations of the gods virtual reality by devising rituals that would "open their mouths" and make them vehicles of divine revelation, sight, hearing and speech. But the Biblical creation narrative, abbreviating the Hebrew prophetic, legal, sapiential and liturgical traditions declares that man is himself the being whom God has endowed with eyes that see, ears that hear, a heart that understands, lungs that breathe and a mouth that speaks God's word (Isa 6:9f., Exo 20:4, Deut 5:8, Psa 115, 135). Here we have a definition of man as the creature with whom God dialogues.[56] The God of the Bible is not interested in talking to machines which have no heart. He is, in this respect, beneath the consideration of the modern "artificial intelligence" buffs who reduce man to intelligence and intelligence to a limited range of logical operations, which can be embodied in circuitry, which is then credited with a status superior to that of the ordinary human. From a biblical point of view, what has happened is similar to the creation of idols who are credited with powers they do not possess.

4.3.   What is the bulwark against this reductive view of man? We have it implicitly in the first verse of the Bible in the image of God "hovering, brooding over the waters" given that 1:26 implies that the image should also apply to man, i.e. that he also consists of a "spirit over waters" (cf. also Gen 2:6–7). In fact, man loves and fears the play and challenge of deep blue, not the deep blue of virtual reality but the real, foamy, wild thing. In reflecting on the origins of philosophy, Hegel argued that it developed around the Mediterranean because man, at the sight of the sea, was reminded of himself and, wishing to cross it, set out on a voyage of self-realization by yoking his courage and wisdom to the task of shipbuilding. St. Therese of Lisieux, seeing the sea for the first time, was reminded, instead, of God and saw herself as a little vessel afloat in his infinity. God hovering over the waters, spirit hovering over matter, man sailing beyond icy Archangel, to where no man has gone before: the deep blue is something to "drive away the cold November from [man's] soul and make [him] stop involuntarily pausing before coffin warehouses".[57] We have in this image an insight into the anthropological basis of the fundamental goods of play, creativity, and adventure:

> There is nothing surprising in this. If they but knew it, almost all men in their degree, some time or other, cherish very nearly the same feelings towards the ocean with me.[58]

4.4.   In other words, Gen 1 does not supply a static image of God. God hovers over the waters, speaks, creates, is fruitful and rests. All this corresponds in a most interesting manner to the injunctions which God gives to man upon creating him:

---

[56] J. Ratzinger, 'Dogmatic Constitution on Divine Revelation' in H. Vorgrimler, *Commentary on the Documents of Vatican II*, vol. 3, London: Burns & Oates 1969, pp. 155f.
[57] H. Melville, *Moby Dick* (1851), paragraph 1.
[58] *Ibid.*

to be fruitful and multiply, to subdue everything but the sea, and to rest.[59] From these correspondences, it is evident that the commandments direct man to imitate and cooperate with God in His work of creation begun by hovering and brooding over the formless waters, leaving only the final subduing of the sea to God Himself (Rev 21:1).

4.5. In a functional sense, therefore, man realizes the divine image to the extent that he also hovers over the waters, sees, speaks, creates, names, is fruitful, works and rests, and all this in time. Conversely, man fails to realize himself to the extent that he impedes, avoids, or is denied all these, through such adversities as the inability to "hover over the waters" and all that it represents: infertility or sterilization in the realm of fruitfulness; sloth, slavery, restlessness, incapacity for contemplation and enjoyment of goodness in the realm of work. The functional definition of personality as deiform implies that it is a dynamic entity which seeks self-realization in time. As the realization of the image may be impeded it requires a nurturing environment and the exercise of virtue. For it is through the exercise of its faculties in ways appropriate to the challenges of its environment that the "image" grows and realizes itself.

4.6. It is important to subordinate this functional definition to the ontological one: man is, as an image of God, a mystery, essentially indefinable, incommunicable, and having a name which no one but God knows (Job 7:17, 15:14, Ps 8:4, 144:3, Ecc. 6: 10–11, Heb 2:6, Sir 18:18, 4 Ezra 8:34; cf. Rev 2:17).[60] To borrow a gospel phrase: each human being, however small, has a meaning and value understood only by "his angel in heaven who always sees the face of the Father" (Matt 18:10). Do such angels not always see the face of the Father precisely because they see it reflected in the "image" they guard and watch? For this reason, the biblical representation of man as an image of God highlights the dangers of fabricating man according to merely human representations and understandings of man's nature. Man is not to be *made in* the "image of man" but *accepted* as begotten (given) in the "image of God".

## 5. The "image of God", reproduction, generation and the family

5.1. The "image of God" enters existence through human reproduction. The womb and the family are each human person's natural and traditional nurturing environments. But technology allows medicine to establish artificial environments for various stages of embryonic existence (e.g., IVF, surrogacy, and artificial wombs) and consequently allows social policy to redefine or abandon the traditional concept of the family as an optimum environment for begetting and raising children. Alternatively, it allows one to artificially control reproduction and thereby divorce sexuality from procreation. In view of the preceding discussions,

---

[59] E. Stein, *Essays on Woman*, in L. Gelber & R. Leuven, OCD (eds.), *The Collected Works of Edith Stein*, Vol. 2, Washington, D.C.: ICS [Institute of Carmelite Studies] Publications 1987, pp. 57ff.
[60] cf. J. F. Crosby, 'The Incommunicability of Human Persons', 57 (1993) *The Thomist* 403–442.

the ethical wisdom of such practices should be questioned. Is there a danger that these practices actually impede the flourishing of the "image of God" in all those people who actively participate in or passively suffer these practices?

5.2. Such questions require very intricate and detailed discussion. What I intend to do here is to clarify the context for approaching them. More specifically, here and in the next section, I intend to provide an exegetical reflection on the role which the biblical creation accounts accord to the traditional natural family structure in nurturing and supporting the realization of the "image of God" in human beings. This reflection should clarify the nature of biblical opposition to certain incursions of technology into the realm of human generation, reproduction, and parenthood along the lines drawn in the "Frankenstein" section (2.2) above.

5.3. One may begin by asking what the image of God in Gen 1:26 has to do with the commandment in Gen 1:28 to "be fruitful and multiply". Presumably, the commandment directs man towards the good, i.e. towards the realization of the divine image in his life. But one could give a bolder answer: by being fruitful, multiplying, and reproducing, man imitates God and better reflects His image in his own life because God also reproduces in a certain sense. To attribute reproduction to God sounds provocative but it is implicit in the creation narrative. The words of Gen 1:26, "Let us make man in our own image..." identify the stage in the creative process at which God begins to reproduce his own image and likeness. Prior to Gen 1:26, the text depicted creatures yielding seed and begetting offspring each according to their own kind (Gen 1:11–12, 21, 24–25). Given that Gen 5:3 has Noah begetting a son "in his own image and likeness", we may say that when all the creatures are said to reproduce according to their own kind, they are reproducing (according to) "their own image and likeness". The phrase denotes the relationship of offspring to their parents. Thus when, at Gen 1:26, God declares "Let us make man according to our own image and our own likeness," we may legitimately infer that the text has reached the point at which God begins to reproduce His own image. In other words, and in a qualified sense, God is shown here to be becoming a Father and beginning His family. Luke's identification of *Adam* as a son of God (Luke 3:38) supports this reading. Humanity therefore may be said to be the result of the "generation/begetting of heaven and earth" in the poetic sense of being sprung from both, heaven and earth (Wis 7:1). Perhaps this reflection throws light on the meaning of the formula "these are the generations/begettings of heaven and earth" in Gen 2:4 which in slightly altered form introduces so many units in the Pentateuch that many scholars see it as the key to its structure.[61] If this is the case, the Bible as a whole may be read as a book about the *genesis* of man through the generations or begettings of heaven and earth.

5.4. Gen 1:26 declares that God is the father of *Adam* (Luke 3:38) but also of every *son of Adam*. His hands and breath fashion not only the first but every man

---

[61] On the Tôledôth framework in the Pentateuch, see T. L. Thompson, *The Origin Tradition of Ancient Israel*, JSOT Supp. 55, JSOT, Sheffield, 1987, p. 64, and E. Scarry, *The Body in Pain*, Oxford: OUP 1985, *passim*.

coming into the world (Gen 2:7, 5: 1f.; 6:4, John 1:9) through sexual union and gestation in a mother's womb (Gen. 4:1, 4:25; Ruth 4:12,13; Psa 139:13; Job 12:10, etc.). What does it mean to say that God becomes a father and what image does the Bible present of His paternity? As noted, the creation process is described in language reminiscent of ancient near eastern creation myths but corrective in key respects. These myths, like the better known Greek ones, describe creation as driven by inter- and intra-generational *eros* and *eris*, or, in more popular modern terms, by Oedipal rivalry. Each generation of pagan deities fears and struggles with preceding and following generations. The Greek myths are powerfully suggestive in their imagery: Kronos swallows his children for fear that they will supplant him as he has supplanted Uranus. Indeed one may have an Oedipal view of time inasmuch as it may be visualized as devouring its children from both ends, eating away at their memories, their senses, intelligence. It seems that it is death that creates this relationship to time. If one could only kill time, it seems, one could hold on to beauty, love, laughter, Aphrodite... It is of course a grace to be given laughter in old age (18:12–15, 21:1–3; "Isaac" means "he will laugh" in Hebrew) and there is nothing wrong with seeking to look good,[62] or with seeking to alleviate the hardships of senescence. But there is something horribly Oedipal in the drive to stay young at any cost, e.g. at the cost of harvesting anti-wrinkle cream from aborted foetuses, or at the cost of conquering and arresting the process of generation altogether through cloning.[63] As we shall see, this Oedipal attitude derives from a wrong, mythical view of time.

5.5.   The creation narratives do provide a contrasting image of paternity. The pagan idea of God as an Oedipal, rivalrous father who fears to share his divine primacy with his children and with man is attributed to a serpentine slander (Gen 3:4f.). It is ultimately defined as a demonic misrepresentation of the divine father-son relationship (John 8:44). As there is no inter-generational rivalry among the plant and animal species of Gen 1, so there is no shadow of it in Gen 1:26. The Oedipal relationship, however, remains an important backdrop against which the character of divine paternity can be understood. This pagan backdrop reveals the Biblical understanding of divine paternity as *kenotic*, self-emptying, self-opening, self-surrendering, like the seed which falls into the ground and dies to give the ground its life. Although the term *kenosis* is usually applied to Christ (Phil. 2:5–11), these reflections reveal that Christ's *kenosis* is simply an imitation of his Father (John 5:19, 8:28, 38; 10:37f., 14:9, etc.) so that through him the goal of the Book of Generations envisioned as the unity of heart among siblings (Gen 33:10; Ps 133) and between parents and children (Gen 22:6f.; Exod 20:12; Deut. 5:16; Mal 4:6) reaches its fulfilment.

5.6.   Pagan and biblical reflections on the importance of generation agree in the knowledge of the curses of barrenness, fratricide, genocide, plague and natural

---

[62] L. Kass, *Toward a More Natural Science: Biology and Human Affairs*, pp. 318ff.
[63] P. Ramsey, 'The Issues Facing Mankind', 1:3 (1985) *Ethics and Medicine* 37–43; L. Kass, 'The Wisdom of Repugnance: Why we should ban the cloning of humans', *The New Republic* June 1997: 17–26.

catastrophe. The patriarchal generations are shown seeking fruitfulness through aphrodisiacs, surrogacy, incest, the law of levirate, and subterfuge (Gen 30:14f.; Gen 16.1f.; 30:3f.; 9f.; Gen 19:30–36; Gen 38 Gen 38, Deut 25:5f., Ruth 3:12, 4:5; Exod. 1:15–2:10).[64] All of the resulting conceptions, because they are rooted in inequalities, engender further and deadly familial, social and political rivalries (Gen 16.1; 30:8; Gen 33:2; 37:2f.; 1 Sa 1:6; Gen 19:37–38; Exod. 1f.). It proves even impossible to avoid rivalry for twins as one of them has to be born first (Gen 25:21ff.). The joy of fruitfulness and multiplication is difficult to achieve: suspicion between the spouses, rivalry between parents and children, fratricide among siblings: what is intended to be a tree of life becomes fraught with so much pain and suffering, that it becomes a tree of mixed experiential knowledge, a knowledge of (both) "good and evil". Through all this, one can begin to surmise that the return to the tree of life involves departing from evil (Job 28:28, Psa 31:14, 37:27, etc.) and the undoing of Oedipal rivalry between parents and children and of murderous rivalry among siblings through the redemption of all the rivalries created through all the surrogacies, seductions, incests, rapes, adulteries and harlotries of history (Matt 1:1–18f.; Luke 3:23–38).

5.7.   The kenotic return to God through respect for the family and its past and future generations stands at the heart of the biblical vision of the way in which human beings find fulfilment and receive a meaning and a name. Two narratives are particularly outstanding in this respect: those about the journeys and trials of Abraham and the book of Ruth. Both narratives concern a journey in faith, a journey through sterility to "laughter", something seemingly rare in the Bible but sublime when present.

5.8.   Abraham's stories are narrated around the call of God to leave what he knows in search of the promised land and around the Covenant promising him land and children as many as the stars of heaven. The narrative illustrates the call is constitutive of personality. No call – no reason for response, no responsibility, no drama, no character. The call makes Abraham's life a life of question and answer, a seeking, a wandering, a dialogue, a story. By responding to the call in faith, he acquires a story and becomes a story. Through his sterile wife Sarah, he is promised a son and laughter, since Isaac means "laughter" or "he shall laugh". But the laughter is not secured except through the ultimate, last trial,[65] a kenotic trial that should fill anyone who thinks about it with sleep-depriving fear and trembling.[66] In the call to sacrifice Isaac, Abraham displays such awesome faith that his capacity to contain anguish makes him the only real-life prototype of the suffering servant, a man seemingly cut off from his generation (Isa 53) like the victims and eunuchs of his and subsequent Exilic ages and holocausts whom God promised to honour with an everlasting "hand and name (Yad vaShem) that is better than sons and daughters" (Isa 56:3–5).

---

[64] cf. E. Scarry, The Body in Pain.
[65] Spiegel, Sh., The Last Trial: On the Legends and Lore of the Command to Abraham to Offer Isaac As a Sacrifice: The Akedah, New York: Schocken 1967.
[66] See Kierkegaard's Fear and Trembling.

5.9.    The book of *Ruth* also turns on the passage from bitter sorrow to joy through sublimely controlled laughter. Ruth is the female Abraham of the Bible, a descendant of Lot through incest (Gen 19:31f.). She leaves her land, mother and father and national gods in pursuit of the call of love for her grief-stricken and bereaved mother in law, Naomi. "By chance" she enters the field of Boaz, who being a distant kinsman of Naomi is a potential Levir – someone who can beget a child in the name of her deceased son and Ruth's husband (Dent 25:5). As the story of Onan illustrates, fulfilling the levirate was a burdensome duty which entailed spoiling one's own name and inheritance. Women like Tamar sought to obtain it through trickery (Gen 38) while custom sought to protect it through rituals of shaming by likening the unwilling kinsman to Onan through the ritual of spitting and sandal-removal (Deut 25:9, Ruth 4:7,8).[67] Naomi and Ruth also tried to trick Boaz. In the middle of the night of the harvest festival he woke up semi-drunk with Ruth at his feet and his skirt lifted up. But he recognized the dedication behind her offer of marriage and pledged her his own loyalty. Only one obstacle impeded the marriage: a closer kinsman. But the kinsman declined Ruth in fear of "spoiling his own inheritance" and "name" (Ruth 4:5,6). It is a pointed irony of the text that by selfish attachment to his own name, this man became the only character in the story whose name tradition forgot. Ruth and Boaz, on the other hand, by dedicating themselves to the name of Naomi and Elimelech, were remembered for all generations and, by being overshadowed by the wings of God (Ruth 2:12; 3:9), became the ancestors of her who uttered creation's second "fiat" and, being overshadowed with God's Spirit, occasioned a new "book of generation" (Mat 1ff.), thus bringing the story of the generation of heaven and earth one step closer to completion.

5.10.    To sum up, the Bible puts a lofty value on kenotic dedication to the family and to our ancestors and descendants because it is through *kenosis*, the giving of self, that the image of God in man is realized. This is not to say that kenosis is impossible without it. Of course it is (cf. Matt. 19:29; 10:35–37). But as all kenosis requires examples and experiences of love, the family is its first and natural school. To protect civilization, one must oppose all that threatens to dismantle and eviscerate its structures.


## 6.  "Knowledge", "Autonomy" and "Quality of Life": *The Seed and the Fruit*

6.1.    The relevance of all the preceding section to ethical, including medical-ethical discussions may be further clarified by a final set of reflections on the type of "autonomy" and "quality of life" which, according to the biblical creation narratives, man is intended to have.

6.2.    Let us conclude by focusing again, with some help, on Genesis 2–3. In this narrative, Man, *'Adam* is formed by Yhwh out of moistened earth, *'adamah*. He

---

[67] A. Phillips, 'The Book of Ruth – Deception and Shame', 36 (1985) *Journal of Jewish Studies* 1–17.

is thus quite literally an Earthman. This Earthman is animated by the divine spirit and receives a commandment to keep the Garden and not to eat of the Tree of the Knowledge of Good and Evil lest he die (Gen 2:15, 17). The commandment not to eat of the Tree in question is the primary commandment which he is to keep but which he transgresses (4 Es 3:7).

6.3.   Now to understand the implications of this, one must bear in mind the way in which biblical scribal traditions link the semantic fields of the concepts pertaining to "keeping", "commandments", "knowledge" and "life" as well as their opposites.[68] Briefly, "keeping" or "guarding" is linked to "knowing" (Gen 4:9, Pro 24:12, Sir 12:11). As commandments are words that should be "kept" in the sense of "obeyed", "done", "revered" and "hearkened unto", scripture links "keeping" of God's commandments to "knowing" God (John 7:17, 8:55, 17:6,7; I John 2:3). Moreover, such keeping or doing leads to life (Lev 18:25, Deut 30:16, Prov 4:4, 23, 7:2, 19:16, Matt. 19:17) and is therefore identified with true wisdom, understanding and knowledge (Deut. 4:6; Psa 118:100; Sir 1:26). Life and knowledge may therefore be regarded as the fruit of the keeping of good commandments. Biblical wisdom traditions often represent life-giving Wisdom under the metaphor of a tree (Pro. 3:18, Sir 24). Similarly, the man who wisely keeps the commandments, i.e. the righteous man, is metaphorically described as a fruitful tree or planting (Psa 1, Isa 5:7, 60:21, Sir 27:6) whose fruit is knowledge of God (Col. 1:10). In keeping with this metaphorical field, the word of God may be compared to a seed (Isa 55:10,11; Luke 8:11, Mark 4:14) and the heart of man to earth or soil (Luke 8:15, 4 Es 4:30,31). The symbolism is made explicit in Jesus' interpretations of his Parable of the Sower (Math. 13; Mark 4; Luke 8). The key point is that the entry of man into life and fruitfulness in the knowledge of God is a process that begins with the keeping and interiorization of divine words and commandments (Pro. 3:18, 11:30, Rev. 2:7, 4 Macc 18:16).

6.4.   The concept sketched out by means of these reflections may now be applied to the commandment given to Adam to keep at Gen 2:17. Thus, as good earth which, by keeping a seed, enters the life of that seed, and is raised into a fruit-bearing tree, so 'Adam, as an Earthman, receives a seed-word which has the power to admit him into its life and raise him into a Treeman, bearing the fruit of the knowledge of the inner goodness which was contained in the seed he was given. Accordingly, the intention of the divine injunction to 'Adam in the Garden was to direct him to become both a Tree of the "Knowledge of God and Goodness" and a "Tree of Life" (Ps 1). By not keeping the seed-commandment, 'Adam put himself outside the possibility of life and fruition in the knowledge of God.

6.5.   Why did 'Adam not keep the commandment? The reasons, like the divine and anthropological meanings of the "seed", "earth", "trees", "fruit", etc., are explained in the sapiential strata of the Bible, and form the subject of Jesus' first parable, the Parable of the Sower (Math. 13; Mark 4; Luke 8). In response to ques-

---

[68] cf. L. Khamor, *The Revelation of the Son of Man*, Geneva, N Y: Ben Yamin Press 1989 (1992), *passim*.

tions about this parable, Jesus asks: "Do you not understand this parable? How then will you understand all the other parables?" (Mark 4:13). Understanding that true life, real understanding and knowledge begin with the keeping of the commandments is prerequisite to everything else. In effect He explains that Earth-man does not keep the word of God because he is tempted by more instant forms of self-gratification and lacks the patience which entry into divine life requires of him (Luke 8:14; cf. Matt 13:22; Mark 4:19).

6.6.   Understanding the Parable of the Sower involves not only understanding the point of the parable but also its symbolism which likens the human heart to soil and divine words to seeds. Here we have a theological anthropology which states that "Man's relationship with his Maker is basically that between earth and Sower; ground and Seed; garden and Gardener; matter and Life."[69] Furthermore, the content and symbolism of the parable is closely related to its form. Parables require a special type of attention and hearing. They are a form of communication which presupposes and teaches that what one sees and hears depends on how one sees and hears (Luke 8:18; 11:34–36): "The eye is the lamp of the body" (Mat 6:22, Luke 11:34).

6.7.   The biblical wisdom of the Parable of the Sower and of the Garden of Eden story is applicable to many realms and levels of life. We could, for example, begin to delineate here the biblical response to the New-Age denial of the link between deeds and destiny (cf. 2.7 above). A good illustration relevant to medical ethics is furnished by issues pertaining to the use of psychoactive and psychedelic drugs. There is a "natural exaltation attached to the completion of the greatest endeavours – victory in a just war, consummated love, artistic creation, religious devotion and discovery of the truth".[70] Drug-induced simulation of the experience of achievement is no substitute for the experience of actual achievement. One could not be actually enjoying the fruits, for by cutting out the naturally required effort, virtue, talent and exercise required in raising them, one would be having only an illusory experience of enjoying them. As the extrinsic substitute makes virtue pointless, the addict becomes internally impoverished and incapable of it. It is at this point also that one may appreciate the wisdom of the biblical riposte to the western "New-Age" denial, reviewed above, of the link between ethics and destiny (see 2.6 and 2.7 above). The tree one becomes and the fruit one bears is a function of the seeds one keeps.

6.8.   Debates about medical ethics give prominence to the idea of securing "quality of life" through "autonomy" and "knowledge". Judeo-Christianity values "autonomy" and "knowledge" but false conceptions of their value constantly threaten to distort our lives. A key aspect of the "original sin" described in Genesis 2–3 involves not so much the desire for divinity, quality of life, autonomy and knowledge as such, as the grasping for instant self-realization in a way that proves, in its inception or conception, to be completely extrinsic and, in its end or fruit, the contrary of any real freedom and autonomy. True autonomy and

[69] L. Khamor, *The Revelation of the Son of Man*, p. 4.
[70] A. Bloom, *The Closing of the American Mind*, New York: Simon and Shuster 1987, p. 80.

quality of life require patient self-donation to maturation, development and growth (Luke 8:15; Rom 2:7; 8:25; Jam 1:3–4). They thus require an assent, a *fiat*, to being in generation, to being at one end of generation a seed, an embryo, a baby, a child, and so on, and at the other end a wasting and withering away (2 Cor 4:16; Isa 40:7–8; Gen 3:19; Eccl 12:1–7). In other words, they require a non-Oedipal perception of time. Time should be seen not as a devouring enemy but as a gift, "a moving picture of eternity".[71] In this perspective, faith brings a radiant willing-to-be at all stages of life.[72]

## 7. Conclusion

7.1.  Getting the wheel of generation right is what the Bible is all about. As God's son, Man also shares the honour of cooperating with God in begetting His family. Man gains his meaning, just as he receives his name, by taking a stand within the generations. In this biblical affirmation we have a fundamental critique of the pagan, Oedipus-complex-driven world-view which understands salvation and self-fulfilment to lie in the escape from generation and domination over it and time. Of the latter there are many examples: liberation of one's career ("name and inheritance") and sexuality from the burdens of family life but at the expense of family life and sex marked by faith; liberation of reproduction through technological replacement of motherhood and fatherhood, but not without the evisceration of inter-generational love, pity and compassion; immunity from the watery mess and power relations of sexual generation through IVF and surrogacy but not without giving the offspring the consciousness of being the objects and products of total self-control; immortality and conquest over generation through cloning, but at the price of freezing or inhibiting the development of past and future generations.

7.2.  As bodily, man feels determined by the laws of nature; as thinking, he is conscious of being a free, responsible agent. This can now be rephrased again: to be bodily, is to be dependent upon generation and thus to receive a name from others and know that one's life is not one's own property. To be a body is to be dependent on love. To live otherwise, is to make "desperate anger one's basic attitude to life ... to insist on procuring [love] by oneself ... and reduce it to the satisfaction of those needs that require no adventure of the spirit or the heart for their filling".[73] When man distinguishes himself from his body, its desires engulf him and shame him. When he loves through it in purity of heart, it becomes the medium of revelation, of grace. What one sees depends very much on how one

---

[71] Plato, *Timaeus* 37d. In E. Hamilton and H. Cairns (eds.), *The Collected Dialogues of Plato*, Princeton: Princeton University Press 1963.

[72] J. Ratzinger, *Eschatology: Death and Eternal Life*, p. 128; K. Barth, 'The Will to Be Healthy'. In S. E. Lammers and A. Verhey (eds.), *On Moral Medicine: Theological Perspectives in Medical Ethics*, Grand Rapids: Eerdmans 1987, pp. 6–10.

[73] Ratzinger, *Eschatology: Death and Eternal Life*, p. 96.

sees, and what one is depends very much on how one does. The great problem is to find a metaphor by which one may instructively represent these truths.

7.3. The obvious is the most difficult to see. The ultimate separator between matter and life is the seed (meaning a "fertilized egg"). It is the small seed that makes all the difference between being soil and being soil that is integrated with air, water and light in a living plant. The most subtle distinctions in the world will not erase the truth of this principle and its applicability to anthropogenesis in this world and in the next (1 Cor 15:42f.). But it is precisely such *subtle* distinctions (e.g. the meaningless post-1984 neologism "pre-embryo",[74] or the distinction between the "pre-syngamy zygote" and the "post-syngamy zygote",[75] let alone the distinctions between "genetic individuality" and "developmental individuality"[76] in discussing the "hominization" of the "pre-embryo"[77]) that blur the fact that individual life begins with the seed thereby paving the way for practices by which individuals are *over-produced, selectively reduced, turned-over,* and thrown out.

7.4. The Christian Bible responds to modernist and post-modernist, new age resentments of Christianity's bondage to the pre-enlightened past by proclaiming the good *news* of having concretely witnessed and come to experiential knowing of the principal desires of both: the attainment of freedom, autonomy, knowledge and quality of life through the conquest of pain and death, not to mention the reception and entry into a mystery beyond the imagination of post-enlightenment *new*-age man (1 Cor 2:9). But the knowing which forms the substance of Christianity's hope for the future is the fruition of its keeping, through thankful *remembering* and *meditation*, a seed sown in the historical past (Luke 2:19; 22:19; 1 Cor 11:24–25).

---

[74] [The Australian] Senate Select Committee on the Human Embryo Experimentation Bill 1985, *The Tate Report*, Canberra: Australian Government Publishing Service 1986, p. 11; S. Chalmers, *The Status of the Human Embryo and the Problem of Embryo Freezing With Particular Reference to Britain*, Licence Dissertation, Pontifical Lateran University, Alphonsian Academy, Rome 1997, Appendix (1), 'The Inaccuracy of the Term "pre-embryo"', pp. 87–89.

[75] N. Tonti-Filippini, 'Further comments on the beginning of life', 59/3 (1992) *The Linacre Quarterly* 76–81.

[76] M. Johnson, 'Quaestio Disputata: Delayed Hominization', 56 (1995) *Theological Studies* 742–763; J. Porter, 'Quaestio Disputata: Delayed Hominization: Reflections on Some Recent Catholic Claims for Delayed Hominization', 56 (1995) *Theological Studies* 763–70.

[77] B. Ashley, 'A critique of the theory of delayed hominization', in A. Morazewski (ed) *An Ethical Evaluation of Fetal Experimentation: An Interdisciplinary Study*, St Louis, MO: Pope John Center 1976, pp. 113–33; Ashley, 'Delayed Hominization: Catholic Theological Perspectives', in Russell Smith (ed) *The Interaction of Catholic Bioethics and Secular Society*, Braintree, MASS: The Pope John Center 1992, pp. 163–79.

# Sexual ethics

# 8

# The nuptial meaning of the body and sexual ethics

JORGE V. ARREGUI

## 1. The coordinates of the theology of the body

WHEN ESTABLISHING the philosophical sources of John Paul II's thought, most authors rely heavily on his declaration in the Preface to the English edition of *The Acting Person*. In this Prologue, written in 1977, he explains that "he owes everything to the systems of metaphysics, of anthropology, and of Aristotelian-Thomistic ethics on the one hand, and to phenomenology, above all in Scheler's interpretation, and through Scheler's critique also to Kant, on the other hand".[1] In consequence, there is a tendency to highlight the attempt developed by Karol Wojtyla to reconcile Thomist metaphysics and phenomenology, his effort to enlarge classical metaphysics with subjects and methods coming from the phenomenology of the Göttingen Circle and from personalist philosophies. For, as Cardinal Wojtyla himself explains in the Prologue to the Polish edition of *The Acting Person*, he tries to overcome the division of philosophy into a philosophy of being and a philosophy of consciousness, endeavouring to make the most of a philosophy of consciousness which remains embedded in a philosophy of being. So, it is usual to maintain that Karol Wojtyla reverses the way followed by Aquinas. Whereas the latter starts from a metaphysical consideration of man as an ontological being in order to arrive at an analysis of his actions, the former follows the opposite direction: he starts from a phenomenological analysis of human actions in order to illuminate the way in which such actions reveal the person as their subject. Cardinal Wojtyla would thus apply a phenomenological method to an ontological problem: he would analyze human experience to arrive at an understanding of the human person. In accordance with this understanding of his approach, it is also usual, especially after his explicit statements in *The Threshold of Hope*, to emphasize the influence of the philosophers of dialogue, such as Buber, Rosenzweig and Levinas.[2]

---

[1] See K. Wojtyla, *The Acting Person*, Dordrecht: Reidel 1979, p. xiv.
[2] See, for example, J. L. Lorda, *Antropología: Del Concilio Vaticano II a Juan Pablo II*, Madrid: Palabra 1996, pp. 95–132 and J. L. Illanes, Prologue to Juan Pablo II, *La redención del corazón*, Madrid: Palabra 1996, pp. 7–23. On the role of phenomenology in the philosophical background of John Paul II see R. Buttiglione, *Il pensiero di Karol Wojtyla*, Milan 1982.

However, in his most recent writings, at least in his expositions on the theology of the body, the philosophical approaches and methodologies that he employs are the hermeneutic ones. It is as if John Paul II has followed the same road, and almost for the same reasons, which has led other contemporary philosophers from phenomenology to hermeneutics. In this sense, the philosophical journey of Ricoeur can illustrate the way followed by John Paul II, because if Cardinal Wojtyla quotes several times in *The Acting Person* the *Philosophie de la Volonté* of Ricoeur, the works of the French philosopher quoted in the General Audiences on the theology of the body and on Christian chastity are *Finitude et Culpabilité* and *Le Conflit des Interpretations*. Even apart from the fact that John Paul II presents his theology of the body as a commentary on the texts of *Genesis*, he seems to have followed Ricoeur's claim that the analysis of immediate self-consciousness should give way to a hermeneutics of the texts in which subjectivity expresses itself. With the recognition that the method for reaching a complete and true self-knowledge is not psychological introspection but the hermeneutics of the objective expressions in which subjectivity takes shape, Ricoeur's work tends progressively to focus on the analysis of symbolical systems and languages, which have – against the alleged private character of self-consciousness – a public and social nature.

From this point of view, the methodology followed by John Paul II is not fortuitous, because, even if it is under the rubric of "the nuptial meaning of the body" that he wants to explain the way in which we men live or experience our own bodies and our attitude towards our own corporality (a subject which Ricoeur has also approached), he does so by clarifying the symbols contained in a story, and not by invoking an alleged immediate self-consciousness.

In this sense, it is worth keeping in mind that, if in his *The Threshold of Hope* he refers explicitly to Ricoeur's studies on metaphoric and symbolic language, in his General Audiences on chastity he quotes Paul Ricoeur after mentioning the philosophers of 'suspicion' (Marx, Nietzsche and Freud). And the text of Ricoeur quoted by John Paul II at the bottom of the page is precisely the one in which Ricoeur explains that, while not doubting the existence of the external world but on the evidence of self-consciousness itself, Marx, Nietzsche and Freud break with one of the most basic postulates of phenomenology: consciousness is not the omnipotent source of meaning. Since that break, Ricoeur concludes, understanding is a hermeneutic task. After the philosophies of suspicion, to look for meaning is not to spell out the meaning we are conscious of but to decipher the objective expressions of consciousness.[3]

Furthermore, the philosophical equipment of John Paul II is always put at the service of a theological reflection which – to some extent – has a hermeneutic

---

[3] See P. Ricoeur, *Le conflit des interprétations*, Paris: Ed. du Seuil 1969, pp. 149–50. [P. Ricoeur, *The Conflict of Interpretations. Essays in Hermeneutics*, edited by Don Ihde. Evanston: Northwestern University Press 1974, pp. 148–50.] Quoted in General Audience, 29.10.1980, n. 1, note 2. I am following the English translation published by The Daughters of St Paul, Boston, 1981.

structure, because, in his reflection on the mystery of man, he always alludes to another two mysteries: the mystery of creation and the mystery of redemption. Christian anthropology exhibits a hermeneutic structure insofar as it is illuminated from two sources which are two divine initiatives: creation and redemption. Creation shows us that man is an image of God whereas redemption shows us that only Christ "fully reveals man to man himself and makes his supreme calling clear."[4] In consequence, as Lorda has summed it up, "the Christian definition of man has a starting point and an arrival point. It starts from the fact that man is an image of God and it reaches its highest point in the new man, Jesus Christ. Between both poles, creation and redemption, lies the mystery of sin with the whole of its anthropological meaning."[5]

Thus, in his theology of the body, John Paul II makes an effort to illuminate hermeneutically the experience that man possessed of his body during the original state of justice starting from the experience that we have of our body after the Fall and, at the same time, he clarifies our historical experience of the body contrasting it with the original one. The approach is a hermeneutic one because, different as the state of justice and the state of sin may be, Christ's reference to the beginning in his answer to the Pharisees indirectly establishes a link between both states.[6] The state of sin can only be understood by beginning with an idea of our original state, and vice versa. Besides, theological reflection on the body has to have as one of its starting points the experience that man has of himself and of his own corporality. For, according to John Paul II, "our human experience is, in this case, to some extent, a legitimate means for the theological interpretation, and is, in a certain sense, an indispensable point of reference, which we must keep in mind in the interpretation of the 'beginning'."[7] In consequence, what John Paul II usually calls "the truth of man" alludes to the hermeneutic circle which exists between the design of the creator, the fall and the redemption. But, since in order to clarify this hermeneutic circle John Paul II uses both the network of symbols contained in the *Genesis* narratives and human experience, his thought seems to engage in a complex hermeneutics which cannot be reduced to unity.[8]

---

[4] Second Vatican Council, *Gaudium et Spes*, n. 22.

[5] J. L. Lorda, *Antropología*, p. 144.

[6] See General Audience, 12.12.1979, n. 4.

[7] General Audience, 26.9.1979, n. 4.

[8] Even if John Paul II has underlined the importance of classical metaphysics in his thought, he seems to be very conscious of the impossibility of reducing the human sciences or the phenomenological and hermeneutic approaches to the metaphysical one. For this reason, he clearly employs a plurality of different points of view which cannot be reduced to a unity. Insofar as classical metaphysics is in his writings a point of view – and not the only one – all his thought exhibits a hermeneutic structure or a pluralistic one: there are several possible true descriptions of the same reality. In *The Threshold of Hope* he applies this pluralism – which does not imply any kind of relativism, as Putnam has shown – to the realm of the Church. When answering a question on the division among Christians, he asserts: "It is necessary for humanity to achieve unity through plurality, to learn to come together in the one Church, even while presenting a plurality of ways of thinking and acting, of cultures and civilizations. Wouldn't such a way of looking at things be, in a certain sense, more consonant with the wisdom of God, with His goodness and providence?" (John Paul II, *Crossing the Threshold of Hope*, London: Jonathan Cape 1994, p. 153).

It seems to be the case that the study of human corporality can be brought into focus from two different perspectives, each one allowing for two different approaches.[9] From a third-person perspective, the human body can be studied, firstly, by the biological and medical sciences as an object of external observation. On this approach, the human body appears to us as a physical reality, as a thing in the world, which presents certain precise characteristics. Roughly: it is a living organism. In consequence, what appears in this approach is the body of somebody else or, even, one's own body as if it were the body of somebody else, because the way of finding out whether I have cholesterol is essentially the same as the way one finds out whether any other person has cholesterol.

Secondly, but still from a third-person viewpoint, the human body can be analyzed ontologically. In this kind of analysis, the aim is to find out what kind of being is a living being, or what kind of being is a human being. In this approach, the question about what kind of being is a living being is simply made more specific in the questions: what is a plant, an animal or a human being? In this metaphysical approach, the one typical of Aristotle or Aquinas, the problem of the body is replaced by the question about the nature of living beings. Precisely because a human being is a living human body, the study of the body is directly the study of its act, that is to say, the study of the soul, because the soul is the act of the living body, that is, the 'being alive' of the living body. It is not fortuitous that Aquinas maintains that a corpse is a body only metaphorically.[10] In a nutshell, then: just because an animal or a human being is a living body, the problem of the body disappears: there are no human bodies, there are human beings.

The origin of our modern notion of the body is, indeed, to be found not in a third-person perspective, but in a first-person perspective, in the philosophical reflection which has as its starting point the analysis of self-consciousness in the relevant sense. For, as Professor Anscombe has shown, the self-consciousness implied by the relevant use of the first person pronoun "I" – the one in which it is asymmetrical with the pronouns "he" or "she" – cannot be reduced to a simple knowledge of the thing or the human being which I am. Neither can this self-consciousness be understood in terms of an inner observation.[11] From this first-person perspective, the aim is to analyze the way in which one's own body appears to one's own self-consciousness. This is the reason why, just because a human being is not identified with a living human body, but with an ego, which is understood as the subject of consciousness, what becomes the focus of attention is the very concept "human body". This does not happen in the metaphysical approach. For, in the first-person perspective, what is distinguished from the living human body is precisely the self, the alleged subject of consciousness.

---

[9] The existence of four different perspectives in the study of the human body is spelt out in J. Choza, *Manual de antropología filosófica*, Madrid: Rialp 1988, pp. 161–85. See also J. V. Arregui and J. Choza, *Filosofía del hombre*, Madrid: Rialp 1991, pp. 127–44.

[10] See Thomas Aquinas, *In II De Anima*, lect. 2, n. 239.

[11] See G. E. M. Anscombe, 'The First Person', in G. E. M. Anscombe, *Collected Philosophical Papers, Volume II: Metaphysics and the Philosophy of Mind*, Oxford: Blackwell 1981, pp. 21–36.

It is well known that, when identifying the *ego* with the *res cogitans*, Descartes pushes the body outside the realm of subjectivity and places it in the sphere of the *res extensa*. This Cartesian move reduces the body to something to be studied by the sciences of anatomy or physiology. However, from within the first-person viewpoint, and accepting the analysis of self-consciousness as the starting point of philosophical reflection, some French philosophers, especially after the work of Gabriel Marcel, began to consider more carefully the way in which one's own body is given to one's self-consciousness. To some extent, the remarks of John Paul II on the nuptial meaning of the body should be placed within this current of thought, for he emphasises that human subjectivity also includes the meaning of the body,[12] pointing out that the linguistic expression "nuptial meaning of the body" should not be understood only in conceptual or theoretical terms. The meaning of the body determines our attitude towards it: it is the way of living one's own body.[13] This is the reason why the phrase "the nuptial meaning of the body" includes the whole affective experience of our body in its masculinity and femininity.

The philosophical discussion of the experience of one's own body, as developed after Marcel by authors like Merleau-Ponty and Ricoeur, has included a strong criticism – even from within the philosophy of consciousness – of hard Cartesian dualism, a criticism which has pointed to the corporeal character of human self-consciousness. Against Descartes, the analysis of the phenomena of self-consciousness shows unambiguously its corporeal nature. Human self-consciousness is not a self-consciousness attached to a body, rather like the light of a lighthouse, but is an intellectual light belonging to a physical structure. It is an incarnated self-consciousness. The body is one of the inescapable dimensions of subjectivity. The whole of our subjectivity turns out to be incarnated. The body belongs to subjectivity, and not to the *res extensa*. Thus, against hard Cartesian dualism, this new phenomenological approach opens up what, from a Thomist point of view, could be called "soft dualism":[14] the body expresses the person; it is the vehicle of the person in the world. The frequency with which the Pope uses sentences like "the body expresses the person", "the body is the expression of the spirit" or "the body constitutes the sign of the presence of the person in the world" seems to place his entire theology of the body within this approach.

Critical of hard dualism as the new phenomenological approach can be, it seems to remain dualist in as much as the claims according to which the body expresses the person or is the vehicle of subjectivity in the world seem to imply the existence of a person, an ego, or a subject of consciousness, which is different from the body. The person (or the ego) seems to be an ontological reality different from the human body, which is characterized as its expression in the world. Perhaps, it is worth remarking, in face of some facile interpretations of the

---

[12] General Audience, 31.10.1979, n. 3.
[13] General Audience, 25.6.1980, n. 5.
[14] I have tried to justify the label "soft dualism" in my book *El horror de morir: El valor de la muerte en la vida humana*, Barcelona: Tibidabo 1992, pp. 319–405.

relationship between phenomenology and classical metaphysics, that, for Aquinas, only the living human body is a human person whereas self-consciousness or the disembodied soul are not.[15]

Finally, there is a fourth approach which may also be located within a first-person perspective. I am referring to studies of the different images and archetypes of our own corporality that we human beings have constructed in the course of history and across different cultures. Not only do we experience our own bodies: we express the experience objectively in different ways, in works of art, for example. So, it is possible to study the historical variations on the way in which human beings have experienced their bodies by considering the different objective expressions of these experiences. This analysis makes up the starting point for a history of the body.

Even if the four perspectives on the body, the scientific, the ontological, the phe-nomenological and the cultural ones, are legitimate as well as necessary in order to understand what a human body is, they cannot be reduced one to another. Since they cannot be held together within a single viewpoint, our understanding of human corporality is essentially pluralistic: there are different true descriptions of the human body. Anatomy does not allow us to guess the lived experience that men have of their own bodies, nor does metaphysics make it possible for us to deduce the images and archetypes that men have constructed of the human body.

Even if reflection on the human body should attend to all four viewpoints, preoccupation with one of them frequently leads people to forget the others. As a consequence of a scientistic and objectivistic bias, it is common for people to think that the scientific perspective monopolizes the truth about the human body. The lived experience of the body becomes merely "subjective" and without any cognitive interest. What Putnam has called "scientific realism" (the belief that the positive sciences can offer 'The True Description of Things') has led many people to think that the body is actually only what anatomy or physiology explain. Against this view, John Paul II has stressed that the biomedical sciences deal with man only under a precise and unique aspect and, therefore, offer a partial view.[16] And he has also stressed the danger implicit in such a one-sided consideration of the body; there is not only the risk of manipulating others, but also the danger of increasing the subjective distance between subjectivity itself and corporality. Inso-far as someone believes that his or her body is simply what anatomy or physiology explain, the lived distance between his or her subjectivity and his or her body increases. According to John Paul II, if the human body is deprived of the meaning and dignity which derives from the fact that it is the body of a person, if the human

[15] There are many texts in which Aquinas maintains that the human person is the living human body or, as it is frequently said, that the human person is the compositum of body and soul. In consequence, for him, the disembodied soul is not a human person. (See, for example, *De Potentia*, q. 9, a. 2 ad 14; *Summa Theologiae* I, q. 29, a. 1 ad 5). Neither can the I be identified with the soul (See *In I ad Cor.* XV, lect. 2, n. 924). On this point see P. T. Geach, *God and the Soul*, London: Routledge and Kegan Paul 1969, pp. 22, 40, and C. F. J. Martin, 'Tomás de Aquino y la identidad personal', 26/2 (1993) *Anuario Filosófico* pp. 249–59.
[16] See General Audience, 8.4.1981.

body becomes an object of manipulation, men no longer identify themselves with their own bodies.[17]

The scientific approach to the study of the human body cannot, however, be the only one, since it presupposes what it studies: the corporality of the scientist. It is only to a subject who is in origin corporeal that the living human body can appear as a physical reality, as an object. A body can appear as a visible thing only because we have eyes, and can be reduced to something to manipulate just because we have hands. Now the point about our own corporeality is that the way in which we experience something when touching it is not the same as the way in which we experience the finger with which we do the touching. And the difference cannot be explained by postulating an inner observation of one's own body.

## 2. The nuptial meaning of the body

It is well known that John Paul II developed the basic concepts of his theology of the body in the Wednesday General Audiences beginning in September 1979 as a preparation for the Synod on the Mission of the Christian Family. To explain the evangelical doctrine on the indissolubility of marriage, he recalls its deepest roots, the fundamental truths about man and, especially, the anthropological meaning of corporality and sexuality. Following Christ's words when answering the Pharisees, he looks for light on the deepest anthropological truths in both of the narratives of the creation of man in the book of *Genesis*. For, even after the Fall, a sense of our original state is still present in the depths of the human heart and should shape our moral orientation, our way of living. The original state, the creative design of God, contains the deepest truth about man.[18]

To be precise: the anthropological truth revealed by the book of *Genesis* refers to the meaning of the human body in the structure of the personal subject. Thus, what is at issue is the presentation of sexuality "as a value and task of the whole created person, created male and female in the image of God".[19] For, in referring to the beginning, Christ directs man to go back in some sense to the threshold of his theological history. He directs man to place himself at the point between original innocence and beatitude, on the one hand, and the legacy of original sin, on the other; which implies that the Redemption of the body consists in the recovery of that original dignity of the body which fulfils its true meaning, both with regard to the personal subject and with regard to interpersonal relationships.[20] That which in the original state was a gift is, after the fall and the redemption, a task.

[17] See General Audience, 8.4.1981, n. 3.
[18] See General Audience, 2.4.1980, n. 1. An excellent exposition of John Paul II on sexuality can be found in J. I. Bañares, 'Masculinidad y feminidad en el pensamiento de K. Wojtyla', 16 (1987) *Persona y derecho* 85–153.
[19] John Paul II, *Familiaris Consortio*, n. 32.
[20] See General Audience 2.4.1979, n. 4.

The theology of the body – as a specific part of theological anthropology – is thus established on the basis of God's revelation.[21] John Paul II is in this way applying to the doctrine on sexuality and marriage the programmatic principle established by the influential text of *Gaudium et Spes:* "The truth is that only in the mystery of the incarnate Word does the mystery of man take on light [...] Christ [...] fully reveals man to man himself and makes his supreme calling clear". The Church, depository of revelation, becomes aware that it is also an expert in humanity and, consequently, it achieves a renewed consciousness of the necessity of giving to the world – Christian or not – its theological wisdom. Because, according to *Redemptor Hominis,* if redemption presents a divine dimension – which is the revelation of the intimacy of a God who is merciful love – it exhibits also a humane dimension – which is the revelation of man to man in the figure of Christ. Human amazement at this new creation which redemption involves makes clear to man his infinite dignity, his value and his vocation to love. In other words: the figure of Christ proves to man "the surpassing worth of his own dignity" and shows him "the meaning of his existence". What the loving redemption brought about by Jesus Christ manifests to man is exactly that he "cannot live without love" and that "he remains a being that is incomprehensible for himself, his life is senseless, if love is not revealed to him, ... if he does not experience it and make it his own, if he does not participate intimately in it. This [...] is why Christ the Redeemer 'fully reveals man to himself'."[22]

For John Paul II, the first of the two *Genesis* narratives of the creation of man, the Priestly, is "of a theological nature, [and] conceals within itself a powerful metaphysical content", whereas the second, the Yahwist, focuses more on man's subjectivity, presenting man's creation in its subjective – or even psychological – dimensions, in those phenomenological aspects which illuminate human self-experience. "The second chapter of Genesis", the Pope explains, "constitutes in a certain manner, the most ancient description and record of man's self-knowledge, and together with the third chapter it is the first testimony of human conscience."[23] Notwithstanding their distinct character, the two narratives – the one with its metaphysical revelation of what man is in himself, the other with its phenomenological manifestation (the phenomenological *aletheia*) of what he is to himself – do not oppose each other, because the subjectivity described in the second one perfectly corresponds to the objective reality of man, as it is ontologically described in the first one.[24]

The Priestly narrative of the creation of man exhibits a theological character and gives a definition of man "on the basis of his relationships with God ('in the image of God he created him'), which at the same time contains the affirmation

---

[21] See General Audience, 19.9.1979, n. 4.

[22] See John Paul II, *Redemptor Hominis,* nn. 10 and 11, where the literal quotations can be found. See also J. L. Illanes, 'Antropocentrismo y teocentrismo', in *Iglesia en la historia. Estudios sobre el pensamiento de Juan Pablo II,* Valencia: Edicep 1997, pp. 97–120.

[23] General Audience, 19.9.1979, n. 1.

[24] See General Audience, 19.9.1979, n. 1.

of the absolute impossibility of reducing man to the 'world'".[25] Man is thus defined directly in terms of his ability to have a personal relationship with God. As John Paul II himself will explain on a later occasion, *"that same man in his own humanity* receives as a gift a special 'image and likeness' to God. This means not only rationality and freedom as constitutive properties of human nature, but also, from the very beginning, the capacity of having a *personal relationship* with God as 'I' and 'you', and therefore the capacity of having a covenant, which will take place in God's salvific communication with man."[26] Thus, the Pope, following the most characteristic personalist approaches of the philosophy of dialogue, seems to define man in relational terms: man is the being who is *capax Dei,* the being who can establish a dialogue with God, who can have a personal meeting with Him. Not only the relation to his Creator belongs to the very essence of man: he is precisely defined by his capacity for having a personal relationship, as an "I" and "you", with God.[27]

In his commentary on the Yahwist narrative of the creation of man, John Paul II begins by clarifying the significance of the original solitude of man, which should be understood not as the loneliness of Adam without Eve but as the original situation of every human being who has realized his own superiority to the world, which is manifested in his ability to give names to all the animals in the world. To become aware of being conscious, to realize that one is a being capable of intellectual knowledge, brings with it the realisation of one's superiority to the world and, so, the sense that one lacks a companion in the world. Hence it is just because he is an image of God that man is alone in face of the world.[28]

When he reaches this point, John Paul II remarks on the positive function of the human body in establishing human self-consciousness and the correlative awareness of man's solitude, because the experience of his own body, which in principle places man in the world, does not lead man to identify himself with the world; rather, it brings him to realize his own dignity. The first reason leading man to distance himself from other creatures in the world is his experience of his own body. Consequently, to John Paul II's mind, the original solitude of man is not only the product of a theoretical reflection, it is also a consequence of a specifically human activity, which is made possible by the human body: work. "The premise of man's distinguishing himself in this way is precisely the fact that only he is capable of 'tilling the earth' and 'subduing it'."[29]

The first way in which man inserts himself in the world is not an exclusively intellectual one; human self-consciousness is not founded in the experience of being an Impartial Spectator of the world, but it originally involves a praxis, the specific human activity of work. For, as the Pope explains in *Sollicitudo Rei Socialis,*

---

[25] General Audience, 12.9.1979, n. 4.
[26] John Paul II, *Dominum et Vivificantem,* n. 34. See also General Audience, 23.4.1986.
[27] John Paul II explains more carefully his position on this point in General Audience, 23.4.1986.
[28] See General Audience, 24.10.1979, n. 2.
[29] General Audience, 31.10.1979, n. 1.

"the fact is that man was not created, so to speak, immobile and static".[30] Since the activity of naming is intimately connected with dominion over the earth, the basic character of work seems to belong to the definition of man as established by the Yahwist narrative.[31] The praxis of work contains the meaning of the human body in relation to the world: the task of having dominion over the earth. "Man is a subject not only because of his self-awareness and self-determination, but also on the basis of his own body. The structure of this body is such as to permit him to be the author of a truly human activity. In this activity the body expresses the person."[32]

Only after having explained the meaning of the body in relation to the world, does John Paul II approach the relation between man and woman. For him, "corporality and sexuality are not completely identified. Although the human body, in its normal constitution, bears within it the signs of sex and is, by its nature, male or female, the fact, however, that man is a 'body' belongs to the structure of the personal subject more deeply than the fact that he is in his somatic constitution also male or female."[33] This conceptual priority of corporality over sexuality provides grounds for the equality of both sexes. Being male and being female appear as two different forms of the unique bodily being of the human being. If the experience of his or her own body leads the human being to distance himself or herself from the world, it is this very original solitude which sets the human being on the road to a real companionship, recognition of difference from the world being conducive to open personal relationships. The only relationship which is adequate to the person is that of interpersonal communion, which can only be established as an encounter on the common ground made possible by the detachment of both man and woman from the world. This detachment from the world is thus the real meeting point between man and woman. It is

---

[30] John Paul II, *Sollicitudo Rei Socialis*, n. 30.

[31] See General Audience, 24.10.1979, n. 4. The Pope himself has summarized his exegesis of the connection between both biblical narratives: just because man is an image of God, his task is to dominate the earth. In *Sollicitudo Rei Socialis* he writes: "The fact is that man was not created, so to speak, immobile and static. The first portrayal of him, as given in the Bible, certainly presents him as a creature and image, defined in his deepest reality by the origin and affinity that constitute him. But all this plants within the human being, man and woman, the seed and the requirement of a special task to be accomplished by each individually and by them as a couple. The task is 'to have dominion' over the other created beings, 'to cultivate the garden'." (n. 30)

[32] General Audience, 31.10.1979, n. 2. In the activity of work, the body expresses the person because, even if labour is a corporeal activity which conveys the presence of man – as a corporeal being – in the world, its real subject is the whole human person. Manual labour is made possible by specifically human intellectual capacities: "Man has to subdue the earth and dominate it, because as the 'image of God' he is a person, that is to say, a subjective being capable of acting in a planned and rational way, capable of deciding about himself, and with a tendency to self-realization. As a person, man is therefore the subject of work." (John Paul II, *Laborem Excercens*, n. 6).

[33] General Audience, 7.11.1979, n. 1.

precisely this common detachment, and, correlatively, the common original solitude, that opens up the possibility of being and existing in a particular kind of reciprocity.[34]

Interpersonal communion converts man and woman into an "image of God" in a new sense when compared to the sense identified in the Priestly narrative, since communion between human persons reflects the communion between the divine persons. Masculinity and femininity express, besides the dual somatic constitution of the human body, a new recognition of the meaning of one's own body which consists precisely in mutual enrichment. Consciousness of the possibility of mutual enrichment transforms humanity into a communion of persons. As the search for personal identity is always pursued within a communion of persons, marriage presupposes a renewal of the mystery of creation. As John Paul II himself spells it out, "this means reliving, in a sense, the original virginal value of man, which emerges from the mystery of his solitude before God and in the midst of the world. The fact that they become 'one flesh' is a powerful bond established by the Creator, through which they discover their own humanity, both in its original unity, and in the duality of a mysterious mutual attraction."[35]

The original solitude of the human being and the original unity between man and woman make up the context in which it is possible to understand the original nudity of Genesis. For, the change of attitude after the fall, the change from not knowing that they were naked to knowing they were, implies not a change in perception (as if they were blind before) but a radical transformation of the meaning of nudity, which in its turn presupposes a change in the meaning of the body. Now, after the Fall, corporality itself is experienced in a different way.[36] Shame after the Fall manifests, beyond the emergence of sexual modesty, the collapse of the original acceptance of the body as a sign of the person in the world.[37] In other words: after the Fall, the body's function of expressing the person shrinks. Shame at his own nudity discloses the non-identification of the human person with his body, and thereby manifests a specific difficulty about realising the essential personal character of one's own body.[38] That is to say, mediation between personal subjectivity and the world turns out to be opaque.

Hence, the original absence of shame or shyness should not be interpreted as any kind of primitivism. Rather, it implies a perfect understanding of the meaning of one's own corporality, whose loss is precisely manifested in shame at one's naked corporality; because, if at the beginning, even after the creation of woman, man was not ashamed of his nakedness, that could happen only because man recognized and met in the woman – and, therefore, in sexual difference – his own humanity at the same time that he experienced that openness to the world which is made possible by his corporality. The original nudity thus manifested a

---

[34] See General Audience, 14.11.1979, n. 2.
[35] General Audience 14.11.1979, n. 5.
[36] See General Audience, 12.12.1979, n. 5.
[37] See General Audience, 14.5.1980, n. 4.
[38] See General Audience, 28.5.1980, nn. 1 and 2.

special plenitude both in interpersonal relationships and in the relation with God and with the world.[39]

It is precisely at this point in the exposition that John Paul II introduces into his comments on the book of *Genesis*, the hermeneutics of the gift and the concept of "the nuptial meaning of the body". In order to understand how the sexual body is an image of God, it is necessary to consider the original nudity by reference to that self-giving which constitutes the most radical being of persons. For "creation" means above all "gift". When creating man in his image, God – who is substantial self-giving – makes man capable in his turn of self-giving. "In fact the gift reveals, so to speak, a particular characteristic of personal existence, or rather, of the very essence of the person. When God Yahweh says that 'it is not good that man should be alone', He affirms that 'alone' man does not completely realize this essence. He realizes it only by existing *'with someone'* – and even more deeply and completely: by existing *'for someone'*." Since to be a person means to be relationally – to be for another – human beings only fulfil their essence when they exist for someone else. From this perspective, the sexual body becomes a sacrament, a sign of God. As John Paul II himself asserts: "man appears in the visible world as the highest expression of the divine gift, because he bears within him the interior dimension of the gift. And with it he brings into the world his particular likeness to God, with which he transcends and dominates also his 'visibility' in the world, his corporality, his masculinity or femininity, his nakedness."[40] Through his sexual corporality, man becomes a visible sign of the economy of love which has in God himself its source, and which was revealed in the mystery of creation.

From this perspective, in the original state the human body turns out to be a sacrament: that which makes visible the invisible, that which conveys grace, that is, a sign of God himself. In John Paul II's words, "the sacrament, as a visible sign, is constituted with man, as a 'body', by means of his 'visible' masculinity and femininity. The body, in fact, and it alone, is capable of making visible what is invisible: the spiritual and the divine. It was created to transfer into the visible reality of the world the mystery hidden since time immemorial in God, and thus be a sign of it."[41] Through his own sexual corporality man becomes a visible sign of the economy of truth and justice which has its source in God himself and which was revealed in the mystery of creation.[42]

The outcome of the original solitude of man, of his becoming aware of his solitude in face of the world, is his conscious realisation of his donative nature: persons are persons for one another; and the first expression of this being-for of the human person is the sexual body. From this point of view, John Paul II can define the concept of "the nuptial meaning of the body": sexual corporality manifests the fact that to be a person is to be someone whose self-fulfilment consists in self-giving. The phrase "the nuptial meaning of the body" means, therefore, that

[39] See General Audience, 19.12.1979, nn. 2–4.
[40] General Audience, 20.2.1980, n. 3.
[41] General Audience, 20.2.1980, n. 7.
[42] See General Audience, 20.2.1980, n. 8.

"the body, which expresses femininity [for masculinity, and vice versa, masculinity for femininity], manifests the reciprocity and communion of persons. It expresses it by means of the gift as the fundamental characteristic of personal existence. This is the body: a witness to creation as a fundamental gift, and so a witness to Love as the source from which this same giving springs. Masculinity-femininity – namely, sex – is the original sign of a creative dimension and of an awareness on the part of man, male-female, of a gift lived so to speak in an original way. Such is the meaning with which sex enters the theology of the body."[43]

Thus, the body, precisely because it is the body of a person, because it is not a thing among other things, but the vehicle of our being in the world, has a nuptial character in as much as it can express the love with which man becomes a gift, verifying the profound meaning of his being and existence. In virtue of its nuptial character, the body is the expression of the spirit,[44] for through the nuptial meaning of the body the physical is transcended in opening man to the affirmation of the other as such. For if, on the one hand, the nuptial meaning of the body is shown in a particular aptitude for expressing the love in which man becomes a gift, on the other, this love is directed towards the other person, and therefore the object of this love is the person in his or her reality, that is to say, as he or she has been loved by God.[45]

Obviously, the Fall, and the concupiscence which resulted from it, disturb in different ways the nuptial meaning of the body. But "in the whole perspective of his own 'history', man will not fail to confer a nuptial meaning on his own body. Even if this meaning undergoes and will undergo many distortions, it always remains the deepest level, which demands to be revealed in all its simplicity and purity, and to be shown in its whole truth, as a sign of the 'image of God'."[46] The difference between the original state of justice and the historical one of sin is that what before was lived tranquilly and unproblematically has now become a difficult task. After the Fall, concupiscence does not destroy the nuptial meaning of the body, but threatens it. Sexuality becomes autonomous in some sense, constrains the self and limits both the expression of the spirit and the experience of mutual self-giving.

## 3. The nuptial meaning of the body and sexual ethics

The redemption of the body carries with it the task of gaining control over the concupiscence of the flesh in such a way that the original nuptial meaning of the body is restored. The theology of the body expounded by John Paul II is pedagogical in intent. For, John Paul II explicitly states that the theology of the body lays the foundations for the most appropriate method in the pedagogy of

---

[43] General Audience, 9.1.1980.
[44] See General Audience, 23.7.1980, n. 1.
[45] See General Audience, 16.1.1980, n. 4.
[46] General Audience, 16.1.1980, n. 1.

the body, that is to say, in the education or self education of man.[47] Furthermore, he has maintained on several occasions that the complete truth about man constitutes the normative basis which determines whether actions, types of behaviour, social customs and states of affairs are good or wrong.[48]

Now, the question is: do these claims assume that Christian sexual ethics is founded on an anthropology or theology of the body? In some sense, the answer is: obviously, yes. For one of John Paul II's projects has been to illuminate the deepest truths about man which make the Christian doctrine of marriage intelligible. He has been making a huge effort to identify those features of human sexuality which of themselves require that sexual union should take place only within marriage. Those features are, on the one hand, the specific way in which sexual corporality expresses the person, and, on the other, the specific way in which sexual union expresses interpersonal communion. A well known text of his Apostolic Exhortation *Familiaris Consortio* perfectly sums up his thought: "sexuality, by means of which man and woman give themselves to one another through the acts which are proper and exclusive to spouses, is by no means something purely biological, but concerns the innermost being of the human person as such. It is realized in a truly human way only if it is an integral part of the love by which a man and a woman commit themselves totally to one another until death. The total physical self-giving would be a lie if it were not the sign and fruit of a total personal self-giving, in which the whole person, including the temporal dimension, is present: If the person were to withhold something or reserve the possibility of deciding otherwise in the future, by this very fact he or she would not be giving totally."[49]

But, it would be a mistake to think that John Paul II has laid the foundations of sexual ethics in the description of the anthropological meaning of sexuality in the sense demanded by typical foundationalist doctrines. Because foundationalism seems to require that, in order to found ethics in philosophical anthropology, value judgements in factual judgements, we should be able to give a description of the facts which, in its turn, does not imply any judgements of value. But, as Putnam has proved, this pure description of facts is impossible. There is not a sharp distinction between judgements of value and statements of facts, "because factual statements themselves, and the practices of scientific inquiry upon which we rely to decide what is and what is not fact, presuppose values."[50] What we call the "empirical world" depends upon our criteria of rationality, which manifest what we understand by an optimal rationality.

My point is that both the usual criticism of moral naturalism, the idea that the *ought* cannot be founded in the *is*, because facts are not moral criteria, and the attempt to deduce morals from a pure descriptive anthropology or metaphysics share the same mistake: the mirage of the existence of something like "a pure

[47] See General Audience, 8.4.1981, n. 3.
[48] See, for example, General Audience, 29.4.1981, n. 3.
[49] John Paul II, *Familiaris Consortio*, n. 11.
[50] H. Putnam, *Reason, Truth and History*, Cambridge: Cambridge University Press 1981, p. 128.

description of facts". The question, therefore, is not whether or not values can be founded on facts; there is no level of facts apart from some order of values. This is the reason why, when defending nature as a moral criterion, the acute remark of Spaemann should be kept in mind: "the interpretation of instinct does not happen by itself; it is not nature, but what we call 'reason'. Only through reason is nature manifested to us as nature."[51]

John Paul II's approach, his effort to show the anthropological roots of sexual ethics, cannot be understood either as a naturalism or as a foundationalism. Obviously, he criticizes strongly and accurately the Humpty-Dumpty idea according to which our mind projects unilaterally on things the meanings that it privately wants. For corporeal gestures have meanings of their own. But he does not think it possible to offer a pure anthropological description free from any moral evaluation. This is the reason why I began my paper by stressing the hermeneutic dimension of his thought. For, the idea that he is a phenomenologist trying to arrive at classical metaphysics, could lead, if not correctly understood, to a foundationalist interpretation of his thought. By contrast, his theology of the body exhibits a clear hermeneutic character. His aim is to illuminate some mysteries by starting from others, to understand human experience – as it has been given objective expression in texts – starting from the divine creative design, and to illuminate the divine creative design from the textual witness to human experience. In this hermeneutic engagement there is no room for foundationalism. John Paul II never pretends that he is giving an anthropological, morally neutral, description of the meaning of sexuality. Perhaps that is the reason why he so much emphasises the fact that God saw that what He created was good.

[51] R. Spaemann, *Glück und Wohlwollen*, Stuttgart: Klett-Cotta 1989, p. 244. See also his 'La naturaleza como instancia de apelación', in R. Alvira (ed.), *El hombre: inmanencia y trascendencia*, vol. 1, Pamplona: Servicio de Publicaciones de la Universidad de Navarra 1991, pp. 49–67.

# 9

# Formation in chastity: the need and the requirements

BARTHOLOMEW KIELY SJ

## Present circumstances

"THE TRIVISIALISATION of sexuality is among the principal factors which have led to contempt for new life. Only a true love is able to protect life." (*Evangelium Vitae*, no. 97) Here, very plainly stated, we have the link between the virtue of chastity and bioethics in general. The Encyclical continues, "There can be no avoiding the duty to offer, especially to adolescents and young adults, an authentic education in sexuality and in love, an education which involves training in chastity as a virtue which fosters personal maturity and makes one capable of respecting the 'spousal' meaning of the body".

Such a programme of education faces notable difficulties at present. On August 29, 1997, a story on the front page of *The Times* announced that four ten-year old boys had been charged in connection with the rape of a nine-year old girl in a London school. This was just one of many items which appeared, this past summer, in the newspapers of Great Britain and Ireland, dealing with sexual misdeeds on the part of very young people, clergy, persons in public life, and others. The tone of the reports seem to range from mere matter-of-fact recounting to one of outrage. It is rare to encounter any proposal for improving the situation; rather, the very same media tend to exalt sexual gratification (within the limits defined by the conventions of the moment) as an important part of life. These trends seem to represent the tip of a contemporary iceberg.

Chastity has always been more or less problematic. "About sex especially men are born unbalanced; we might almost say they are born mad. They scarcely reach sanity until they reach sanctity"; thus wrote Chesterton in *The Everlasting Man*.[1]

C.S. Lewis, almost 50 years ago, gave expression to common Christian doctrine: "Chastity is the most unpopular of the Christian virtues. There is no getting away from it: the Christian rule is, 'Either marriage, with complete faithfulness to your partner, or else total abstinence'. Now this is so difficult and so contrary to our instincts, that obviously either Christianity is wrong or our sexual instinct, as it now is, has gone wrong. One or the other. Of course, being a Christian, I think it is the instinct which has gone wrong." The citation is from *Mere Christianity*, first

---

[1] G.K. Chesterton, *The Everlasting Man*, Book 1, Chapter 6, at the start.

published in 1952.[2] The confidence of Lewis's assertion may even come as a surprise to the contemporary reader; there is, surely, a deep divergence of views between contemporary Western culture and the Christian tradition. The roots of this divergence lie deep and merit some comment.

A rapid survey of some present circumstances will serve to underline both the difficulty and the importance of formation in chastity. Divorce is easy in many societies. Premarital sex is a worrying problem in many countries, even pre-teens becoming parents. The decision of the Supreme Court of the United States, *Planned Parenthood versus Casey*, 1992, recognised explicitly that abortion is often used as a backup measure when contraception has failed:

> The *Roe's* limitation on state power could not be repudiated without serious inequity to people who, for two decades of economic and social developments, have organized intimate relationships and made choices which define their views of themselves and their places in society, in reliance on the availability of abortion in the event that contraception should fail.[3]

This statement is quite frank and stands as a sort of milestone in the separation of sex from responsibility.

The second Humanist Manifesto (*Humanist Manifesto II*)[4] urged that contraception, divorce, abortion, suicide and euthanasia should all be recognised as basic human rights. Here we have a group of humanists expressing themselves in their own words; and the world they hope for is surely one in which it would be hard to find a place for chastity.

On February 8, 1994, the European Parliament at Strasbourg voted in favour of a resolution that homosexuals be given rights equal to those of heterosexuals, including the right to marry, to adopt children, and to political asylum.

Even the spread of AIDS has led only to a measure of caution, and in general (so far as I can gather) to the recommendation of "safe sex" or "safer sex" which is far from safe; given the well-documented fallibility of the condom as a contraceptive, it can hardly be very secure as a protection against the sexual transmission of AIDS, while the only sure protection, apart from total abstinence, would be a monogamous relationship between persons initially free from infections.[5]

Another circumstance, of special interest to Catholics, has been the devaluation of the teaching authority of the Church connected with dissent from *Humanae Vitae*. Such dissent appears to have been the context in which emerged the crisis in moral teaching and thinking to which the Encyclical *Veritatis Splendor* was addressed.[6]

---

[2] C.S. Lewis, *Mere Christianity*, Glasgow: Collins (Fount Paperbacks) 1978, p. 86.
[3] Page III of the "Slip Opinion". See also J.E. Smith, 'The Connection between Contraception and Abortion', 93 (April 1993) *Homiletic and Pastoral Review*, pp. 10–18.
[4] 'Humanist Manifesto II', (1973, September–October) *The Humanist*, pp. 4–9.
[5] A recent review of the literature has been provided by J. Suaudeau, 'Le "sexe sûr" et le préservatif face au défi du SIDA', 47 (1997) *Medicina e Morale*, pp. 689–726.
[6] P. V. Mankowski, 'The Prayer of Lady Macbeth: how the contraceptive mentality has neutered religious life', 19 (1993) *Faith and Reason*, pp. 79–93.

This dissent has been associated especially with the moral theory known as "proportionalism". This theory was never in itself very plausible.[7] The only hierarchy of values which can be used in a proportionalist sense (i.e. for "commensurating" different values) seems to be a subjective rank-ordering of values;[8] one can say, the value A is more important to me than the value B, so that I can act *directly* against the value B for the sake of the value A, given some "proportionate reason", that is, some reason that seems proportionately important within one's (subjective) hierarchy of values. Since it does not seem to be possible, in this context, to distinguish between a temptation and a proportionate reason,[9] the proportionalist approach would seem to lead to the conclusion that one should yield to strong temptations and resist weak ones. Yet, in spite of its inherent weakness, this theory came to enjoy very wide acceptance, with negative effects on much of morality, including sexual morality.

A final circumstance is a widespread ignorance of basic or "catechetical" doctrine. This presumably varies from place to place but can at least sometimes be impressive. William Kilpatrick encountered a class of twenty graduate students who were unable (even in collaboration) to list the ten commandments, and of another college student who did not know the meaning of either "abstinence" or "chastity".[10]

Some insight can be gained into the various trends just sketched when they are seen as expressions of the widespread outlook known technically as "liberal individualism".[11] In this approach, the primary human value is freedom understood as "freedom from", so that each person should have the maximum of freedom that is compatible with a like freedom for others, while what one does with one's liberty is basically a private matter. Morality becomes a matter of dealing with boundary-disputes between individual freedoms. One's private sphere of liberty does not seem to be subject to norms, as long as the freedom of others is respected. Since discipline is inevitable in one's work, the area of private freedom will more likely regard the area of recreation or pleasure-seeking, and sexuality risks being interpreted in terms of that kind of freedom from norms. In any view of life, the central values are usually protected strongly; sexual freedom and also abortion can be defended strenuously and even fiercely as symbols of an individualist interpretation of freedom as something that cannot be sacrificed to any lesser value, perhaps to any other value whatsoever (apart from the freedom of others, understood in the same sense).

---

[7] B. Kiely, 'The Impracticality of Proportionalism', 66 (1985) *Gregorianum*, pp. 655–686.
[8] Cf. G. Grisez, *The Way of the Lord Jesus*, Vol. 1: *Christian moral principles*, Chicago: Franciscan Herald Press 1983, pp. 156–159.
[9] Cf. B. Kiely, 'The Impracticality of Proportionalism', pp. 671–672, 676–683.
[10] W. T. Kilpatrick, *Why Johnny Can't Tell Right From Wrong*, New York: Simon & Schuster 1992, pp. 118–119.
[11] J. Rawls, A *Theory of Justice*, Cambridge, Mass.: Harvard University Press 1971, pp. 60, 447, 552–554; D. Hollenbach, *Claims in Conflict*, New York: Paulist Press 1979, pp. 13–20, 91, 189.

## The pressure to conform

Together with the circumstances just sketched goes the great pressure to conformity exercised by conventions of thought. We all live under pressure from our social environment, to a greater extent than we are usually aware of. Books expressing opposed views may stand peacefully side-by-side on the same shelf, but human opinions are not like that. Rather, one tends to seek the agreement of others; "a basic human need appears to be the need for the validation of one's opinions".[12] There is (for example) a rule, nowhere written but widely in force, that one must wear two shoes of the same colour. If some bold spirit were to go around wearing one white shoe and one red, he would come under pressure to conform wherever he went.

Most people do not get beyond conventional moral thinking in the developmental scheme defined by Lawrence Kohlberg,[13] and adolescents never seem to do so. Conventional moral thinking, as Kohlberg noted, "has a vast amount of 'stretch' to absorb arbitrary but socially authoritative content".[14] For the adolescent, conventions or traditions practically are moral principles, so that a choice about principles is in effect a choice among competing traditions or conventions; a choice to be made amid the emotional lability and desire for approval that are usually marked in adolescence. The fact that Kohlberg studied relatively simple problems, involving reasoning about justice, strengthens this argument rather than weakening it; limitations on moral reasoning may be expected to emerge more strongly in dealing with more complex problems.

As to the content of such conventional thinking, the words of C. S. Lewis are still valid: "Poster after poster, film after film, novel after novel, associate the idea of sexual indulgence with the ideas of health, normality, youth, frankness and good humour".[15] Since Lewis wrote, the influence of television has come to be powerful in our lives, and the sheer polish and professionalism of the images it presents lend plausibility to the views which, implicitly or explicitly, accompany those images.

The current situation has been described in strong terms in a recent document of John Paul II.

> *The first challenge* [to consecrated chastity] is that of a *hedonistic* culture which separates sexuality from all objective moral norms, often treating it as a mere diversion and a consumer good, and, with the complicity of the means of social communication, justifying a kind of idolatry of the sexual instinct.[16]

Such pressures find an ally in the weakness that exists in human nature and so in each of us, perhaps especially in the sexual area. We recognise that all the parts (so

---

[12] P. F. Secord and C. W. Backman, *Social Psychology*, New York: McGraw-Hill 1974 (second edition), p. 310.

[13] L. Kohlberg, *Essays on Moral Development: I, The philosophy of moral development* (1981); *II, The psychology of moral development* (1984), San Francisco: Harper & Row.

[14] L. Kohlberg, *Essays on Moral Development: I, The philosophy of moral development*, p. 127.

[15] C. S. Lewis, *Mere Christianity*, p. 90.

[16] John Paul II, Post-Synodal Apostolic Exhortation *Vita Consecrata* (1996), n. 88.

to speak) of human sexuality come from the Creator and are good: the body, sexual differentiation, attraction, falling in love, marriage, pleasure, babies. St Thomas wrote that without original sin, sexual pleasure would have been more intense, because nature would have been healthier and the body more sensitive.[17] At the same time, our tradition and our experience, as well as contemporary psycho-analysis,[18] all reveal a tendency to fragment the unity of human sexuality and so make it egoistic, even though all its parts are in themselves good.

### The need for formation in chastity

The need is evident and especially now, as social trends tend to separate and so deform both the unitive and the procreative meanings of sexuality.[19] If sexual acts can, by contraception or by abortion, be dissociated from procreation, then sex becomes little more than a plaything, and one can no longer see clearly why it should be linked to the permanent commitment of marriage. Likewise, if babies can be produced without sexual union, by in-vitro fertilization or perhaps even by cloning, then the procreative meaning of sexuality is also debased; a child is no longer a gift, but something that can be manufactured according to one's own desires. So we come to a situation in which the trivialization of sexuality leads to contempt for new life; see again the citation from *Evangelium Vitae* with which this article began.

Such tendencies reduce both sexual union and procreation to the level of consumer goods, to the level of the *bonum utile* or *delectabile*, to which the logic of utilitarianism can be quite naturally applied. Utilitarianism is quite at home within the context of liberal individualism. It is clear that utilitarianism, taken here as a natural expression of liberal individualism,[20] cannot lead to an adequate account of love, but only to a "harmonization of egoisms".[21] The ideal of making a gift of oneself does not find a place here.

### Requirements for such formation: general

Formation in chastity has a better chance of succeeding, especially in today's world, if it begins from the context of faith. This starting-point is used several

---

[17] St Thomas Aquinas, *Summa Theologiae*, I, q. 98, art. 2, ad 3.

[18] For example, O. Kernberg, 'Boundaries and Structures in Love Relations', 25 (1977) *Journal of the American Psychoanalytic Association*, pp. 81–114.

[19] Cf. *Humanae Vitae*, no. 12.

[20] A Kantian approach to ethics is also compatible with liberal individualism; cf. Rawls, *A Theory of Justice*. However, Kohlberg found that Kantian reasoning (stage 6 in his scheme) does not seem to occur naturally, and that utilitarian reasoning (stage 5) is usually the end-point of natural development in reasoning about problems of particular justice.

[21] K. Wojtyla, *Love and Responsibility*, New York: Farrar, Strauss, Giroux 1981, pp. 37–39.

times in *Educational Guidance in Human Love*[22] (nos. 1, 21, 29, 43); and the later document, *The Truth and Meaning of Human Sexuality*,[23] also moves constantly on a theological basis.

Here I do not intend any devaluation of natural law. Natural law (understood, roughly, as what we can know as non-arbitrary, in the light of reason) is indispensable as a defence against various forms of positivism (individual, social or even theological) and the impositions which go with positivism.[24]

Chastity will certainly stand to reason as a virtue. One might build up quite a strong argument for chastity on the basis of reason alone, taking friendship as the starting-point, then trust as a condition of friendship, and finally chastity as a requirement of trust between men and women or (more generally) between persons.[25] But as faith provides a fuller understanding of friendship, it also provides a fuller understanding of chastity.

There are at least two ways (not completely distinct) in which revelation can complete our understanding of natural law. One is in answering the question, "who are the persons involved in a given action?" Take murder, which even apart from faith is clearly a great evil. When we see that both the murderer and the victim have been made in the image and likeness of God, and that what one does to the least of Christ's brethren one does to Christ Himself, then the evil becomes more clear. The second way is in answering the question, "of what story (or drama) is this action a part?" In other words, what are the *possibilities* given in human life? Does everything finish with death, or does our present life lead into eternity? After all, the possibilities which life offers are the first moral "facts". We make our choices among the possibilities that are given.

Reasons of this nature indicate that chastity has a stronger basis in faith than in pure reason. It seems quite difficult to teach or learn chastity on the basis of reason alone; it would require in the learner an unusual degree of consistency and independence, and (presumably) the support of stable social and/or religious traditions. Otherwise chastity (as Augustine found) can be very difficult.

If pure reason, in today's world, does not seem a sufficiently strong basis for the teaching or learning of chastity, still less will it be possible to communicate the value of chastity on the basis of some bland humanism which proclaims that life is nice and love is nice and chastity is nice (at least in moderation) and they all go nicely together.

---

[22] From the Congregation for Catholic Education, 1983.

[23] From the Pontifical Council for the Family, 1995.

[24] A. MacIntyre, for example, states that "emotivism entails the obliteration of any genuine distinction between manipulative and non-manipulative social relations" (*After Virtue: A study in moral theory*, second edition, Notre Dame, Indiana: University of Notre Dame Press 1984, p. 23).

[25] One may, indeed, find quite strict accounts of the requirements of chastity in codes of professional ethics, concerning for example the relations between psychotherapist and client; see H. I. Kaplan et al., *Synopsis of Psychiatry*, 7th edition, Baltimore: Williams & Wilkins 1994, pp. 1185–1186. The context is that of legal liability for malpractice, and the chapter-title is 'Forensic Psychiatry'.

Chastity, like other moral virtues, involves the integration of different human goods according to different modes of responsibility, and in keeping with a view of the integral good of the human person. Lonergan's analysis of three kinds of finality[26] is very useful, especially his treatment of "vertical finality", by which goods on one level, while remaining values in themselves, may be integrated so as to lead to a good on a higher level.

Here, however, rather than pursuing an analysis of goods and forms of finality, I wish to examine some of the presuppositions and components of chastity, especially those that are important in the architectonic sense, concerning which the Christian tradition is so often different from the view of the world around us. In other words, I wish to discuss chastity within the context of a Christian anthropology, that is to say, within the context of that view of the human person and his or her integral good which has been repeatedly proposed by the recent Magisterium of the Church.[27]

The same idea, of the person's integral good, can be recognised in the definition of chastity given in the *Catechism of the Catholic Church*, no. 2337:

> Chastity means the successful integration of sexuality within the person and thus the inner unity of man in his bodily and spiritual being. Sexuality, in which man's belonging to the bodily and biological world is expressed, becomes personal and truly human when it is integrated with the relationship of one person to another, in the complete and lifelong gift of a man and a woman.
>
> The virtue of chastity therefore involves the integrity of the person and the totality of the gift ["*et totalitatem doni*" in the *editio typica latina* of the *Catechism* (1997)].

Chastity, as involving "the integrity of the person and the totality of the gift", means much more than sexual restraint or an absence of desire. "Charity is the form of all the virtues. Under its influence, chastity appears as a school of the gift of the person. Self-mastery is ordered to the gift of self" (*Catechism*, 2346). Chastity is necessary in the life of the human person as the animal made in the image and likeness of God, the eternal animal.

Three points of Christian anthropology are particularly relevant to this virtue.

First of all, every life is a vocation (*Populorum Progressio*, 1967, no. 15). A Christian view of life is here radically different from that of liberal individualism.

[26] B.J.F. Lonergan, 'Finality, Love, Marriage', in F.E. Crowe (ed.) *Collection: Papers by Bernard J.F. Lonergan S.J.*, New York: Herder 1967, pp. 16–53.

[27] "The question of the birth of children, like every other question which touches human life, is too large to be resolved by limited criteria, such as are provided by biology, psychology, demography, or sociology. It is the whole man and the whole complex of his responsibilities that must be considered, not only what is natural and limited to this earth, but aso what is supernatural and eternal." (Paul VI, *Humanae Vitae*, no. 7) See also *Gaudium et Spes*, 35, 61; *Populorum Progressio*, 13–21; *Octagesima Adveniens*, 40; *Familiaris Consortio*, 32; *Donum Vitae*, Introduction, 1,2,3; II.7; *Sollicitudo Rei Socialis*, 1, 9, 10, 29–33, 38. Cf. also *Veritatis Splendor*, 83, which speaks of the "integral truth about man".

All Christians are called to holiness (*Lumen Gentium*, 39–42): "All the faithful of Christ, of whatever rank or status, are called to the fullness of Christian life and the perfection of charity (ibid., 40), called to virtue and even heroic virtue." (*The Truth and Meaning of Human Sexuality*, 18)

We find important explanations of the Christian vocation in *Veritatis Splendor*. At least six times this encyclical presents the Christian vocation as the following of Christ (nos. 12, 19, 66, 89, 119). In particular, the Christian life is the following of Christ in *making a gift of oneself*. This idea recurs at least nine times in the text (15, 17, 20, 21, 48, 85, 87, 89, 120) and is one of the key themes of the whole encyclical. Synthetic expressions are found in no. 20, "Jesus asks us to follow him and to imitate him along the path of love, a love which gives itself completely to the brethren out of love for God", and in no. 85, "The Crucified Christ reveals the authentic meaning of freedom; he lives it fully in the total gift of himself and calls his disciples to share in his freedom". In brief, human freedom finds its full expression only in making a gift of oneself: "Perfection demands that maturity in self-giving to which human freedom is called" (no. 17; see also no. 87).

This point is much more than a pious paranesis; it is the basis of the Christian answer to the question, "why be moral at all?" The Christian *can* really make a gift of himself to God and neighbour; the gift will be received and conserved. This is one way of formulating the basic criterion for judging all his actions.

Further, the ontological status of the possibility of making a gift, not of some possession, or function, or instrumental service to others, but of one's very self, can be grasped only in the light of our faith. It does not seem to be a possibility that can be discovered by empirical observation or by introspection. I have not found the idea in any contemporary psychological author, with the exception of some whose inspiration is explicitly Christian.[28] The idea is also missing, or at least largely missing, from contemporary moral philosophy.[29]

The idea of self-giving, however, is not new within the Christian tradition; one may cite Lewis once more:

> For in self-giving, if anywhere, we touch a rhythm not only of all creation but of all being. For the Eternal Word also gives Himself in sacrifice: and that not only on Calvary. For when He was crucified he "did that in the wild weather of His outlying provinces which he had done at home in glory and gladness" [citing George Macdonald]. From the foundation of the world He surrenders begotten Deity back to begetting Deity in obedience.... From the highest to the lowest, self exists to be abdicated, and by that abdication becomes the more truly self, to be thereupon yet the more abdicated, and so on forever. This is not a heavenly law which we can escape by remaining earthly, nor

---

[28] See for example L. M. Rulla, *Anthropology of the Christian Vocation, I: Interdisciplinary Bases*, Rome: Gregorian University Press 1985, especially pp. 276–284.

[29] Cf. A. MacIntyre, *Three Rival Versions of Moral Inquiry*, Notre Dame, Indiana: University of Notre Dame Press 1990, p. 192.

an earthly law which we can escape by being saved. What is outside the system of self-giving is not earth, nor nature, nor "ordinary life", but simply and solely Hell.[30]

The possibility of self-giving in Christian life has its foundations not only in the doctrine of the Blessed Trinity, but also that of the Mystical Body of Christ and the Communion of Saints; we Christians, forming one body and one spirit with Christ, are called to participate[31] in the "whole Christ".[32] "In the 'communion of saints', 'none of us lives to himself, and none of us dies to himself' (Rom 14,7)".[33]

When Christian moral living is seen (as in *Veritatis Splendor*) as the following of Christ in making a gift of oneself to the Father and to one's brothers and sisters, then we are already beyond the horizon of any merely rational morality based on the data of experience as discoverable outside the context of faith; for the approach of the Encyclical clearly implies the existence of a dimension in our lives and actions that is hidden and can be discovered only by the light of faith. Our relationship to God and to our neighbours is much deeper and closer than we can know apart from faith. We are perhaps used to thinking of a hidden dimension to some of our acts, such as prayer or vicarious penance; but this dimension is present in all of our acts. No action, good or bad, no virtue, and no vice, can be a purely private matter. An individualistic ethic in any form can provide only an impoverished basis for moral living; and the same holds for any approach to morality that is based only on the application of reason to data accessible outside the light of faith.

To summarise: all Christians are called to holiness and self-giving, prior to a specification of one's particular vocation as marriage, the priesthood, or whatever.

A second basic point of Christian anthropology, closely related to the virtue of chastity, is the value of the body as participating fully in the dignity of the person (this too has been stressed in *Veritatis Splendor*, 46–50). Any dualism which, explicitly or implicitly, would reduce the body to some kind of sub-human instrument must undermine all of sexual morality, and not just a few particular points. Any such dualism was foreign to the Old Testament and is not discussed there. The problem appears in the Bible when Paul, in 1 Corinthians, addressed the problem of sacred prostitution at Corinth. Paul denies that the relationship of sex to the body is like that of food to the stomach. Rather, "the body is for the Lord and the Lord for the body. And God raised the Lord and will also raise us up by his own power. Do you not know that your bodies are members of Christ ( . . . ) You are not your own; you were bought with a price. So glorify God in your body." (1 Cor 6,12–20).

---

[30] C. S. Lewis, *The Problem of Pain*, Glasgow: Collins (Fount Paperbacks) 1978, Chapter 10. A remarkably similar account of the theology of self-giving has been proposed more recently by H. Urs Von Balthasar, *Theodramatik*, III: *Die Handlung*, Einsiedeln: Johannes 1980, especially pp. 297–305, ('Kreuz und Trinität').
[31] *Catechism of the Catholic Church*, nn. 259, 260.
[32] *Catechism of the Catholic Church*, n. 795.
[33] *Catechism*, n. 953.

The body has a nuptial or spousal meaning,[34] destined to fulfilment in the resurrection of the flesh, and explained by John Paul II in pages of particular value.

When God is seen face to face, love will completely absorb human subjectivity in both body and soul. The blessed will share in the inner life of the Trinity, and at the same time have a new and perfect communion with each other. This will be the definitive fulfilment of the spousal meaning of the body.[35]

The third point of Christian anthropology lies in being freed from a compulsion to seize such fulfilment or satisfaction as one can during this present life. In any view of life whatsoever, it does not seem possible to abandon the value that is seen as supreme; that would mean abandoning one's ultimate hope. Someone who finds the meaning of life in having as many gratifying experiences as possible does not have much chance of living chastely; pleasure will become a "symbol of immortality", an idol offering one some protection against death and insignificance.[36] It is clear that every decision requires renunciation; to choose one thing is to abandon alternatives. It is not easy to make sense of renunciation if this is seen as a demand of impersonal rules;[37] but renunciations which are part of the following of Christ in making a gift of oneself to God and neighbour can be more easily endured.

### Requirements: particular

If these basic elements – a sense of vocation, a respect for the body, and a hope rising beyond immediate gratifications – are present, at least as a healthy embryo which can grow, then one can think of the more particular requirements of formation in chastity. These are abstracted from recent documents of the Magisterium, especially those already cited (*Educational Guidance in Human Love* and *The Truth and Meaning of Human Sexuality*; see notes 22 and 23, above). Here they can only be dealt with in outline; I have concentrated on the more basic issues, because that seems to be where the real battleground lies. All are explicit in those documents except perhaps one, which I take first of all.

This particular requirement is a willingness to learn from the Tradition of the Church, including the attitude of expecting that even if I do not now grasp the meaning of some point, I can presume that it is true and hope to understand it later. This, surely, is part of entering into any difficult discipline. Students of

---

[34] *The Truth and Meaning of Human Sexuality*, no. 10. And see the previous chapter, by Professor Arregui, in this volume.

[35] John Paul II, *Uomo e donna lo creò. Catechesi sull'amore umano*, third edition, Vatican: Città Nuova – Libreria Editrice Vaticana 1992, p. 271 (conference LXVIII, in the third catetechetical cycle). A condensed version of the relevant conferences may be found in December (1981) *The Pope Teaches*, 355–359.

[36] B. Kiely, *Psychology and Moral Theology: lines of convergence*, Rome: Gregorian University Press 1987, pp. 189–200.

[37] See again MacIntyre, *Three Rival Versions of Moral Inquiry*.

physics, chemistry, and so on, have to accept many ideas that are initially obscure. Moral problems are no easier than those of physics or chemistry; yet, amid the widespread dissent in the years since *Humanae Vitae* appeared, a casual rejection of parts of the Tradition has become common and even fashionable.[38]

Correspondingly, the tradition has to be presented confidently and without ambiguity; otherwise one will be sending a "double message" in which the manner of presentation contradicts the content and the hearer understands that the message is not meant to be taken seriously.[39]

Other particular requirements for the teaching and learning of chastity include the following four:

(i) Sexual information that is proportionate to the young person's age and level of knowledge. I expect that nowadays this will rarely be a question of enlightening a totally ignorant youngster, but of correcting and completing information already possessed, and of adding knowledge about the human and Christian meaning of sexuality to merely biological information.

(ii) There needs to be an apprenticeship in prayer and sacramental life; otherwise the idea of life as a vocation will remain merely notional. Together with this should go an awareness of our dependence on the grace of God, something that must be more acutely felt the less we are supported by social or personal routines.

(iii) Catechesis and learning also need to include the themes of sin, repentance, and the Sacrament of Reconciliation. These are certainly difficult topics to teach well, but they cannot be avoided. The Sacrament of Reconciliation can also be a valuable occasion for individual guidance.

(iv) A training in self-mastery is a part of the Christian life in general and of chastity also. And as the *Catechism* (no. 2342) reminds us, "Self-mastery is a long and exacting work. One can never consider it acquired once and for all. It presupposes renewed efforts at all stages of life. The effort required can be more intense in certain periods, such as when the personality is being formed during childhood and adolescence."

This need for self-mastery goes well beyond the control of youthful sensuality. There is an unrelenting asceticism in marriage, in sharing the whole of one's life with a spouse and in the raising of children.

In brief, what is needed is an *integral* communication and appropriation of the Christian message. One cannot skip the bits that one finds difficult or distasteful. John Paul II in *Catechesi Tradendae* (1979) reminds us that "no true catechist can lawfully, on his own initiative, make a selection of what he considers important in the deposit of faith, as opposed to what he considers unimportant, so as to teach the one and reject the other" (no. 30; see also

---

[38] A striking example can be found in C. E. Curran, 'Ten Years Later: reflections on the anniversary of *Humanae Vitae*', (7 July 1978) *Commonweal*, pp. 425–430.

[39] The classic article of A. M. Johnson and S. A. Szurek, 'The Genesis of Antisocial Acting Out in Children and Adults', 21 (1952) *Psychoanalytic Quarterly*, pp. 232–343, is highly instructive.

no. 49).[40] The parts of Christian doctrine depend on each other like the different organs of a living body.

### Causing pain?

There is of course a psychological problem here which cannot be overlooked: the fear that one may have of causing unnecessary suffering, anxiety or scruples, in teaching about sin or about chastity. This difficulty has no complete solution, as far as I can see. In all areas of life, one has to begin learning before one can fully understand. In any psychological account of development, such as that of Kohlberg or Erikson, learning begins with what is concrete and particular, and only later moves on to what is more abstract, general and nuanced. (An Irish child is said to have answered the question, "Why shouldn't you cast your pearls before swine?", "Because the swine might skid on the pearls"). In learning about dealing with one's neighbour, one does not start from the principle of treating the person always as an end and never as a means. One first learns, perhaps, that one must not pull one's little sister's hair – or else! Similarly, in learning chastity one does not begin with the ideal of the gift of self and of sharing in the life of the Blessed Trinity; one starts perhaps with the rule of avoiding pornographic reading or fantasy. Conscience tends to be rigid initially; distinctions come later.[41] A young person becomes able to objectify the notion of an intention as distinct from an action only at the third of the developmental stages defined by Kohlberg, which presupposes the attainment of formal cognitive operations and so can emerge (roughly speaking) only when the child is able to pass from arithmetic to algebra.

Nevertheless, a fear of causing anxiety about sin in general, or in the particular area of chastity, cannot be an excuse for simply avoiding these topics. It would be unrealistic to think that one can leave (so to speak) blank pages in the mind, which will remain blank until they are correctly filled in as an adult. The pages will not simply remain blank; rather, habits of living will form, with a blind spot on the level of conscience, and these will not easily be remedied later on.

[40] In this connection a recent piece of psychological research is of interest. About one hundred persons were asked to write in their own words "a summary of what is important in living as a Christian, as revealed in the Gospels by the words and actions of Jesus". The subjects who were less mature in the living of their own Christian lives (as judged from detailed reports on interviews and psychological tests, analysed with the consent of the subjects) tended to recall selectively the more consoling or agreeable parts of the Gospel's teaching and to forget selectively the more demanding parts. Those who were more mature in their own living were better able to recall both components of the Gospel, although even they showed some tendency to forget the "hard sayings". The statistical patterns were quite clear. The persons (relatively few) who showed signs of psychopathology had difficulty also in recalling the more consoling aspects of the Gospel (B. Dolphin, *The Values of the Gospel: personal maturity and thematic perception*, doctoral thesis [no. 3749], Rome: Gregorian University 1991).
[41] B. Bettelheim, "Moral Education", in J.G. Gustafson et al., *Moral Education: five lectures*, Cambridge, Mass: Harvard University Press 1970, pp. 85–107.

I do not think that there is any totally painless way of learning to live as a Christian, about conversion or sin or chastity, because I do not think that there is any painless way of growing up. One's first encounters with death (of a grandparent, even of a pet), with loneliness, with failure, with the vicissitudes of friendship, with adult responsibilities: all of these involve suffering, and I do not see any way of altogether avoiding that kind of pain. As we grow older we may become wiser and calmer, but is there any way of avoiding pain in our early encounters with the great problems of life? I do not think so.

Surely there is need for care, tact, and individual attention, in teaching people to be Christians or to be chaste. Unnecessary suffering is to be avoided as far as possible, but the hope of an integral formation that avoids all anxiety, all suffering, and every occasion of scruple, seems beyond what is possible.

It is helpful to keep in mind the difference between material and formal sin, and also the "law of gradual growth".

In *The Truth and Meaning of Human Sexuality*, note 136 to section 105, we read:

> ...the Church teaches the serious character [of sexual sins] because of the object of the act, but this does not exclude the absence of grave guilt, owing to the imperfection of the will. Indeed, in no. 10 of *Persona Humana*, it is made clear that in this area such imperfection is quite possible.

It may be suggested that such "imperfection of the will" is linked to the great plasticity of sexual symbolism,[42] as a result of which sexual tension can be accentuated by difficulty or frustration in any area of life, especially when subconscious motives are aroused.[43]

The "law of gradualness, or step-by-step advance" is expressed in *Familiaris Consortio*, no. 34. There we read:

> ...it is part of the Church's pedagogy that husbands and wives should first of all recognise clearly the teaching of *Humanae Vitae* as indicating the norm for the exercise of their sexuality, and that they should endeavour to establish the conditions necessary for observing that norm.

The "law of gradualness" does not imply any radical separation between a fundamental option and the observance of particular norms; but it does imply that even a sincere commitment to a particular norm may not lead immediately to success in observing that norm.

The "law of gradualness" seems to have an area of application not confined to the context, that of contraception, in which it was first enunciated. The same idea appears more recently in the *Catechism*, no. 2359, in connection with homosexuality: "Homosexual persons are called to chastity...they can and should

---

[42] See M. A. Friedrich, "Motivations for Coitus", 13 (1970) *Clinical Obstetrics and Gynecology*, pp. 691–700.

[43] L. M. Rulla, J. Ridick and F. Imola, *Anthropology of the Christian Vocation, II: Existential Confirmation*, Rome: Gregorian University Press 1989, pp. 280–315.

gradually and resolutely approach Christian perfection": "*gradatim et obfirmiter appropinquare*", in the *editio typica latina* of the *Catechism* (1997).

Further study of the meaning and application of the "law of gradualness" is, I think, needed. It does not seem applicable to a problem like abortion, given "the irreparable harm suffered by the innocent who is killed" (*Catechism*, no. 2272). It can also be very difficult to assess the degree of freedom possessed by a person to whom one is listening, in some pastoral situation; but it will usually be easier to be sure about the direction in which the person is striving, as an index of good faith and good will.

In conclusion, it is well to recall that if the learning of chastity can include suffering, the failure to do so means suffering of another and less fruitful kind. Having listened to the stories of many young people over the last 25 years, I still have to find one for whom the "sowing of wild oats" had been a happy experience. The words of the *Catechism* (2339) are borne out by those stories: "The alternative is clear. Either man governs his passions and finds peace, or he lets himself be dominated by them and becomes unhappy". There is great humiliation in being a slave to passion. Nor should one forget the anger of those whose feelings have been manipulated, with or without physical intimacy. A great bitterness can follow from that kind of experience, and a difficulty in being able to trust others again.[44] One hears about the experience of those whose parents have divorced. And so on. Those young people are happiest who have learned to live chastely,[45] however they have come to this virtue; perhaps by way of an initial rigidity, perhaps by way of failure and recovery. The experience of listening to such stories has been, for the present author, a strong confirmation of the value of the Church's tradition.

In any case, the stakes are high. If we hope that future generations will enjoy trust between the sexes, committed and stable and loving marriages, dedication of parents to children, and the joy of making a total gift of oneself in marriage or in the consecrated life, then we must do our best, whatever the difficulties encountered, to pass on our tradition on love and chastity.

---

[44] H. Hendin, *The Age of Sensation: a psychoanalytic exploration of youth in the 1970s*, New York: McGraw-Hill 1977, especially chapters 1–4.

[45] R. McCown, 'American Sexual Morality's Decline', 17/4 (1996) *Human Development*, pp. 15–18.

# Situating health care

# IO

# Health care as part of a Christian's vocation

## GERMAIN GRISEZ

## I. What a Christian's vocation is

FOR ALL PRACTICAL purposes, heaven and hell can be ignored. That at least is the impression one gets by comparing even the soundest Christian teaching and preaching of the past thirty years with the Synoptic Gospels. In them, Jesus talks constantly about the kingdom and often emphatically calls attention to the awful possibility of being found unworthy to enter it. But unless one takes a lively interest in heaven, thinking about vocation will be pointless. And unless one regards hell as a real possibility, the kingdom seems a sure thing, so that one takes it for granted rather than takes a lively interest in it.

Therefore, as a necessary presupposition for what follows I call attention to a repugnant truth about myself: I could go to hell. Despite all God's graces, I could freely choose to do something I know to be gravely sinful, gambling on the chance to repent. I could even resist the grace of repentance and persist in some habitual grave sin, telling myself that, being well-behaved in other respects, I can count on the merciful Lord not to hold this one thing against me but to find a way to get me into heaven despite it.[1] Then, I could lose my bet or persist too long in my self-deceiving presumption, die, and find myself in hell. Sadly, moreover, this is not true of me due to anything peculiar about me.

Before Vatican II, Catholics often used the word *vocation* to refer to the special calling of some men and women to be priests or religious. The Council broadened the concept by teaching that the whole Church is called to holiness, and every member is bound to respond to that universal vocation by exercising love of God and neighbour in fulfilling the responsibilities of his or her unique *personal vocation*.[2]

---

[1] Such self-deception has been facilitated during the present century, especially since around 1960, by theories of fundamental option according to which one can remain faithfully committed to the Lord deep in one's heart while making concrete choices to do particular acts that one knows to be gravely wrong. But such seductive thoughts should be set aside as groundless. The commitment of faith is the fundamental choice of Christian life, and, even without losing faith, one can lose sanctifying grace, charity, and eternal happiness by committing any mortal sin, as the Council of Trent definitively teaches: sess. VI, *Decree on Justification*, chap. 15 and canons 27–28 (DS 1544/808, 1577–78/837–38); cf. John Paul II, *Veritatis splendor* 65–68: 85 (1993) AAS 1184–88; *L'Osservatore Romano* (English edition), 6 October 1993, x.

[2] See *Lumen Gentium* 39–42; cf. 11, 46; *Presbyterorum ordinis* 6; *Gaudium et spes* 31, 43, 75.

This idea in not entirely new. Scripture tells us: of ourselves we can do nothing good, but God's graces include the gift of good works; apart from Jesus we can do nothing, but if we live in him we will bear fruit.[3] Faithful Christians always have believed that God's providence extends to the details of each individual's whole life, and that one works out one's salvation by trying always to do God's will. However, developing the Council's teaching, John Paul II has greatly enriched previous Catholic reflection on personal vocation.

To organize their lives, people without faith must clarify what they want and figure out how to get it. In affluent, secularist societies, such a plan is likely to call for the self-centered pursuit of emotionally appealing goals: wealth to be accumulated, things to be possessed, status to be achieved, honours to be gloried in, relationships to be enjoyed, and, above all, pleasant experiences.

By contrast, people with faith should try to discern God's plan for their lives, especially, though not only, in respect to the major decisions that shape life as a whole: whether to forgo marriage for the kingdom's sake or to marry and if so whom to marry, what sort of work to do and how to prepare for it, with which persons to cultivate friendships, in which voluntary associations to participate actively, where to live, what hobbies and regular forms of recreation to adopt, and so on. To discover God's plan about these major decisions, one must compare one's gifts and talents with others' needs that offer opportunities for service; take into account one's own genuine needs, already existing responsibilities, and other unavoidable limits; and ask how one can fruitfully serve others and, in doing so, truly fulfil oneself.[4]

God's providential plan directs everything toward creation's eventual consummation in his heavenly kingdom – in the new heaven and new earth, where the blessed, though still created persons, will be like God by seeing him as he is, and also, without losing their individuality, will be members of Jesus' body, sharing his resurrection life, and joining him and one another in an unending wedding feast. Of course, nothing we can do will bring about the kingdom; it will be God's new creation. Still, as Vatican II teaches, good works in this life are important for God's kingdom, because, in a mysterious way, he will salvage what is good in those works and use it as material for the kingdom. So, those who during this life promote human goods in God's Spirit and in accord with his plan will find those goods again in heaven – purified, completed, and transformed.[5]

Therefore, if we put on Jesus' mind to discern God's will for our lives and follow him in taking up our cross and faithfully fulfilling our personal vocation, we will effectively seek the kingdom and prepare material for it, and will use the unique

---

[3] See Eph 2.9–10, Jn 15.1–11; cf. Council of Trent, sess. VI, *Decree on Justification*, chap. 16 (DS 1548/810).

[4] For a more detailed summary of John Paul II's teaching and for references to the places where it may be found, see Germain Grisez, *The Way of the Lord Jesus*, vol. 2, *Living a Christian Life*, Quincy, Illinois: Franciscan Press 1993, pp. 113–29. (This volume will be referred to hereafter by *LCL*.)

[5] See *Gaudium et spes*, 38–39; cf. Germain Grisez, *The Way of the Lord Jesus*, vol. 1, *Christian Moral Principles*, Chicago: Franciscan Herald Press 1983, pp. 459–68, 814–22; *LCL*, pp. 78–87.

gifts we have received as different members of Jesus' one body to build up that body. If we walk in the life of good works God prepared in advance for us and with each step more fully engage our minds, hearts, souls, and strength, the divine love poured forth in our hearts by the Holy Spirit when we were baptised will gradually suffuse our whole being and transform us into the saints God wishes us to be forever. If we do the truth of faith in love, we will bear credible witness to that truth by our lives, which also will be the living sacrifice, holy and acceptable to God, that we will offer the Father in the Mass along with Jesus' self-sacrifice.

## II. The place of health care in every Christian's vocation

Health is not a sensible good: feeling well or being pain free. Someone suffering from a fatal disease might feel fine, and experiencing and responding to pain, as to other sensations, normally is part of healthy functioning. Health does include psychic functions. But it is an intelligible good, an element of true human well-being, though not the whole of it. Human well-being includes intellectual knowledge, acquired skills, moral virtues, harmonious relationships, and God's supernatural gifts – none of which pertains to health. Health is the aspect of well-being that is common to human beings and other animals: functioning well as integrated, psychosomatic wholes. Health is functioning that tends toward growth to maturity, the ability to reproduce, and continuing survival. Its contrary is organic and/or psychic functioning that tends toward stunted growth, the inability to have and raise offspring, and death.

Because human persons are not subjects that merely have and use bodies but are sentient, bodily beings, human life and health are intrinsic elements of human well-being and flourishing.[6] As such, they are not merely instrumental goods; they are good in themselves and can by themselves provide reasons for health care – that is, for choosing to do what promotes and protects them and to avoid what adversely affects them. Still, life and health are necessary conditions for sharing in many, it not all, other intrinsic human goods. So, other human goods usually provide additional reasons for health care. Some but not all behaviour that pertains to health care also is naturally, and often powerfully, emotionally motivated. Intense pain, anything obviously interfering with a vital function, and any clear and present threat to life always arouse strong emotions. Known but subtler and less immediate threats and risks to life and health usually arouse little or no emotion and do not directly motivate health care behaviour even when one has good reasons for choosing it.

---

[6] See *Catechism of the Catholic Church*, 362–65; *LCL*, pp. 460–67; cf. John Finnis, Joseph M. Boyle, Jr., and Germain Grisez, *Nuclear Deterrence, Morality and Realism*, Oxford: Oxford University Press 1987, pp. 304–9; Patrick Lee, 'Human Beings Are Animals', in Robert P. George (ed.) *Natural Law and Moral Inquiry: Ethics, Metaphysics, and Politics in the Thought of Germain Grisez*, Washington: Georgetown University Press 1998, pp. 135–151.

We have a large field of possible health care action. It includes regulating exercise, rest, and what one ingests; abstaining from behaviour that risks injury or the transmission of disease; regulating behaviour to protect and promote a healthful environment; and seeking professional help. Moreover, competent people can care not only for their own health but for that of their children and other non-competent dependents, and also can care for one another's health, especially by abstaining from doing various things that might adversely affect others' health.

Some moral responsibilities regarding health care are independent of one's personal vocation. It is always wrong to choose to kill or injure anyone or damage anyone's health, and it is always obligatory to choose in accord with a reason for behaving in a way conducive to health when that reason is opposed only by an emotional motive. In health care as in everything else one must be fair to everyone concerned, and one may never do anything wrong on some other ground for the sake of health.

Since the vocations of personal friends and of members of families and family-like communities include being one another's keepers, they should help one another in health care, encourage and support appropriate self-care, and avoid behaviour likely to harm one another's health. Parents and others caring for children should not only deal with their obvious health problems but adopt a healthful style of life, engage the children in it, and encourage them to follow it in their own choices. Spouses should take health into account in deciding whether and when to engage in marital intercourse; health considerations, whether or not related to a possible pregnancy, often are serious reasons for abstaining.

One's other vocational responsibilities often provide morally compelling reasons for taking care of one's own health. Students should avoid unhealthful behaviours, which impede intellectual development and acquisition of skills. Parents should try to stay alive and healthy to bring up their children, and spouses to help each other as they age. Priests, professionals, and other people in positions of special responsibility should take care of themselves so that they will be able to do well by those who are counting on them. In general, other vocational responsibilities can morally require people, in caring for their health, to take measures that involve sacrifices and cause burdens so great and so serious as to constitute sound and even morally compelling reasons for forgoing or avoiding such measures in the absence of such responsibilities.

At the same time, one's other vocational responsibilities compete with health care. Sometimes the competition is direct – fulfilling a responsibility can harm one's health, yet the responsibility can justify and even require that one accept the harm. Sometimes the competition is for resources: time, energy, money and capacity to endure stress. Many people could use most of their resources for their own health care, but doing so seldom is reasonable except for short stretches.

As one's other vocational responsibilities drop away, they no longer provide reasons for taking care of one's health. Yet greater resources for doing so often simultaneously become available. Of course, the intrinsic goodness of life and health always is a reason for health care. However, in these circumstances, established practices and strong emotional motivation generated by the prospects of pain, impaired functioning, and death can lead people to go to unreasonable lengths in caring for their health, sometimes neglecting other goods, and sometimes unfairly burdening others or using resources on which others have better claims. Even if not unfair to others, Christians often may – and then as a matter of mercy should – forgo health care to which they otherwise are entitled so that the resources will be available for others in need.[7]

## III. Health care as part of a health care professional's vocation

My wife and I began having children while I was studying at the University of Chicago. We lived in public housing and made do on the salary I earned working nights at a bank. Like other poor people in our neighbourhood, we took our children when they needed care to the emergency room of the nearby Catholic hospital. There we got to know a paediatrician, who lingered after completing morning rounds with patients from his private practice, for which he kept hours during the afternoon and evening in an office some miles away. At the emergency room, he would see whatever babies were brought in, but, not having an office there, he was casual about being paid. He was wonderful with children, and I thought he must be a great father. But he told me that, though he had planned to marry and have a family once he completed his training and got into practice, when the time came he realised that, with all there was for him to do for babies needing care, it would hardly be fair to a wife and children if he married and had a family of his own.

That paediatrician had an adequate income from his work but did not care for babies so as to make money. He was well respected but not ambitious for status and honour. He enjoyed his work and found fulfilment in doing it, but did not live for gratifying experiences. He had become a paediatrician in response to God's call and was using his gifts and training in dedicated service to children who needed care.

Of course, many Christians are called both to have a family of their own and professionally to help others care for their health. But if such people practise their profession as they should in response to God's call, they will be like our Chicago paediatrician in using their gifts and training in dedicated service. Indeed, like Jesus, who came not to be served but to serve, they will not hesitate to play the part of slaves.[8]

---

[7] Still, I disagree with Daniel Callahan, *Setting Limits: Medical Goals in an Aging Society*, New York: Simon and Schuster 1988, pp. 115–58, who argues that age can be a valid principle for cutting off governmental support for various forms of health care. People age at different rates, so that some eighty-year-old persons can get greater real benefit from various health care measures than most people who are sixty. My point, rather, is that as people get less real benefit from health care measures that impact on others, fairness and mercy increasingly require them to limit or even forgo such measures.

[8] See Mt 20.24–28, Mk 9.3–37, Lk 22.24–27, Jn 13.1–20; cf. Eph 6.5–8, Col 3.22–24.

They will serve each patient in solidarity with other health care professionals, but will give any patient's interests priority over solidarity with a professional who wrongs that person or is negligent. They will support making public the facts about differences in quality among professional health care providers and measures so that every patient will be able to make prudent judgments about whose services to seek and what measures to prefer. They will not enter into any relationship with a public entity, an insurance company, a health care business, or any other party likely to generate interests in conflict with those of any patient.

A patient who is untidy, smelly, poor, uneducated, of low class will be treated with no less courtesy, respect, consideration, and kindness than his or her betters; each will be dealt with as a very important person, as a member of Jesus' body. A patient will not be made to wait and wait, or to suffer other inconveniences and discomforts without a good reason, fairly applied and candidly explained. A person suffering from an unusually repugnant condition will not be avoided if possible or turned away, but welcomed. A patient who is difficult – who nags, insults, and fails to cooperate – will not be punished, as such a patient often is in subtle ways, and sometimes significantly and with gross injustice. Instead, a difficult patient not only will be dealt with fairly but mercifully; his or her special need for sympathetic understanding, gentleness, reassurance, and friendly good humour will be recognised and met.

No system of paying for health care adequately covers every person or every need for professional help. Confronted by a person with genuine but uncovered needs, Christian professionals responding to their vocation as they should will not make it their first priority to determine how payment will be made. Instead, they will recognise their profession's co-responsibility to meet such needs, and will generously do more than their fair share toward fulfilling that responsibility – *more* to make up for those who will not serve. Moreover, their readiness to serve will not necessarily be limited to their homeland and to the normal length of a professional's career there. They will hear that Jesus needs health care in other lands and after their retirement, and will be willing to help meet those needs if they can.

They will always bear in mind that they are helping others care for their own and their dependents' health. They will educate and encourage each patient to carry out his or her own responsibilities. They will gently but candidly tell all the truth each patient might need to plan ahead, not least to prepare for death, and will never conceal such information, much less lie, 'for the patient's good'.

They will not suppose that health care is ever the only thing or is usually the most important thing a patient should think about. So, they will take the time to provide each patient with all the information, about his or her problems and the suitable options for dealing with them, that the person might need in order to judge what to do in view of his or her other responsibilities, resources and limitations. In providing this information, they will take care not to prejudice the decision by their tone of voice, gestures, the way they present the options. They will neither pre-empt a patient's judgment in order to save time nor presume to judge for a patient as if their competence, like parents' over children's lives, extended to the person's every concern and responsibility. Pressed by a patient anxiously seeking to evade his or her responsibility to make a decision, "What would you do if you were in my place?" they will reply softly: "I'm sorry, but I cannot take your place. So far as I can see, both [all] the options I've described could be reasonable, so you must decide what is right for you."

Christian health care professionals responding to their vocation as they should will be humble and self-critical. They will acknowledge not only the limitations of medications and technologies but their own limitations and shortcomings: their uncertainty, ignorance, lack of skills, weaknesses, mistakes and faults. Knowing that they can only try to bring about some state of affairs with a reasonable expectation that doing so will benefit health, that the expected benefit may not he realised, and that whatever they do may have unexpected bad effects, they will realise that the success of even the simplest and most effective measures always depends on a kindly providence. So, they will hope in God, put their trust in him, constantly ask him to give success to the work of their hands, and thank him for any good result they seem to achieve. And they will not hide their faith and prayerfulness from other professionals or a patient they serve. "Just a moment – before we begin, I need to pray"; "Would you like me to pray with you?"; "I think this is worth trying, but I'm not sure it will work; we could try it and pray that it does"; "I made a stupid mistake, but no harm's done; and I thank God for that."

Always responding to genuine needs rather than wishful thinking and never nurturing false expectations, such Christian professionals will not do or cooperate with what they consider unreasonably burdensome and costly in view of its minimal likely benefits. Of course, they will never abandon a patient and will do what they can to mitigate suffering. But when their well-trained hands no longer have any work for whose success they can honestly pray, they will put aside their white coats and whatever else distinguishes them from other visitors, sit down by the person they had helped or tried to help, grasp the person's hand, and share his or her helplessness and feeling of despair.[9] They will neither pretend that death can be avoided nor suggest it is a friend to be welcomed. They will recall that death remains the last enemy to be destroyed, whose temporary victory must be endured and whose horror can be mitigated only by hope for the resurrection of the dead and the life of the world to come.

For the foreseeable future, Christian health care professionals responding to their vocation as they should will work as aliens in the world.[10] They find it more and more difficult to maintain their standards in doing their work. Their

[9] See Sheila Cassidy, *Sharing the Darkness: The Spirituality of Caring*, Maryknoll, New York: Orbis Books 1991, pp. 1–71.

[10] Of course, all Christians should use every morally acceptable means to resist and strive to overcome secularists' injustices against not only themselves but all theists. Realistically, however, though true believers can win some battles, they cannot expect to avoid persecution and suffering. And Jesus' faithful disciples can hope to overcome the world only as he did: by rising from the dead.

consciences are increasingly disrespected. Some fields of activity already are closed to them, and others will be. They are being pressured to help manufacture babies, prevent them, and kill them; they soon will be pressured to help people commit suicide and to kill people unwanted by those close to them or by society. Some committed people will not be able to keep their jobs, maintain their practices, continue to operate their facilities unless they betray their commitments by doing wicked things.

They will be urged and tempted to make an arrangement with a third party who has no objection to doing the wicked things – so that they will be able to satisfy the evil demands while keeping their own hands clean. But those who are clear-headed and faithful will realise that they can make no such arrangement without *intending* that the third party carry out his, her or its undertakings to do the wicked things. And, rather than intend that, they will lose their jobs, give up their practices, close their facilities.[11] They will regret not being able to continue to follow their vocation of helping others care for their health. But having undertaken to follow Jesus in responding to their vocation, they will remember that, though he regretted accepting the unsuccessful end of his effort to gather up the lost sheep of the house of Israel, he endured the cross for the sake of the joy that was set before him.[12]

And so they will endure their cross, looking forward with confident hope to finding again in heaven not only all the goods they have nurtured – purified, completed, and transformed – but many, if not all, the persons they have served: gloriously, joyously, permanently alive.

---

[11] See Germain Grisez, *The Way of the Lord Jesus*, vol. 3, *Difficult Moral Questions*, Quincy, Illinois: Franciscan Press, 1997, pp. 292–318, 325–28, 355–60, 370–80, 391–402.
[12] See Mt 10.5–7; 23.37–38; Heb 12.2.

# 11

# The encounter with suffering in the practice of medicine in the light of Christian revelation

DAVID ALBERT JONES OP

## What do we mean by suffering?

WHAT DO WE MEAN by suffering? Well I think characteristic of *modern* people (which we are, like it or not) is that we think of suffering first and foremost as an experience. Suffering is the felt experience of evil rather than simply the presence of the evil. (Using "evil" here in the general sense of something bad or harmful, rather than the more restricted sense of the moral wickedness of people.) In this way the characteristic modern notion differs from an older notion of suffering which focused on the evil suffered (rather than the experience of it). We still talk of someone suffering ill fortune, as say a mild stroke or a tax increase, but even here I suspect we have in mind primarily the experience of suffering these things rather than the misfortune itself. Thus it may be a surprise for people to hear that St Thomas Aquinas thought that, whereas the greatest good is a pleasure, the greatest evil is not a pain or a sorrow.[1] For pleasure springs from an awareness of some present good and is an aspect of that good. Pain or sorrow, however, in as much as they are an appropriate response to the presence of some great evil, are themselves good and true. St Thomas thought that it was clearly worse that some great evil was present but one wasn't even aware of it, than that one was aware of it. Thus the greatest evil involves a lack of appropriate felt sorrow. I mention this not to advocate this position (though I think it correct) but rather to illustrate how different are the immediate connotations of the notion of suffering in a modern context. In a modern context suffering means felt suffering. This is why the modern theological understanding of evil focuses so much on evil suffered rather than on evil done. For moderns the problem of evil has become the problem of pain. When someone reads a title like "the encounter with suffering in the practice of medicine" he legitimately expects some account of human pain.

## Christian theodicy

How then does the Christian tradition reconcile the fact of human pain with the doctrine that God is love? Well there are some thinkers who have recently

---

[1] St Thomas Aquinas, *Summa Theologiae* 1a 2ae q.34 art.3; q.39 art.4.

argued that the tradition doesn't in fact reconcile these facts and that we shouldn't try to either. Just one example:

> For the early Christians, suffering and evil, which for present purposes I do not need to distinguish, did not have to be "explained" . . . Indeed it was crucial that such suffering or evil not be "explained" – that is, it was important not to provide a theoretical account of why such evil needed to be in order that certain good results occur, since such an explanation would undercut the necessity of the community capable of absorbing the suffering.[2]

I have heard people argue, in this vein, that it would be immoral or impious to seek to reconcile these two facts, of God and human pain, for it would endanger either our acknowledgment of the reality of suffering or our commitment to the holiness of God.

It is often remarked that modern formulations of this question have their roots in the philosophical attitudes of the 17th and 18th century.[3] It is during this period that Leibniz coined the word "theodicy" to describe his attempt "to plead the cause of God", that is – to justify the ways of God to human beings. One might well wonder what an earlier generation of Christians would have made of the notion of seeking to justify God's actions to human judges. The account of God commonly given in the 17th and 18th centuries, that now characterized by the term "Deism", is certainly open to criticism. The transcendent mystery of God as put forward by the classical metaphysical tradition had given way to a morally upright infinite Spirit about whom one could have "a clear and distinct idea".[4]

It is even possible for a modern practitioner of theodicy to put forward a meditation in which one actually becomes an all powerful spirit. "You also come to see things from any point of view which you choose, possibly simultaneously, possibly not. You remain able to talk and wave your hands about, but find yourself able to move directly anything which you choose, including the hands of other people . . . - You would think and reason as men often do in words uttered to yourself. Surely anyone can thus conceive of himself becoming an omnipresent spirit. So it seems logically possible that there be such a being".[5] From a traditional perspective this meditation is a better portrait of the Devil than of God. In truth we cannot imagine what it is to be the source and creator of all things though we can have an idea what it is to be an ambitious spiritual creature growing more powerful at the expense of others. The idea that we could aspire to become like God is the basis of the fall of Satan and the fall of Adam and Eve. God is not the creature of our imagination that we would like to be when we would like to be some super powerful spirit.

---

[2] S. Hauerwas, *Naming the Silences*, Edinburgh: T & T Clark 1993, p. 49.
[3] K. Surin, *Theology and the problem of evil*, Oxford: Basil Blackwell 1986, p. 4.
[4] Descartes, *Meditations on First Philosophy* (especially the "Third Meditation").
[5] Richard Swinburne *The Coherence of Theism*, Oxford: Oxford University Press 1977, p. 105.

Certainly any theodicy which gives an account of God as a morally upright person, with a certain duty of care for his creatures, is doomed to failure. On the one hand, though the sorts of arguments brought forward (the free will defence, the benefit of suffering to bring maturity, to give a chance for courage and endurance) are easy to understand, they are generally dissatisfying in the face of great evils. They would not justify the case of human parents treating their children in such a way. On the other hand the account given of God bears little resemblance to the transcendent creator of the Scriptures and of the classical Christian metaphysical tradition. If this is all that theodicy means then it is not a fit pursuit for Christian thinkers.

However this modern intellectual pastime is hardly the only or the greatest attempt to understand the reality of evil in the context of the reality of the good God. Further, we can hardly dismiss the honest questions of those for whom the reality of evil has become an obstacle to acknowledging the reality or even the possibility of a transcendent good God. It is not enough just to offer practical help and comfort in the face of suffering. The question has been asked and deserves some sort of reply.

## Evil as a privation

The classical tradition starts with a very general observation. An evil is always a lack or a failure of some expected good.[6] Evil is always parasitic upon good. Good things can exist without defects but defects are always defects in otherwise good things. Each good thing has its own proper cause that brings it to be and causes that sustain it. Rabbits are brought to be by rabbits (and the power of the Sun). The order and integration and continued existence of good things may be traced back to a single cause. There is however no single or general cause for defects. Defects are due to a lack in a cause or the interference of causes. There may be many reasons why something does not happen, or why it happens wrongly, but if it happens aright this can only be because of some proper cause. That a rabbit breaks its leg is an accident. That a rabbit grows a leg in the first place cannot be an accident. If we were to put matters anthropomorphically we could say that when a washing machine works that is because it has been designed to do so but if it breaks down that is not because it has been designed to do so but because of some failure or impediment. There is then one principle of good that is the source of all good things, in as much as the universe is one thing and that there is an order or harmony among the good things within it. There is not however any one principle of badness which is responsible for all bad things because badness is not unitary in that way. Evil always lies in some privation, in the failure of some cause, not in the presence of some proper cause.

---

[6] See e.g. St Augustine, *Enchiridion* 11–15; Dionysius, *On the Divine Names* IV; St Thomas Aquinas *Summa theologiae* 1a q.48.

## Pain

But pain doesn't feel like a lack; it is a robust and a harsh reality. As I have already said, pain is the positive awareness of negative experience. Sometimes people talk of pain as though it were a thing or a quality. They talk of "pain sensors" and "pain receptors" as though pain was a quality like light, heat or pressure which could be sensed. Pain sensors are in fact damage sensors. The awareness of damage becomes pain because we recoil and are distressed at the first and most basic level of bodily sensitivity or awareness. We sense that something is very wrong. Pain is then the sense knowledge of some evil (damage which can, itself, only be understood as a lack, a disintegration, a loss, a failure of what is expected). In as much as it is sense knowledge then it is not a privation but a positive reality and indeed a limited good! It can be true (apt, appropriate, accurate). It is a sort of awareness of our state. It orients us in the world, guards, cautions us and prevents further injury. Pain is not under conscious control because it is an aspect of our first fundamental bodily awareness prior to other emotions, prior to reasonings and deliberations. It necessarily impinges on our consciousness for it is the alarm of damage. Even while we understand that an experience is for our greater good and not seriously threatening us our nature still recoils from it. Our awareness of pain does depend on what else is going on (our attention, our general well being) but the worst pains distort any mind. Pain then is not an absurdity but is a reality that makes sense within the context of the imperfections and deprivations of this life.[7]

## Theism, dualism, nihilism

What though is the point of this exposition? Is it supposed to domesticate evil and render it innocuous? Are we saying that suffering isn't so bad after all? On the contrary, suffering which is the encounter with evil (with failure, loss or damage) is real and terrible. This account is not meant to explain suffering away, it is rather an attempt to understand what is the true nature or meaning of suffering.

The notion of evil as a privation may seem to be an arid intellectual abstraction of little interest to ordinary people. Yet it underlies fundamental differences of attitude in facing and coping with suffering. Sheila Cassidy recounts her experience at a conference on the Church's healing ministry.

> I found, to my surprise, that the conference members (doctors, nurses and clergy) were split into two groups: those who believed in a concept of cosmic struggle in which the powers of evil personified in the devil were at war

---

[7] Since writing this it has been pointed out to me by Professor Germain Grisez that pain sensors often alert us to situations of impending damage. They alert us to danger, to the proximate presence of damaging circumstances. This does not alter the outlines of the present account. Pain is still an awareness logically (not contingently) related to damage, a 'reality' which can only be understood as a certain lack.

with the powers of goodness personified in Christ; the other group, in which I found myself infinitely more at home, believed in a God who, somehow, had his world totally in hand.[8]

These two groups represent two fundamentally different accounts of the nature of evil. Those who believe in a great cosmic struggle display a tendency to dualism, a tendency to think of evil as a principle alongside good. There are, it is true, many dualities in Christianity and there is a fallen angel, that ancient serpent who is the enemy of the human race, but these dualities are premised on the overarching sovereignty of God as creator of all. The Devil is a mere creature like us; there is no sinister equivalent to God.

As well as these two there is another attitude, which reflects a third account of the nature of evil. There is the view which takes the contradiction of goods and evils as evidence that there can be no overall principle (good or evil), no funda-mental order, no deeper meaning to things. Those who hold this view would deny the very possibility of a good God and so it is hardly surprising that they were not represented at a conference on the Church's healing ministry!

The notion of evil as a privation is in fact of great importance. If one accepts this very general account then it becomes clear that there can be a single transcendent cause of all that is good but not a cause of all that is bad. There is a good God responsible for all good things but not a bad god responsible for all bad things. There is no such thing as pure evil. Evil is always some lack. So when we encounter suffering this does not reveal some great and malign "force of evil" for evil consists not in such a cause but in the lack of a proper cause. Suffering does not reveal or reflect some dark presence but it obscures and fails to reflect the goodness of the Creator. Suffering is opaque. That is why it is hard to bear.

### The loving Father

So far I have talked about a principle of all good things but not about a God of love. If the existence of a principle and source of all good things is metaphysically compatible with the reality of evil, nevertheless how can one talk of God showing his love if his creatures continue to suffer?

God shows his love first by creating many different sorts of creatures. It is in fact a mark of God's love and generosity that he creates imperfect and corruptible creatures. God had no need in himself to create anything. He contains all things in himself and has no need of anything. The goodness of angels is one thing, of human beings is another, of lower animals is another. Each sort of creature is good in some way but also vulnerable or corruptible in some way. Animals of their very nature are the sorts of things that can fall apart, can suffer and die. Even the angels could fall and sin, at least initially. In each case the weakness

---

[8] Sheila Cassidy, *Sharing the Darkness*, London: Darton, Longman and Todd 1989, p. 67.

and corruptibility of the creature is intrinsic to the sort of creature it is. Adam need not have died had he not sinned. He could have lived a long life and then been transferred to a life of glory without death intervening. Yet Adam would be vulnerable to death if ever he turned away from God which, alas, he did. It is a mark of God's generosity that God did not desist from creating us even though we are, of our very nature, the sorts of creatures who could turn away from him.[9]

The second way God shows his love for his creatures is by redeeming them from their sufferings. According to the Christian account of things the world is not as it should be. It has been traumatised by a primeval fall. Now human beings are liable to suffering and death and prone to sin more readily than in the innocence of the youth of our race. This bad state, compounded by many sins, could have been justly left by God. In creating he had shown his generous love. All the good which remained was the work of God. He had no need to work further to demonstrate his love. Yet he added one gift to another. The characteristic pattern of the Christian Gospel involves God bringing good out of evil, overcoming evil to bring a greater good from it.

Christian doctrine, then, gives a twofold pattern to the relation of God and evil. First God shows his generosity by creating weak and imperfect creatures, second God comes to them to be with them and rescue them when they fall. The crucifixion and resurrection of Jesus give a picture of suffering overcome by a redeeming love. It is essential to realise that this Christian pattern does not make evil good or good evil. God overcomes the evil of sin and death but it remains evil in itself. It is nothing intrinsic to suffering, sin or death that makes these things life giving. It is rather the power of God that takes what is evil and brings good out of it.

## False pieties

A proper understanding of Christian doctrine is clear that suffering is never in itself a good thing. However there have been, and are, examples of false piety and perverse spirituality that would romanticise suffering and so add to the sum of human misery. I recall a scene in a film by Louis Buñuel in which a Jansenist nun has herself nailed to a cross. Would that this caricature were less on target, but the tradition of welcoming any opportunity to suffer is not far away even in these days. When opponents of Christianity reject the systematic cruelty and killjoy spirit of some advocates of the faith they correctly identify what is really a perversion of true Christianity.

Jesus healed the sick and lifted the burden of those who were suffering. The world would be better if it were free of suffering, and it is good for us to act to relieve suffering. But if someone has not suffered, aren't they in danger of remaining shallow and self regarding? This may be an accurate observation. St Thomas

[9] I am indebted to Simon Tugwell OP for the insight that the creation of imperfect creatures is a demonstration of God's generosity. He claimed that this was something that St Augustine had learned from the Platonists.

comments that "those who regard themselves so fortunate and powerful as to imagine that no evil can befall them show no pity".[10] Yet it would be better still if we did not need to suffer to shake us out of our self absorption. This tendency to shallow pitilessness is, itself, a result of the fall, as is the ubiquity of suffering. Suffering is moreover not universally useful, even in this way. Sometimes misfortune just adds to someone's desperate state and his indifference to the suffering of others. For it is the work of God that uses suffering to bring about some good when something good is brought about. It is not that the suffering itself is ever good. St Thomas discusses the various human emotions of joy, sadness, love, hate, hope, fear and anger, outlining their causes and effects, but only with regard to sadness (*tristitia, dolor*) does St Thomas give remedies. Why does he give remedies? Because pleasure is a good and pain is an evil. Jesus healed the sick and lifted the burden of those who were suffering. In the garden there was no suffering and for the saints, at least in the next life, there shall be none; for then every tear will be wiped away.

## Intellectual asceticism

It is possible then to give a very general metaphysical account that shows that the reality of suffering and the reality of a single source of all that is good are compatible. It is also possible to recognise the love of God in creation, but more especially in redemption.

What it is not possible to do is explain the reason why God *allows* suffering despite loving us. There is a mystery at the heart of suffering. We do not know what it is to be God or what it is to create. Creation is not like making or begetting or causing in the way that created causes cause things. The Creator is at the heart of all things, and everything, and gives to each thing the gift of its own self and its own nature. We cannot view the whole of providence nor can we understand the significance of events even in our own life. Occasionally we will be given a glimpse of what our life is or could be about, but in general we walk by faith not by sight. It is necessary, then, for us to be very limited in the sorts of explanations we give of things, and renounce the desire to plead God's cause for him in the face of suffering. This wish to practise theodicy in the modern sense puts us in the position of Job's comforters. These notoriously were of no comfort to Job and were no help to God either. They were advocates only of their own fear and a wish to add to the sufferings of Job the burden of a supposed explanation. (So in fact writers such as Hauerwas are quite right when they oppose this self justifying sort of theodicy). The alternative to the wish to act as advocate for God's cause is to cultivate a sort of *intellectual asceticism*, which realises the limits of our intellectual mastery of the world. Faith differs from rationalism in that it freely admits the limits of its knowledge and the place of darkness and trust.

[10] *Summa theologiae* 2a 2ae q.30 art.2.

## Virtue

The real problem of evil is not in fact how to account for evil, but how to face it. In the ancient world the problem was how wisdom could secure happiness (the end of human life) in the face of suffering and ill fortune. The question of how to face suffering (as opposed to how to explain it) becomes essentially a matter of virtue. Nobody likes to suffer. Nobody likes to see someone else suffer. Yet everybody does suffer (physically, emotionally, in their bodies and in their dignity). Anaesthetics are not without cost, and cannot deal with all suffering. Apart from brute pains there is also the problem of loss of dignity (in, for instance, not being able to wash oneself or feed oneself). To face such suffering one needs grace and virtue. One needs a source of hope and happiness by which to bear the burden of suffering. Suffering is a test of faith, not simply an intellectual puzzle, because faith is a matter of trust. It is difficult to trust someone in the face of some negative experience. One says something like "What is all this? I don't understand. I can't make any sense of it," and one is left with trust. Now virtues such as trust and hope do not come from nowhere; they are given directly by God and in a mediated way through the Church. The answer to the problem of suffering is one of grace and virtue.

Is this then a sort of craft – something that can be learnt or at least picked up? We need to learn how to be weak. God himself has shown us how to do this because he, who was strong, became weak for our sake. It is this weakness of God in Jesus that is imitated by the martyrs. A martyr is someone who faces death for the sake of witnessing to Jesus. Someone who is sick is not facing persecution but he or she can make of his or her sufferings a witness by the patience with which they are borne and the place that person continues to have in the Christian community. It is all too easy simply to tell someone who is ill that one must identify one's sufferings with those of Christ. Yet some suffering, which we cannot avoid, will come upon us all and finally we must face our own death and here at least we must identify ourselves with Christ in his death so that we might be like him in his resurrection.

## Anger and grace

Perhaps then it is our attitude that can transform suffering and make sense of it as Christian martyrdom. Except that this leaves too little room for the anger and mourning we should have in our suffering. It is right for us to rail against our sufferings and recoil from the evil that they represent. This may not seem very pious but it is the attitude of Job, Jeremiah and many of the Psalms. Jesus himself did not welcome suffering but shrank from it, praying "My Father, if it be possible, let this cup pass from me" (*Matthew* 26:39). If we are to imitate Christ then we too should accept suffering as our lot only when it cannot be avoided or when it is for some great good. We should rejoice when we can but there is no requirement that we should suppress altogether our pain and anger and accept an imposed joy. This hardly characterises Jesus in Gethsemane nor does it take notice of the proverb "He who sings songs to a heavy heart is like one who takes off a garment on a cold day, and like vinegar on a wound" (*Proverbs* 25:20)

In a way it is harder to accept suffering which is not a sacrifice, has no political or religious significance, is simply part of our general lot. In this case, especially when the suffering is very great, it presents a test for our faith and we face the prospect of losing even that little consolation which we have when we do hold on to our faith. The Gospel "ups the stakes", as it were, and threatens the possibility of greater suffering, of loss of meaning for those who cannot sustain their trust.

The bringing of good out of evil remains then a paradox, a sort of miracle. Suffering leaves us weak and without our own resources. It is at such moments that we are faced most strongly with our stark dependence on God. It is not through strength of character alone that suffering can be borne, for this will often break down under the strain; but those who do come through are preserved by God's grace, even though they seem to have no resources left. This at least seems to be the experience of the saints and martyrs of Jesus. This is the meaning of the word of God to St Paul, "my grace is sufficient for you, for strength is made perfect in weakness" (2 *Corinthians* 12:9)

## Medicine

So far I have said much about suffering and little about medicine. Now it seems to me that what is most specific to the encounter with suffering in medicine is that it is the encounter with *other people's* suffering. These others are in a close relationship of care with those who minister to them. This relationship is different from the caring of a friend or relative; for it is shaped by a professional ethos and specific medical skills meeting specific medical needs. Medical professionals will also have to impose sufferings on their patients (for their benefit, and with their consent, of course); but more relevant, and in fact more problematic, they have the task of relieving suffering.

It is precisely this role of relieving other people's suffering which puts medical professionals in the role of the saviour, giving the solution to human suffering. Such a role is impossible to fulfil; yet it is perpetuated by the hubris of modern technical knowledge, and the desperation of those who turn to it. In fact, however, all the patients will die and all will suffer. Though medicine can and should alleviate this suffering, it cannot eradicate it, and eventually there will come a stage when medicine can do nothing. Medical professionals have therefore to cope with continually coming up against the limits of their craft and the inadequacy of their tools. It is a very difficult thing to be closely involved with another who is suffering. The position of medical professionals as relievers of suffering only makes this relationship more difficult when there is in fact little medical that can be done. It is in this context that people look to secular accounts of suffering to help them cope with the burden of caring.

## Utilitarianism

Most comprehensive among the secular systems of coping with the realities of suffering is utilitarianism. Utilitarianism is a system of weighing up positive and negative experiences so as to calculate the best possible (which is therefore the only morally acceptable) proposal for action. This calculation does not consider past suffering but present and future suffering. It is a theoretical enterprise but it has as its conclusion a proposal for action. Thus the difficulty of present compassion can be alleviated by the promise of future action. The raw materials for this calculation are the predicted pains and pleasures associated with different courses of action. So in fact suffering, in the modern sense of felt suffering, is vital to the utilitarian project. This does not seek to explain suffering, but by putting it in the context of proposed action it offers a sort of practical solution to the difficulties of facing suffering. Also it has as its clear aim the end of human happiness. In these things it is to be commended. However the utilitarian approach to things is still seriously misguided from a Christian point of view.

## A comparison with Christianity

One could draw a comparison between utilitarian and Christian projects. When discussing the nature of pain and sorrow, St. Thomas quotes the saying of Jesus, "Happy are they who mourn, for they shall be comforted."[11] He uses this to make the point that pain can be an indirect cause of pleasure. Present woes can lead to future happiness. At first glance this thought has the characteristics of a utilitarian calculation. Happy are the unhappy for they will be happy. This is in fact the form of all the beatitudes; the comparison between present state and future prospects can serve to highlight the differences between the two approaches.

First and foremost the two approaches involve different notions of happiness. Utilitarianism is concerned with feelings, experiences, pains and pleasures, which can be measured on a single scale. From a Christian perspective this is too shallow. There are many different human goods, some more important, some more profound than others. A miserable man is unable to enjoy even his simple pleasures. A happy man can more easily bear up when in pain. Christianity is concerned with the real and most fundamental fulfilment of human beings and the pleasures that flow from the presence of our true end. Its pleasures are the sign but not the measure of this fulfilment.

Further, the mourning and happiness which are the concern of Christianity are the mourning and happiness of the same individual; there is no attempt to offset the sorrow of one by reference to the happiness of another. Those who mourn will themselves be comforted, if their mourning is indeed a case of grace and Christian virtue.

---

[11] *Summa theologiae* 1a 2ae q.35 art.3 obj.1, quoting *Matthew* 5:4.

Christianity is concerned with suffering because it is concerned with the virtues necessary to cope with suffering; hope and courage before one's own suffering, mercy before another's. St. Thomas, following the Latin tradition, interprets the saying of Jesus as referring to the need to mourn over anything which could be an obstacle of our return to God;[12] in particular our sins, and the attachments which are the vestiges of our sins. Mourning in this sense is not simply an experience but is a firm disposition given and sustained by God's grace. The utilitarian calculation concerns itself only with experiences: so the agent, the virtue, the grace are all invisible. Yet these are the essentials of the Christian understanding.

## Evil remains evil

None of these differences is trivial yet for our present purposes there is a further difference that is of great importance. The utilitarian calculation by producing a single sum and a measure tends to justify the evil that is done or experienced. The particular evil, as it were, dissolves and is completely assimilated into the calculation. It becomes something that can licitly be accepted, desired, done as a means to the desired end. Whereas in Christianity, as has been said before, evil remains evil even if God brings good out of it. A proper understanding of the Christian Gospel leaves the beatitude as a paradox. For sin and its consequences are still evils and suffering is never a good thing in itself, yet it has become a means of finding salvation. Suffering remains an evil never to be sought for itself or accepted outside the context of virtue (faith, hope, courage, mercy, prudence, justice and of course charity).

There is no intrinsic good to our sufferings. God Himself does not cause them (for there is no universal cause of evil) but allows them. He does not justify the suffering by reference to some calculation, but He does console those who suffer and redeems the world of its suffering for those who will accept His grace. Evil is not His direct and deliberate means to achieve some end (as it would be for us) but is a lack in His world and an aspect of the sort of imperfect world He has chosen, in His generosity to create and one which He brings good out of. Evil remains evil and not in itself the work of God or willed by God (except in the sense that everything in this world must be tolerated by Him and that the world only continues to exist as it is sustained by Him). It is therefore still right to voice anger and pain and to be outraged by sin, suffering and death. Those who reject God, sometimes think that belief in God means having to accept evil as a relative good: "What he longed for was that he might not believe in God; that he might walk out from the darkness into a clear morning, in which the sky was empty and things had no meaning but simply were; in which one might be able to hate suffering without trying to believe that it could be just or

---

[12] *Summa theologiae* 1a 2ae q.35 art.3 ad 1; cf. *Catena Aurea* on *Matthew* 5:4.

could be corrected later."[13] This is another example of the sort of false piety commented on more than once. Those who reject it are right to do so, but wrong in thinking that in doing so, they reject Christianity properly conceived. If I were to say, in one phrase what was false about this view I would say that it makes God into a utilitarian.

### Misericordia

Medicine properly concerns the suffering of others. It is still the case that to face suffering we need more than an account of suffering, we need virtue. To cope with the suffering of another, we need, not so much hope, courage, patience, endurance, as with our own suffering, but rather the virtue of mercy, what is called in Latin *misericordia*. Mercy is compassion for another's misery, and so the same thing that makes a man merciful makes him grieve over another's misfortune.[14] It is a virtue, a mean between two vices. To be merciful is to grieve over another's distress in the right way, not being cold and unfeeling but neither being overwhelmed or sentimental. This virtue is the highest of all the moral virtues and second only to charity which is directed specifically to God. Mercy is the direct effect of charity on our dealings with those in need.

The virtue of mercy, properly understood, is especially important for medical professionals. In their dealings with patients they must accept their distress without becoming so affected as to be unable to help. Though I have talked about utilitarianism, because it is a clear and systematic secular alternative to a Christian approach to suffering, few doctors or nurses are consistent utilitarians. Only in the area of resource allocation is utilitarianism actually popular. Instead concerns focus around the issues of patient autonomy (which sets up an immediate and safe distance when coping with another's suffering), over and against various forms of paternalism ("doctor knows best" still prevalent on this side of the Atlantic and not without its benefits) whereby the appearance of control in managing the disease wards off the helplessness of watching the patient suffer. In general the ethos of professionalism offers protection and distance which enables someone to emotionally sustain continued work with suffering people. These are necessary safeguards, for much harm is done, not only by emotional burn-out, but also by taking difficult decisions in emotionally charged circumstances. The norms of prudence and justice, which should shape all our decisions, are endangered by an over-sentimentalism. This is the opposite vice to cold indifference and between these two lies the virtue of true mercy. In particular the difficulty of coping with another's suffering can lead to the professional seeking to escape this by cutting short the life of the patient rather than helping the patient live well and as comfortably as possible his or her last remaining days.

[13] Jill Paton Walsh, *The Knowledge of Angels*, London: Black Swan 1995, p. 278.
[14] *Summa theologiae* 2a 2ae q.30 art.2; cf. St Augustine, *City of God*, IX 5.

## The medical role

Doctors, it is said, make bad patients. Perhaps they are used to being in control and so lack the virtue of patience. Whether or not this is true it is not obvious that for that reason they would be bad doctors. Of course everyone will themselves suffer one day, and it is not enough to hold to one's professional self; still in this context we are considering not, primarily, the virtues of being a good patient (which will include patience and impatience, the willingness to accept help when it is useful but the desire to be as independent as is practicable) rather we are considering the virtues of being a good health care professional, a good doctor, or nurse, or physio. The virtues of being a good coach are not identical with those of the athlete. The virtue of mercy concerns the suffering of another and professional concern with the suffering of others is not an easy role. It has its own trials and its own virtues. In certain areas like care for the dying, especially, I am told, care for the young dying of AIDS, the burdens are often too great to allow people to work in this area for long.

I have met people who say that they have received more help from self-help support groups of people who are themselves going through the same trials, than from professional carers. This also is something to openly acknowledge. There is a sort of support that someone who shares one's situation can give which others cannot. There is a sort of shared knowledge, which is the basis for shared support. Yet this is a different thing from medical support and neither is a substitute for the other. In general (as a friend of mine once remarked in a different context) ''nothing is a substitute for anything else''. Medical professionals should not feel, or be made to feel, inadequate to their role, just because they cannot identify with the persons suffering as though they had actually been through it. That is not their place. Their place is to act well in the role of medical carers and care in a way that is sustainable and appropriate to that role and relationship. Often if a carer is too closely involved with the patient that will adversely affect his or her medical judgement. This might lead to over-caution or over-treatment or simply to an inability to cope with the prolonged suffering of someone under one's care. To be sucked in or overwhelmed by the person's suffering is a more kindly and attractive vice than the opposite vice of cold indifference but it is in truth a vice, a sort of weakness or indulgence and an obstacle to effectively caring for someone who is suffering.

## Scriptural examples

What examples can be drawn from the Scriptures and tradition to flesh out the virtues of the professional carer? If facing one's own sickness is not exactly like martyrdom, then caring for the sick is even less so. We are more concerned here with healing and compassion than with persecution and courage. Does the healing ministry of Jesus offer a good example to help health care workers understand their role? Here, I think, one must be very cautious. A danger with medicine, which has already been pointed out, is its tendency to accept the role of saviour and solution to the problem of human suffering. Yet this is a role that is doomed to failure; for all the patients will die, and all will suffer, in some way or another. Given the reality of this it is imperative that real goods are not sacrificed in vain while searching for a medical solution when none exists. The reality and possibility of failure (the failure of the doctor, say, to save the life of a child) is something to be acknowledged and coped with. This will be easier if the role of saviour is eschewed in the first place.

## The unity of Christian virtue

There is a unity of the virtues and none makes complete sense without the others. So although I have repeated that the primary virtue of the carer is mercy rather than courage there is also a sort of courage and endurance that a carer must have. Likewise the shape of mercy in practice depends on understanding well the requirements of justice and having the practical virtue of prudence to be able to act well in particular circumstances. If one has to deal with the relatives as well as with a patient who is dying then mercy is nothing without discretion and the ability to relate well with strangers in difficult situations.

Finally for a Christian there is always the need for prayer to find the strength to act well but also to put before God one's concern for the patient and for oneself. In relating providence to the ordinary decisions of the day it is very important to pray for those who will be affected by one's decisions. Only then can one be at ease with the fulfilling of one's own role and acknowledge the limits of one's own control, while continuing to express some concern and solidarity with the suffering person. The relationship of carer and 'cared for' is in a way that of the strong caring for the weak, those not suffering caring for those who suffer. That is why it presents its own particular problems. One contribution that Christian revelation brings is the realisation of our own weakness and our reliance on God's grace. Medicine in fact is also the weak caring for the weak, though this is disguised in certain ways. There is no one who is so strong as to be invulnerable. Nor from a Christian perspective is invulnerability a thing to be sought after, at least not in this life. This realisation frees us to be able to show mercy. As St Thomas says, "It follows that the reason why one person has mercy on another is because he himself suffers some weakness".[15] This weakness does not debilitate nor does this mercy overwhelm but both are infused with charity, the love of God, which is shared with us by the power of the Holy Spirit and becomes the form of all the virtues. It is finally in the Spirit that we hope to find a way of coping with the suffering we encounter in medical practice or elsewhere. The problem of suffering does not admit of a satisfying intellectual solution (though we can show that there is no metaphysical incompatibility in a good God having created a world that includes suffering, we cannot fathom why he has in fact done so); but it does admit of a practical answer – which is grace and virtue through the Holy Spirit.

[15] *Summa theologiae* 2a 2ae q.30 art.2.

# 12

# Medicine as a profession and the meaning of health as its goal

## LUKE GORMALLY

W HEN I STARTED work at The Linacre Centre twenty years ago I went to live in a part of London where the then professor of obstetrics and gynaecology at our local teaching hospital was well known for what people refer to as "liberal" views on abortion. But his position was more interesting than that of the standard liberal gynaecologist, who wants to strike a muddled compromise between maintaining pretensions to professional status while in certain respects behaving like a mere technician. What I mean by this contrast should become apparent in the course of this paper. Our local professor of obstetrics and gynaecology, however, was lucid about his status as a technician. What I have acquired through my training, he tended to say, is mastery of a range of techniques. It is not for me to say to what ends those techniques should be employed. If the techniques could be employed to meet the wishes of his patients then it was his job, as he saw it, to employ them to those ends. It was not for him as a doctor to say which ends were morally acceptable and which unacceptable. Hence the question of abortion on demand was not an issue of moral principle; the interesting question was why more gynaecologists were not clear-headed enough to see that they should be providing it. This position struck me at the time as exhibiting a bold perception of what was at issue for the profession of obstetrics and gynaecology in the legalization of abortion.

It betrays a fundamental misunderstanding of what a profession is to say that it has no normative goals. Professions exist precisely because there are some goods so necessary to human well-being, and which can be secured only by the exercise of skills which are informed by a complex body of knowledge, that we require a body of learned practitioners dedicated to securing those ends and to cultivating the necessary knowledge and skills. The human good of justice should be the good to which the practice of the law is directed. The human (albeit instrumental) good of a dwelling place suitable for domestic life is the good to which the practice of domestic architecture is directed. A client who needs the services of a member of such a profession submits himself to the professional in a way which determines in some respect his future condition.[1] Because of one's dependence on the expertise of the professional it is necessary to "come clean" with all the relevant facts, for what

---

[1] R. Sokolowski, 'The fiduciary relationship and the nature of professions', in E.D. Pellegrino, R.M. Veatch, and J.P. Langan (eds.), *Ethics, Trust and the Professions. Philosophical and Cultural Aspects*, Washington: Georgetown University Press 1991.

one conceals may be precisely what the professional needs to know to serve one's good. A student may have reason to be ashamed of his ignorance of certain matters. But if knowledge of those matters is presupposed by a particular course of study he would do well to confess his ignorance to his teacher so that some attempt can be made to dispel it. Otherwise the course of study is likely to be a waste of time.

The exposure or "client nakedness" which is necessary if a professional is to be well-placed to do his best in securing the good one needs is one reason for a professional ethic. The client is in a position of naked dependence; this is, of course, often literally true in the practice of medicine. The vulnerability which goes with naked dependence is bearable if one knows that the professional is dedicated to the human good which is at stake in one's encounter with the professional. One's confidence in this dedication must be something one can infer precisely from the status of the professional as a professional. I'm in no position to check out the individual ethic of a doctor if I'm rushed into the Accident and Emergency Department. Since what is needed is an ethic characteristic of practitioners, then the inculcation of the ethic must be part of the formation of practitioners, and must be known to be professed by them as a requirement of admission to the profession.

Central to the existence of a profession, then, is our need for knowledge-based expertise to secure a particular human good and our need for the practitioners of the expertise to be dedicated to securing this good in the lives of their clients and so being prepared to follow norms which protect and express this dedication. A professional ethic does not merely support and warrant the relationship of trust between professional and client, but maintains the profession in existence. A norm-governed dedication to the good of a profession is constitutive of that profession. That is why maintenance of a professional ethic is the proper business of a profession. If the practitioners of the skills employed in law or medicine or teaching or architecture reject the ethic which has served to secure dedication to the proper good of the profession, we are left with no reason to think of them as dedicated to that good and no reason to recognise any authority as attaching to their advice. By authority here I mean what would warrant our following their advice if we wish to secure the good their expertise should serve.

A clear example, I believe, of the precise role of a professional ethic in maintaining a profession in being is provided by the physician's undertaking in the Hippocratic Oath not to kill those whom he attends. The moral law as it has been understood in every half-decent society forbids murder, since a licence to murder negates the most elementary possibility of human flourishing. But this is not the precise reason for the prohibition in the Hippocratic Oath. The oath forbids killing because if doctors feel free to kill this will have the effect of destroying the profession. For people look to doctors for cure and care, and they entrust themselves to them in the confidence that doctors are dedicated to those ends. If it ceases to be clear that doctors are dedicated to those ends a fiduciary relationship with them is no longer possible. In face of the collapse of an ethic internal to the practice of medicine, people increasingly look for ways of exerting external control on the practice of medicine. But the more medicine is perceived to be in need of external control the more technical medical expertise becomes cooptable for purposes which have no warrant in the proper ends of medicine.

The recent attempt by the British Medical Association's Ethics Committee to produce a revised version of the Hippocratic Oath[2] provides some evidence for thinking that the rejection of professionalism which I encountered in my local professor of obstetrics and gynaecology in 1977 is the wisdom now embraced (perhaps unconsciously) by the in-house experts of the doctors' trade union in 1997. About abortion the proposed revision of the Oath reads: "Where abortion is permitted, I agree that it should take place within an ethical and legal framework." This phrasing betrays the view that the practice of abortion has no relationship to an ethic constitutive of medical practice and therefore internal to it. Medicine is seen as properly governed by whatever ethical and legal framework happens to hold sway in a given society. And that framework can differ to the extent of criminalising or decriminalising abortion. So a doctor uttering the suggested sentence is making no substantive commitment which would serve to define him as a doctor. What is the point of such an utterance except to maintain a simulacrum of professionalism?

The problems of restoring a sense of a professional ethic are, however, deep and may reasonably be thought intractable. In a society characterised by moral pluralism, how can a substantive ethic of medicine continue to define the profession of medicine? Even if, however, the general practice of medicine in a society seems unlikely to recover and maintain its professional integrity we might still suppose that an authentic practice of medicine could survive in subcultural enclaves (such as Catholic hospitals). But if that is to be possible a good deal requires to be done.

One thing which requires to be done – not necessarily the most important thing – is to get clear about just what the human good is which medicine exists to serve in the lives of patients. There is a large degree of verbal agreement that the central good of the practice of medicine is the good of *health*. But the verbal agreement masks dramatically different understandings of the concept of "health", of which the most notorious is the one enshrined in the Constitution of the World Health Organization (1946) which defines health as "a state of complete physical, mental and social well-being". This comes close to identifying health with human happiness. No body of technical expertise based on systematic knowledge of natural causes can have human happiness as its goal, because human happiness is not secured by modifying the operation of natural causes. But the breadth of the definition has the ominous advantage of making room for a range of social engineers who describe their objectives as "health policy". When the WHO definition of health is married (as it frequently is) to a subjectivist understanding of what is worthwhile, for which "the good" is defined as "whatever people happen to desire or prefer", then we appear to have legitimation for

[2] See British Medical Association, *Annual Report of Council, 1996–97*, Appendix 1: 'Draft revision of the Hippocratic Oath', London: March 1997.

understanding the role of the doctor as that of a technician whose job it is to satisfy client's desires or preferences.

There has been a vigorous debate in recent years in journals concerned with the philosophy of medicine about the meaning of health. The debate has been polarised around two opposed positions. One is labelled "empiricist" (or sometimes "reductionist"), the other is labelled "relativist". Proponents of an empiricist type of position are opposed to the idea that health is an essentially value-laden notion. Proponents of a relativist position claim that our idea of health is determined in its content precisely by our interests and preferences, interests and preferences which may vary between individuals and societies; hence the label "relativist".

Typically, an empiricist claims that when we talk about health what we really have in mind is statistically normal functioning of organs and organ systems. Conversely, disease is defined as "species atypical diminishment of species typical functional ability".[3] Medical judgements about normal functioning are essentially statistical judgements, and one can think of sick people as "merely statistical outriders".[4]

The objection to this position is fairly obvious. One need only think of the high incidence of conditions such as cardiovascular disease in our society to realise that we have good reason for not identifying health with "statistically normal functioning". And it may be clear that in relation to some conditions – for example, tooth decay – it is precisely the statistical outriders that are healthy.

The motivation behind reductionist empiricism about the nature of health arises from a basic assumption which it shares with relativism – the assumption that values lack objectivity. The reductionist proposes to define health in terms of observed statistical regularities precisely in order to provide an objective basis for health-care policy.

The relativist thinks that health is a policy goal only because people desire it, but precisely what they desire in desiring health depends on a variable range of subjective interests. A prominent exponent of this position is the Swedish philosopher and health-policy analyst Lennart Nordenfelt.[5] For Nordenfelt, health is "a person's ability, in standard circumstances, to reach his vital goals"[6] where the latter "constitute the set of goals necessary and together sufficient for a person's *minimal* degree of happiness".[7] It depends on an individual's ambitions, abilities and hierarchy of goals what he decides to count as his level of minimal happiness. It follows that, for Nordenfelt, what is to count as health for an individual is relative to that individual's decisions.

[3] See Christopher Boorse, 'The distinction between disease and illness', *Philosophy and Public Affairs* 5 (1975), pp. 49–68, and *idem*, 'Health as a theoretical concept', *Philosophy of Science* 44 (1977), pp. 542–573.
[4] See the discussion of Boorse's position (references in previous footnote) in James G. Lennox, 'Health as an objective value', *The Journal of Medicine and Philosophy* 20 (1995) pp. 499–511, at p. 500.
[5] L. Nordenfelt, *On the Nature of Health. An Action-Theoretic Approach*. Dordrecht: Kluwer 1987.
[6] Nordenfelt, *On the Nature of Health*, p. 145.
[7] *On the Nature of Health*, p. 89.

Since it is for many practical purposes necessary to give "health" a meaning in social contexts, Nordenfelt believes that what is to count as health should be "decided upon" by the members of a particular society, who also decide on what is to count as "minimal real happiness". But the process of arriving at such decisions seems fraught with insuperable difficulties since Nordenfelt offers no principled way of excluding any decisions about what is to count as "happiness" and, therefore, about what is to count as "health".

As I have already remarked, the common assumption which lies behind these polarised views on the nature of health is the assumption that values are not objective. We can trace the source of this assumption about a value like health a long way back to one of the major figures in the history of modern thought, the greatly influential French philosopher and mathematician of the seventeenth century, René Descartes.

It is worth dwelling briefly on a short passage in the Sixth of Descartes' *Meditations on First Philosophy*[8] – for two reasons: first to gain some sense of how deeply entrenched in the history of modern thought is the assumption which underlies the polarization of positions I have been describing. Secondly, to help us see what is required to overcome that polarization.

As is well known, Descartes thought of human beings as a conjunction of two distinct substances: a conscious substance is mysteriously conjoined to a materially extended substance, the body. For Descartes, the body was to be understood in mechanistic terms. To say that something is to be understood as a machine is to say that we can explain the kind of thing it is exclusively by reference to the natural laws governing the parts of the thing together with the arrangement of the parts. If you want to understand something as simple as a bicycle pump – how it works – what you need to understand is how its parts are so fitted together that they take advantage of the natural laws which govern its parts. But it is the natural laws governing the parts which ultimately explain how it works.

Descartes illustrates his mechanistic understanding of the human body when he compares it to a clock in his *Sixth Meditation*. Descartes says that a clock does not function well in virtue of a nature intrinsic to it as a clock. The parts of a clock, whether it is functioning well or badly, are true to their natures. The human body is like a machine, not merely in having functional parts (which anyone would admit the body to have) but in not having intrinsic to it any nature which tends to the good of the body, any nature which is gone against by disease. It is only because we impose our ideas of what a body ought to be like onto a body that we can say that a diseased body falls short of its nature. In this sense of the word "nature" a body's nature, as Descartes says "is something extrinsic to the object it is ascribed to". Our ideas of healthy functioning and unhealthy functioning derive not from any understanding of how the body in its very nature is meant to function – for precisely as a body it has no nature which characterises it as a

---

[8] The passage in question can be found at p. 120 of Descartes, *Philosophical Writings. A Selection* translated and edited by Elizabeth Anscombe and Peter Thomas Geach, Edinburgh: Nelson 1954.

unified body. No truly explanatory description of the workings of the human body could yield, according to Descartes, an insight into the good constituted by the well-ordered organic functioning of the body.

A mechanistic understanding of living bodies is contrasted with a teleological understanding. According to a teleological understanding, though a body may be differentiated into parts, those parts are hierarchically integrated in such a way that the operation of parts serves the well-functioning of the body as a whole. Living organisms have natures intrinsic to them, the dynamic operation of which is directed to the well-functioning of the organism as a whole. The well-functioning of an animal body is what we call health. How we should understand this in relation to the human animal I shall come to shortly. Before doing so, however, I should say something about mechanism and teleology in relation to medical science.

Medical science is indeed interested in mechanisms and in explanation, therefore, in terms of the laws governing the parts of a mechanism. But we cannot understand why the various mechanisms are in play except in terms of the roles they play in the human organism. The mechanisms are understood at each level as serving an outcome; that outcome is what makes their existence intelligible. Thus biochemical transformations in the liver have as their function or purpose "bile secretion"; bile secretion as that is modulated by changing stimuli has as its function to contribute to the workings of the entire intestinal tract, which in turn have as their role to contribute to the "vital function" of digestion, which in turn exists for the sake of the whole organism.[9]

Twentieth century medical science, and specifically physiology, integrates mechanistic and teleological explanation. In doing so it subverts the polarisation in the philosophical debate about the meaning of health between an empiricist, purportedly "value-neutral", understanding of health as "statistically normal functioning", and a relativist understanding the content of which is determined by people's subjective preferences. This polarisation has been parasitic upon a mechanistic understanding of the human body of the kind advocated by Descartes which expelled teleological understanding and thereby denied itself the possibility of understanding bodies as organisms.

Those who have polarised the philosophical debate about the meaning of health appear to have overlooked the contemporary scientific understanding of the human organism which underpins medicine. For an adequate scientific understanding is essentially teleological in this sense: that it consists in knowing what things are about in doing what they do. Now it is of course true that what human beings are about in engaging in distinctively human activities is acting to achieve human happiness (under some conception of happiness). But within the ongoing life of a human being there are ends subordinate to the achievement of happiness and ends which are ingredients of happiness. One such end, certainly

---

[9] S. Toulmin, 'Concepts of functions and mechanism in medicine and medical science', in H.T. Englehardt and S.F. Spicker (eds.), *Evaluation and Explanation in the Biomedical Sciences*, Dordrecht: Reidel 1974.

subordinate to the achievement of happiness, and arguably a component of it, is the end which makes a range of organic functions more or less immediately intelligible – namely, the well-ordered organic functioning of the body; and that is what is referred to when we speak of *the good of health*. That good is given with the kind of organisms we are and is not a construct from some variable list of human desires.

The organism we are talking about here is the living human body. Now the human person is not something separable from the living human body. This does not, however, mean that personal life is reducible to the functioning of subsystems of the organism. For the life which gives unity to the human organism is the life of the human soul which is essentially rational life. All bodily activities are activities of the soul, but not all human activities are bodily activities. All bodily activities are activities of the soul because they are only properly intelligible in terms of the role they play in that unified life which is caused by the rational soul.

The function of some bodily activities is maintenance of what Claude Bernard called the "milieu intérieur" – a certain normal inner condition of the organism. Some of the body's homeostatic systems are designed to keep its inner state normal in face of a constantly changing environment (including factors like temperature, light and moisture). Other bodily activities are designed to protect the primary homeostatic systems from stress and shock, from bacteria and viruses, and to help restore normal functioning.

Yet other bodily activities function as the organs of powers such as sensation, imagination and memory, which provide the materials for our rational activities.

Our rational activities as such – the grasp of meaning, the affirmation of the truth about what is the case and what is worthwhile, and the practical reasoning which leads to choice – are not bodily activities, though they are not possible for us without bodily activities.

So the malfunctioning or non-functioning of the organic systems of the human body can affect our life at every level internal to its unity.

If we understand health as the well-ordered organic functioning of the body, then we will not characterise in terms of health – as "healthy" or "unhealthy" – the full range of dispositions and associated activities which exhibit the nature of human life. Virtue and vice, understanding and misunderstanding, knowledge and false belief, can be described only by remote analogy as states of health and disease.

I am here proposing *somatic health* – defined as the well-ordered organic functioning of the body – as at the very least the central case of what we mean by health, and as the distinctive good which is the proper goal of medicine. It is the proper goal of medicine because

- it is the subject of a unified or potentially unified field of knowledge of natural causes;
- it is at least an instrumental and arguably an ingredient good of human flourishing, the lack of which through disease, damage or congenital defect

creates occurrent needs for the expertise of doctors to restore health (or the best achievable approximation to well-ordered organic functioning);

- the restoration and maintenance of health in the lives of patients is therefore a proper object of that dedication characteristic of a profession, a dedication which is informed by a professional ethic. It is the human need for that dedication which grounds the requirement that doctors should act precisely for the good of somatic health and not in ways which undermine that dedication. There is a dual presupposition behind such dedication: the first (just mentioned) that health is a good important to human flourishing, a good which may be diminished and threatened in ways that create occurrent needs for its restoration. The second, more fundamental presupposition is that any human being who because of need comes under the care of a doctor is to be respected as possessing the dignity characteristic of human beings. It is this presupposition that demands of doctors in their dealings with patients dispositions of justice, truthfulness, respect for the fundamental responsibilities of the patient, courtesy and kindness. The practitioner of medicine should of course be governed in his behaviour not just by the ethic distinctive of his profession but also by the ordinary requirements of morality.

There are various objections that should be considered to this account of somatic health as the proper goal of medicine.

The first is that it is sometimes said that there are a number of disparate goals of medicine. One standard list is:

- the restoration and maintenance of health;
- the alleviation of pain; and
- the prolongation of life.

About such a list I would simply say that the second and third goals are not to be understood independently of the first, which is the controlling goal of medicine. Consider alleviation of pain as a goal of medicine. Any "doctor who thought the relief of pain *as such* was his goal would make a very bad doctor. Pain is a monitoring system vital for health (which is why post-operative analgesics have to be so carefully and sparingly administered). Health must be the overriding goal."[10] In what sense the goal of health controls the doctor's dedication to prolongation of life is a topic I shall not address here since it requires a paper to itself.[11]

A much more strongly felt objection to the account I offer of the goal of medicine is likely to be that it is too narrow. This is not primarily a theoretical objection. The problem with confining the notion of health to "somatic health", and more particularly interpreting the correlative notion of ill-health in terms of bodily disorder, disease or defect, is that it seems inadequate to the reality of

[10] J. Cottingham, 'Medicine, virtues and consequences', in D. Oderberg and J. Laing (eds.), *Human lives: Critical Essays on Consequentialist Bioethics*, London: Macmillan 1997.
[11] For some brief observations on this topic see Luke Gormally (ed) *Euthanasia, Clinical Practice and the Law*, London: The Linacre Centre 1994, p. 134.

what is expected from doctors by patients. Patients come to doctors not necessarily with identifiable somatic disorders but with a range of "complaints" only some of which are diagnosable in terms of the dominant physiological/biochemical account of disease. This certainly makes it necessary for doctors to be sensitive to the fact that the only genuine solutions to the complaints of some patients will be better moral dispositions in the patient, or legal redress for wrongs done to the patient, or a religious conversion which would recognise a redemptive meaning in suffering.

But the need for such sensitivity on the part of doctors does not argue to the conclusion that doctors should be competent precisely as doctors at providing this range of solutions. To think so would be similar to thinking that because a priest should be sensitive to the different kinds of help those approaching him may need, he should himself be competent to provide all those forms of help.

The complaint that "somatic health" represents too restrictive a notion of health is likely to be felt most acutely in relation to what are called mental illnesses. Here we need to distinguish between

- mental afflictions which are, so to speak, causal side-effects of bodily disorders, and
- mental afflictions with no detectable organic cause but which are related to factors ranging from unresolved conflicts of emotion to self-destructive vices.

The first group of "mental afflictions" seems to fall fundamentally within the ambit of a medicine which has somatic health as its goal. The remedies for the second group of afflictions could not reasonably envisage the restoration of somatic health as their goal. What may be required, for example, is recognition of some painful truths about oneself, or recognition of the need to forgive someone whom one habitually perceives as an enemy. Whatever is envisaged as the goal of "therapy" is likely to vary considerably in character from one practitioner to another of what we call psychological medicine. The absence both of a unified body of knowledge-based expertise and of a central controlling goal of therapy in the treatment of non-somatically based mental afflictions suggests to me that it merely creates confusion in our understanding of mainstream medicine if we seek to include all forms of psychological medicine within its ambit.

It isn't a passion for neat classification which motivates this observation. I should like to conclude by offering a number of considerations which argue to the great utility of recognising somatic health as the central, controlling goal of medicine.

First, it allows for a coherent understanding of medicine as a profession. This is not some merely theoretical gain, since what is at issue is whether we are able to conceive of medicine as a profession with an ethic constitutive of the practice of medicine. If we cannot sustain such a conception then what we are left with is medicine as expertise in the deployment of technical skills. If medicine is a profession then we can expect a doctor to exhibit in his or her work a range of virtues or dispositions of character conducive to achieving the good of the profession. But if the doctor sees himself as a technician, prepared to exercise technical skills to secure whatever objectives patients have in mind, there is no possibility for him of acquiring or retaining those dispositions of character necessary for serving the good of health in his patients. When that happens to doctors on a significant scale medicine becomes much more vulnerable to political manipulation.

The second reason for recognising the usefulness of thinking of the goal of medicine in terms of somatic health is that this conception of the goal of medicine provides us with an indispensable element in a rational basis for the allocation of healthcare resources. Without a well-grounded understanding of the goal of medicine, or more broadly of what counts as healthcare, many allocation decisions are likely to be irrational.

Thirdly, a defensible account of the proper goal of medicine as somatic health would, if invoked, save us from some of the more gravely damaging applications of the Bolam test in English law. *Bolam* is the leading case in regard to medical negligence. "It establishes that a doctor will not be judged to be in breach of his duty if, on the evidence of peers [i.e. fellow doctors], he has behaved as a reasonable doctor."[12] But the application of the Bolam test has been extended from a test of competence in the assessment of medical negligence, to a much more general test of what it is reasonable, in the sense of being ethically acceptable, for doctors to do. Perhaps the most disturbing example of this extension was in the *Bland* case, the principal case in English law concerning the withdrawal of tubefeeding from a patient diagnosed as in what is termed "persistent vegetative state". In delivering his judgement on the case the then senior Law Lord, Lord Keith of Kinkel, said:

> ...a medical practitioner is under no duty to continue to treat such a patient where a large body of informed and responsible medical opinion is to the effect that no benefit at all would be conferred by continuance. Existence in a vegetative state with no prospect of recovery is by that opinion regarded as not a benefit, and that, if not unarguably correct, at least forms a proper basis for the decision to discontinue treatment and care. [And His Lordship then refers to the *Bolam* case.][13]

In the *Bland* case, then, what is made pivotal to the reasoning is that a body of medical opinion existed which considered the continued existence of Tony Bland "not a benefit" or not worthwhile. Since the worthwhileness of Tony Bland's existence is made the subject of medical judgement, the point of discontinuing "treatment and care" becomes that of putting an end to an existence judged no longer worthwhile. Hence three of the five Law Lords in the case agreed (the others not dissenting) that the conduct they declared lawful (of withdrawing tubefeeding) had as its deliberate and precise purpose that of terminating the life of the patient. What emerged from the reasoning in *Bland* was in effect, then, a judgement that euthanasia by a course of planned omission was lawful.

[12] I. Kennedy, *Treat Me Right. Essays in Medical Law and Ethics.* Oxford: Oxford University Press 1988.
[13] [1993] WLR at p.362.

I have the impression that at least some of the Law Lords would have preferred to avoid that outcome. Be that as it may, their line of reasoning was entirely avoidable had they recognised the possibility of keeping a firm focus on the normative limits of a doctor's duty precisely as a doctor. It was arguable that the precise goal of somatic health was no longer achievable in the case of Tony Bland, and there was every reason to discontinue specifically medical treatment (as distinct from ordinary care). Such a line of reasoning would certainly have warranted the discontinuance of antibiotic treatment, for example. I am not myself of the view that tubefeeding for someone in what was Tony Bland's condition is medical treatment. Nonetheless, given the fact that the Courts accepted the medical testimony asserting that tube-feeding was medical treatment, then, had the reason for withdrawing it been that there was no continuing duty of medical care because the goal of medical treatment was no longer achievable, the reasoning would have borne on the futility of treatment rather than the supposed futility of Tony Bland's existence. We might then have been spared an explicit endorsement of euthanasia by deliberate omission.

The recognition that the restoration and maintenance of somatic health are the proper ends of medicine is, I think, implicit in a variety of legal judgements which rely on the distinction between what is therapeutic and what is not therapeutic. But, unsurprisingly, there is little or no explicit discussion among the lawyers about the normative goal of medicine, and about somatic health as the concept which best defines that goal.

My discussion of that concept has been intended as a contribution to restoring an adequate understanding of medicine as a profession. The aspiration to do so may seem wildly optimistic, since medicine as a truly independent profession with a distinctive ethic appears to be unravelling in face of a number of forces: notable among them are ethical pluralism, bureaucratic control, and the drive to reduce costs, whether it comes from Government or the insurance industry. But if the practice of medicine does succumb to these forces and ceases to be a recognisable professional occupation, then the consequence will be increasing alienation between doctors and patients, since the vital conditions of a relationship of trust will have been undermined.

# Integrity in health care

# 13

# Collaboration and integrity: how to think clearly about moral problems of cooperation

## JOSEPH BOYLE

C OOPERATION WITH EVIL is the name created in Catholic theology and used in Church teaching to discuss a class of cases in which complex circumstances make it difficult to correctly apply the general norm that one should not contribute to or participate in the wrongdoing of others. Clarity in thinking about the Catholic teaching on cooperation with evil requires some attention to the character of the complexity which makes impossible the straightforward application of this norm.[1]

## I. The Catholic idea of cooperation with evil: the idea and its use

Scandal is understood as leading another into sin. It is plainly itself morally evil. When one induces another to join in one's own sin, then one sins doubly: one sins and one scandalizes. And if the one induced to join in one's sin does so, then he too sins; and if he induces the original sinner to sin more or worse, then he too sins doubly.

It does not stretch our sense of language to say of such a pair, for example, partners in satisfying their desires for pleasure or status, that they are "cooperating" or collaborating in doing wrong. This, however, is not what the Catholic moral tradition has meant by cooperation with evil. The tradition's concern here has been focused on cases where one party is the primary agent and the other an accomplice or supporter playing a subordinate role in carrying out or facilitating the primary agent's evil action, in other words, on cases where the cooperating party is not actually doing the evil act, but something to facilitate it.

But even this narrowing of focus does not isolate exactly what the tradition was concerned with, as a moral issue distinct from scandal. For when one party

---

[1] The analysis in this paper is heavily indebted to Germain Grisez's recent work on cooperation, which I helped him develop. This presentation is not meant to be a summary of Grisez's analysis but a brief fresh statement of some of the salient points, thus allowing ample opportunity for my own mistakes. See *The Way of the Lord Jesus*, Volume III, *Difficult Moral Questions*, Quincy, Illinois: Franciscan Press 1997, Appendix 2, pp. 871–897. Grisez's index entry under cooperation suggests how frequently this category must be used in dealing with difficult moral questions. Since I think there is considerable confusion on this subject in the literature, aspects of my analysis will involve implicit criticism of other treatments; for the most part I will leave the polemics implicit.

is the fully willing agent or accomplice of another, even if one party is the primary moral agent and the other a partner playing a subordinate role, there is not a special moral obscurity calling for clarification. There is likely to be mutual scandal in such cases, but they are not morally complicated in ways that make problematic either the application of the norm prohibiting contributing to another's wrongdoing, or plausibly excuse or justify the willing agent or accomplice: by sharing the wrongful goals or participating voluntarily in the project of the primary agent, an accomplice or agent clearly makes a free and unconstrained choice contrary to the norm. The fact that sometimes such helpers do not actually carry out the evil action has no tendency to obscure what is going on morally: we are not disposed to think that a gang member assigned look-out duty is less a part of the heist just because of a role at the edge of the action.

Not all scandalizing and wrongdoing by a group of people depend on the parties sharing common desires and, as it were, a common will to evil. For one can induce another to participate in sin by causing him or her to fear the consequences of not sinning. In other words, one can scandalize by coercion or duress. Calling actions responsive to such coercion "cooperation" or collaboration does stretch our sense of the meaning of these words. The coercive aspect of this kind of scandalizing removes the associations of community (already stretched by the sinfulness of the project) which these words have.

Attending to the possibility of coercive motivation in inducing help for wrongdoing usefully narrows the focus to the sorts of cases the category of cooperation with evil was intended to deal with. For coercion always changes the voluntariness of actions done in response to it, and sometimes alters some of the obligations of those who are coerced.

Coercion affects voluntariness in the way explained by Aristotle in his account of the mixed voluntary, what is called *voluntarium secundum quid* by St. Thomas and the later tradition. In action of mixed voluntariness, a person chooses to do what the person would prefer not to do, and does so only because of the coercing circumstances: if they were not present the person would choose otherwise. The responsible sea captain who throws his cargo overboard to avoid shipwreck in a storm prefers not to act in this way and would not do so unless the necessity of the situation required it. When a person in such cases chooses as the situation requires, he or she is willing to act as he or she does, contrary to preference, so the action remains voluntary. Indeed, the action is more voluntary than not.[2]

Of course, coercive circumstances may sometimes transform the voluntariness of actions more radically than this. They sometimes cause fear so great that no voluntary action is possible, with the result that actions caused by such fear are not human actions and their agents are completely excused. More commonly, such circumstances provide grounds for mitigating the responsibility of those who weakly do even great evils. But they do not justify evil actions: as Aristotle noted, sometimes we praise people for what they do under compulsion, sometimes

---

[2] See *Nicomachean Ethics*, Book 3, 1110a12; the reasoning is accepted and used by St. Thomas and the subsequent tradition; see *Summa theologiae* 1a 2ae q.6 a.6.

we blame them, sometimes we pardon them for bad things done under compulsion, and sometimes we think people should suffer anything rather than do some unthinkable acts – his example is matricide.[3]

As Aristotle's comments suggest, the coercive character of a situation can change the obligations of those coerced. This change occurs because the threatening circumstances put into play within one's practical thinking considerations not normally in view, such as saving one's life or keeping one's job. These considerations indicate that there are options for action which (1) in noncoercive situations do not ordinarily arise except as temptations to choose wrongly, but (2) in these situations are morally good. Thus, when faced with a storm at sea, Aristotle's captain does not violate owner's property rights or otherwise fail in his responsibilities by throwing cargo overboard. Similarly, one is not collaborating in banditry when one hands over even urgently needed goods in response to a credible threat of "your money or your life". These responses to coercion are not the morally evil acts they would be in less constrained circumstances. They are not evil actions more or less excused by the circumstances, but completely good actions. However similar the chosen behaviour might be to behaviour carrying out bad choices, the choice to throw over or to hand over goods in these circumstances is for the sake of preserving life, a good end. In the circumstances that need not be unjust since goods are instrumental to persons. When just, this choice is also morally good.

But as Aristotle's example of matricide makes clear, coercion does not justify any action needed to respond to the coercion. Idolatry, murder, adultery, perjury and other absolutely forbidden actions are simply out, morally speaking, and no coercive circumstance can change that. Moreover, the creation of new options by conditions of coercion and the consequent variation of the moral significance of behaviour chosen under coercion do not constitute a basis for setting aside all non-absolute obligations. Much of a person's life is structured by non-absolute duties based on one's commitments to others, and one often is pressured to set them aside. But sometimes others' welfare so depends on one's doing one's duty that deliberately setting it aside to avoid bad consequences would be gravely wrong. So, the appallingly coercive conditions of a battlefield do not ordinarily justify a soldier's abandoning his post.

Consequently, the fact that coercion can but does not necessarily change one's obligations indicates a general area where moral clarification is needed, namely, to distinguish things one might do because of the impact on one's obligations of coercive circumstances from the things which even in coercive circumstances one may not do. A specific version of this need arises when a person committed to wrongdoing uses coercion to enlist the help of others in support of his wrongdoing. The previous discussion suggests that when the inducement to help in wrongdoing is coercive, the person induced might be able to render some kinds of assistance to the wrongdoer without himself or herself doing wrong. That would occur whenever the assistance given was not wrong for some other reason than that it contributed to wrongdoing, and when the coercive

[3] *Nicomachean Ethics*, Book 3, 1110a19–30.

circumstances transformed the ordinary obligation to avoid helping people do wrong.

In other words, there is need to distinguish, in actions in which one person helps another do wrong, cases in which a coercive context can change one's ordinary obligations, most importantly the obligation not to contribute to wrongdoing, from those cases in which one acts wrongly under duress.

The Catholic moral tradition came explicitly to isolate this moral issue, as distinct from issues concerning scandal, in the period of casuistry leading up to St. Alphonsus' important synthesis of moral theology. The issue came to be called cooperation with evil. One kind, called formal cooperation to indicate a moral union between the cooperative action and the wrongdoing was rejected as always wrong, another, called material cooperation, because it contributed to the wrongdoing without the moral union with wrongdoing characteristic of formal cooperation, was taken to be morally permissible under certain circumstances.[4]

The assumptions of the discussion were that (1) the cooperator was a subordinate participant motivated to help the primary wrongdoer, not actually to do the latter's wrongful act; (2) the cooperator and primary wrongdoer were not functioning as a community having shared goals, at least as far as the latter's wrongdoing was concerned, and thus (3) the cooperator's will towards assisting in the wrongdoing was mixed: he or she would not consider rendering the assistance without some constraining circumstance such as the threat of dismissal from employment.

The recognition that the assisting action in question would ordinarily be wrong, because of its facilitating wrongdoing, is not sufficient for the mixed voluntariness relevant here. For the relevant reluctance to assist evil is not necessarily present in people of bad character or of weak will. Plainly people can be wholeheartedly involved in what they judge wrong.

More importantly, however, the constraining circumstances necessary for mixed voluntariness are not limited to those strictly or narrowly coercive. For one can think that one has no choice but to contribute to another's wrongdoing because of other duties whose fulfilment curtails the effort completely to avoid helping others do evil. And moral impossibility, plainly, is not the only relevant form of impossibility: the complete avoidance of help to evildoers is beyond human power – and divine power too if keeping sinners existing and alive is helping them sin. Thus, citizens pay taxes to governments committed to immoral practices; grocers sell food to gluttons. What constrains in the first case, besides fear of governmental use of force, is the moral necessity imposed by the duty to pay tax; in the second ultimately it is the limits of human capability. So, the relevant kind of mixed voluntariness is also present when we cannot fulfil our responsibilities without making some contributions to others' evildoing or otherwise cannot altogether avoid the contribution. My initial focus on coercion can, in short, mislead; it provides a paradigm of the sort of circumstance that generates mixed

---

[4] For some of the relevant history see Roger Roy C.SS.R., 'La Cooperation selon Saint Alphonse de Ligouri', 6 (1968) *Studia Moralia* 377–398.

voluntariness. Other forms of constraint, including moral limits on what one may do, also create the relevant sort of mixed voluntariness.

There is a corollary, which is perhaps more important than the analysis so far for clear practical thinking about cooperation issues: the coercion induced reluctance of one motivated to assist wrongdoing does not by itself indicate that the assisting actions are permissible. Reflection on the nature of coercion makes plain that, excusing factors aside, it has no tendency to justify a general suspension of moral norms. Coercion does transform one's options so that some chosen behaviours wrong in most circumstances can be morally justified. But it is often not clear even to the conscientious when this happens and how it affects the obligation not to contribute to wrongdoing. So the constraining circumstances raise the moral question, they do not answer it. In other words, if one were motivated without such circumstances to assist wrongdoing, the casuistical question of how to distinguish those helping actions whose moral character is changed by coercion from those that are not does not arise, and we would face only the unperplexing, common case of people working together to do wrong.

## II. The tradition's approach to the complexities of applying "do not help others sin"

The tradition provided the clarification needed to apply the norm prohibiting contributing to wrongdoing (a) by providing a morally significant basis for distinguishing the two kinds of cooperation noted above, and (b) by providing some general normative considerations relevant to the determination of whether material cooperation is justified in given cases. I will consider these in order.

### A. The difference between formal and material cooperation and why it matters ethically

St. Alphonsus provided the classic analysis of this problem; his analysis became the framework for subsequent Catholic discussions, including this one. A fundamental element of this framework is supplied by his definitions of formal and material cooperation, which provide a basis for the normative significance of the distinction between them. He formulates the definitions as follows:

> That [cooperation] is formal which concurs in the bad will of the other and cannot be without sin; that [cooperation] indeed is material which concurs only in the bad action of another, outside the intention of the cooperator.[5]

---

[5] St. Alphonsus Ligouri, edited by L. Gaude, *Theologia Moralis*, Rome 1910, Volume 1, p. 357; Lib. II, Tract. III, Cap.II, Dubium V, Art. III, #63. "Sed melius cum aliis dicendum, illam esse formalem quae concurrit ad malam voluntatem alterius, et nequit esse sine peccato; materialem vero illam quae concurrit tantum ad malam actionem alterius, praeter intentionem cooperantis."

These definitions assume that concurring in willing is necessary and sufficient for moral union in acting; when that union obtains, the cooperation is formal and the cooperator morally shares in the wrongdoing he or she wills; when one cooperates without such union in willing the wrongdoing, then, although one's act may be morally flawed because of the help it provides to wrongdoing, one does not morally share in the wrongdoing in the way that makes it one's own.

This reading implies that formal cooperation provides a kind of limit case for thinking about the application of the requirement not to contribute to wrong-doing. For when one cooperates formally one does not so much contribute to wrongdoing as do it, or do part of it, oneself, in the morally relevant sense of "do it". So, it is not this norm, but whatever norm is violated by the principal's wrongful action that one primarily violates in cooperating formally. Thus, a formal cooperator in abortion is guilty of abortion, not primarily of cooperation with it.

Of course, the application of St. Alphonsus' definitions requires understanding his contrast between concurring in another's bad will and concurring only in another's action. The meaning of the contrast is not transparent.

One thought, apparently embraced by some in the tradition, is that one concurs in another's bad will only if one acts cooperatively with the intention that the other formally sin, that is, if one of the things one wants to achieve by the cooperation is the other's sinning, as distinct from his or her possibly inculp-able wrongdoing.[6]

This understanding of formal cooperation would reduce it to assisting in wrongdoing with the added intention that the other sin, and so would explain the specific moral evil of formal cooperation as a kind of scandal: one's intent is to get the person to sin or sin more or to be more fully involved in it. St. Alphonsus does not indicate any such understanding in his definition of formal cooperation.[7]

More importantly, the Catholic conception of morality sees sin as bad for humans even apart from its specifically moral malice. Even those who inculpably do what is immoral harm human goods and persons. So there is something morally amiss in supporting the bad actions of people independently of whether they are culpable. And consequently there is a moral issue here distinct from leading others to sin.

A more promising approach to elucidating St. Alphonsus' contrast is to consider the elements of human willing involved in a person's acting and then to consider how they can concur with those of another person.

When one acts, one's will in so doing centrally includes the benefit or end one seeks in acting and the particular behaviour one chooses for the sake of realizing that end. Normally, one's action also includes some side effects, themselves neither chosen nor intended, of choosing to do some definite thing for the sake of some end. A performance chosen for the sake of some end sometimes fails to bring

---

[6] For references to this position see Grisez, *The Way of the Lord Jesus*, Vol. III, *Difficult Moral Questions*, Appendix 2, pp. 891–893, 895.
[7] See Grisez, *op. cit*, p. 891.

about the end and often is understood by the person choosing it to be insufficient by itself to bring about the end. Such facts do not make it any less a chosen means. Thus, when a person tries to get another to do something he wants done to achieve his ends, the effort to induce the other is a means to his end, and the other's action, seen as something the person brings about for his purposes, is also his means. Perhaps we might prefer to call this action an intermediate end. However it is named, it plainly falls in the line of what the primary agent is actively seeking to bring about.

Since one's intended end is the ground for what one chooses to do, both ends, ultimate and intermediate, and means are within one's intention in acting, but side effects are not; they are outside one's intention – *praeter intentionem*, in language used in the tradition at least since St. Thomas. Side effects are not what we are after in acting, or what we do to get what we are after, but we do bring them about voluntarily: we often know or should know that our actions will have certain bad side effects and this prospect might provide a reason to avoid that action. There is, however, a kind of inevitability about causing bad side effects: sometimes we cannot avoid causing them in the fulfilment of serious duties; sometimes we cannot avoid creating some bad results whatever we do.

Actions involving no intention to contribute to wrongdoing can have the effect of contributing to it; the conscientious taxpayer and grocer mentioned above are examples. Such actions are what St. Alphonsus and the later tradition regarded as material cooperation; they do contribute to wrongdoing, and that is why they are morally problematic. But they do not involve the kind of willing – intending and choosing – which could identify one's moral act with that of the wrongdoer. That one's action contributes to wrongdoing is a side effect. As St. Alphonsus explains, one's anticipation of the misuse of one's action by the principal wrongdoer does not make that misuse morally one's own.[8]

So the idea of concurring only in the action of the wrongdoer, with the wrong-doing itself remaining beyond one's intention is clear enough. But some unclarity remains in the idea of concurring in another's bad will. When does the intention or choice involved in an action that assists wrongdoing concur with the intention or choice of the wrongdoer?

The general answer: one's choice or intention concurs with that of a wrong-doer just in case something one chooses or intends is included within what is wrongful in the will of the wrongdoer. I believe that this general answer is frequently difficult to apply in cases where help is provided to wrongdoing under constrained circumstances, but that the underlying idea of one person's willing concurring with another's is not difficult.

Examples reveal this: let us consider a variation on the taxpayer. Consider a pro-abortion citizen who pays his taxes willingly, in part because they go to

[8] St. Alphonsus, *loc. cit.* : "Nec valet dicere quod tua actio, etsi indifferens, conjuncta tamen cum circumstantia pravae intentionis alterius, evadit mala; nam revera actio tua non est per se conjuncta cum mala intentionis illius, sed illud conjungit suam malam voluntatem cum actione tua; unde tua actio non erit causa per se influens in peccatum, sed tantum occasio, qua ille abutitur ad peccandum."

supporting abortion. This is not the kind of complex case the tradition was dealing with under the rubric of cooperation with evil, but it does illustrate the idea of concurrence in bad will: the government's relevant end is facilitating abortions and that very end is shared by this taxpayer. This is not an ultimate end for either, but clearly it is a state of affairs both intend. Cases become more complex when there is not this sharing of a common end.

So, let us now consider a variation on the grocer. This one is not a conscientious grocer; his concern about the gluttony of shoppers is quite opposite to that of the conscientious grocer: he wants them to overeat and to spend on fancy but unhealthy food. That pays his bills. So, he develops enticing ads and a style of salesmanship to appeal to people's intemperate desires; in so doing his will concurs with that of his gluttonous customers. This is also, and perhaps primarily, scandal, unless we can suppose that the gluttony is a fixed moral disposition his advertising can neither create nor enhance. But what his customers do as a means of satisfying unreasonable desire is something he does what he can to promote as a means to his end of paying the bills. There is a concurring in the means: theirs to buy food; his to cause them to do just this. So this is not a case of their abusing his action of providing food, but of his choosing to do what he can to bring about that abuse.

We might easily imagine a grocer acting this way doing so reluctantly because of his recognition of the evils of gluttony, but still carrying on in order to pay the bills. This would be a case approximating those in which helping in wrongdoing is perplexing in ways that call for moral analysis. Here, however, the reluctance does not point to a coercion-induced change of obligations. For the choice remains still a choice to cause others to buy for wrongful reasons and the morally induced regret does not transform the situation. The cooperation is formal.

Another variation: suppose the grocer is unwilling to induce people to gluttony; but the bills still need to be paid and he knows that will happen only if he has a pool of customers that includes the gluttonous. His will still seems to concur with those of his gluttonous customers, but it is now unclear whether there is a cooperative action. If he does nothing, literally zero, nothing at all, to get the gluttonous to act on their vice, even if their doing so is necessary for his goal, then his will to gluttony is a sin of thought only: he's happy they do it and hopes they will continue, but that's all. The difference between a wish and an intention is one's willingness to do something to realize the desired object. I am not aware that the tradition considered this as a distinct possibility, but it is a situation that arises often enough: one does not do anything to assist wrongdoing but has plans that cannot succeed unless the wrongdoing occurs, so one hopes it will. And that, at the very least, is a near occasion of sin to cooperate wrongly.

The main point of these examples has been to illustrate the concept of concurring in another's bad will. This idea is clear enough to apply. But the examples I have used tend to suggest that there are not likely to be difficult cases of formal cooperation: it will be obvious at least upon a moment's reflection when one's will concurs with another's wrongdoing, and so the hard cases arise only in the area of material cooperation.

I believe that this suggestion begins with a valid observation. Surely, there is no special obscurity when a person shares the bad end of another. And it certainly seems that when the intersection between the cooperator's and the principal's wills is only in the means, the cooperator formally cooperates only by a further intention to support wrongdoing. For in virtually all these cases the cooperator's means to his or her end are misused by the principal, and could be chosen by the cooperator without intending wrongdoing. Thus, the grocers discussed above are far less common than the grocer who does not induce the misuse of the food he sells but only accepts that as a side effect of performing a needed service for people. My manipulative grocer would need only the slightest self awareness to realize he was morally out of line.

More generally, I think it is true that most of the simple behaviours people choose to carry out in response to constraining circumstances in the knowledge that they contribute to wrongdoing can be material cooperation only, just as long as they are not actually carrying out the wrongdoing itself. So nurses can choose behaviours very closely and immediately related to abortion for the sake of keeping their jobs and be cooperating with abortion only materially (though not necessarily justifiably), and can without formal cooperation sedate a person carrying out a suicidal plan by refusing food and liquid.

Contrast these cases with the physician who gives a lethal injection at a patient's request: although the patient may be the main moral agent, the physician, by carrying out the patient's suicidal will, formally cooperates: one wants to be dead, the other wants to help bring about that state of affairs because asked to help. The only thing that could obscure this is rationalizing confusion about the patient's being in good faith and acting sincerely. When that condition obtains, the physician nevertheless chooses precisely to carry out the patient's objectively bad will. So even when the potentially obscuring condition is introduced into the description of the action, the action is formal cooperation, and does not present a difficult moral problem.

These considerations do not, however, show that there are no cases in which formal cooperation is difficult to detect. They show only that cases in which a simple behaviour supportive of wrongdoing is elicited by some kind of force are hardly the most difficult cases to see through. Generalizing from the cases I have found difficult to analyze, the cases requiring careful moral analysis are not so much those involving close behavioral connections with wrongdoing but are those in which one participates in organizing institutional and contractual relationships to keep wrongdoing at a distance by providing it, as it were, some social space. Thus, for example, a potential contractor won't come to an agreement unless one provides immoral services; one needs the deal, but finds providing the immoral services repugnant. So one decides to accept the deal with a provision that the immoral services will be provided by another party.

It is not immediately clear from this description whether or not this case involves formal cooperation. If the provision is simply an explicit statement that providing the immoral services is not part of one's contract, then it would seem that there is no cooperation, indeed the refusal of cooperation, with the other party's wrongdoing. But if one must do something to guarantee the provision, even if by someone else, of these services, then there seems to be formal cooperation: the means to getting the contract is providing for immoral services.

So keeping wrongdoing at a distance is compatible with formally cooperating in it, and I think that this is the main reason why the cases of institutional cooperation with evil are so difficult. (Another reason is the difficulty of understanding how formal groups, like institutions, can act, decide or intend.)

Catholic hospitals, at least in North America, are pressed by financial exigency and sometimes governmental demands to work closely with health care providers who routinely do very bad things. They are not asked to sponsor abortions and provide for euthanasia, but they are asked to integrate into a system that provides for such things. It is easy to suppose that, as long as the Catholic institution keeps its hands clean, there is no serious problem about formal cooperation and good grounds for thinking justified such material cooperation as is needed. But the supposition that the only cooperation in such cases is material is not generally justified. The details of the arrangements must be carefully considered to determine how exactly the Catholic institution's participation is related to the immoral activities; if it must guarantee them, then the cooperation is immoral, and if the cooperative venture cannot succeed unless the wrongdoing is carried on, even with no help from the Catholic partner, then the temptation and corporate sin of thought raise questions that are distinct from those of material cooperation.[9]

The preceding clarifications are meant to show that the tradition's first recommendation in responding to perplexities caused by the fact that one's actions contribute to wrongdoing is not trivial. In effect, the tradition says to the person thus perplexed: the fact that your action is behaviourially distinct from the wrongdoing to which you contribute does not guarantee that the wrongdoing is not your own. So before going on to consider whether the obligation not to contribute to wrongdoing might be set aside by other responsibilities, be sure that you are not more fully involved as one who oneself is willing the wrongdoing, however reluctantly.

### B. The conditions under which material cooperation is justified

The development of the contrast between formal and material cooperation suggests the nature of the reasoning that justifies some instances of material cooperation. In material cooperation the contribution to wrongdoing is real but a side effect of an action done for other reasons. The obligation not to contribute to wrongdoing is not a moral absolute and sometimes must be set aside in favour of the obligations grounded in those other reasons. So, the moral reasoning is an application of the complex ethics of accepting bad side effects. Thus, one reasonable reconstruction of the tradition's second recommendation to a person

[9] For a full discussion of this kind of case, see Grisez, *The Way of the Lord Jesus*, Vol. III, *Difficult Moral Questions*, question 87, pp. 391–402.

perplexed because his or her action provides support for wrongdoing is: when you know that the wrongdoing is not your own, you may do what supports it as a side effect only if it is justified to perform an act having this bad side effect along with other side effects the action has because of its contributing to wrongdoing.

The ethics of accepting bad side effects seems to me to be one of the under-developed parts of moral theology. The clearest part of this discussion concerns the norms which frame the evaluation of actions possibly wrong because of their side effects: the action having the side effect, considered in itself or independently of the side effect, must be morally permissible, and there must be a morally good reason for performing it. Beginning with St. Alphonsus, the tradition has insisted on these as conditions for justifiable material cooperation. St. Alphonsus puts it as follows:

> But the latter [material cooperation] is licit when the action is good or indifferent in itself, and when one has a reason for doing it that is both just and proportioned to the gravity of the other's sin and to the closeness of the assistance given for carrying out the sin.[10]

The reference to an action good or indifferent in itself and to a justifying reason ("*justa causa*") capture these necessary conditions for doing what has bad side effects. St. Alphonsus adds a third condition: the reason must be proportioned to the gravity of the wrongdoing and to the proximity of the help. This too is closely related to the usual rule for accepting bad side effects: that there must be a proportionate or a proportionately grave reason for doing what has a bad side effect. It is with respect to this condition, in which the moral weight of the side effects themselves is somehow assessed in comparison to the reasons for doing what causes them, that the tradition seems to me in need of development.

Some have suggested that the relevant comparison be carried out by consequentialist calculation. But even limited to this context, the attempt to compare the strength of reasons for action just as such, that is, just as the stronger, better reason, is in vain.[11] And there is little evidence that moralists in the tradition meant any such thing by proportionate reason. They tend to leave the determination of proportionate reason to the discernment of a prudent person.

This may have led some to be unreasonably permissive about accepting bad side effects. But there are rational steps which those of us less than fully prudent can take to imitate its perception. First, we can submit ourselves to the forms of reflection which can reveal whether our willingness to accept certain side effects is due to unreasonable limitations in our feelings toward others, towards spiritual realities and other aspects of human good to which our feelings cannot be adequately responsive.

The best known of these forms of reflection is the Golden Rule. This is a procedure for testing our feelings about the impact of our actions on those for

[10] St. Alphonsus, *loc. cit.*: "Haec autem est licita, quando per se actio est bona vel indifferens; et quando adest justa causa et proportionata ad gravitatem peccati alterius, et ad proximitatem concursus, qui praestatur ad peccati exsecutionem."
[11] See Grisez, *The Way of the Lord Jesus*, Vol. III, *Difficult Moral Questions*, pp. 884–885.

whom we do not have natural feelings of solidarity. By putting ourselves in their place, this procedure often shows that we would not stand for harm to the same goods our actions harm as side effects when they are the goods of those we love. Thus, unreasonable partiality, rooted in the natural limits of our affections, can be exposed by the Golden Rule. Plainly, this is an important consideration in evaluating any action having bad side effects that harm others. Since wrongdoing harms the wrongdoer at least morally and usually in other ways as well, and ordinarily harms other people as well, moral assessment of actions that assist wrongdoing must take into account not only the fact that wrongdoing is facilitated but also the further consequences for others of this fact.

Other natural limits on the way we feel about the side effects of our actions are also important in thinking about material cooperation. The bias of feeling against spiritual reality is especially relevant here: in cooperating with evil we place ourselves and others in occasions of sin; we compromise our capacity to give witness against the evil we support; we alienate ourselves from those harmed by the wrongdoing, and so on.

Second, after testing our feelings about the effects of materially cooperating, we can consider the entire set of reasons for and against doing what has these bad side effects in the light of the most general moral considerations and judge which comports better with them. Does doing an act with bad side effects or its alternative fit better with the common end of the whole of human life? The option that better fits is proportionate.

This suggests that St. Alphonsus' idea of proportion may be too narrow: his justifying reason must be proportioned to two things: the seriousness of the wrongdoing and the proximity of the help. But surely the overall moral importance of the action that supports wrongdoing in comparison with the choice not to do it is the whole of which St. Alphonsus' first proportion between the reason for acting and the seriousness of the sin is only a part.

Moreover, the issue of the proximity of the help, which the manualists treated as an important consideration for or against material cooperation, seems to me more a sign, and a fallible one at that, of the more fundamental moral considerations. It is easy to suppose that the closer one's act is to the wrongdoing, the more likely it will be itself to be wrongdoing or to support it unjustifiably. I argued above that this is a mistake. Indeed, the tradition implicitly acknowledges this: cooperation with evil that is quite immediate, in the sense understood by the manualists, that is, cooperation in which one does something that actually carries out the wrongful act – like opening the safe under duress – is routinely justified. It is true that the proximity of the action to the wrongdoing it helps affects people's awareness of the connection: helping that is closer in to wrongdoing is less ambiguously connected to it than helping that is more remote. That can affect how others will react to the action – surely an important side effect of cooperation. But it is these considerations about the often neglected side effects of material cooperation and not proximity as such that are morally decisive.

To sum up briefly: it is possible to think about material cooperation; and if we attend to the moral category of the thinking we can do so well and clearly: this thinking is an application of the complex ethics of accepting bad side effects. When we consider an action that facilitates wrongdoing, if that action is not morally flawed by features other than its doing just this, then our task is to pay careful attention to the further effects that the action may have just as cooperative with wrongdoing. If we pay attention to these effects of cooperation, then it becomes clear that significant, avoidable material cooperation is not presumptively permissible, but in fact difficult to justify. It is a mistake to think that because the ethics of accepting side effects is not settled by moral absolutes it is an area where permissiveness reigns. Bad side effects are really bad – they harm people, and the harm of wrongdoing includes damage to the moral selves of sinners and their victims. We need not and should not be casual in approaching this matter.

# 14

# Is there a distinctive role for the Catholic hospital in a pluralist society?

ANTHONY FISHER OP[1]

## 1. Introduction

MY OPENING STORY is of two imaginary hospitals. It aims to illustrate the ways some Catholic hospitals have gone in recent times and the things they offer or might offer a secular, pluralist society. Each hospital is a collage of aspects of various institutions in several countries, caricaturing some features to bring them more effectively to notice, to highlight similarities and differences, and to invite reflection upon what might lie behind them. Neither is a description of any actual hospital. After telling this somewhat provocative tale, I shall identify some of the challenges to which Catholic hospitals are responding, before outlining my position on whether there should be any difference(s) between them and secular institutions. I will suggest three differences in particular, and then propose six crucial matters for the future of Catholic hospitals.

### 1.1. A tale of two hospitals

St Mary Magdalen's Hospital is a large modern acute-care hospital in the middle of a major city. Founded in 1880 as a hospice for the poor, a century of devoted service by dozens of religious women has seen "The Magdalen" grow into one of the most highly reputed hospitals in the country. It offers "state of the art medical technology" in "hotel-style comfort", and is favoured by politicians and society leaders.

[1] Thanks to the following organisations for their assistance: the Australian Province of the Order of Preachers; the Australian Catholic University; the Beswick Family Foundation; the John Plunkett Centre for Ethics in Health Care; the Research Department of the Australian Catholic Bishops' Conference. The following individuals contributed ideas or commented upon drafts of the paper: Rev. Richard Finn OP (Blackfriars, Cambridge); Dr Warwick Neville (Research Department, ACBC); Dr Hayden Ramsay (Department of Philosophy, La Trobe University Melbourne); Mr Francis Sullivan (Australian Catholic Health Care Association); Dr Bernadette Tobin (Plunkett Centre); Mr Nicholas Tonti-Filippini (Consultant ethicist, Melbourne).

Since writing and presenting this paper the author has been appointed Episcopal Vicar for Health Care in the Archdiocese of Melbourne, Australia. The paper is not a policy statement of that Archdiocese and the issues raised and examples used are not directed at or taken from any institutions in that Archdiocese in particular.

While at one time The Magdalen had a staff of a handful of heroic sisters and a few lay staff, it now employs over a thousand people in various capacities. In 1979, on advice from a city firm of health management consultants, the hospital was independently incorporated and an expert health administrator, Mr Tecknay, was poached from a nearby hospital and appointed as CEO. Mr Tecknay has no religious affiliations but is well-disposed to the Christian ethos. He promises to lead the hospital into the twenty-first century with top-of-the-range services at competitive prices, the highest standards of patient comfort and choice, maximum throughput, big efficiency gains, tough labour relations, and a greater public profile. There are no longer any sisters on the hospital board or in any administrative or nursing positions, but the congregation continues to sponsor the hospital and, as far as their lawyers can work out, to own it; the sisters have reserved the right to determine the hospital's mission statement and to veto the appointment of any future CEO. There are still two sisters employed by the hospital: Kay, who is the chaplain, and Beth, who is mission officer.

Kay and Beth both have modest budgets, but ever since the cutbacks to all departments (except administration) the chaplaincy team – formerly a priest, two sisters and two lay people trained in clinical pastoral education – has been reduced to Kay working alone. Social workers have taken up some of the slack, e.g. bereavement counselling. Kay visits patients and is keen to try some new pastoral strategies such as the enneagram. Beth has been especially active in regularly revising the policy statements on mission, vision, patient empowerment, and affirmative action in employment. She consults widely with other hospitals – and usually with the staff – with a view to making such statements up-to-date and inclusive of plural opinion. She is very conscious of the need to maintain "our mission and values" and so has conducted conversations with staff about how they might better integrate policy and practice. In all this she sees herself as a "catalyst, tone-setter and facilitator". Kay and Beth have helped preserve some tangible signs of the congregation's traditions despite the massive redevelopments and relocations of the hospital complex in recent times. Some new religious symbols have been commissioned for the prayer room and a sculpture of the Foundress for the lobby. What was formerly the convent and chapel have been turned into offices, but provision has been made for an interfaith "quiet space", with a welcoming decor, some encouraging posters, and refreshment facilities.

Like all hospitals, The Magdalen has felt the pinch of resource constraints of late, but it has fared better than most. The hospital is on a firm financial footing, has significant endowments, and has entered a series of co-operative arrangements with various secular service providers to ensure that it maintains its competitive advantage. It enjoys particularly close co-operation with Mr Tecknay's former employers, the City General Hospital, with whom it operates an "integrated service delivery network" and health maintenance organisation. For example, the two hospitals operate a joint fertility programme, with City General doing the human embryo experimentation and IVF and The Magdalen offering various procedures called "GIFT". The hospital is proud of its reproductive technologies which are widely regarded as "Catholic IVF", paralleling natural family planning, "the Catholic contraceptive". It also has a large prenatal diagnosis and genetic counselling programme and this is one of its principal research strengths.

Among other things The Magdalen boasts "top of the range women's services". The sometimes frustrating Church strictures in this area are in general accepted with good humour, if not entirely understood by the staff. The hospital's lawyers and ethics consultants are skilled in finding ways around some of the harsher Church guidelines. Commonly patients wanting forbidden procedures are simply referred to City General for treatment. The Magdalen has an official "no abortion" policy but allows the early induction of handicapped children and is rather less squeamish than other church facilities about curettes (especially after rape) and drugs inducing miscarriages, either directly (in problem pregnancies) or indirectly (in certain other situations). Again, while an official "no sterilisation" policy is included in the mission statement, some women, several of whom were mentally handicapped, have been sterilised though usually in association with some other operation (such as a caesarean section or appendectomy) or "in order to" regulate the woman's menstruation. Likewise, a "no contraception" programme is applied flexibly, especially in situations where pregnancy would pose a threat to a woman's health, where natural methods of family planning have proved difficult, or as prophylaxis against diseases other than pregnancy. None of these 'exceptions', it should be said, is trumpeted abroad: the hospital is concerned to avoid public scandal, does not want to embarrass Church officials, the sponsor congregation or the benefactors, and if asked insists that it provides only "life-affirming" services.

At the opposite end of the city is St Norbert's Hospital founded by an order from somewhere in the Austro-Hungarian empire. Like St Mary Magdalen's, St Norbert's is a nineteenth century foundation, but it is rather more obviously so, given how little the buildings, religious decor and even the staff have changed. Originally an asylum for lunatics, waifs and disgraced girls, St Norbert's became a hospital in the modern sense and diversified in various ways. Yet it resisted expansion into every medical specialty or hi-tech test or therapy, and so never achieved the size or status of The Magdalen, remaining a much more local concern. The hospital relies on an unpredictable mix of bequests, benefactions, government grants, fundraising activities, and user and insurer contributions. Staff and community relations are very good and Mother Administrator is something of a genius at finding funds when urgently required. But only prayer and Mother's peculiar talents have kept the hospital from bankruptcy to date.

The smaller scale of St Norbert's made it rather easier for the sisters to hold onto the management of the hospital, although they have an advisory board of local Catholic worthies and grateful former patients. The sisters provide several of the nurses, and semi-retired nuns are encouraged to chat with patients and staff, and generally be obvious and welcoming. The favourite of all is Sr Mary Philomena who, it seems, attended the births of everybody's grandparents and wanders around the wards distributing rosary beads and a kindly word to all, Muslims and atheists included. The sisters are ageing and professing too few to replace those who die on the job, and so must employ a significant number of lay staff. Nonetheless the sisters are sufficiently numerous and immersed in their congregation's charism to unselfconsciously communicate it to the rest of the staff and, no doubt, the patients. They continue to prefer staff with a strong faith (although this has gotten them into a few scrapes with the unions and the Anti-Discrimination Board), they require all staff to undertake professional development in Catholic bioethics, and they encourage them to take part in retreat days.

Pastoral care is perhaps the most distinctive feature of the hospital. In addition to Sr Philomena's attentions, patients are guaranteed regular visits from a pastoral care team (which includes sisters, a priest and others), and ready access to the sacraments, daily Mass, daily prayer and other devotions. In addition to its particular identification with the local ethnic communities, St Norbert's is chosen by many non-Catholics because they think it is different: they report it is "a peaceful place", "prayerful", "personal", "a real community hospital". Responding to developments in the surrounding society, the sisters have decided to focus their energies on those they think are most neglected nowadays or most at risk of harm in other hospitals, and on areas of healthcare unfashionable in most institutions. Preference is given to poorer patients; more affluent patients are asked to help contribute to this by sponsoring an underprivileged patient with the same condition as their own, and some do so willingly. Other hospitals regularly divert patients who are unlikely to meet their bills to St Norbert's and this is certainly putting a strain on the finances. In conjunction with some friendly parishes and reporters, the hospital has been active in promoting a Christian health maintenance organisation; it has also actively sought greater co-operation among like-minded services with a view to establishing an "integrated Christian healthcare network".

The jewel in St Norbert's crown is its hospice for the dying. Highly regarded throughout the city, it has successfully tendered to provide palliative care services to other hospitals and the district. Many of the patients are suffering from end-stage AIDS. All are treated with special love and respect, and assisted to live their last days in comfort, surrounded by those they love, and well-prepared for death both emotionally and spiritually. The hospice stands resolutely against the contemporary tendency either to withdraw all care (even feeding and hydration) from patients thought better off dead, or to deliberately overdose them. It is equally resistant to the trend to ration limited resources on the basis of so-called "quality of life" judgments which, the sisters observe, always seem to put their "favourites" at the bottom of the heap. Not that St Norbert's is inclined to over-treatment either: the technological imperative and immoderate expectations of medicine and lifespan are discouraged by the sisters.

Less well-known than the hospice is St Norbert's ovulation clinic which provides natural alternatives not only to the contraceptive pill but also to the reproductive technologies offered to the infertile elsewhere in the city. The hospital is also involved in several community and home-care programmes: accommodation and support for women with unplanned pregnancies, for drug-addicts, and for street kids; physiotherapy, special education and respite care for the handicapped; a rescue and support service for mental health patients abandoned to 'care in the community'; home visitation and community nursing for shut-ins; a state of the art hospice-in-the-home programme; and respite for families over-burdened with the care of a dependent. Despite its old-fashioned ethos these particular specialties have attracted some research projects to the hospital.

### 1.2. Current challenges

My story suggests two kinds of response to the challenges of modernity made by Catholic hospitals in recent years: one has been to offer top-quality healthcare on competitive terms, but at some cost to "Catholic identity"; another maintains religious traditions and particular, often fairly low-tech, forms of care, but at the expense of becoming rather marginal. No-one should doubt the enormous contribution which both styles of hospital have made over the centuries and still today, and the extraordinary self-spending by their staff, especially religious women, almost always without having enjoyed the opportunity of studying theology, philosophy or even "healthcare ethics". Many hospitals have moved in directions which involve elements of both our imaginary hospitals, or perhaps different directions altogether; and no-one pretends that any is completely ideal. Both styles are in danger of extinction, the second perhaps more immediately than the first. Why is that?

The Catholic Church is the oldest and largest provider of healthcare in the world. From the time the apostles healed a paralytic at the Beautiful Gate in Jerusalem (Acts 3:1–10), Christians have cared for the sick as part of *hospitalitas*. St John Chrysostom records that already in his day the sick and the convalescent in Antioch were nursed in Christian hospitals.[2] Monks established hospices and welcomed sick pilgrims and neighbours. In the mediaeval period there were fraternities and orders of hospitallers. In the early modern and modern periods, many new nursing congregations were founded and large hospitals such as St Mary Magdalen's and St Norbert's evolved as part of an extraordinary network of institutions established largely by religious women and their benefactors. Today there are over 7,000 acute-care hospitals, 4,000 day-care centres, and 10,000 nursing and long-term care centres operating under Catholic auspices

---

[2] *In Mat. Hom*; 66, 3; *Ad Stagyr. Conc*; 3, 13; *In Act. Hom.* 45, 4. On the history of Christian/Catholic health care see: D Amundsen and G Ferngren, 'Medicine and religion: early Christianity through the Middle Ages', in M Marty and K Vaux (eds.), *Health, Medicine and the Faith Traditions*, Philadelphia: Fortress 1982, pp. 93–132; Jesús Alvarez Gómez, 'The care of the sick in the history of the Church', 31 (1996) *Dolentium hominum* 45–47; George Rosen, *From Medical Police to Social Medicine: Essays on the History of Healthcare*, New York: Science History 1974. On the documents of Catholic identity see Benedict Ashley OP, 'The documents of Catholic identity', in Russell E Smith (ed.), *The Gospel of Life and the Vision of Health Care: Proceedings of the 15th Workshop for Bishops*, Braintree, Massachusetts: Pope John Center 1996, pp. 10–16.

throughout the world.[3] In the United States alone, 10% of all hospitals – 625 in total – are Catholic, and there are approximately 700 Catholic nursing homes and growing numbers of clinics, ambulatory care, home health and assisted-living programmes; the US Catholic health system treats 65 million people a year, employs three quarters of a million, and spends $45 billion per annum.[4] The Church is even more involved in some countries' health systems, but rather less so in others. In Britain, for instance, the Church's principal contri-bution is at the level of nursing home care. This means that the rôle of a Catholic hospital will vary enormously in the various countries represented at this conference and much of what I say would have to be modified to apply, if at all, to some.

Overall, however, this century has seen a huge growth in the scale and activ-ities of all hospitals, Church hospitals included, with a parallel growth in public expectations.[5] Catholic hospitals have commonly evolved from "family concerns"

---

[3] See Pontifical Council for Pastoral Assistance to Healthcare Workers, *Ecclesiae Instituta Valetu-dini Fovendae Toto Orbe Terrarum* (Index: 'Catholic Health Care Institutions in the World'), Vatican City: 1994. The Pontifical Council reported that there are 21,757 Catholic healthcare facilities in 135 countries (7,193 hospitals, 4,104 nursing homes, 4,824 aged care centres, 166 homes for long-term patients, 455 medical facilities for the disabled, 291 rehabilitation centres, 32 day hospitals, 4,169 dispensaries, 49 consulting rooms, 151 leprosariums, 323 home care services). This includes: 273 facilities in Australia (78 hospitals, 132 nursing homes, 50 aged care centres and 8 centres for the disabled); 199 facilities in Britain (24 hospitals, 48 nursing homes, 112 aged care centres, and 15 other centres); 106 facilities in the Republic of Ireland (49 hospitals, 10 nursing homes, 27 aged care centres, and 18 other centres); and 1,592 facilities in the USA (811 hospitals, 451 nursing homes, 267 aged care centres, and 62 centres for chronic, disabled, rehabilitation, daycare or out-patients). The index runs to over 1,000 A4 pages.

[4] Patricia Cahill, 'The environment in which Catholic healthcare finds itself', 27/2 (1997) *Origins* 27–29.

[5] On the enormous historical, economic and cultural developments which challenge the identity and existence of Catholic hospitals see: Henry J Aaron, *Serious and Unstable Condition: Financing America's Healthcare*, Washington DC: Brookings Institution 1991; John R Amos et al., *The Search for Identity: Canonical Sponsorship of Catholic Healthcare*, St Louis: Catholic Health Associa-tion 1993; Australian Catholic Bishops Conference, *Statement of the Australian Catholic Bishops' Conference in support of the Process of 'Integration 2000'*, Canberra 1997; John Beal, 'Catholic hospitals: how Catholic will they be?', (1994–95) *Concilium: Catholic Identity*, London: SCM Press 1995, 81–90; Joseph Bernardin, 'Crossroads for the Church's health care ministry', 22/24 (1992) *Origins* 409–411; Bernardin, 'Medicine's Moral Crisis' (AMA Address), 25/27 (1995) *Origins* 454–457; Catholic Health Association of the United States, *No Room in the Marketplace: The Healthcare of the Poor*, St Louis 1986; Charles E Curran, 'The Catholic identity of Catholic institutions', 58 (1997) *Theological Studies* 90–108; Richard A McCormick, 'The Catholic hospital: mission impossible?', 24/39 (1995) *Origins* 648–653; Joseph J Piccione, 'Catholic healthcare: justice, fiscal realities, and moral norms', in Russell E Smith (ed.) *The Gospel of Life and the Vision of Health Care: Proceedings of the 15th Workshop for Bishops*, Braintree: Pope John Center 1996, pp. 95–108; Francis Sullivan, 'Dreaming the impossible dream', 73/2 (1996) *Australasian Catholic Record* 131–135; Doctrine Committee of the National Conference of Catholic Bishops, *Ethical and Religious Directives for Catholic Healthcare Services*, Washington DC: NCBC 1994 (also in 24/27 (1994) *Origins* 450–462).

into something more like "franchise operations".[6] The very Catholic sub-culture in which they were founded has largely vanished, and declining vocations and new priorities have meant their founder congregations no longer lead or staff the hospitals. Day-to-day management has been handed over to lay trustees, administrators and clinical staff who, believers or not, represent a wide range of value perspectives. Relying less and less on the institutional Church and private donors for finance and more and more upon government and private insurers, these institutions have also lost considerable financial and administrative autonomy.

Escalating healthcare costs have led governments, insurers and hospitals recently to engage in budget cutbacks, aggressive cost containment, rationalisation such as closures and mergers, and rationing of services. In some places, the very survival of religious and other charitable hospitals is threatened by such cut-backs and by competition from for-profit hospitals. The market is increasingly shaping healthcare relationships: healthcare is more and more regarded as a commodity subject to the consumer market, supplied by "healthcare providers" to "healthcare consumers" under the direction of "healthcare managers", rather than as a priceless form of compassionate service between a professional and a patient. "No margin, no mission" has become the catchcry.

As a result there has been some radical questioning of the goals and usefulness of Catholic hospitals in recent years. Richard McCormick, for instance, has argued that, in order to be genuinely Catholic, hospitals must sustain an appropriate culture. But that goal is compromised today by the depersonalised atmosphere in which medicine is practised, the trend to viewing it as a mere business, and the pressures to "exit" patients quicker and quicker.[7] That same surrounding culture "tries to transcend mortality, investing bigtime in sick-care and medicalizing more basic human problems". Meanwhile hospitals are declining in importance as healthcare moves away from major institutions towards out-patient, community-based care. With respect to their specifically Catholic *raison d'être*, Catholic hospitals have, McCormick concludes, "become practically dysfunctional... The heart of the Catholic healthcare culture is gone. The mission has become impossible".[8]

---

[6] John Beal ('Catholic hospitals: how Catholic will they be?') uses the term "family businesses" to denote the former free-standing institutional apostolates of religious congregations, owned, operated and in large measure staffed by their members immersed in their congregation's charism, and "franchise operations" to denote situations where sponsoring congregations have independently incorporated their hospitals, handed over their administration to others and radically reduced their involvement, but maintain some connection – lending the institution its name and patrimony, retaining powers over the corporate statutes and the appointment to certain key positions, setting the corporate philosophy and mission statement, approving budgets, and perhaps participating in pastoral care or at board level.

[7] I presume McCormick here means "pressures to discharge patients quicker", although another possible interpretation, "pressures to commit euthanasia upon patients", is also true.

[8] Richard A. McCormick, 'The Catholic hospital: mission impossible?'; cf. John Cardinal O'Connor, 'The temptation to become just another industry: healthcare', 25/27 (1995) *Origins* 452–454 at 452.

Recently there has been a trend, especially in the US, for healthcare providers to reorganize into horizontally and vertically integrated systems, becoming part of what Joseph Piccione has called a "healthcare ecosystem" instead of relatively self-contained, stand-alone institutions.[9] Catholic and secular providers are co-sponsoring joint delivery networks or health maintenance organizations which can better provide the full spectrum of services and compete for the business of third-party payers and for market share. But this survival strategy is not without its own difficulties. Benedict Ashley and Germain Grisez have recently argued that such arrangements often involve wrongful co-operation in evil, whether formal[10] or material.[11] When such arrangements lead Catholic hospitals to engage in such wrongful practices, Ashley suggests that this radically erodes their Catholic identity while doing no real service to the poor, sick and dying.[12] Those responsible for Catholic hospitals must never subordinate their mission to their (otherwise quite necessary) concerns for economic stability, professional reputation and cultural acceptability.

> When to do good by evil means is the only option our culture and our government seem to allow us, we should create new channels for our service to the poor, remembering the admonition of the Lord, If they will not hear you, "shake the dust from your feet" and go elsewhere (Lk 9:5).[13]

After examining various strategies to avoid this grave result, Grisez also concludes that since Catholic hospitals may not always be able to avoid wrongful co-operation and remain financially viable, we ought to be prepared (and should now be preparing) to give them up. "Institutions like hospitals are only means for carrying out a healthcare apostolate. Like other means, their usefulness is

---

[9] Joseph J Piccione, 'Catholic healthcare: justice, fiscal realities, and moral norms', p. 97.

[10] Grisez argues that unlike hoteliers, the administrators of a hospital ordinarily do sponsor any immoral activities which are done in it or done by associated providers because they ordinarily intend each and every procedure carried out by the parties, or at least that any such procedures, if and when they occur, are performed well and with consent. Even if considerable care is taken to "isolate" the hospital from the immoral activities of one of its collaborators, the negotiators and subsequent managers will probably intend that those services are indeed provided, if only by the collaborators; those strategies which succeed in avoiding formal co-operation are usually impractical. "In sum, entirely avoiding formal co-operation in immoral practices will be difficult indeed. It can arise in ways that are not obvious and it seems unavoidable in any arrangement that would satisfy a mandate to provide all services." See Germain Grisez, 'How far may Catholic hospitals co-operate with providers of immoral services?', in *The Way of the Lord Jesus*. Vol. 3: *Difficult Moral Questions*, Quincy, Illinois: Franciscan Press 1997, q. 87. (First published in 62/4 (1995) *Linacre Quarterly* 67–72 and subsequently revised.)

[11] Grisez argues that the material co-operation of Catholic hospitals with others in immoral activities of those others is usually morally unacceptable because it is an occasion of formal co-operation or other corruption, causes scandal (in the theological sense), impairs the hospital's (and its members' and the wider Church's) capacity to give credible witness against evil, and/or is unfair to injured parties.

[12] Benedict Ashley OP, 'The documents of Catholic identity', p. 15.

[13] Ashley, 'The documents of Catholic identity', p. 16.

limited. Remaining attached to them as their usefulness diminishes will entail infidelity to the good they formerly served."[14]

McCormick, Ashley and Grisez's views have been contested by several authors, and ways of maintaining identity and avoiding moral compromise proposed, even within integrated delivery networks.[15] But clearly very careful thought must be given to any such arrangements in advance, various procedural safeguards put in place, and eternal vigilance exercised by all concerned, all with respect to the maintenance of a specifically Christian and Catholic character.

### 1.3. Is there any difference between a Catholic and a secular hospital?

Which leads us to the questions: is there such a thing as a specifically Christian institutional character? Should Catholic hospitals be different to secular institutions? I suspect a resounding "yes" would be given by almost anyone uneducated in or uncorrupted by moral theology. But ever since the Second Vatican Council celebrated a new "openness to the world"[16] there has been a heated debate in theological circles over the specificity of Christian ethics. In many ways it is a replay of the age-old matches between philosophy and theology, between different styles of theology, between Catholics and Protestants, and between fans and foes of the Enlightenment. Indeed the debate goes back at least to deuteronomistic and prophetic utterance against following other gods, consorting with their devotees and adopting their practices, and the Pauline suspicion of the wisdom of this world and insistence on the need of Christians to abandon their former ways and "put on the new man". In Tertullian it famously had voice in the questions: "What has Athens to do with Jerusalem, the Academy to do with the Church?

[14] Germain Grisez. 'How far may Catholic hospitals co-operate with providers of immoral services?'. The US Bishops, though more optimistic, point out that "new partnerships can pose serious challenges to the viability of the identity of Catholic healthcare institutions and services, and their ability to implement these directives in a consistent way, especially when partnerships are formed with those who do not share Catholic moral principles. The risk of scandal cannot be underestimated when partnerships are not built upon common values and moral principles. Partnership opportunities for some Catholic healthcare providers may even threaten the continued existence of other Catholic institutions and services, particularly when partnerships are driven by financial considerations alone. Because of the potential dangers involved in the new partnerships that are emerging, an increased collaboration among Catholic-sponsored healthcare institutions is essential and should be sought before other forms of partnerships." (Doctrine Committee of the NCCB, *Ethical and Religious Directives for Catholic Healthcare Services.*)
[15] M Cathleen Kaveny and James F Keenan, 'Ethical issues in healthcare restructuring', 56 (1995) *Theological Studies* 136–150; Kevin D O'Rourke, 'Making mission possible', 76/6 (1995) *Health Progress* 45–47; Russell E Smith, 'Ethical quandary: forming hospital partnerships', in Russell E Smith (ed.) *The Gospel of Life and the Vision of Health Care: Proceedings of the 15th Workshop for Bishops*, Braintree: Pope John Center 1996, pp. 109–123. (First appeared in 63/2 (1995) *Linacre Quarterly*, 87–96, and subsequently revised.)
[16] *Lumen gentium* 21, 36–37; *Gaudium et spes* 36, 41, 43, 56.

What concord can there be between heretics and Christians?...Away with all attempts to produce a mottled Christianity of Stoic, Platonic and dialectic composition. We want no curious disputation after possessing Christ Jesus, no research after enjoying the gospel!"[17] Ancient as this debate is, Servais Pinckaers observes that

> The question has become particularly acute in the discussion of concrete moral problems presented to public opinion in a pluralistic society. Christians have been struggling to establish renewed bases for friendly collaboration with those who do not share their faith. Faced with the difficult problems of contraception, abortion, euthanasia [and so on]...may Christians follow their own lights, norms, and criteria implying special standards, or should they remain on the same level with others and form their judgments according to merely rational criteria, with the help of philosophy and the behavioural sciences? If the second alternative were preferable, could they go still further and reinterpret Christian morality in its entirety according to purely human values?[18]

In the 1970s and early '80s this debate took the form of the impasse between "autonomous ethics"[19] and the "faith ethics". Influential authors such as Josef Fuchs argued that "Christian ethics is...a morality of authentic humanness...- not specifically Christian values but universal, human ones."[20] Or as Charles Curran put it recently in a review of the literature on Catholic institutional identity: "what Catholics are obliged to do in this world is at the very least not that much different from what all others are called to do".[21] What, on this account, does being a Christian add? Christian intentionality (the "transcendental" inspiration of faith, hope and love) and a certain clarity (because of the sublime teaching and example of Jesus). On this account the Catholic hospital in a pluralist society would not be expected to have a particularly distinctive identity, except that it would aim to be the humanly best hospital, demonstrating the greatest respect for human dignity and rights, for goods such as life and health, for human norms and virtues, and the technically best hospital, demonstrating the highest standards of rescue, healing and care.

---

[17] Tertullian, *De praescriptione haereticorum* 7.

[18] Servais Pinckaers, *The Sources of Christian Ethics*, trans. Mary Noble, Washington DC: Catholic University of America Press 1995, p. 98.

[19] Advocates of "autonomous ethics" included Böckle, Curran, Fuchs, Gustafson, Häring, McCormick and Schüller. Many of these were collected in and popularised by the second Curran-McCormick reader (Charles E Curran and Richard A McCormick (eds.), *The Distinctiveness of Christian Ethics*, New York: Paulist 1980), which stayed on the list of compulsory readings in Anglophone seminaries and theology schools until superseded by new theological fashions in the late '80s.

[20] Joseph Fuchs, 'Gibt es eine spezifisch Christliche Moral?', 185 (1970) *Stimmen der Zeit* 99–112; English translation in Curran & McCormick, *The Distinctiveness of Christian Ethics*, pp. 3–19, at p. 8.

[21] Charles E Curran, 'The Catholic identity of Catholic institutions', 58 (1997) *Theological Studies* 90–108, at p. 92.

But where, some have asked, is Christ in all this? Critics of "autonomous ethics" have suggested that it is a radical misreading of the call of Vatican II[22] and have posited instead a morality derived entirely, or at least very largely, from Christian revelation, personal religious vocation, the experience and wisdom of the Christian community, and so on.[23] These writers insist that Christian faith makes many demands upon the disciple that no non-Christian would be bound to or even likely to consider; Christian revelation subverts mere human reasoning about moral matters, putting faithful Christians very often in a position *contra mundum*. On this account a Catholic hospital would be expected to offer a pluralist society something rather different in the way of healthcare at many levels.

Space precludes a fuller analysis of the aforementioned controversy, but it will obviously have implications for how one views the difference or not between religious and secular hospitals. For now let me simply assert that the rapprochement between faith and reason in ethics proposed by writers such as Germain Grisez and Servais Pinckaers is a way forward. Reason, on their account, will indeed take us a long way to discovering and applying moral norms, and to cultivating good character. We will have much common ground with non-believers without undue appeal to revelation. Christian faith has a largely confirmatory, inspirational and empowering function here. But it is more than this. Revelation affects the whole way we understand God, each other, the world, and ourselves: it will thus inevitably colour any application by the believer of 'natural' principles, and perhaps bring some additional norms as well.[24] There is an ongoing dialectic between the human and the divine, the reasoned, philosophical natural law and the faith-given divine law, the natural virtues and the supernatural ones. So Christian faith and love operate not merely at some abstract 'transcendental' level of intentionality, but in concrete virtues, norms and actions; Christian morality is more than "spirituality" narrowly understood. While Christian faith does not annul nor contradict natural law and virtue, it inwardly transforms them and calls the disciple to be what she can be and to do what she can do by virtue of being not only human but also a child of God. How else could we make sense of the consecrated celibacy, the total self-giving, the particular priorities, the way of relating to patients, demonstrated by the sisters of St Norbert's? Any description

---

[22] Kasper, for instance, argues that the autonomy of secular disciplines and affairs proposed anew by Vatican II has been commonly misread as reducing the field of the specifically religious to certain spiritual tasks (such as worship, narrowly defined) and the Church's internal problems; equally problematical has been the "overadaptation" of Christian morality "whether to secularized bourgeois civilization or to revolutionary liberation movements". He asks whether Christianity cannot make some particular contribution to the transformation of our life and our world? (Walter Kasper, 'The power of Christian love to transform the world: the relationship between Chritianity and society', *Faith and the Future*, trans. R Nowell, London: Burns & Oates, 1985, p. 86.)

[23] e.g. Hauerwas, Kasper, Schürmann, Ratzinger and von Balthasar.

[24] Germain Grisez, *The Way of the Lord Jesus*, Vol. 1, *Christian Moral Principles*, Chicago: Franciscan Herald Press 1983; Pinckaers, *The Sources of Christian Ethics*, pp. 102–103, 132–133; cf. Kasper, *Faith and the Future*, pp. 96ff.

of their vocation as merely one more "mode of authentic humanness" seems rather too limp. On this account, like other institutional apostolates of the Catholic Church and other activities of individuals and groups of Christians, a Catholic hospital might be expected to have much in common with others but also much that is different.

Vatican II described the Church as a sacrament – a sign and instrument of our union with God.[25] Walter Kasper suggests that this is effected "by means of its prophetic utterance and symbolic action (*martyria*), through the celebration of its worship (*leitourgia*), and above all…through its entire life and its whole pattern of behaviour (*diakonia*)".[26] Insofar as healthcare ministry is an expression of this broadly sacramental character of the Church,[27] Catholic hospitals should be signs and instruments of union with God effected by service of the sick, witness given to Gospel truth, and worship offered in prayer and pastoral care. In what remains of this paper I will explore what these three "sacramental" aspects of healthcare might say about the distinctive rôle of the Catholic hospital in a pluralist society.

## 2. Catholic hospitals as diakonia

### 2.1. *Preferential option for the poor*

The Old Testament is replete with references to God's siding with the poor and the requirements of justice towards them. The Torah requires special provision to be made for the poor, weak and outcast, the widows, orphans and refugees.[28] "Since the poor will always be with you," says the Lord, "I command you to open wide your hand to the poor and needy" (Dt 15:11). When Israel fails in this regard God "rages in the prophet's voice":[29] "What do you mean by crushing my people, by grinding the face of the poor?" says the Lord of hosts.[30] In his programmatic reading from the same prophet at the beginning of his ministry, Jesus declares himself anointed to bring good news to the poor (Lk 4:17) and later in the same Gospel he beatifies them (Lk 6:20; cf. 14:13–23; 16:19–31; 19:8).

Much has been written in recent years, not least by John Paul II, about the Church's preferential love for the poor.[31] But it has a long history in Christian

---

[25] *Lumen gentium* 1, 9, 48; *Gaudium et spes* 42, 45.

[26] Kasper, *Faith and the Future*, p. 95.

[27] cf. John E Curley, 'Catholic identity, Catholic integrity', 72/8 (1991) *Health Progress* 56–60, at p. 57.

[28] e.g. Ex 22:25–27; 23:6, 10–11; Lev 19:10; 23:22; Dt 24:14–15, 19–22.

[29] Juliana Casey, *Food for the Journey: Theological Foundations of the Catholic Healthcare Ministry*, St Louis: Catholic Health Association, 1991, p. 76, quoting Abraham Joshua Heschel, *The Prophets*, New York: Harper and Row Torchbooks 1969, vol.2, p.5.

[30] Isa 3:15; cf. 10:1–2; 11:4; 14:30; 25:4–6; 32:7; 58:3–7; Jer 2:34; Amos 2:6–8; 4:1–2; 5:11; 8:4–6; Zech 7:10.

[31] e.g. John Paul II, *Sollicitudo rei socialis. Encyclical on Social Concerns*, London: Catholic Truth Society 1987; *Centesimus annus: Encyclical on the Centenary of 'Rerum novarum'*, London: CTS 1991.

social teaching and practice, especially in institutional apostolates such as hostels, orphanages, schools and soup kitchens. This same mandate was behind the foundation of hospitals like St Mary Magdalen's and St Norbert's. And one of the principal reasons given by the hierarchy for their continued commitment to hospitals is that in societies where access is inadequate, at least for some, Catholic institutions can pay particular attention to the needs of the poor.[32] This is perhaps most obvious in those countries where universal access to healthcare is yet to be achieved: but even in those countries where such access is more or less guaranteed, there will be those who "slip through the safety net" and there will be pressures to limit some people's access even to reasonable care whether out of partiality, for the sake of cost-containment or otherwise. 'Charity' hospitals will always have their place.

### 2.2. Preferential option for the sick

In the Old Testament God's preferential care is not reserved for the poor only but to a larger group of those disadvantaged in various ways. Thus the prophet Ezekiel (34:1–6) rails against "the pastors of Israel": "You eat the fat, you clothe yourselves with wool ... but you do not feed the sheep. You have not strengthened the weak, you have not healed the sick, you have not bound up the injured, you have not brought back the strayed ...". The Psalmist (147:2–3) and the prophets respond, as it were, trusting that the Lord God is the One to "gather the outcasts of Israel, heal the broken-hearted and bind up all their wounds".

This divine physician came among us in Jesus Christ. And heal he did, serving people not only by preaching to and absolving them, but also by curing them. He restored sight to the blind (Mk 8:22–26; 10:46–52; Mt 20:29–34), hearing to the deaf (Mk 7:32–37; Mt 11:5) and speech to the mute (Mt 9:32–33; 12:22; Lk 11:14). He cured the woman with a haemorrhage (Mk 5:25–34), lepers (Mk 1:40–45; Lk 17:12–19) and the paralysed and lame (Mk 2:3–12; Mt 8:6–13; 21:14; Jn 5:3–8). He even restored dead people to life (Mk 5:35–43; Lk 7:12–17; Jn 11; cf. Mk 9:17–29). For Mark Jesus is very much the exorcist-healer. Luke records that in initiating his ministry, Jesus declared programmatically that he had been anointed not only to bring good news to the poor but also sight to the blind (Lk 4:17) and that he later compared himself with a physician (of bodies and souls: Lk 5:31), with a miraculous preacher-healer (Lk 7:22–23),

---

[32] e.g. Directive 3 of the US Bishops' *Ethical and Religious Directives for Catholic Healthcare Services*. "In accord with its mission, Catholic healthcare should distinguish itself by service to and advocacy for those people whose social condition puts them at the margins of our society and makes them particularly vulnerable to discrimination: the poor, the uninsured and the underinsured; children, the unborn, single parents and the elderly; those with incurable diseases and chemical dependencies; and racial minorities, immigrants and refugees. In particular, the person with mental or physical disabilities, regardless of the cause or severity, must be treated as a unique person of incomparable worth, with the same right to life and to adequate healthcare as all other persons."

and with a Good Samaritan nursing a Jew mugged and left for dead (Lk 10:29–37). His many cures are summed up by Luke (14:40): "Now when the sun was setting, all those who had any sick with various diseases brought them to him; and he laid his hands on them and healed them." Likewise Matthew (15:30–31; cf. Mk 7:37) tells us: "Great crowds came to him, bringing with them the lame, the maimed, the blind, the mute, and many others. They put them at his feet, and he cured them, so that the crowd was amazed when they saw the mute speaking, the maimed whole, the lame walking, and the blind seeing. And they praised the God of Israel." Indeed so replete was his life with the cure of every kind of ailment and disease (Mt 9:35) that Matthew interpreted Jesus' mission as the fulfilment of the prophecy of Isaiah: "He took away our infirmities and bore our diseases" (Mt 8:17; cf. Is. 53:4).[33]

Why have Christians always engaged in healthcare and institutionalized it so? The most obvious reason is: so as to make patients well – a goal which is self-evidently good and choice-worthy.[34] By establishing hospitals the Church has enabled people who would not otherwise have had access to certain kinds of healthcare to have a chance of it and what it enables, reflecting respect for human dignity, active compassion and service of the common good – human values well-supported in Christian faith. But there is more to it than this: Jesus told his disciples *to continue his own healing mission*: he commanded them to "heal the sick, raise the dead, cleanse lepers" (Mt 10:8) and to embrace the likes of these sick people as part of the kingdom (Lk 14:12–14). In all their tasks he promised them his divine assistance: "Truly, truly, I say to you, whoever believes in me will also do the works that I do; and even greater works than these will that one do" (Jn 14:12; cf. Lk 10:17–20). Thus, in serving the sick, Christians claim to be engaging not merely in a job but in an "apostolate", a "ministry", a holy service, mediating the healing compassion of God to a suffering world, serving the suffering Christ in their patients.[35] Other writers in this volume have described how professional healthcare can be a genuinely Christian vocation.[36] Even if much of what Catholic hospitals actually do is very similar to what occurs in other hospitals, the commitment of the hospital's sponsors, administrators and personnel to healthcare as diakonia to the poor and sick should colour its whole life. Embracing the whole person – body, mind and spirit – with compassion and love, Catholic hospitals say to the sick, the infirm

---

[33] On the very common use by the Fathers of this title for the Lord see G Dumiege, 'Le Christ Médecin dans la littérature chrétienne des premiers siècles', 48 (1972) *Revista di archeologia christiana* 115–141.

[34] cf: Grisez, *The Way of the Lord Jesus*, Vol. 1, *Christian Moral Principles;* Bonifacio Honings, 'The Charter for Healthcare Workers: A synthesis of Hippocratic ethics and Christian morality', 31 (1996) *Dolentium hominum* 48–52.

[35] Pontifical Council for Pastoral Assistance to Healthcare Workers, *Charter for Healthcare Workers*, Vatican City: 1995, §§4,5; National Conference of Catholic Bishops, *Health and Healthcare*, Washington DC: NCCB 1981 (also in 11 (1981) *Origins* 396–402); NCCB, *Ethical and Religious Directives for Catholic Healthcare Services*, cf. Mk 25:31–46.

[36] See in particular Germain Grisez's contribution, chapter 10.

and all those in need of healthcare, "As Christ would reach out to touch and heal you, so too do we."[37]

### 2.3. Preferential option for the dying

A third group to whom tradition directs our preferential love and care is the dying. Even from the cross Christ showed his care for a dying thief. And the task of medicine is to care even when it cannot cure. Christians have been at the forefront of the hospice movement, in specialized care for the dying, including but not limited to the increasingly effective science of pain management. As the U.S. bishops suggest:

> Christ's redemptive and saving grace embrace the whole person, especially in his or her illness, suffering and death. Catholic healthcare ministry faces the reality of death with the confidence of faith. In the face of death – for many, a time when hope seems lost – the Church witnesses to her belief that God has created each person for eternal life. Above all, as a witness to its faith, a Catholic healthcare institution will be a community of respect, love and support to patients or residents and their families as they face the reality of death.[38]

The task of caring well for the terminally ill is especially challenging in a world increasingly inclined to discrimination, abandonment and homicide, all dressed up as efficient pursuit of the common good and as mercy for those who cannot be cured and no longer contribute in any obvious way. We must rebuild the "covenant between the generations" so that the elderly and the dying can trust that they will be treated with pietas, reverence and genuine compassion, even unto death.[39]

---

[37] Administrative Committee of the National Conference of Catholic Bishops, *The Bishops' Pastoral Role in Catholic Healthcare Ministry*, Washington DC: NCCB 1997. (Also in 26/43 (1997) *Origins* 700–704, at p. 704.) John Paul II (*Vita Consecrata: Apostolic Exhortation on the Consecrated Life and its Mission in the Church and in the World*, CTS 1996, §83) describes the *diakonia* of nursing religious in terms which might be applied more generally to all those who share in the Catholic healthcare apostolate: "The Church looks with admiration and gratitude upon ... [those] who, by caring for the sick and the suffering, contribute in a significant way to her mission. They carry on the ministry of mercy of Christ, who 'went about doing good and healing all [who were oppressed by the devil]' (Acts 10.38). In the footsteps of the Divine Samaritan, physician of souls and bodies, and following the example of their respective foundresses ... [they] should persevere in their witness of love towards the sick, devoting themselves to them with profound understanding and compassion. They should give a special place in their ministry to the poorest and most abandoned of the sick, such as the elderly, and those who are handicapped, marginalized, or terminally ill, and to the victims of drug abuse and the new contagious diseases."
[38] *Ethical and Religious Directives for Catholic Healthcare Services*, Part 5, Introduction.
[39] John Paul II, *Evangelium Vitae: Encyclical on the Value and Inviolability of Human Life*, London: CTS 1995, §94.

No-one should underestimate the difficulty of this task. Cardinal O'Connor relates a disturbing example:

> Our own Calvary hospital is considered, I believe, by professional observers to be one of the very finest hospitals in the US for those who are currently ill with cancer, from a human perspective incurable. Until not too many years ago, patients referred to Calvary from acute-care hospitals had an average length of stay of approximately six weeks. They lived for those six weeks in great comfort and in love, given tender, gentle care by incredibly warm and dedicated doctors and nurses, administrators and staff. Now, because of various new wonder drugs, patients may live six months or longer in the same loving and virtually pain-free environment, with added time to prepare both materially and spiritually for the death they know is coming, often strengthening bonds with their families, finding peace at the end. I have never known a relative or friend of a Calvary patient who has not been deeply grateful for the extraordinary care given their loved ones. Some time back, however, the storm clouds gathered. A major insurance carrier, I am told, called the leadership of Calvary hospital to say: "You are keeping your patients alive too long. If you continue to do this, we will discontinue your insurance."[40]

As O'Connor noted, that sort of thing has "a chilling effect" on "people trying to do good".

Against such opposition, institutional and communal support is crucial. Resources are not all that are at issue here. In 'Salvation and health: why medicine needs the Church' Stanley Hauerwas argues that in the face of the grave demands put upon healthcarers today – to rescue, to respond to pain and sickness, to engage in the "hard slog" of caring for chronic and dying patients, to give of self not just with great physical energy and technical skill, but from the heart – something very much like a church is necessary. Human sympathy and high ideals, important as they are, will not, he thinks, be sufficient to sustain such care. Nor will the technical, ethical and people skills required for this kind of care simply come "naturally": they must be acquired in a community of care. "Medicine needs the church not to supply a foundation for its moral commitments, but rather as a resource of the habits and practices necessary to sustain the care of those in pain over the long haul."[41]

Fundamental, then, to what Catholic hospitals offer a pluralist society is the alternative of healthcare institutions committed to a preference for the poor, the

[40] O'Connor, 'The temptation to become just another industry: healthcare', p. 453.
[41] Stanley Hauerwas, 'Salvation and health: why medicine needs the Church'. In Earl Shelp (ed.), *Theology and Bioethics. Exploring the Foundations and Frontiers*, Dordrecht: Reidel 1985, pp. 205–224, at p. 222. (Reprinted in Hauerwas, *Suffering Presence: Theological Reflections on Medicine, the Mentally Handicapped and the Church*, Notre Dame, Indiana: University of Notre Dame Press 1986, pp. 63–86.)

sick, the suffering and the dying. And how the most vulnerable are treated is properly the litmus test of any civilisation.[42]

## 3. Catholic hospitals as *martyria*

### 3.1. Healing as evangelization

In *Ethics After Babel* Jeffrey Stout, a non-believer, deplores the "nearly complete breakdown of fruitful dialogue between secular philosophical thought and the religious traditions", suggesting that this impoverishes both and is the result not only of secular moral philosophers adopting "tropes and fetishes" that virtually preclude such conversation but also of theology failing to offer anything that might make an educated public sit up and listen.

> To gain a hearing in our culture, theology has often assumed a voice not its own and found itself merely repeating the bromides of secular intellectuals in transparently figurative speech... Meanwhile, secular intellectuals have largely stopped paying attention. They don't need to be told, by theologians, that Genesis is mythical, that nobody knows much about the historical Jesus, that it's morally imperative to side with the oppressed, or that birth control is morally permissible. The explanation for the eclipse of religious ethics in recent secular moral philosophy may therefore be... that academic theologians have increasingly given the impression of saying nothing atheists don't already know.[43]

Stout's assessment of the potential contribution of religious ethics to a secular, pluralist society, and his diagnosis of the failure of communication, might be applied not only to academic theology but also to the enacted theological discourse of institutions such as hospitals. Religious assumptions and categories still play a large part in medical and nursing practice, form the backdrop to any secular alternatives, and have a distinctive wisdom to offer. But Catholic hospitals must re-establish that they "have something to say", so to speak, that they have an

---

[42] Holy See, *Statement of the Holy See for the International Year of Disabled Persons*, 4 March 1981 (in Austin Flannery (ed.), *Vatican II: More Post-Conciliar Documents*, Grand Rapids: Eerdmans, 1988, pp. 518–528), §3.

[43] Jeffrey Stout, 'The voice of theology', in his *Ethics after Babel: The languages of morals and their discontents*, Boston: Beacon Press 1988, p. 164; cf: Hauerwas, 'Salvation and health: why medicine needs the Church'; Alasdair MacIntyre, 'Can medicine dispense with a theological perspective on human nature?' in D Callaghan and H T Englehardt (eds), *The Roots of Ethics*, New York: Plenum, 1981, pp. 119–138; MacIntyre, *After Virtue* (second edition), Notre Dame, Indiana: University of Notre Dame Press 1984; Gilbert Meilaender, 'Are there virtues inherent in a profession?'. In Edmund Pellegrino et al (eds.), *Ethics, Trust and Professions*. Washington DC: Georgetown UP 1991, pp. 139–155; Gilbert Meilaender, *Body, Soul, and Bioethics*, Notre Dame: University of Notre Dame Press 1995; LeRoy Waiters, 'Religion and the renaissance of medical ethics', in Earl Shelp (ed.), *Theology and Bioethics: Exploring the Foundations and Frontiers*, Dordrecht: Reidel 1985, pp. 3–16.

approach to healthcare worthy of being a competitor in the market of ideas, of competing not just for resources but for people's commitment, their souls. Might it be that in engaging in constructive but compromised "ecumenical" dialogue with our co-religionists, fellow believers and non-believers, we risk selling our birthright for a social acceptability and political power, real or imagined, which amounts to no more than a "mess of potage"? How much does "the world" require us to compromise of those things we hold most dear in the project of achieving respectability in its eyes and co-operation from its policymakers? Are we really the movers and shakers we imagine we are, or are small phyrric victories such as Catholic hospitals funded by the state, insurers and others tolerated only as long as this serves an ultimately very different, non-Christian agenda? Is that agenda hidden from our eyes or have we become blinded to it by comfortably consorting for so long with those who really set it? Without courting or glorying masochistically in unpopularity, should a prophetic people not expect to be significantly at odds with a world which does not share its faith and morals?[44] And isn't our 'alternative' lifestyle precisely the particular gift we have to offer a pluralist society?

If Catholic hospitals allow *diakonia* to large numbers of people, especially the poor, the sick and the dying, they also allow such holy service to be integrated with the proclamation of the Gospel. "Jesus", we are told by Matthew, "went about Galilee, teaching in the synagogues, preaching the gospel of the kingdom, and healing every disease and infirmity among the people" (4:23; 9:35). Sometimes the hearings preceded and evoked faith; at other times the cure was a response to faith.[45] Thus Jesus' *diakonia* and his *martyria* were intimately related. The linking of these two ministries is extended to his disciples: "As you go," he tells them, "proclaim the good news that the kingdom of heaven is at hand. Heal the sick, raise the dead, cleanse lepers, cast out demons" (10:7–8). Whether for Jesus or for his disciples, healing and preaching are, as it were, two sides of the same redemptive coin.

## 3.2. Witnessing to what?

Catholic healthcare, then, must be not only *diakonia* but also *martyria*, a lived proclamation of the Gospel. As John Paul II told healthworkers when he visited

---

[44] On the other hand, sectarianism has its own temptations. How comforting it might be to retire to the relative safety of a Catholic ghetto on the margins of political and social life, sneering at outsiders as damned or invincibly ignorant. But such sectarianism involves the abandonment of any attempt to be the leaven in the loaf, the preachers to and baptizers of all nations, the servants of all.

[45] When the leper was cured it was "as a testimony (*marturion*) to them" (8:4) and when the blind, the mute and even the dead were cured it evoked human and religious awe among the people (9:26, 31, 33). On the other hand, when the centurion's servant was saved, the woman with a haemorrhage cured, and the blind men restored to sight, it was in response to some pre-existing faith and thus a prayer of faith (8:5–13; 9:20–22, 27–30).

Melbourne, theirs is both a "a very valuable service to life" and "a form of Christian witness".[46] Leaders and staff must therefore have a genuine appreciation not merely of some "code of ethics" but of the fundamental commitments of their institution as a hospital which (a) is heir to a particular tradition, articulated by the Magisterium, the Hippocratic ethic, the goals of the founders and benefactors, and so on, (b) has certain resources, financial but above all human and spiritual, and (c) has particular opportunities to serve the surrounding community and beyond. In the face of pressures of secularism, bureaucracy and the market and the perennial temptation to "jump into bed with the *Zeitgeist*", religious leaders have recently sounded a state of ethical alert, even emergency, and called on Catholic hospitals to regain their sense of identity and fight back.[47] Central commitments will include: respect for the dignity of every human person as made in the image of God; reverence for life from conception to death as a sacred trust; love of neighbour and a concern for the common good, including universal access to a reasonable level of care and the just allocation of resources; a desire to humanize medical practice; and a preferential option for the disadvantaged.[48]

Catholic hospitals give *martyria* to the Gospel the more consistently and luminously they exemplify Christian morality; they obscure and ultimately abandon their *raison d'être*, the muter and more compromised is their moral witness. Stanley Reiser identifies several cases of "ethical bifurcation" increasingly commonplace in hospitals.[49] First, major differences between the goals of the founder-sponsors and those of the current administrators and staff. Secondly, the growing chasm between the traditional professional ethic of healthworkers and the new bureaucratic-commercial mindset of health administrators. Thirdly,

[46] John Paul II, Address to health workers at the Mercy Maternity Hospital, Melbourne, 28 November, IX/2 (1986) *lnsegnamenti* 1734, cited in Pontifical Council for Pastoral Assistance to Healthcare Workers, *Charter for Healthcare Workers*, §1. Likewise John Paul II describes health workers as "servants and guardians of life, witnesses to the Church's presence alongside sick and suffering people" (*Vita Consecrata: Apostolic Exhortation on the Consecrated Life and its Mission in the Church and in the world*, 7).

[47] Joseph Bernardin, 'The case for not-for-profit healthcare', 24/32 *Origins* 538–542; O'Connor, 'The temptation to become just another industry: healthcare'.

[48] cf. Bernardin, 'Medicine's Moral Crisis', p. 456; Catholic Health Association of the United States, 'How to approach Catholic identity in changing times', 75/3 (1994) *Health Progress* 23–29; John Paul II, *Sollicitudo rei socialis*; Thomas Murphy, 'What is the bottom line in Catholic healthcare?', 26/4 (1996) *Origins* 56–60; New Jersey Bishops, 'The rationale of Catholic healthcare', 25/27 (1995) *Origins* 449–452; O'Connor, 'The temptation to become just another industry: healthcare', p. 452; Pontifical Council for Pastoral Assistance to Healthcare Workers, *Charter for Healthcare Workers*; US Bishops, *Ethical and Religious Directives for Catholic Healthcare Services*. As Directive 1 of the *Ethical and Religious Directives* puts it: "a Catholic institutional healthcare service is a community which provides healthcare to those in need of it. This service must be animated by the Gospel of Jesus Christ and guided by the moral tradition of the Church."

[49] Stanley Joel Reiser, 'The ethical life of healthcare organizations', 24/6 (1994) *Hastings Center Report*, 28–35.

inconsistencies between official ethical commitments and the array of organizational policies never subjected to explicit ethical analysis. Fourthly, the gap between official rhetoric and actual practice.

Catholic hospitals must be especially aware of the scandal – both in the theological and the ordinary senses – that some actions occasion, whether engaged in by particular hospital staff or the hospital as a whole, whether alone or with other providers, and with or without the administration's permission.[50] Practitioners, managers and ethicists who use theology or ethics as vehicles to accommodate and/or justify certain kinds of practices rather than as a standard against which they should be judged do no service to the Gospel, their patients or their profession. Benedict Ashley suggests that some Catholic hospitals have wrongfully co-operated in

> intrinsically evil means, as these have been defined by magisterial instructions, some of which are common practices in today's culture (abortion, contraception, sterilization, reproduction in the laboratory, and euthanasia), on the mistaken view that these are pragmatically necessary ways of promoting human health. The various efforts to justify these intrinsically evil practices in hardship cases or by wrong application of the notion of material co-operation under duress has already gone far to erode Catholic identity in our healthcare facilities and medical education... When seeming conflicts arise between the concern for the poor, [the sick and the dying] and the ethical limitations on the means that can be used, Catholics should remember that it is no real service to the poor to help them abort, contracept, sterilize themselves, or commit suicide.[51]

Faithful witness requires vigilance on the part of sponsors and administrators to ensure not only that nothing unethical occurs in the hospital, but also, more positively, that its whole approach accords with the core commitments and values of

---

[50] James H Provost, 'Approaches to Catholic identity in Church law', *Concilium 1994–95: Catholic Identity*, London: SCM 1995, pp. 15–25, argues that any institution which works at cross purposes to those of the official Church "lacks the very inner reality to be considered 'Catholic', whatever its formal title". Germain Grisez ('How far may Catholic hospitals co-operate with providers of immoral services?') suggests that the compromised witness and scandal given by some Catholic hospitals may not only lead people into sin but mean that some individuals die or otherwise suffer in ways that might have been prevented "if those who profess the sacredness of life and the dignity of persons consistently avoided complicity in wrongful behaviour. Accepting these bad consequences is likely to be unfair unless the victims themselves freely consent to what they suffer."

[51] Benedict Ashley OP, 'The documents of Catholic identity', pp. 15–16. Likewise Piccione, 'Catholic healthcare: justice, fiscal realities, and moral norms', p. 101: "The instinct of the Catholic provider is to serve the poor, yet our concern to meet the needs of the underserved cannot exclude Catholic moral norms, otherwise we would formally co-operate with, or even do, evil for the sake of other goods. The charitable instinct is not served by performing services that are not truly charitable, denying the dignity of the human person, marriage, or life itself. Catholic healthcare cannot provide morally objectionable services as if healthcare were simply a commodity, driven by market needs or state mandate."

the hospital. In recent years Church leaders have repeatedly recommitted the Church to the healthcare ministry, but also insisted that this must be in accord with sound morality as articulated by the Church's Magisterium.[52] The US Bishops, for instance, have ordered that all Catholic healthcare services in that country adopt their published directives[53] as "policy", "require adherence to them within the institution as a condition for medical privileges and employment, and provide appropriate instruction regarding the directives for administration, medical and nursing staff and other personnel".[54]

Apart from giving the example of Catholic moral teaching in action, Catholic hospitals are also appropriate places for more overt evangelisation.[55] Catholic teaching hospitals should never be merely providers of 'value-free' technology

[52] e.g. John Paul II, *Evangelium Vitae*; Pontifical Council for Pastoral Assistance to Healthcare Workers, *Charter for Healthcare Workers*; National Conference of [U.S.] Catholic Bishops, *Health and Healthcare and Ethical and Religious Directives for Catholic Healthcare Services*; see also Congregation for the Doctrine of the Faith (CDF), *Quaestio de abortu: Declaration on Procured Abortion*. CTS 1974; CDF, *Haec sacra congregatio. Declaration on Sterilization in Catholic Hospitals*. CTS 1975; CDF, *Declaration on Certain Questions concerning Sexual Ethics*. CTS 1976; CDF, *Jura et bona: Declaration on Euthanasia*. CTS 1980; CDF, *Donum vitae: Instruction on Respect for Human Life in its Origin and on the Dignity of Procreation*. CTS 1986; Committee for Pro-Life Activities of the National Conference of Catholic Bishops, *Nutrition and Hydration: Moral and Pastoral Reflections*. Washington DC: NCCB 1992; Kevin D O'Rourke and Philip Boyle, *Medical Ethics: Sources of Catholic Teachings* (second edition), Washington DC: Georgetown University Press 1993.

[53] General directives were issued to hospitals in 1971, 1975 and 1994, as well as directives on various specific issues such as nutrition and hydration (1992).

[54] US Bishops, *Ethical and Religious Directives for Catholic Healthcare Services*, Directive 5.

[55] As Honings ('The Charter for Healthcare Workers: A synthesis of Hippocratic ethics and Christian morality', p. 49) recently observed: "The profession, mission and vocation of the healthcare worker naturally requires a solid training and a constant ethical-religious formation in moral questions in general and in questions relating to bioethics in particular." John Paul II (*Vita Consecrata*, §83) likewise reminded nursing religious "that a part of their mission is to evangelize the healthcare centres in which they work, striving to apply the light of Gospel values to the living, suffering and dying of the people of our day. They should endeavour to make the practice of medicine more human, and increase their knowledge of bioethics at the service of the Gospel of life. Above all therefore they should foster respect for the person and for human life from conception to its natural end, in full conformity with the moral teaching of the Church. For this purpose, they should set up centres of formation and co-operate closely with those ecclesial bodies entrusted with the pastoral ministry of healthcare." Pontifical Council for Pastoral Assistance to Healthcare Workers, *Charter for Healthcare Workers*, §7: "The continuous progress of medicine demands of the health care worker a thorough 'preparation and ongoing formation' so as to ensure, also by personal studies, the required competence and fitting professional expertise. Side-by-side with this, they should be given a solid 'ethico-religious formation', which "promotes in them an appreciation of human and Christian values and refines their moral conscience". There is need "to develop in them an authentic faith and a true sense of morality, in a sincere search for a religious relationship with God, in whom all ideals of goodness and truth are based." "All health care workers should be taught morality and bioethics. To achieve this, those responsible for their formation should endeavour to have chairs and courses in bioethics put in place." Cf. Paul VI, *Evangelii Nuntiandi: Apostolic Exhortation on Evangelization in the Modern World*, CTS 1975, §14; Vatican Council II, *Ad gentes divinitus: Decree on the Church's Missionary Activity* (1965), various editions, §35.

and art: rather, they offer in a pluralist society the real alternative of a training in full accord with a particular tradition. We should not shy away from this, for fear of losing funding or respectability. Indeed, I suspect that it is precisely as a high-quality *alternative* to the run-of-the-mill that Catholic hospitals will best be able to justify continued tolerance and support of funders and regulators. Unashamedly Catholic codes of ethics and practice, ethics committees, staff education programmes etc. will not only help ensure that the hospital fulfils its primary mission of providing sound care but also offer it a 'market niche'.[56] This will have its attractions not only for many patients but also for many staff: for it is already the case in some countries that trainees and practitioners in certain specialties such as obstetrics and gynaecology, family planning, genetics, paediatrics, geriatrics and intensive care, are pressured to conform to immoral practices and even refused positions if they will not. Without Catholic hospitals in which to train and work some healthworkers might either compromise their consciences and objective morality, or have to quit their specialty.[57] In such a world Catholic hospitals may offer not only a place for a distinctively Catholic healthcare vocation but also a refuge for those still committed to genuinely Hippocratic medicine.

In fact both staff *and patients* are appropriate targets of evangelisation. This need not involve "forcing the Gospel down people's [unwilling] necks" any more than in any evangelical or catechetical activity; it should not involve abusing the healthcare situation or the relative vulnerability of the sick and the employee. A simple word of encouragement or explanation, coming from hospital staff, may well be the occasion of enlightenment, and even perhaps a deeper conversion.

### 3.3. More than just the rules of the Catholic club

Contemporary ethics has turned away from the two ascendant models of the previous generation – the buffet (ethics is about choosing according to taste from the range of possibilities and then getting what I want) and the accountants' ledger (ethics is about balancing "pre-moral" debits and credits) – and towards a more richly textured ethic of various human goods, norms, commitments, virtues, beliefs, narratives, communities and traditions. In general I think this has been

---

[56] Pontifical Council for Pastoral Assistance to Healthcare Workers, *Charter for Healthcare Workers*, §8.

[57] I think Grisez underestimates the difficulties outside Catholic hospitals when he asserts that "Catholic teaching hospitals offer a valuable opportunity for Catholics to be trained in full accord with their faith only if their programmes are consistently Catholic, and if nurses and doctors completing those programmes will be able to practise without moral compromise in the fields for which they trained. But where such principled practice remains possible, the technical training for it is likely to be available outside Catholic teaching hospitals, and individuals can acquire their indispensable moral and spiritual formation by private study and from faithful Catholic mentors whose concerns extend to healthcare." (Grisez, 'How far may Catholic hospitals co-operate with providers of immoral services?')

very healthy, though we must beware the old liberal and utilitarian wolves dressing up in neo-Aristotelian and neo-Kantian sheep's clothing. New age varieties of proportionalism are already disguising themselves as old-fashioned *phronesis*. Nonetheless, what these new approaches highlight is that Catholic hospitals must address themselves not only to promoting fidelity to norms, but also to cultivating certain kinds of character. Amongst staff: respectfulness, pietas, compassion, understanding, benevolence, spontaneity, honesty, fidelity, thoroughness, patience, humility – virtues summed up in the Good Samaritan;[58] amongst patients: virtues such as patience and courage, moderation in expectations, and hope.[59] Leaders and staff of Catholic hospitals should be especially wary of the institutionalization of vices such as cavalier disrespect for human life and dignity, blindness or indifference to effects of policy on particular people, avarice and ageism, the technological imperative, and so on. They will resist the sacrifice of persons for the sake of efficiency, progress or profitability, and promote a certain asceticism in response to the drive to medical maximisation, and a certain contemplativeness in response to the busyness of the average hospital.

Another respect in which Catholic hospitals can give *martyria* to the faith is in subtle and more overt advocacy of Gospel values to the wider society. There are many situations in which large institutions have a voice which can communicate the richness of Christian values which individuals and smaller groups do not.[60] In *Evangelium vitae* John Paul II exhorted healthcare institutions to take every opportunity to make "impassioned and unflinching affirmations" of the sacredness and inviolability of every human life.[61] In a world where recourse to medical homicide

[58] Benedict Ashley OP, 'Does the "Splendour of Truth" shine on bioethics?', 19/1 (1994) *Ethics and Medics* 3–4; Ashley, *Living the Truth in Love: A Biblical Introduction to Moral Theology*, New York: Alba 1996; Bernardin, 'Medicine's Moral Crisis', 457; Romanus Cessario OP, 'From casuistry to virtue ethics', 19/10 (1994) *Ethics and Medics* 1–2; Augustine Di Noia, OP, 'The virtues of the Good Samaritan: healthcare ethics in the perspective of a renewed moral theology', 31 (1996) *Dolentium hominum* 211–214; Gilbert Meilaender, 'Are there virtues inherent in a profession?'; Edmund Pellegrino, 'The moral status of compassion in bioethics', 20/10 (1995) *Ethics and Medics* 3–4; Pellegrino, 'Toward a virtue-based normative ethics for the health professions', 5 (1995) *Kennedy Institute of Ethics Journal* 253–277; Edmund Pellegrino and David C Thomasma, *For the Patient's Good: The Restoration of Beneficence in Health Care*, Oxford: OUP 1988; Pellegrino and Thomasma, *The Virtues in Medical Practice*, Oxford: OUP 1993; Servais Pinckaers, *The Sources of Christian Ethics*; Pontifical Council for Pastoral Assistance to Healthcare Workers, *Charter for Healthcare Workers*, §2.

[59] Ashley, *Living the Truth in Love: A Biblical Introduction to Moral Theology*; Richard M Gula, *Euthanasia: Moral and Pastoral Perspectives*, Mahwah, New Jersey: Paulist 1994; Stanley Hauerwas, 'Practising patience: how Christians should be sick'. In Hilary Regan et al (eds.), *Beyond Mere Health: Theology and Health Care in a Secular Society*, Melbourne: Australian Theological Forum 1996, pp. 80–102; Pinckaers, *The Sources of Christian Ethics*.

[60] Thomas Murphy, 'What is the bottom line in Catholic healthcare?', p. 58; Francis Sullivan, 'Dreaming the impossible dream', p. 135.

[61] John Paul II, *Evangelium Vitae*, §§87–89. Likewise: *Catechism of the Catholic Church*, §2288; New Jersey Bishops, 'The rationale of Catholic healthcare', p. 451; Pontifical Council for Pastoral Assistance to Healthcare Workers, *Charter for Healthcare Workers*, §1; [U.S.] National Conference of Catholic Bishops, *Ethical and Religious Directives for Catholic Healthcare Services*.

is increasingly common and "banalized",[62] Catholic hospitals should represent a stark contrast to the prevailing culture. But the prophetic voice must be heard not only by consistently refusing to engage in any anti-life practices, but also by unmasking the ideologies which underpin them. Amongst the latter identified in the encyclical are: individualism, materialist and reductionist accounts of the human person and value, consumerism and hedonism, Prometheanism and pragmatism, and ethical scepticism, all of which contribute to what John Paul II has immortally labelled as "the idolatry of the market" and "the culture of death".[63] Testimony to higher values, to better ways of relating and to the culture of the kingdom, is crucial to the distinctive rôle of the Catholic hospital in a pluralist society.

All in all, Catholic hospitals must not allow the scope of their moral concerns to be narrowed to the stereotypical "Catholic club rules" against contraception, abortion and euthanasia – important as those are in themselves and as litmus tests of professionalism and of the Catholicity of the institution.[64] Rather they should see as one of their fundamental purposes the thoroughgoing conversion of patients and health professionals, community and culture – spiritual heart transplants to match the physical, health of soul paralleling health of body, the goal of eternal life beyond any extension of earthly life.


## 4. Catholic hospitals as *leitourgia*

### 4.1. Dulia *without idolatry*

Just as Jesus' healing miracles at once expressed the healing compassion of God and provided signs and foretastes of the coming of God's kingdom, so Catholic hospitals "see their ministry not only as an effort to restore and preserve health, but also as a spiritual service and a sign of that final healing which will one day bring about the new creation that is the ultimate fruit of Jesus' ministry and God's love for us".[65] The life of Catholic hospitals should thus testify to more than just Christian morality even richly understood. Christian beliefs about a loving, provident God, about creation and anthropology, about sickness and death, the communion of saints, the forgiveness of sins, the resurrection of the body, and life ever-lasting: all these should inform and be proclaimed by Christian

[62] Pontifical Council for Pastoral Assistance to Healthcare Workers, *Charter for Healthcare Workers*, §139.
[63] John Paul II, *Evangelium Vitae*, §12 etc.; see Joseph Bernardin, 'The case for not-for-profit healthcare', 24 (32) (1995) *Origins* 538–542, at p. 539; Anthony Fisher OP, 'A guided tour of *Evangelium vitae*', 72/4 (1995) *Australasian Catholic Record* 445–462; Kasper, *Faith and the Future*.
[64] Reiser, 'The ethical life of healthcare organizations', p. 29.
[65] US Bishops, *Ethical and Religious Directives for Catholic Healthcare Services*.

healthcare.[66] Of course, Christians have no monopoly on beliefs such as the dignity of the human person, the importance of community, or 'liberal' values such as care and respect. Yet their faith means they see the person as much more than autonomous agency, a locus of rational preferences, or the like: the human person is the image of God and the human community is the image of the Trinity. We are, therefore, brothers and sisters in the Lord and we are our brothers' and sisters' keepers; "care and respect", important as they are, are too lame a description of that sacred relationship and trust. Reverence, wonder, what St Thomas called *dulia*,[67] this attitude should mark our relating. How that pans out in the particulars of day-to-day hospital care is not easy to define: perhaps in the courtesy and compassion, the patience and perseverance, the hopefulness, the willingness to engage in apparent inefficiencies such as listening and careful touch, a reverential language and touch and awe not unlike that with which we treat the holy things.[68]

Catholic hospitals, then, might be said to engage in a kind of liturgical drama as they invoke the presence of God, retell the sacred stories, enact the creed, intercede for the sick and dying, deliver God's healing mercy to them, stand in wonder and reverential silence before the mysteries of birth, suffering and death, celebrate the sacredness of life, and recall the promise of a life beyond the present. Words like "vocation", "mission" and "apostolate", which roll so easily off the Christian tongue, must mean more than "job" or even "profession" here: they must bespeak

---

[66] New Jersey Bishops, 'The rationale of Catholic healthcare', p. 451: "We are a community of faith and worship and fraternal love and care, who know who we are and become who we are through the life, death and resurrection of Jesus... [In him we recognize] the God who suffered along with us... In his resurrection we acknowledge not only the power of God, but also the new life given by God... God dwells with us and within us through the power of the Holy Spirit and that makes us really and truly different... We who have been touched and saved and changed by God must make all this visible not only by our grateful faith-filled praise of God, but also by our loving presence with each other and our compassionate care for one another. Catholic healthcare exists as a practical sign of living faith; it exists 'to be Jesus' love for the other in the healthcare setting'." US Bishops, *Ethical and Religious Directives for Catholic Healthcare Services*: "For the Christian, our encounter with suffering and death can take on a positive and distinctive meaning through the redemptive power of Jesus' suffering and death. As St. Paul says, we are 'always carrying about in the body the dying of Jesus, so that the life of Jesus may also be manifested in our body' (2 Cor. 4:10). This truth does not lessen the pain and fear, but gives confidence and grace for bearing suffering rather than being overwhelmed by it. Catholic healthcare ministry bears witness to the truth that, for those who are in Christ, suffering and death are the birth pangs of the new creation. "God himself will always be with them. He will wipe every tear from their eyes and there shall be no more death or mourning, wailing or pain, for the old order has passed away." (Rev. 21:3–4.) Cf. Casey, *Food for the Journey: Theological Foundations of the Catholic Healthcare Ministry*; MacIntyre, 'Can medicine dispense with a theological perspective on human nature?'.

[67] *Summa theologiae* 2a 2ae q.25 art. 1; qq. 103–109; 3a q.25 art.2.

[68] Space precludes further exploration of the Genesis theme of the human person as *eikon* so richly explored in Eastern theology. Cf. John D Zizioluas, *Being As Communion: Studies in Personhood and the Church*, Crestwood, NY: St Vladimir's Seminary Press and London: Darton, Longman and Todd 1985.

a kind of "liturgical" ministry of mediating and praising the God who is the lover of life and health.[69]

If Catholic healthcare is so high a calling, those charged with it must be wary of secularization, accommodation and compromise, and wary too when medicine exceeds its legitimate sphere, colonizing the whole of reality, promising to alleviate people of the human condition, offering them false hopes of earthly immortality, engaging in therapeutic overkill, attempting to tame even death by making it part of the medical armoury, or pretending health is salvation. Like the anathemas against witch-doctors in the Old Testament (Lev 20:27; Dt 18:10–14; 1 Chr 10:13–14; cf. Acts 13:6–12) and against the pharmacists (*pharmakois*) in the New (Rev 21:8; 22:15), worshippers of true religion must always be ready critics of healthcare messianism and medical idolatry.[70] Whatever the values of Hippocratic medicine, we do not swear by Asclepius, Hygieia, Panacea or even Apollo the Great Physician.

### 4.2. Pastoral care

Jesus healed whole persons, body and soul. When he cured the paralytic he first forgave him his sins (Lk 5:17–26; cf. Mk 2:1–12). The links between physical and spiritual sickness, and physical and spiritual healing, have long been appreciated by Christians and other believers. Yet already by St Thomas' day different monks dispensed the medicaments and the absolutions. He recognised the connection, however, when he compared the duty of the sinner not to delay seeking a priest for confession with the duty of a sick man not to delay sending for the physician.[71] As the US Bishops have observed that "without health of the spirit, high technology focused strictly on the body offers limited hope for healing the whole person. Directed to spiritual needs that are often appreciated more deeply during times of illness, pastoral care is an integral part of Catholic healthcare."[72]

A strong, well-prepared pastoral care team is clearly desirable in any large hospital. But *Catholic* pastoral care to the sick is different from social work, counselling, other human supports, even if it includes elements of these things: it is first and foremost about the sacraments. Priests, supported by pastoral teams and co-operative clinical staff, must be ready to engage with people at some of

---

[69] Wisdom 11:26; see Honings, 'The Charter for Healthcare Workers: A synthesis of Hippocratic ethics and Christian morality', p. 49; Pontifical Council for Pastoral Assistance to Healthcare Workers, *Charter for Healthcare Workers*, §3.

[70] cf. Hauerwas, 'Salvation and health: why medicine needs the Church'; Meilaender, *Body, Soul, and Bioethics*.

[71] *Summa Theologiae*, Supp. q.6 art.5 ad 2. On the relationship between faith and healing, see e.g. Rene Latourelle, *The Miracles of Jesus and the Theology of Miracles*, trans. M. O'Connell, New York: Paulist 1988; Leopold Sabourin, *The Gospel miracles. The Gospel According to St Matthew*, vol. 2. New York: St Paul's 1983, pp. 502–514.

[72] US Bishops, *Ethical and Religious Directives for Catholic Healthcare Services*; cf. Pontifical Council for Pastoral Assistance to Healthcare Workers, *Charter for Healthcare Workers*, §3.

the most vulnerable and receptive moments of their lives with the sacraments of God's love.[73] Ever since St James counselled that the presbyters be called to pray over, anoint and absolve the sick (5:14–15), Church leaders have properly been solicitous to ensure that the sick and dying have access to the sacraments.[74] The sacrament of anointing of the sick is obviously central here. But this ministry also includes: baptism, confirmation or reception into the Church for the dying who seek it (or whose guardians seek it); sacramental confession and the apostolic pardon; the Mass and the sacrament of the Eucharist, especially viaticum for those in danger of death; regular opportunities for communal prayer and worship both for patients and staff; blessings, sacramentals, religious art and devotions of various kinds, perhaps most fittingly crucifixes and the stations of the cross. Obviously such spiritual care, like the rest of hospital care, will have to be tailored to the particular needs of the patients: non-Christians, non-Catholics and non-practising Catholics, for instance, will have very different needs to more ''regular'' Catholics. None the less even non-Catholics come expecting a distinctively ''spiritual'', unembarrassedly Christian approach, and we ought not to be afraid that ''showing our Catholic petticoats'' will offend outsiders.

In addition to the sacraments, pastoral care to the sick ''encompasses the full range of spiritual services, including a listening presence, help in dealing with powerlessness, pain and alienation, and assistance in recognizing and responding to God's will with greater joy and peace''.[75] The goal here is to confirm brothers and sisters in the Lord so that they might live, suffer and die well. Seeking to humanize and Christianize sickness, dying and healthcare itself, and offering cause for hope even when medicine can do no more, are crucial ways in which pastoral care complements clinical care.[76] And as Hauerwas has observed:

[73] Patricia Cahill, 'The environment in which Catholic healthcare finds itself', 27/2 (1997) *Origins* 27–29, at p. 28.

[74] e.g. The US Bishops' *Ethical and Religious Directives for Catholic Healthcare Services* direct that ''for Catholic patients or residents, provision for the sacraments is an especially important part of Catholic healthcare ministry. Every effort should be made to have priests assigned to hospitals and healthcare institutions to celebrate the Eucharist and provide the sacraments to patients and staff . . . Particular care should be taken to provide and to publicize opportunities for patients or residents to receive the sacrament of penance . . . Responsive to a patient's desires and condition, all involved in pastoral care should facilitate the availability of priests to provide the sacrament of anointing of the sick, recognizing that through this sacrament Christ provides grace and support to those who are seriously ill or weakened by advanced age . . . All Catholics who are capable of receiving communion should receive viaticum when they are in danger of death, while still in full possession of their faculties . . . . Newly born infants in danger of death, including those miscarried, should be baptized if this is possible . . . When a Catholic who has been baptized but not yet confirmed is in danger of death, any priest may confirm the person.'' (Directives 12–18.) Likewise Pontifical Council for Pastoral Assistance to Healthcare Workers, Charter for Healthcare Workers, §§108–113.

[75] US Bishops, *Ethical and Religious Directives for Catholic Healthcare Services*.

[76] cf. Honings, 'The Charter for Healthcare Workers: A synthesis of Hippocratic ethics and Christian morality'.

> No matter how powerful [medicine] becomes, it cannot in principle rule out the necessity of prayer. For prayer is not a supplement to the insufficiency of our medical knowledge and practice; nor is it some divine insurance policy that our medical skill will work; rather, our prayer is the means that we have to make God present whether our medical skill is successful or not. So understood, the issue is not whether medical care and prayer are antithetical, but how medical care can ever be sustained without continued prayer.[77]

Of course, much of all this can be done by pastoral workers who are part of or visit secular hospitals. In a Catholic hospital what should be different is that *leitourgia* is central to people's understanding of patient care and staff support, not merely "icing on the cake".

## 5. Where to from here?

As Richard McCormick observes:

> Catholic hospitals have beautiful mission statements. We read references to continuing the health mission of Jesus … caring services for each individual, personalised patient care, the holistic approach which weds competence and compassion … [and] option for the poor … [Yet] everywhere I go I see Catholics involved in healthcare doubtful, perplexed, wondering whether they are viable *[sic]*, whether they ought to be in healthcare, asking about their identity, how they differ from non-Catholic institutions. There is a great deal of institutional navel-gazing … [about] rediscovering or re-creating mission in changing circumstances. In sum, there is a gap between institutional purpose and aim, and personal conviction and involvement.[78]

Various responses to these challenges have been proposed and attempted. Sponsorship, mission and vision statements, mission effectiveness programmes, and ethics committees have been in the forefront of strategies to maintain Catholic identity.[79] Far more crucial, in my view, are six matters. First, like individuals discerning their vocations, or reassessing their morally revisable commitments, the sponsors of Catholic hospitals must consider seriously the materially and morally available options, neither engaging in a simple maintenance operation nor abandoning the trust received from their predecessors and the Church

---

[77] Stanley Hauerwas, *Suffering Presence: Theological Reflections on Medicine, the Mentally Handicapped and the Church*, p. 81.

[78] Richard A McCormick, 'The Catholic hospital: mission impossible?', p. 648.

[79] Developed through institution-wide discourse and revised periodically, these documents and programmes are supposed to articulate the traditions, values and no-go areas for the hospital community, clarifying what the institution stands for, instructing members about their responsibilities, and eliciting their commitment to those duties and values; mission officers and ethicists are charged with promoting discourse about the means and ends of the organization. Cf. Reiser, 'The ethical life of healthcare organizations', pp. 33–35.

today. They must, for instance, ask themselves: what healthcare and other needs are now unmet and likely to remain unmet by others? Are we more ready, willing and able to meet some of those needs than others? If Catholic healthcare *is* thought still to be worthwhile and possible, there must be a conscious reappropriation of the distinctively Christian and Catholic in healthcare.

Secondly, with this in view, a "critical mass" of strategically located caregivers, administrators and policymakers dedicated to the hospital's mission and values must be selected, trained and appropriately supported.[80]

Thirdly, there must be far greater co-operation among Catholic (and any other Christian) healthcare and allied services, moving perhaps towards providing integrated delivery networks or towards less comprehensive alliances.[81]

Fourthly, survival will require astuteness on the part of congregations and hospital managers regarding arrangements within their institutions and the broader "healthcare ecosystem" which respond creatively and efficiently to political and financial pressures in ways which promote and do not compromise mission and ethics.[82]

Fifthly, Catholic hospitals and the whole Catholic community must be vigilant in resisting any moves by government, insurers or others to require or pressure Catholic hospitals into such compromises.

And finally, local bishops, in conjunction with leaders of religious congregations and others, must exercise vigorous oversight, co-ordination and forward

---

[80] Beal, 'Catholic hospitals: how Catholic will they be?', p. 86; Bernardin, 'Crossroads for the Church's health care ministry'; Grisez, 'How far may Catholic hospitals co-operate with providers of immoral services?'; Piccione, 'Catholic healthcare: justice, fiscal realities, and moral norms', p. 102; Sullivan, 'Dreaming the impossible dream', p. 134; US Bishops, *Ethical and Religious Directives for Catholic Healthcare Services*. In several countries this need has been recognised by the institution of formal programmes to educate lay leaders of Catholic hospitals in Catholic mission and ethics. The Australian Bishops in 1997 supported an initiative of the Australian Catholic Health Care Association, known as Educare, to provide professional adult formation courses for Catholic healthcare services (*Statement of the Australian Catholic Bishops' Conference in support of the Process of 'Integration 2000'*).

[81] Patricia Cahill, 'Collaboration among Catholic health providers', 24 (12) (1994) *Origins* 212–213; Murphy, 'What is the bottom line in Catholic healthcare?'; Sullivan, 'Dreaming the impossible dream', p. 134; Administrative Committee of the NCCB, *The Bishops' Pastoral Role in Catholic Healthcare Ministry*. The Australian Bishops have supported an initiative of the Australian Catholic Health Care Association, known as "Integration 2000", to promote partnerships and networking between various Catholic services and organisations (*Statement of the Australian Catholic Bishops' Conference in support of the Process of 'Integration 2000'*).

[82] Piccione, 'Catholic healthcare: justice, fiscal realities, and moral norms', p. 102: "Certainly we should utilize the skills presented for good and efficient stewardship of our resources, but must resist the model of corporate life and corporate culture... If we talk like business leaders and think like business leaders and structure personal rewards like business leaders, we will not be effective models of the ministry of service. As laypersons take the leadership rôles of religious sisters and brothers, the laity must understand that they, too, are now symbols of this service, and their concerns for the conduct of the service must extend beyond financial performance."

planning in this area to ensure that hospitals within their sphere of influence do indeed fulfil the functions of service, witness and pastoral care.[83]

Is all this, as some have suggested, "mission impossible"? This much is clear: even Jesus could not call the uncallable (Mt 19:20–22), forgive the unforgivable (Mk 3:29), teach the unteachable (Mt 13:13–15), answer the unanswerable (Mk 13:32), or heal the unhealable (Mk 6:1–6). If even he was bound by the limits of logical and moral possibility, his own powers, and above all the receptivity of those he dealt with, so too the Church, her congregations and institutions cannot expect to do everything they would like. Maybe Catholic healthcare on the scale to which those in some countries have become accustomed and which those in other countries would like to become accustomed, is no longer possible – though we should be reluctant to give up what has been achieved or yet could be achieved through such institutions. But big or small, Catholic healthcare is challenged today to rediscover and deepen its *diakonia, martyria* and *leitourgia*. If it does this it may discover that many apparently impossible things are indeed possible for God (cf. Mt 19:26).

[83] Much has been written in recent years about the rôles of the bishops here: e.g. Beal, 'Catholic hospitals: how Catholic will they be?', pp. 85–87; Cahill, 'The environment in which Catholic healthcare finds itself', p. 28; Piccione, 'Catholic healthcare: justice, fiscal realities, and moral norms', pp. 104–108; James H Provost, 'Approaches to Catholic identity in Church law', pp. 22–23; US Bishops, *Ethical and Religious Directives for Catholic Healthcare Services*; [US Bishops'] Ad Hoc Committee on Healthcare Issues and the Church, *The Responsibility of the Diocesan Bishop for Strengthening the Health Ministry*, Washington DC: NCCB 1996; US Bishops, *The Bishops' Pastoral role in Catholic Healthcare Ministry*; cf. *The Code of Canon Law*, 216, 217, 305.1. They must: initiate and help co-ordinate collaboration among Catholic hospitals, nursing and rehabilitation facilities, clinics, charities, social services, parishes, theologians, schools and religious education programmes; challenge the faithful to take greater responsibility for health and healing; insist upon the doctrinal and moral integrity of the witness and practice of each institution; carefully examine any partnerships with non-Catholic providers that may affect the mission or identity of Catholic providers; make provision for good pastoral, including sacramental, care; and ensure the preservation and deepening of the Catholic identity, apostolic zeal and effectiveness of the institutions or else withdraw formal recognition of them as Catholic institutions.

# Law, public policy
# and
# the prolife cause

# 15

# The legal revolution: from 'sanctity of life' to 'quality of life' and 'autonomy'

JOHN KEOWN

"HOW CAN IT BE lawful to allow a patient to die slowly, though painlessly, over a period of weeks from lack of food but unlawful to produce his immediate death by a lethal injection, thereby saving his family from yet another ordeal to add to the tragedy that has already struck them? I find it difficult to find a moral answer to that question. But it is undoubtedly the law . . . ".[1]

## Introduction

The Western world is undergoing a legal revolution. For centuries the law in both common law and civil law jurisdictions has stoutly upheld the principle of the 'sanctity of life'. Over the past thirty or so years, however, courts and legislatures across the Western world have seriously compromised that principle. Respect for life's inviolability has been increasingly eroded by the notion that only some human lives, those which pass a certain 'Quality' threshold, merit protection, and by respect for more or less unbridled individual autonomy. To many, this revolution has proved less evident than other revolutions of the period. For unlike other revolutions promoted suddenly, violently and outside the law by social radicals, this revolution is being promoted gradually, without violence and through the law by pillars of the legal establishment.

Examples of the abandonment of the principle by legislatures are not difficult to find. In the UK, a country which has done more than most to promote the revolution, the *Abortion Act* 1967, widely imitated around the globe, overturned the historic prohibition on abortion. Abortion was transformed from a serious criminal offence to a minor medical procedure, commonly performed for reasons of social convenience rather than medical necessity. *The Human Fertilisation and Embryology Act* 1990, apart from further relaxing the law on abortion, also permitted destructive experimentation on human *in vitro* embryos until the start of the fifteenth day of development. Since its enactment, thousands of embryonic human beings have been created, frozen, stored and discarded in the name of science and medicine.

---

[1] *Airedale NHS Trust v. Bland* [1993] A.C. 789 at p. 885 *per* Lord Browne-Wilkinson.

233

But legislatures have not been alone in promoting the revolution. Judges too have played a major role: although their involvement has been less obvious to many, it has been no less profound. Examples here too are not difficult to find. In 1973, in judgements of breathtaking invention, showing scant understanding of, let alone respect for, the tradition being trashed, the US Supreme Court swept away that nation's longstanding laws against abortion.[2] In 1988 it was imitated, in judgements of no greater merit, by the Supreme Court of Canada.[3] Now, as the courts turn their attention to the other end of life, they continue to promote the revolution. In 1984, the Dutch Supreme Court held that doctors could lawfully kill their patients in certain circumstances.[4]

This paper illustrates the ongoing legal revolution by examining in detail a landmark English case decided in 1993 by the House of Lords. Arguably the most important case ever decided by that court, it illustrates well the extent to which even a conservative judiciary, without the latitude afforded by a written constitution or Charter of Rights, is advancing the legal revolution.

In *Airedale N.H.S. Trust v. Bland*,[5] the House of Lords held that it was lawful for a doctor to cease tube-feeding his patient who was in a "persistent vegetative state" (pvs) even though this would inevitably lead to the patient's death and even though, in the express opinion of a majority of their Lordships, the doctor's intent was to kill. The implications of the case are profound. A leading utilitarian bioethicist and advocate of euthanasia, Professor Peter Singer, has even commented that the case marks the collapse of the traditional Western ethic – the principle of the sanctity of human life.[6] There can be little doubt that the Law Lords dealt a blow to that principle and, although Singer's comment may be overstated, the blow may yet prove fatal. Whether it does so may well depend on the readiness of their Lordships to reconsider their reasoning in *Bland*.

This paper respectfully argues that they should, not least because their reasoning leaves the law, as Lord Mustill commented, in a "morally and intellectually misshapen" state, prohibiting active but permitting passive medical killing. With few exceptions, notably Professor Finnis's acute commentary,[7] this cardinal case has inspired strikingly little academic analysis. The present paper suggests

[2] *Roe v. Wade*, 410 U.S. 113 (1973)

[3] *R v. Morgentaler* [1988] 1 S.C.R. 30

[4] *Nederlands Jurisprudentie* (1985) No. 106, 451.

[5] [1993] A.C. 789 at p. 885.

[6] Peter Singer, *Rethinking Life and Death* (Oxford: Oxford University Press 1995) at p. 1. I shall use the term 'sanctity' throughout because the 'sanctity of life' has consistently been stated by the courts to be a governing principle of English law: see, e.g., text *infra* nn. 52–53. However, the term runs the risk of seeming specifically religious and anyone who finds this possible connotation distracting could use the phrase 'inviolability of human life'. Again following judicial usage, I shall use 'life' throughout as shorthand for 'human life'. This is not the place to canvass the important reasons for distinguishing human from other animal life.

[7] J.M. Finnis, '*Bland*: Crossing the Rubicon?' (1993) 109 *Law Quarterly Review* 329. An overview of *Bland* and more recent cases on pvs is provided by J.K. Mason and G.T. Laurie, 'The Management of the Persistent Vegetative State in the British Isles' (1996) 4 *Juridical Review* 263.

that the doctrine of the sanctity of life was misrepresented, misunderstood and mistakenly rejected, and argues that the courts should, by reinstating the law's consistent application of that doctrine, restore moral and intellectual consistency, coherence and clarity to the law.

The paper comprises three main parts. Part I outlines three alternative ethical approaches to the valuation of human life: 'vitalism'; 'sanctity of life'; and 'Quality of life' (the reason for the 'Q' will appear later) and concludes that the sanctity of life offers a middle way between two unacceptable extremes. It also sketches how a proper understanding of the moral significance of individual autonomy – of autonomy as enabling us to make decisions which promote rather than frustrate human flourishing – dovetails with that middle way. Part I concludes by maintaining that the common law has historically followed this middle way in its rejection of 'vitalism', 'Quality of life', and unbridled autonomy.

Part II argues that the Law Lords in *Bland* swerved from the middle way towards the ethical extremes of 'Quality of life' and unbridled autonomy; observes that the case indeed leaves the law in a morally and intellectually misshapen state; and suggests that the swerve may well have resulted from a confusion of the doctrine of the sanctity of life with vitalism.

Part III indicates how a coherent understanding of the principle of the sanctity of life – the principle at the heart of the doctrine of the sanctity of life – could have supplied a sound answer to the question raised in *Bland* and left the law in good shape.


## I. Human life and the law

### 1. Vitalism v. sanctity of life v. Quality of life

Before deciding which ethical approach the law ought to take to the valuation of human life, it is important to appreciate that there are at least three competing alternatives.


### (i) Vitalism

Vitalism holds that human life is an absolute moral value and that it is wrong either to shorten the life of an individual human being or to fail to strive to lengthen it. Whether the life be that of an anencephalic newborn (one lacking the cerebral hemispheres) or a dying centenarian, vitalism prohibits its shortening and requires its preservation. Regardless of the pain, suffering or expense that life-prolonging treatment entails, it must be administered: human life is to be preserved at all costs. Vitalism is as ethically untenable as its attempt to maintain life indefinitely is physically impossible. Its error lies in isolating the genuine and basic good of human life, and the duty to respect and promote that good, from the network of standards and responsibilities which make up our ethics and law as a whole; and its neglect of concepts and distinctions (such as between intention and foresight) vital to that network.

### (ii) The sanctity of life

#### (a) The prohibition of intentional killing

The principle of the sanctity of life is often advocated but much less often understood. In Western thought, the development of the principle has owed much to the Judaeo-Christian tradition.[8] That tradition's doctrine of the sanctity of life holds that human life is created in the image of God and is, therefore, possessed of an intrinsic dignity which entitles it to protection from unjust attack. With or without that theological underpinning, the doctrine that human life possesses an intrinsic dignity grounds the principle that *one must never intentionally kill an innocent human being*.[9] The 'right to life' is essentially a right not to be intentionally killed.

The dignity of human beings inheres because of that radical capacity inherent in human nature, which normally results in the development of rational abilities such as understanding and choice. Some human beings, such as infants, may not yet be in possession of rational abilities. But a radical capacity to acquire abilities must not be confused with exercisable abilities: one may have, for example, the capacity but not the ability to speak Swahili. All human beings should be presumed to possess the radical capacity characteristic of their nature, even though, because of infancy, disability or senility, they may not yet, not now, or no longer have the abilities that characteristically issue from possession of that capacity.[10]

As this account of human dignity might suggest, the principle can also be articulated in non-religious terms, in which 'inviolability' might be more apt than 'sanctity'. Indeed, a prohibition on killing is central to the pre-Christian fount of Western medical ethics – the Hippocratic Oath[11] – and the modern reaffirmation of that Oath by the (arguably post-Christian) Declaration of Geneva,[12] and many non-believers recognise the right of human beings not to be intentionally killed. Lord

---

[8] Respect for life is, however, also deeply rooted in Eastern thought: see Damien Keown, *Buddhism and Bioethics* (London: Macmillan 1995).

[9] 'Innocent' excludes anyone actively contributing to, or guilty of, unjust aggression and the principle has, therefore, traditionally allowed the use of lethal force in self defence, the prosecution of a just war and the execution of capital offenders. This has little relevance to doctors and patients.

[10] See Luke Gormally, ed., *Euthanasia, Clinical Practice and the Law* (London: The Linacre Centre 1994) at pp. 118–119.

[11] "To please no-one will I prescribe a deadly drug, nor give advice which may cause his death. Nor will I give a woman a pessary to procure abortion". J.K. Mason and R.A. McCall Smith, *Law and Medical Ethics* (4th ed, 1994) at p. 429.

[12] "I will maintain the utmost respect for human life from the time of conception; even under threat, I will not use my medical knowledge contrary to the laws of humanity": *ibid.*, at p. 430.

Goff noted in *Bland*[13] that the sanctity principle has long been recognised in most, if not all, civilized societies throughout the modern world, as is evidenced by its recognition by international conventions on human rights. Article 2 of the European Convention, for example, provides:

> Everyone's right to life shall be protected by law. *No one shall be deprived of his life intentionally* save in the execution of a sentence of a court following his conviction of a crime for which this penalty is provided by law.[14]

The right not to be killed intentionally is enjoyed regardless of inability or disability. Rejecting any such distinctions as fundamentally arbitrary and inconsistent with a sound concept of justice, the principle (whether in its religious or secular forms) asserts that human life is not only an instrumental good, a necessary precondition of thinking or doing, but a basic good, a fundamental constituent of human flourishing. It is, in other words, not merely good as a means to an end but is, like other integral aspects of a flourishing human life, like friendship and knowledge, something worthwhile in itself. Of course some people, like those who are pictures of health in the prime of life, participate in the good of life and health to a greater extent than others, such as the terminally ill, but even the sick and the dying participate in the good to the extent they are able.

Although human life is a basic good it is not the highest good, a good to which all the other basic goods must be sacrificed in order to ensure its preservation. The sanctity doctrine is not vitalistic. *The core of the doctrine is the principle prohibiting intentional killing, not an injunction requiring the preservation of life at all costs.*

## (b) Intention and foresight

Sanctity prohibits *intentional* life-shortening. Conduct which is intended to shorten life – 'intention' bearing its ordinary meaning of *purpose* – is always wrong. Conduct which may foreseeably shorten life is not always wrong. Whether it is will turn largely on whether there is a sufficient justification for taking the risk of shortening life.[15]

---

[13] [1993] A.C. 789 at pp. 863–864.

[14] 1953 Gr. Brit. T.S. No. 71 (Cmd.8969). Emphasis added.

[15] The precise ethical criteria have traditionally been articulated in terms of the long-established principle of 'double effect'. This principle, recently endorsed by the House of Lords Select Committee on Medical Ethics (*Report of the Select Committee on Medical Ethics* H.L. Paper 21-I of 1993–94, at para. 242.) holds that an act which produces a bad effect is morally permissible if the action is good in itself, the intention is solely to produce the good effect, the good effect is not achieved through the bad effect, and there is a sufficient reason to permit the bad effect: see Luke Gormally *The principle of respect for human life* (Paper 1, Prolongation of Life Series; London: The Linacre Centre, 1978) at p. 10. For a fuller discussion of the moral distinction between intended and foreseen consequences see J.M. Finnis, 'Intention and Side-Effects' in R.G. Frey and Christopher W. Morris (eds), *Liability and Responsibility* (Cambridge: Cambridge University Press 1991) at p. 32; and J.M. Finnis, 'Intention in Tort Law' in David Owen (ed.), *Philosophical Foundations of Tort Law* (Oxford: Clarendon Press 1995) 229 at pp. 243–246.

A doctor treating a terminally-ill cancer patient suffering pain clearly has a sufficient justification for administering palliative drugs with intent to ease the pain, even though a foreseeable side-effect may or will be the shortening of life. Similarly, a doctor may properly withhold or withdraw a life-prolonging treatment which is futile (that is, cannot secure a significant therapeutic benefit) or which the patient would find too burdensome, even though the doctor foresees that non-treatment may or will result in the patient's life ending sooner than would otherwise be the case. Doctors may not, on the other hand, take unreasonable risks with patients' lives. It is one thing for a doctor to perform neurosurgery to remove a malignant tumour, even though the operation may prove fatal; quite another to perform it merely because the patient has a headache.

## (c) Acts and omissions

In the medical context, there are no exceptions to sanctity's moral prohibition of intentional killing: the doctor who intentionally shortens the life of a patient, whether a terminally ill adult or a child with Down's syndrome, breaches the principle. It matters not, moreover, whether the shortening is brought about by an act or an omission. Intentionally shortening a patient's life by withholding treatment, or food, water or warmth, is no less wrong than injecting a lethal poison. Nor does a good motive, such as the alleviation of suffering, of the patient or relatives, redeem a bad intent. In short, any conduct which is intended to shorten a patient's life, whether as an end or as a means to an end and whatever the further motive, offends against the principle.

## (d) The worthwhileness of treatment: its benefits and burdens

As the above distinction between intended and foreseen life-shortening indicates, the sanctity doctrine accepts that in many cases it is perfectly proper to withhold or withdraw life-preserving treatment. That one need not try to preserve life *at all costs* is sometimes expressed in a quotation from A.H. Clough's ironic poem *The Latest Decalogue* that while one must not kill, one "needst not strive *officiously* to keep alive". More precisely, however, the sanctity principle holds that there can be no moral obligation to administer or undergo a treatment which is not worthwhile. A treatment may be not worthwhile either because it offers no reasonable hope of benefit or because, even though it does, the expected benefit would be outweighed by burdens which the treatment would impose, such as excessive pain. Notice, however, that the question is always whether the *treatment* would be worthwhile, not whether the patient's *life* would be worthwhile. Were one to engage in judgements of the latter sort, and to conclude that certain lives were not worth living, one would forfeit any principled basis for objecting to intentional killing.

Where the benefit of a proposed treatment is not outweighed by the burdens it would impose, it has traditionally been referred to as 'ordinary' and, where the converse is the case, as 'extraordinary'. Problems associated with this terminology (not least the fact that 'ordinary' was often mistakenly interpreted to mean 'usual' and 'extraordinary' to mean 'unusual') have resulted in the increasing use of terms such as 'proportionate' and 'disproportionate'. But whichever terms are used, the moral question is the same: whether a proposed treatment is worthwhile, that is, whether its benefits, if any, would outweigh its burdens, if any.

Take Angela, a baby born with Down's syndrome and an intestinal blockage. Her doctor informs her parents that the blockage can be removed by a straight-forward surgical operation and that, if it is not so removed, Angela will die. The doctor and parents, judging that the treatment will clearly benefit Angela by saving her life while involving only minimal burdens, such as the usual discomfort associated with the operation, decide that the operation would be worthwhile or proportionate and should be performed.

Contrast Angela with Bertha, a baby born with a terminal illness which will inevitably lead to death in a matter of hours. Her doctor informs her parents that, due to respiratory difficulties, she may stop breathing at any time and asks whether they would like attempts at artificial ventilation to be made should her breathing falter. Given that such efforts could not hope to reverse Bertha's inevitable decline, and might impose significant burdens on her, they decide against ventilation as it would be disproportionate. In short, they decide to allow Bertha to die in peace. Yet their judgement in no way contravenes the principle of the sanctity of life; it is, indeed, wholly consistent with it.

But what if the decision in either case were made not on the basis that the proposed *treatment* was not worthwhile, but on the basis that the child's *life* was not worthwhile? Here we encounter another extreme avoided by the sanctity doctrine: 'Quality of life', the opposite pole to vitalism.

### (iii) 'Quality' of life

The doctrine of the Quality of life is not concerned with assessing the worthwhileness of the treatment but with the worthwhileness of the patient's life. It holds that the lives of certain patients fall below a quality threshold, whether because of disease, injury or disability. This valuation of human life grounds the principle that, because certain lives are not worth living, it is right intentionally to terminate them, whether by act or omission. Some who subscribe to this philosophy would require the patient's request as a precondition of termination. Others would not. After all, they argue, if the life of an incompetent patient is of such low quality that it is no longer worth living, and death would be a benefit, what is wrong with terminating it?

### 2. quality v. Quality: a crucial distinction

### (i) Patient's condition v. worth of life

'Quality of life' judgements purport to assess the worthwhileness of the patient's life. The sanctity doctrine opposes such attempts and merely takes the patient's condition into account in determining the worthwhileness of a proposed treatment. For, in order to decide whether a proposed treatment would be worthwhile, one must first ascertain the patient's present condition and consider whether and to what extent it would be improved by the proposed treatment. This exercise is often described as involving an assessment of the patient's 'quality of life' now and as it would be after the treatment. At no point in the sanctity assessment is one purporting to pass judgement on the worthwhileness of the patient's life, but the use of the term 'quality of life' clearly risks confusion with its use in that sense. Such confusion is, regrettably, rife in ethical and legal discourse. To avoid any confusion in this paper, 'quality' of life will hereinafter be used to refer to an assessment of the patient's condition as a preliminary to assessing the worthwhileness of a proposed treatment and 'Quality of life' to refer to assessments of the worthwhileness of the patient's life.

### (ii) Illustrating the distinction

To illustrate the differences between the two approaches, let us return to Angela. The sanctity approach concluded that the blockage should be removed because – on a fair measure, that is, one commonly used by people in relation to their own situation – the benefits promised by the treatment, the improvement the operation would make to her condition (or 'quality of life'), would significantly outweigh any burdens. However, a Quality of life approach might well deny the operation on the ground that *life with Down's syndrome* is simply not worth living. The focus is not on the worthwhileness of the treatment: indeed, the problem is thought to arise by the Quality of life advocate precisely because the treatment would be entirely successful.

### (iii) Sanctity v Quality

From the standpoint of the sanctity doctrine, a central objection to the Quality of life philosophy is that it denies the ineliminable value of each patient and engages in discriminatory judgements, posited on fundamentally arbitrary criteria such as physical or mental disability, about whose lives are 'worthwhile' and whose are not. The arbitrariness is highlighted when it is asked *which* disabilities, and to which *degree*, are supposed to make life not worth living?[16] Such discrimination seems, moreover, inconsistent with national and international declarations of human rights, which recognise the inherent rights enjoyed by all human beings simply because of their common humanity, not because they pass some Quality threshold.

---

[16] See Gormally, *op. cit. supra* n. 10 at pp. 123–124.

### 3. The good of autonomy

In determining whether a proposed treatment would involve excessive burdens to a particular patient, the views of the patient are clearly crucial. Individuals differ, for example, in their ability to tolerate pain, and what may be excessively painful for one patient may not be so to another. Indeed, the distinctions between proportionate and disproportionate treatments were devised by moralists not primarily for the purposes of health care professionals faced with decisions about which treatments they were morally bound to offer, but for patients facing decisions about which treatments they were morally bound to accept.

Moreover, the responsibility for safeguarding and promoting the good of health lies primarily with the patient, not with the doctor, at least where the patient is competent. Choices by patients which promote the good of health therefore merit respect and it is reasonable to allow patients considerable leeway, given the considerable variation between patients, in deciding what treatments they would find excessively burdensome.

This does not mean that just *any* choice by the patient merits respect, such as a choice to refuse treatment as a means of committing suicide. The value of individual choice lies in the fact that it is through our choices that we are able to promote our own flourishing as human beings (and that of those around us). Such choices, moreover, serve to reinforce dispositions to act in ways conducive to our flourishing. For our choices have internal as well as external effects: they shape our character. A's murder of B results not only in B being murdered but in making A a murderer. As the ancient adage attests, an act tends to form a habit, a habit tends to form a character, and a character tends to form a destiny.[17]

The capacity to choose brings with it the responsibility of making not just any old choice, but choices that do in fact promote, rather than undermine, human flourishing. Given the legitimate diversity of lifestyles and life-choices which are consistent with human flourishing, many choices are consistent with human well-being. We should, therefore, think carefully before restricting another's autonomy. But it is difficult to see why patently immoral choices, choices clearly inconsistent with human well-being, such as my starving you to death, or my starving myself to death, merit respect. An exercise of autonomy merits respect only when it is in accordance with a framework of moral truths. For example, A's decision to murder B is an exercise of autonomy, but it hardly merits respect since it breaches a grave moral norm. This is particularly clear when the decision, such as a decision to murder, seriously harms another person. But it is also true when the decision is morally wrong, whether it 'harms' another or not, such as a decision to buy and smoke 'crack' cocaine, or to commit incest with a consenting relative, or perform female circumcision on a consenting woman, or to commit suicide.

Autonomy is, in other words, like the pointer in a compass. The pointer itself is of little value, indeed makes little sense, in the absence of the points of the compass. When the pointer indicates a morally valuable course – and there may be a

[17] *Ibid.*, at pp. 130–131.

number of morally valuable courses – the choice merits respect. But when the choice is immoral, whether because it would harm another, or oneself, or breach some other moral norm, what claim to moral respect can it have? This is not to say that all morally worthless choices should be overridden, merely that they lack moral force.

Much contemporary talk about autonomy consists of little more than the bare, uncritical assertion that a person's choice merits respect simply because it is his or her choice, whatever the choice may be; that self-determination is a moral absolute. The focus is on a self-justifying 'right to choose' rather than on what it is right to choose. The 'right to choose x' often serves as a slogan with powerful emotional appeal. But crude slogans are no substitute for rational reflection, and one can hardly sensibly assert a right to choose 'x' until one has considered whether it is right to choose 'x'. The right to choose only arguably makes any moral sense in the context of a moral framework which enables us to discern what it is right to choose, what choices will in fact promote human flourishing. And not only our flourishing, but that of others. For we do not live as atomised individuals, as much loose talk about absolute respect for personal autonomy seems to assume, but in community, where our choices can have profound effects not only on ourselves but on others.

If the principle of the sanctity of life is accepted, and it has hitherto been a hall-mark of civilised societies, its implications for the right to self-determination should be patent. If it is seriously immoral intentionally to kill an innocent person, it is difficult to see how a choice to kill, whether another or oneself, can command moral respect. As the Anglican and Catholic Bishops stated in their joint submission to the House of Lords Select Committee, autonomy is not absolute and is valid "only when it recognises other moral values, especially the respect due to human life as such, whether someone else's or one's own".[18]

Indeed, given the fundamental value of life, society is fully justified in using the criminal law to deter the implementation of such choices. This is not to say we must use the law against individuals who have attempted suicide, who typically need understanding and help rather than condemnation and punishment, though it remains reasonable to use it against those who would assist or encourage suicide.

To conclude, just as the patient's life is not the highest moral value requiring preservation at all costs, neither is the patient's self-determination a moral absolute requiring respect in all circumstances, and certainly not when it involves a choice to kill, whether oneself or another.

## 4. The law

### (i) Homicide

The doctrine and principle of the sanctity of life have long informed the common law. The law prohibits, as murder, the intentional shortening of a patient's life,

---

[18] *Euthanasia – No!* (London: Catholic Truth Society 1993) para. 8.

regardless of the motive of the doctor[19] or the age, medical condition or wishes of the patient. Though the blameworthiness of the killer may of course be mitigated, it remains as much murder intentionally to shorten the life of an aged terminally-ill cancer patient who pleads for death as it is to kill a young person in the prime of life who strenuously objects to death.[20] It also remains murder regardless of "necessity"[21] or duress.[22]

### (ii) Acts and omissions

Nor is the criminal law concerned only to punish active killing. Although there is, generally, no liability for an omission to preserve life, it is well-established that it is murder to omit to discharge a duty to preserve life if the omission is with intent to kill or cause serious harm. Examples would be a parent's omission to feed a child, as in *Gibbins and Proctor*,[23] or a doctor's to feed a patient, with such intent.

### (iii) Intention and foresight

The important moral distinction between intention and foresight which charac-terises the sanctity principle has also, at least since the decision of the House of Lords in *Moloney*,[24] been more or less clearly incorporated into the English law

---

[19] As Lord Goff has pointed out: "... if I kill you from the motive of compassion (so-called mercy killing) I nevertheless intend to kill you and the crime is one of murder". Lord Goff, 'The Mental Element in the Crime of Murder' (1988) 104 *Law Quarterly Review* 30 at p. 42. Footnote omitted.

[20] At York Assizes in 1812, two women who drowned a dying and deformed newborn child were convicted of murder, even though they thought they were acting rightly and lawfully. The trial judge stated: "I think this prosecution may be of great use to the public, in removing an erroneous opinion, that the law allows the right of deliberately taking away the life of a human being under any circumstances whatever." *Woodger and Lyall* (1812) 54 *Annual Register*, Chronicle at p. 97.

[21] In *Dudley and Stephens* (1884–85) 14 Q.B.D. 273 Coleridge L.C.J., rejecting necessity as a defence to murder, observed (at p. 287): "It is not needful to point out the awful danger of admitting the principle which has been contended for. Who is to be the judge of this sort of necessity? By what measure is the comparative value of lives to be measured? Is it to be strength, or intellect, or what?"

[22] In *Howe* [1987] A.C. 417 Lord Mackay stated (at p. 456): "It seems to me plain that the reason that it was for so long stated by writers of authority that the defence of duress was not available in a charge of murder was because of the supreme importance that the law afforded to the protection of human life and that it seemed repugnant that the law should recognise in any individual in any circumstances, however extreme, the right to choose that one innocent person should be killed rather than another." He concluded that the law should continue to deny that right. See also *McKay v. Essex A.H.A.* [1982] Q.B. 1166.

[23] (1918) 13 Cr. App. R. 134. In this paper, "his" includes "her" unless the contrary is apparent.

[24] [1985] A.C. 905. See also *Hancock and Shankland* [1986] A.C. 455. Regrettably, the House of Lords in *Woolin* [1998] 4 All E.R. 103 appears to have thrown doubt on this crucial distinction in the criminal law.

of homicide. Murder requires proof of intention in its ordinary sense of *purpose*. Foresight, even of consequences which are certain, is not equivalent to intention and is, at most, evidence of intention.

It will be recalled that the sanctity principle prohibits conduct intended to shorten life but that conduct which is foreseen to be certain or likely to shorten life may or may not be culpable, depending on the circumstances. So too with the criminal law. Intentional killing is punished as murder, but conduct which foreseeably shortens life is at most manslaughter and may be perfectly lawful, depending on the reasonableness of the doctor's conduct. For example, a doctor who follows reasonable medical practice in administering palliative drugs to a dying patient, intending thereby to alleviate suffering, acts lawfully, even if the drugs, as an unintended side-effect, hasten death.

In *R v. Cox*, a physician who had administered a lethal drug to a dying patient at her request was convicted of attempted murder. In his summing-up, Mr Justice Ognall said:

> It was plainly Dr Cox's duty to do all that was medically possible to alleviate her pain and suffering, even if the course adopted carried with it an obvious risk that, as a side effect [note my emphasis, and I will repeat it – even if the course adopted carried with it an obvious risk that as a side effect] of that treatment, her death would be rendered likely or even certain.[25]

There was no doubt, he added, that the use of palliative drugs would often be fully justified even if they hastened death. What could never be lawful, however, was the use of drugs with the "primary purpose" of hastening death.[26]

### (iv) Autonomy

Historically, the law has adopted the traditional ethical understanding of the value of autonomy sketched above. Consequently, it has proscribed, and continues to proscribe, many exercises of autonomy on the ground that they are wrongful. Their wrongfulness often inheres in their infliction of harm upon others or in the exposure of others to the risk of harm, whether or not, as in duelling, the other consents to the risk of harm. But an exercise of autonomy may also be prohibited because it exposes oneself to harm, or to the risk of harm, such as buying and snorting cocaine or, less seriously, driving a vehicle without wearing a seat-belt. In short, the law has, historically, provided scant support for an absolutist understanding of individual autonomy.

---

[25] [1992] 12 B.M.L.R. 38 at p. 41. The bracketed words appear in the extract from the summing up in Ian Kennedy and Andrew Grubb, *Medical Law: Text with Materials* (2nd. edn. 1994) at p. 1309. See also *Adams* [1957] Crim. L.R. 365; *Re J (A Minor) (Wardship: Medical Treatment)* [1991] 1 F.L.R. 366 at pp.374–375 *per* Lord Donaldson M.R.
[26] *Ibid.*

## II. From sanctity to Quality

### 1. The facts

Before his death on 3 March 1993, Tony Bland had lain in Airedale Hospital for over three years in pvs, a state in which, it was believed, he could neither see, hear nor feel. The medical consensus was that he would never regain consciousness. Neither dead nor dying, his brain stem still functioned and he breathed and digested naturally. He was fed by nasogastric tube, his excretory functions regulated by catheter and enemas. Infections were treated with antibiotics. His doctor and parents wanted to stop the feeding and antibiotics on the ground that neither served any useful purpose. The hospital trust applied for a declaration that it would be lawful to do so.

The application, supported by an *amicus curiae* instructed by the Attorney-General, was opposed by the Official Solicitor, representing Bland. The declaration was granted by Sir Stephen Brown, President of the Family Division of the High Court, whose decision was unanimously affirmed by the Court of Appeal and the House of Lords.

### 2. The court's reasoning

Counsel for the Official Solicitor, James Munby Q.C., argued that stopping treatment and feeding would be murder or at least manslaughter. Three of the Law Lords accepted his submission that the doctor's intention would be to kill Tony Bland, a submission which the remaining two neither rejected nor accepted. One of the three, Lord Browne-Wilkinson, said:[27]

> Murder consists of causing the death of another with intent to do so. What is proposed in the present case is to adopt a course with the intention of bringing about Anthony Bland's death. As to the element of intention..., in my judgment there can be no real doubt that it is present in this case: the whole purpose of stopping artificial feeding is to bring about the death of Anthony Bland.[28]

Why, then, would it not be murder? Because stopping treatment and feeding was not a positive act but an omission. Lord Goff stated[29] that withdrawing life-support was no different from withholding it in the first place; the doctor was simply allowing the patient to die as a result of his pre-existing condition. More-over, tube-feeding was medical treatment: there was, he said, "overwhelming

---

[27] [1993] A.C. 789 at p. 881.
[28] Why the majority assumed it was the doctor's intention to kill is not entirely clear: it does not follow that because the doctor foresaw the patient's death as certain he therefore intended it. However, to the extent that the basis of the decision was that withdrawal was justified as ending a life judged no longer worthwhile an intention to kill seems implicit in the reasoning.

evidence" that in the medical profession tube-feeding was so regarded and, even if it were not strictly treatment, it formed part of the patient's medical care. The provision of food by tube was, he added, analogous to the provision of air by a ventilator.

The House further held that the doctor was under no duty to continue tube-feeding. *Re F*[30] decided that a doctor could treat an incompetent patient only if it was in the patient's best interests; *Bland* held that the same criterion should govern the withdrawal of treatment. As continued feeding was no longer in the patient's interests, the doctor was under no duty to continue it. The tube-feeding was not in Bland's best interests because it was futile and it was futile because, in the words of Lord Goff,[31] "the patient is unconscious and there is no prospect of any improvement in his condition". In deciding whether treatment was futile, the doctor had to act in accordance with a responsible body of medical opinion and thereby satisfy the '*Bolam* test' – the test which determines whether, in an action for medical negligence, a doctor has fallen below the standard of care required by the law.[32]

### 3. Misunderstanding the sanctity of life

Their Lordships' reasoning appears, with respect, vulnerable to several criticisms.

### (i) Tube-feeding: futile treatment or basic care?

Why was tube-feeding not basic care which the hospital and its medical and nursing staff were under a duty to provide? The Law Lords held that tube-feeding was part of a regime of "medical treatment and care".[33] The insertion of a gastrostomy tube into the stomach requires a minor operation, which is clearly a medical procedure. But it is not at all clear that the insertion of a nasogastric tube is medical intervention. And, even if it were, the intervention had already been carried out in Tony Bland's case. The question in such a case is why the pouring of food down the tube constitutes medical treatment. What is it supposed to be treating? Nor does the difficulty evaporate by classifying it, as did the Law Lords, as medical treatment or medical care. As Professor Finnis observes:[34]

> The judgments all seem to embrace a fallacious inference, that if tube-feeding *is* part of medical 'treatment or care', tube-feeding is therefore *not* part of the non-

[29] [1993] A.C. 789 at 868.
[30] [1990] 2 A.C. 1.
[31] [1993] A.C. 789 at 869.
[32] *Bolam* v. *Friern H.M.C.* [1957] 1 W.L.R. 582. Lord Mustill reserved judgement about the appropriateness of this test in this context: see text *infra* n. 57.
[33] See, e.g., [1993] A.C. 789 at p. 858 *per* Lord Keith.
[34] *Op. cit. supra* n. 7 at p. 335. Original emphasis.

medical (home or nursing) care which decent families and communities provide or arrange for their utterly dependent members. The non-sequitur is compounded by failure to note that although naso-gastric tube-feeding will not normally be established without a doctor's decision, no distinctively medical skills are needed to insert a naso-gastric tube or to maintain the supply of nutrients through it.

Their Lordships seemed to place great weight on the fact that tube-feeding is regarded by the medical profession as medical treatment.[35] But whether an intervention is medical is not a matter to be determined by medical opinion, nor by the mere fact that it is an intervention typically performed by doctors. A doctor may do many things in the course of his practice, such as reassuring patients or fitting catheters, which are not distinctively medical in nature. And, if it is opinion which is crucial, the answer one gets may well depend on whom one asks. Tube-feeding may be regarded as medical treatment by many doctors, but many nurses regard it as ordinary care.[36]

Further, Lord Goff's analogy between tube-feeding and mechanical ventilation is (although accepted by Mr. Munby Q.C.[37]) unpersuasive. Ventilation is standardly part of a therapeutic endeavour to stabilise, treat and cure: tube-feeding is not. Moreover, ventilation replaces the patient's capacity to breathe whereas a tube does not replace the capacity to digest and merely delivers food to the stomach. Nor have all patients who are tube-fed (including, it appears, those in pvs) lost the capacity to swallow. Tube-feeding may be instituted solely to minimise the risk of the patient inhaling food and/or because spoon-feeding is thought to be too time-consuming. Even if the patient has lost the capacity to swallow, the tube would still not be treating anything. A feeding-tube by which liquid is delivered to the patient's stomach is surely no more medical treatment than a catheter by which it is drained from the patient's bladder.

Even if tube-feeding were medical treatment, why was it futile? Was it because it would do nothing to restore Tony Bland to the condition towards which *medical* practice and procedures are directed, namely some level of health, an explanation consistent with the sanctity ethic?[38] Or was it rather because Bland's *life* was thought futile, an explanation inconsistent with it? Dr. Keith Andrews, director of medical services at the Royal Hospital for Neurodisability, and a leading authority on pvs, recently wrote:[39]

> It is ironic that the only reason that tube feeding has been identified as 'treatment' has been so that it can be withdrawn.... I would argue that tube-feeding is extremely effective since it achieves all the things we intend it

[35] See, e.g., [1993] A.C. 789 at p. 870 *per* Lord Goff.
[36] See, e.g., *Nursing Times*, 10th February 1993 at p. 7.
[37] [1993] A.C. 789 at p. 822.
[38] See Luke Gormally, 'Reflections on Horan and Boyle' in Luke Gormally, (ed) *The Dependent Elderly* (Cambridge: Cambridge University Press 1992) at p. 47.
[39] (1995) 311 *British Medical Journal* 1437 (letters).

to. What is really being argued is whether the patient's life is futile – hence the need to find some way of ending that life.'

Are there, then, grounds for concluding that the judges in *Bland* condoned the withdrawal of tube-feeding because they felt the patient's life, rather than the "treatment", was futile?

### (ii) Misunderstanding the sanctity of life

Lord Mustill rejected the notion that the state's interest in preserving life was attenuated "where the 'quality' of the life is diminished by disease or incapacity". If correct, he added, that argument would justify active as well as passive euthanasia and thus require a change in the law of murder.[40] The proposition that because of incapacity or infirmity one life is intrinsically worth less than another was, he said, the first step on a "very dangerous road indeed" and one he was unwilling to take.[41] Yet even he held that Tony Bland had no interest in being kept alive[42] and no best interests of any kind.[43] How do these propositions differ from a judgment that the patient's life was no longer worthwhile?

The concept of the worthless life is even more pronounced in other judgements, particularly in those passages which espouse what one may call 'dualism', the notion that human beings comprise two separate entities: a 'body' and a 'person', the former being of merely instrumental value as a vehicle for the latter. Sir Stephen Brown, for example, described Tony Bland thus:[44] "His spirit has left him and all that remains is the shell of his body . . . [which is] kept functioning as a biological unit . . . ". Similarly, Lord Justice Hoffmann said:[45] "His body is alive, but he has no life in the sense that even the most pitifully handicapped but conscious human being has a life". Bland's existence was, he added, a "humiliation"; he was "grotesquely alive".[46]

Such judicial endorsement of dualism is both novel and surprising, not only because (as Finnis points out[47]) dualism enjoys relatively little support among philosophers but also because the law has hitherto rejected the notion of "biological units" which are "inhabited" by a non-bodily person and has, on the contrary, taken the traditional, common-sense view that human life *is* personal life, that living human beings are persons and that persons are, applying standard

[40] [1993] A.C. 789 at p. 894.
[41] *Ibid.*
[42] *Ibid.*, at p. 898.
[43] *Ibid.*, at p. 897.
[44] *Ibid.*, at p. 804.
[45] *Ibid.*, at p. 825. He admitted he had been influenced by reading the manuscript of Professor Dworkin's book *Life's Dominion* (1993), a book which espouses dualism and misrepresents the doctrine and the principle of the sanctity of life (see (1994) 110 *Law Quarterly Review* 671).
[46] See also [1993] A.C. 789 at 863 *per* Lord Goff; at 879 per Lord Browne-Wilkinson; at 897 *per* Lord Mustill.
[47] *Op. cit. supra* n. 7 at p. 334.

biological criteria, either alive or dead. As the judges recognised, it would be murder actively to kill Bland, regardless of his permanent unconsciousness. The law does not deny personhood, and the rights it attracts, because the person has lost the ability to think. We are all "biological units", and our mental acts, far from being a separate form of life, something 'added to' our body (from where?), intrinsically involve, just like our physical acts, biological processes, and are an expression of our one life as a human being, a human person. For example, the judge who listens to and evaluates an argument from counsel is not a biological machine with a little mental person inside (reminiscent of "The Numskulls" in the children's comic) but an integrated, dynamic unity, a living human body exercising the capacities (intellectual and physical) which are inherent in his or her nature as a human being. It is because we are human beings, human "biological units", that we have the radical capacity for acts both physical and mental. The fact that a human being has lost the ability to think does not mean he or she has lost his or her life. As Finnis puts it:[48]

> One's living body is intrinsic, not merely instrumental, to one's personal life. Each of us has a human life (not a vegetable life plus an animal life plus a personal life); when it is flourishing that life includes all one's vital functions including speech, deliberation and choice; when gravely impaired it lacks some of those functions without ceasing to be the life of the person so impaired.

And, he adds, the fact that one is in pvs, although a gravely impairing condition which may prevent participation in basic human goods apart from life such as friendship or aesthetic experience, does not mean that one is not participating in the good, the benefit, of life.

But could it have been beneficial to feed and care for Tony Bland even though he could not appreciate it? It is perfectly possible to benefit someone, even if they are unaware of it, as where A, unbeknown to B, deposits a large amount in B's bank account, or speaks well of him to C.[49] And to state, as did Lord Mustill,[50] that Bland had "no best interests of any kind" is, with respect, surely false. Would it not have been contrary to his interests to use him as, for example, a sideboard?

Given the dualistic reasoning uncritically engaged in by the judges, their conclusion that Bland's life was of no benefit, indeed may even have been a harm, a humiliation, comes as little surprise. That it was Bland's life, and not his tube-feeding, that was adjudged worthless is clearly illustrated by the following passage from the speech of Lord Keith:

> ...it is, of course, true that in general it would not be lawful for a medical practitioner who assumed responsibility for the care of an unconscious patient simply to give up treatment in circumstances where continuance of it would

---

[48] *Op. cit. supra* n. 7 at p. 334.

[49] See Joseph Boyle, 'A Case for Sometimes Tube-Feeding Patients in Persistent Vegetative State' in John Keown, (ed) *Euthanasia Examined* (Cambridge: Cambridge University Press 1995) pp. 189–199.

[50] [1993] A.C. 789 at p. 897.

confer some benefit on the patient. On the other hand a medical practitioner is under no duty to continue to treat such a patient where a large body of informed and responsible medical opinion is to the effect that no benefit at all would be conferred by continuance. *Existence in a vegetative state with no prospect of recovery is by that opinion regarded as not being a benefit*, and that, if not unarguably correct, at least forms a proper basis for the decision to discontinue treatment and care: *Bolam v Friern Hospital Management Committee* [1957] 1 W.L.R. 582[51]

But why was discontinuance not a breach of the principle of the sanctity of life, a principle which Lord Keith accepted[52] it was the concern of the State, and the judiciary as an arm of the State, to uphhold? What is remarkable is that, while their Lordships agreed with the fundamental importance of the principle, none of them accurately articulated it.

Lord Goff, for example, in setting out the fundamental principles of law relevant to the case, stated[53] that the "fundamental principle is the principle of the sanctity of life". But he then went on to claim[54] that, although it is fundamental, it is "not absolute". In support of this surprising claim, he made a number of observations which suggest that his Lordship misunderstood the principle.

He observed, first, that it is lawful to kill in self-defence and, secondly, that, in the medical context, there is no absolute rule that a patient's life must be prolonged by treatment or care regardless of the circumstances. Both statements are, as the discussion in Part I made clear, accurate. But they do not show that the principle of the sanctity of life is "not absolute", unless one thinks, as his Lordship appears to, that the principle prohibits all killings or requires the preservation of life at all costs. Neither proposition is, of course, consistent with the principle as traditionally formulated and understood. His Lordship observed, thirdly, that the fact that a doctor must respect a patient's refusal of life-prolonging treatment showed that the sanctity of life yielded to the right to self-determination. Again, his Lordship seems to think that the sanctity of life requires the preservation of life, even against the competent patient's contemporaneous wishes. Again, this is not so. Fourthly, he distinguished between a doctor, on the one hand, omitting to provide life-prolonging treatment or care and, on the other, administering a lethal drug. "So to act", he said[55] "is to cross the Rubicon which runs between on the one hand the care of the living patient and on the other hand euthanasia – actively causing his death to avoid or to end his suffering". But, as we saw in Part I, the intentional killing by one person of another person in his care, even if effected by omission, breaches the principle.

[51] *Ibid.*, at pp. 858–859. Emphasis added. See also p. 857, where he implies that Bland's life was meaningless. See also pp. 878–879 and pp. 884–885 per Lord Browne-Wilkinson.
[52] *Ibid.*, at p. 859.
[53] *Ibid.*, at p. 863.
[54] *Ibid.*, at p. 864.
[55] *Ibid.*, at p. 865.

## (iii) The Bolam test

The Law Lords decided that Tony Bland's doctor was under no duty to continue treatment and tube-feeding if he felt that continuation was no longer in the patient's best interests and if his opinion was supported (as it was) by a responsible body of medical opinion. Indeed, as Lord Browne-Wilkinson pointed out,[56] if the doctor decided that treatment was no longer in the patient's best interests, he was under a *duty* to withdraw it. Since the doctor could only lawfully treat the patient if he believed it was in the patient's best interests, continuing treatment when he did not believe it to be so would consitute the crime and tort of battery.

But why should the judgement about which patients have lives worth living be delegated to a "responsible body" of medical opinion? Even assuming this comprehensive judgement can be made about the worth of another (which the sanctity principle denies), what qualifies a *doctor* to make it? Lord Mustill aptly observed[57] that the decision could be said to be ethical and that there was no logical reason why the opinions of doctors should be decisive. His was, however, a lone voice among the Law Lords. Lord Browne-Wilkinson expressly stated[58] that one doctor could decide, because of his ethical views about the sanctity of life, that his patient was "entitled to stay alive" whereas another doctor who saw "no merit in perpetuating a life of which the patient is unaware" could lawfully stop his patient's treatment.

Their Lordships did observe that, for the present, all cases like Bland's should be brought before the High Court for a declaration. But what is the court's role? Is it, as it appears to be, essentially to confirm that the doctor's opinion is supported by a responsible body of medical opinion? Or is it to lay down judicial criteria for deciding which lives are worthwhile? If the latter, what are those criteria?[59]

## (iv) A 'slippery slope'

Lord Justice Hoffmann said[60] that it was "absurd to conjure up the spectre of eugenics" as a reason against the decision in *Bland*. However, once Quality supplants inviolability, there is no reason in principle why the Quality threshhold should stop at pvs. Finnis has observed that it is one thing to say that one should not treat people in ways which affront their inalienable dignity, but quite another to say that, because of their physical or mental disabilty, they *have* no dignity or, worse, that they *are* an indignity. How can the latter judgement logically be limited to those in pvs? As he maintains:[61]

---

[56] [1993] A.C. 789 at p. 883.
[57] *Ibid.*, at pp. 898–899.
[58] *Ibid.*, at p. 884.
[59] See *Frenchay N.H.S. Healthcare Trust v. S* [1994] 1 W.L.R. 601; John Keown, 'Applying Bland', [1994] 53(3) *Cambridge Law Journal* 456.
[60] [1993] A.C. 789 at p. 831.
[61] *Op. cit. supra* n. 7 at p. 336.

"Epithets of indignity and humiliation could easily be applied (as in recent history) to various classes of severely handicapped people, many of whom, moreover, cannot exercise the distinctively human or 'personal' forms of understanding and response".

Lord Mustill raised,[62] without resolving, the case of the patient who has "glimmerings of awareness" and Lord Browne-Wilkinson[63] the patient with slight chances of improvement or with "very slight sensate awareness".

In May 1995, the Irish Supreme Court, following Bland, permitted (by a 4–1 majority) the withdrawal of tube-feeding from a patient who was not in pvs and had retained some cognitive function.[64] It affirmed the decision of the first instance judge who stated that if she were aware of her condition "that would be a terrible torment to her and her situation would be *worse* than if she were fully P.V.S."[65]

Leaving aside the reasoning of the judges who favoured withdrawal (which is more, rather than less, vulnerable to criticism than the reasoning in *Bland*), the Irish case illustrates the inherently arbitrary nature of Quality of life judgements. The criticism bites even more deeply when the judgement is, *via* the *Bolam* test, delegated to "responsible" opinion. The question then simply becomes whether there is a body of "responsible" medical opinion which supports the doctor's view that the patient's life is worthless, whether or not a larger body of medical opinion disagrees. The inherent arbitrariness of Quality of life judgements, particularly when delegated to doctors, is underlined when it is recalled that medical opinion is often divided and in flux. A patient may be treated by a doctor who thinks his life worthwhile, but that doctor's ethical views may change, or the patient may come under the care of a doctor with different ethical views. The upshot would appear to be that if a doctor responsible, say, for a patient with advanced Alzheimer's disease thinks the patient's life is of no benefit, and the doctor's opinion coincides with that of a "responsible body" of medical opinion, the doctor may, indeed must, cease treating the patient.

A recent case concerning non-treatment of an incompetent adult involved a 23 year-old man ('R') with serious mental and physical disabilities.[66] Frail and weighing five stones, R operated cognitively and neurologically at the level of a newborn infant but responded to comfort, warmth and a safe environment by producing the occasional smile and to pain and to discomfort by becoming distressed and crying. After several hospital admissions in 1995, the consultant psychiatrist in learning disabilities who was responsible for his treatment agreed with R's parents that should R suffer a life-threatening condition involving a cardiac arrest he should not be given cardio-pulmonary resuscitation. As a result of concern expressed at this decision by staff at the day care centre R attended, the hospital trust applied

[62] [1993] A.C. 789 at p. 899.
[63] *Ibid.*, at p. 885.
[64] *In the Matter of a Ward of Court* [1995] 2 I.L.R.M. 410; John Keown, 'Life and Death in Dublin', [1996] 55 (1) *Cambridge Law Journal* 6.
[65] Cited in [1995] 2 I.L.R.M. 401 at p. 432 *per* O'Flaherty J. Emphasis added.
[66] *Re R* [1996] 2 F.L.R. 99.

for a declaration in the Family Division and the Official Solicitor was appointed to act as R's guardian *ad litem*.

Sir Stephen Brown granted a declaration in terms drafted by counsel for the Official Solicitor, James Munby Q.C., and approved by counsel for the plaintiffs and by R's parents. The declaration provided *inter alia* that it would be lawful as being in R's best interests for the plaintiffs to perform a gastrostomy but to withhold cardio-pulmonary resuscitation and, provided R's general practitioner and consultant psychiatrist so advised and one or both of R's parents agreed, to withhold antibiotics in the event of a potentially life-threatening infection.[67]

*Re R* does little to assuage concerns about a slippery slope. Although Dr. Keith Andrews, medical expert for the Official Solicitor, opposed resuscitation on the ground that it would be a futile *treatment* (because of its very small prospect of success and its real risk of inflicting injuries on R), Sir Stephen Brown's judgement omits to distinguish between non-treatment on this ground and on the ground that the patient's *life* is thought futile and, in a number of passages, approves non-treatment on the latter ground.[68]

The risk of a slippery slope is heightened by the practical difficulties which can be involved in accurately diagnosing the condition which is thought to justify non-treatment. Even pvs is not a clear-cut syndrome and misdiagnoses are not uncommon. A study carried out by Dr. Keith Andrews, published in July 1996, disclosed that of 40 patients referred to the Royal Hospital for Neurodisability as vegetative between 1992 and 1995, no fewer than 17 (43%) had been misdiagnosed. All but one of the 17 had been referred by a hospital consultant, mostly by a neurologist, neurosurgeon or rehabilitiation specialist. The study concluded that accurate diagnosis is possible but requires the skills of a multidisciplinary team experienced in the management of people with complex disabilities.[69]

The Practice Note governing applications for declarations in cases of pvs states that there should be two neurological reports on the patient, one commissioned by the Official Solicitor, but does not require the involvement of such a team.[70] Furthermore, the risks of misdiagnosis must increase if time is short. In one case in which the Court of Appeal declared that it would be lawful not to reinsert a feeding tube which had become disconnected, the court did so even though there had been insufficient time for the Official Solicitor to obtain an independent neurological opinion.[71] It seems doubtful whether the patient in that case was in fact vegetative.

---

[67] *Ibid.*, at p. 110.

[68] See *ibid.*, at p. 107 where he applied *Re J (A Minor)* [1991] 1 F.L.R. 366 in which the Court of Appeal adopted a Quality of life approach (see text *infra* nn. 73–78). His reliance on *Re J* rather than *Bland* is puzzling as *Re J* involved a minor. Both cases, however, are at one in adopting a Quality of life approach. Another puzzling aspect of *Re R* is the doctors' willingness to perform a gastrostomy operation but not to administer antibiotics.

[69] Keith Andrews *et al.*, 'Misdiagnosis of the vegetative state: retrospective study in a rehabilitation unit' (1996) 313 *British Medical Journal* 13.

[70] [1994] 2 All E.R. 413.

[71] *Supra* n. 59. See also *Re D* (1997) 38 BMLR 1; *Re H ibid.*, 11.

### (v) A possible explanation?

What accounts for the judges' misunderstanding of the sanctity principle, a principle which has long been central to the law? A plausible explanation is that the principle does not appear to have been accurately set out before them by any of the counsel who appeared in the case. Even counsel for the Official Solicitor appears to have confused sanctity with vitalism. In the Court of Appeal, for example, he argued that if Tony Bland showed signs of life-threatening failure of, in succession, heart, lungs, liver, kidneys, spleen, bladder, and pancreas, the doctor would be under a duty to perform surgery to rectify the failure. Sir Thomas Bingham M.R. observed:[72]

> Such a suggestion is in my view so repugnant to one's sense of how one individual should behave towards another that I would reject it as possibly representing the law.

This observation is, with respect, entirely right since counsel's argument was surely vitalistic.

*Bland* was not the first time Mr. Munby Q.C. had, as counsel for the Official Solicitor, advanced a vitalistic understanding of the sanctity of life. In *Re J (A Minor)*,[73] the previous leading case on the withholding or withdrawal of medical treatment, the question was whether a disabled ward should be artificially ventilated. Mr. Munby Q.C. made two alternative submissions. The first, his "absolute" submission, was "that a court is never justified in withholding consent to treatment which could enable a child to survive a life-threatening condition, whatever the pain or other side-effects inherent in the treatment, and whatever the quality of life which it would experience thereafter."[74]

The alternative, "qualified" submission[75] (based on the reasoning of the Court of Appeal in the earlier case of *Re B*[76]) was that a court could withhold consent to treatment only if it was certain that the Quality of the child's life would be "intolerable" to the child. In *Re J*, then, the court was presented with only two alternatives: vitalism or Quality of life. It preferred the latter, with the rider that the Quality of life was to be judged from the perspective of the child. As Taylor L.J. expressed it:[77]

> the correct approach is for the court to judge the quality of life the child would have to endure if given the treatment and decide whether in all the circumstances such a life would be so afflicted as to be intolerable to that child. I say 'to that child' because the test should not be whether the life would be

[72] *Ibid.*, at p. 815. See also Butler-Sloss L.J. at pp. 822–823.
[73] *Re J (A Minor) (Wardship: Medical Treatment)* [1991] 1 F.L.R. 366.
[74] *Ibid.*, at pp. 370–371 *per* Lord Donaldson M.R.
[75] *Ibid.*, at p. 373.
[76] [1981] 1 W.L.R. 1421.
[77] [1991] 1 F.L.R. 366 at pp. 383–384.

tolerable to the decider. The test must be whether the child in question, if capable of exercising sound judgement, would consider the life tolerable.[78]

It appears, then, that in *Bland*, as in *Re J* before it, the sanctity of life was not heard; that the choice as presented and perceived was between vitalism and Quality of life, and that the judges (unsurprisingly) opted for Quality of life. Despite the fundamental importance attached to the sanctity of life by the judges who sat in *Bland*, it is by no means clear that any had the benefit of an accurate appreciation of it.

## 4. Misunderstanding autonomy

The courts in *Bland* undervalued human life. But this was not their only error. For they also appeared to *over*value human autonomy, even to the extent of suggesting that the latter trumped the former. We noted above Lord Goff's statement that the patient's right to self-determination overrides the sanctity of life and observed that this statement is misleading if it suggests that the sanctity of life is breached when a doctor allows a patient to refuse a life-saving treatment. What *would* breach the principle, however, is a *suicidal* refusal of treatment by the patient and the intentional assistance or encouragement of that refusal by the doctor, whether by act or omission. Whether his Lordship was intending to condone such refusals and assistance in them is unclear. He said[79] that where a patient refused life-prolonging treatment: "there is no question of the patient having committed suicide, nor therefore of the doctor having aided or abetted him in doing so." If he was referring to the refusal of a worthless treatment, this is uncontroversial. But if he included a refusal by which the patient intends to commit suicide, the statement indicates that patients may now lawfully commit suicide by refusals of treatment (or care?) and that doctors may assist or encourage such refusals, albeit by omission. In support of such a proposition could be cited the statement of Lord Justice Hoffmann in the Court of Appeal that the decriminalisation of suicide by the *Suicide Act* 1961 "was a recognition that the principle of self-determination should in that case prevail over the sanctity of life".[80]

However, as the Parliamentary debates leading up to the enactment of the *Suicide Act* 1961 confirm, the reason for decriminalisation was *not* respect for

---

[78] Given that the child had never been capable of making any judgement, invoking the child's viewpoint is, with respect, a confused fiction. It is remarkable that the courts should import 'substituted judgement' in the case of a child who has never been competent, yet reject it in the case of an adult like Tony Bland who once was. Yet even if substituted judgement had been applied in *Bland*, and the court had declared that the feeding should be stopped because he would have chosen to be killed rather than live in pvs, it would still amount to the making of a Quality of life judgement. A Quality of life judgement remains just that, whether made on the basis of best interests or substituted judgement.

[79] [1993] A.C. 789 at p. 864.

[80] *Ibid.*, at p. 827. See also p. 814 *per* Sir Thomas Bingham M.R., who assumed that a refusal of tube-feeding is not suicidal.

self-determination but a belief that the suicidal needed help rather than punishment. In other words, suicide was decriminalised not to help people to commit suicide, but to help them not to. The Government strenuously denied any intention to condone suicide, let alone establish a right to it. Moving the Suicide Bill's Third Reading, the Joint Under-Secretary of State for the Home Department issued the following warning:

> Because we have taken the view, as Parliament and the Government have taken, that the treatment of people who attempt to commit suicide should no longer be through the criminal courts, it in no way lessens, nor should it lessen, the respect for the sanctity of human life which we all share. It must not be thought that because we are changing the method of treatment for those unfortunate people we seek to depreciate the gravity of the action of anyone who tries to commit suicide.[81]

Addressing fears that decriminalisation might give potential suicides the impression that what they proposed to do was no longer regarded as wrong, he stated:

> I should like to state as solemnly as I can that that is certainly not the view of the Government, that we wish to give no encouragement whatever to suicide ... I hope that nothing that I have said will give the impression that the act of self-murder, of self-destruction, is regarded at all lightly by the Home Office or the Government.[82]

That acceptance of a right to commit suicide was not the reason for decriminalisation is confirmed by the fact that assisted suicide was not decriminalised and remains a serious offence.

In *Secretary of State for the Home Department v Robb*,[83] Mr Justice Thorpe cited *Bland* as authority for the proposition that a patient who refuses life-prolonging treatment, which results in death, does not commit suicide and that the doctor who complies with the patient's wishes does not aid or abet suicide. Granting a declaration that the Home Office and medical and nursing staff might lawfully abide by a prisoner's refusal to take food and water, he observed[84] that "The principle of the sanctity of human life in this jurisdiction is seen to yield to the principle of self-determination" adding that, although the state interest in preventing suicide is recognisable, it had no application to a case such as the present where the refusal of food and treatment "in the exercise of the right of self-determination does not constitute an act of suicide".

If Mr Justice Thorpe is of the opinion, as he seems to be, that suicide may only be committed by an act and not by a refusal of food and treatment, then he advances no argument or authority in support, beyond the *dicta* in *Bland*. But

---

[81] (1960–61) 645 Parl. Deb. H.C. cols. 822–823. (Mr. Charles Fletcher-Cooke M.P.)
[82] (1960–61) 644 Parl. Deb. H.C. col. 1425–26.
[83] [1995] 1 All ER 677.
[84] At p. 682.

this is bootstrap authority: those *dicta* are themselves either ambiguous or bereft of authority and the point was simply not argued in that case. Moreover, his apparently unqualified proposition that the right to self-determination takes precedence over the sanctity of life is difficult to square with the prohibition on assisted suicide and murder on request.[85]

## III. From Quality to sanctity

What answer would the traditional ethic, accurately understood and applied, have yielded in the *Bland* case? Sanctity of life ethicists are agreed that since medical treatment such as ventilation (and probably also antibiotics) can do nothing to restore those in pvs to a state of health and well-functioning, it is futile and need not be provided. On the question whether tube-feeding is simply medical treatment or also basic care there is not, at least as yet, unanimity. Some classify tube-feeding as medical treatment which may, therefore, be withdrawn; others (probably advancing the more representative viewpoint) that it is basic care which ought, therefore, to be provided.[86]

However, although the traditional ethic does not, as yet, unequivocally rule out the withdrawal of tube-feeding on the ground that it is futile medical treatment, it certainly rules out its withdrawal on the ground that the *patient is* futile. While the ethic may currently allow for a legitimate diversity of answers, it does insist on asking the right question: "Is tube-feeding 'treatment' and, if so, is it worthwhile?" and not "Is the patient's life worthwhile?"

How, then, could their Lordships have developed the law in accordance with the sanctity of life principle? As Finnis has pointed out, cases such as *Gibbins and Proctor* establish that one who undertakes the care of a dependent person and omits to provide necessary food or clothing with the intention of causing death (or serious harm) commits murder if death results. He adds that those cases do not confront the argument successfully raised in *Bland* – that one who has undertaken a duty of care may yet have no duty to exercise it so as to sustain life – but that "the proper application or extension of their rule to meet that argument was surely this: those who have a duty to care for someone may never exercise it in a manner intended to bring about that person's death".[87]

*Bland* decides the opposite. And it does so at the expense of radical inconsistency, prohibiting as murder intentional killing by an act, but permitting intentional killing by omission. Imagine the following scenario. X is a patient in pvs who is free of any suffering and who has made no request to be killed. X's doctor decides that, because X's life is worthless, he would be better off dead,

[85] For an ethical and legal analysis of pre-incompetence refusals of treatment, see Stuart Hornett, 'Advance Directives: A Legal and Ethical Analysis' in John Keown, (ed) *Euthanasia Examined* (Cambridge: Cambridge University Press 1995), pp. 297–314.

[86] See e.g. Luke Gormally, 'Definitions of Personhood: Implications for the Care of PVS Patients' (1993) 9.3 *Ethics and Medicine* 44 at p. 47. Joseph Boyle, *op. cit. supra* n. 49.

[87] *Op. cit. supra* n. 7 at p. 333.

and stops his tube-feeding with intent to kill. In the next bed is Y, a patient dying in agony who, after serious reflection, begs the doctor to kill him by lethal injection. The doctor, fearful of prosecution, refuses. A third patient, Z, moved by Y's predicament, draws a pistol, holds it to the doctor's head and threatens "If you don't inject Y, I will shoot you dead". The doctor, to save his own life, administers a lethal drug to Y. The doctor's killing of X is lawful; his killing of Y is, at least in English law, murder.

Small wonder that Lord Mustill expressed[88] his "acute unease" about resting his decision on a distinction between acts and omissions given that "however much the terminologies may differ the ethical status of the two courses of action is for all relevant purposes indistinguishable". But it is, with respect, the judges' reasoning in *Bland* which has distorted the legal structure, not *vice-versa*. *Bland* is the culmination of a series of cases in which the courts have veered away from the traditional ethic, which coherently combines sanctity and quality in a consistent and principled legal opposition to intentional killing, toward a new ethic which incoherently combines sanctity and Quality and produces a misshapen opposition to active killing but not intentional killing by omission.

The Law Lords urged Parliament to consider the issues raised by *Bland*. A distinguished Select Committee of the House of Lords, chaired by Lord Walton and including Lord Mustill, was established by the House of Lords to consider the issues raised by the case. It reported in February 1994. The Committee recommended that the law should not be relaxed to permit active intentional killing. Reaffirming the prohibition on intentional killing, the Committee observed:[89] "That prohibition is the cornerstone of law and of social relationships. It protects each one of us impartially, embodying the belief that all are equal."

On the question of tube-feeding patients in pvs, the Committee was divided between those who regarded it as basic care which should be provided and those who regarded it as medical treatment which could properly be withdrawn. Nevertheless, the Committee was unanimous that the question need not, indeed should not, usually arise since it was proper to withdraw medical treatment, including antibiotics, from such patients.[90]

However, by confining itself to considering active killing and ignoring intentional killing by omission the Committee did little to resolve the inconsistency in the law created by *Bland*.[91] Consequently, the law remains in the same misshapen state in which the Law Lords left it. And the question which the Committee said should not arise has continued to do so as hospitals and courts *hasten* to terminate

---

[88] [1993] A.C. 789 at p. 887. See also *ibid.*, at p. 865 *per* Lord Goff; at p. 877 *per* Lord Lowry; at p. 885 *per* Lord Browne-Wilkinson.

[89] *Op. cit. supra* n. 15, at para. 237.

[90] *Ibid.*, at para. 257.

[91] The Committee gave no reason for limiting its definition of euthanasia to active killing (*ibid.*, at para.20) nor did it rule out Quality of life judgements (see e.g. *ibid.*, at para. 255). It did not, therefore, advance a consistent sanctity ethic.

the lives of those they consider to be in pvs.[92] Lord Lowry referred[93] in *Bland* to a gap between "old law" and "new medicine" and observed that it was the role of the legislature to remedy any disparity between society's notions of what the law is and what is right. But if their Lordships were looking to the legislature to render the law consistent by decriminalising active intentional killing, the legislature has declined the invitation and has bounced the misshapen ball back into the judicial forum.

## Conclusions

First, the ethical principle of the sanctity of life, which has long informed the common law, offers a middle way between the extremes of vitalism on the one hand and Quality of life on the other. *Bland* represented a swerve toward the Quality of life extreme, accepting that certain lives are of no benefit and may lawfully be intentionally terminated by omission.

Secondly, accentuating the swerve was a shift from a traditional understanding of the value of autonomy – autonomy as enabling individuals to participate in the moral enterprise of making choiceworthy decisions, decisions which respect objective moral norms and promote the flourishing of the decision-maker and others – to an essentially self-justificatory understanding of autonomy in which choices merit respect simply in virtue of being choices.

Thirdly, *Bland* has indeed left the law in a "morally and intellectually misshapen" state. The law prohibits doctors caring for patients in pvs from actively killing them but permits (if not requires) them to kill by omission. The case also suggests that while doctors may not actively assist competent patients to commit suicide, they may assist them to do so by omission – by intentionally assisting suicidal refusals of treatment. The significance of the decision is profound: although the House of Lords Select Committee reaffirmed that active killing, even on request, should not be made lawful, the Law Lords have decided that killing by omission, even without request, already is. The making of such a fundamental change in the law seems, moreover, difficult to reconcile with the guidelines for judicial development of the law laid down by Lord Lowry in *C. v. D.P.P.*[94]

Fourthly, given that the Law Lords have embraced the Quality of life principle, and effectively delegated the judgement as to which lives are of no benefit to medical opinion, there is little reason to expect that judgement to be confined to patients in pvs. Moreover, the ramifications of the courts' adoption of an individualist and amoral understanding of autonomy are also likely to be profound,

---

[92] *See supra* nn. 59 and 71.
[93] [1993] A.C. 789 at p. 877.
[94] [1995] 2 All E.R. 43 at p. 52. See also *Airedale N.H.S. Trust v. Bland* [1993] A.C. 789 at p. 865 *per* Lord Goff; at p. 880 *per* Lord Browne-Wilkinson; at p. 890 *per* Lord Mustill.

not least in its corrosive effect on the legal prohibition of assisted suicide and consensual murder.[95]

Fifthly, the Law Lords' rejection of the sanctity principle and their adoption of an amoral concept of autonomy appear to have been based on a misunderstanding of the traditional ethic. Lord Mustill, surely rightly, observed[96] that it was a great pity that the Attorney-General had not appeared to represent the interests of the state in maintaining citizens' lives. It is to be hoped that the Attorney will appear in an appropriate future case to represent, articulate and defend the traditional ethic.

Sixthly, the decision whether to withdraw treatment and tube-feeding from a patient in pvs should be based on an evaluation of the worthwhileness of the treatment, not the supposed worthwhileness of the patient. While there appears to be a consensus that it is proper to withdraw treatment in such a case, there is a good argument that tube-feeding constitutes basic care and that it should, at least presumptively, be provided. Even if it were the better view that it may be withdrawn, this should be because it, and not the patient, is judged futile.

*Bland* indeed rendered the law morally and intellectually misshapen, hypo-critical rather than Hippocratic. But the Law Lords are not alone in promoting this legal revolution. For *Bland* is but one of several leading cases in common law jurisdictions that could have been used to illustrate the disturbing tendency of judges across the Western world to turn the traditional ethic on its head. Judges, often regarded as one of the most conservative arms of the state, have played a role no less significant than that of legislatures in subverting that ethic by converting a right *not* to be killed into a duty *to* kill and a right to self-determination into a right to self-termination.

Unless the traditional ethic is restored by the courts or, failing the courts, by legislatures, one of the main pillars of Western civilisation, the sanctity of life, will have been fatally undermined.

[95] See also *Re MB* [1997] 8 Med. L.R. 217 in which the Court of Appeal held that a competent pregnant woman has an absolute right to refuse medical treatment, even if she and the unborn child will die as a result.
[96] [1993] A.C. 789 at p. 889.

# 16

# The Catholic Church and public policy debates in Western liberal societies: the basis and limits of intellectual engagement

JOHN FINNIS

I

THE TERM "liberal" has no core of meaning sufficiently stable and clear for use in a general political philosophy or theory. We could accept that the first liberal ("the first Whig") was Thomas Aquinas, while also accepting the core of right judgment in Pius IX's *Syllabus of Errors* when it rejects the claim that the Church must simply reconcile itself to modern liberalism. That claim was rightly rejected because modern liberalism, then (in 1864) as now, included opinions such as John Rawls defends – that no one should ever act in public life (e.g. as a voter) on the basis of the thought that such-and-such an opinion is *true*.[1] Aquinas was a liberal because, although he rightly defended institutions and practices important in public life on the basis that they are required or authorised by certain moral and metaphysical *truths*, he at the same time insisted that the proper functions of the state's laws and rulers do not include making people morally all-round good by requiring them to abstain from immorality. The role of state government and law, according to Aquinas, is to uphold peace and justice; the requirements imposed, supervised, and enforced by state government and law concern only those sorts of choice and action which are external and affect other people.

But though we can and should do our general critical political reflection without attempting to employ the term "liberalism" as a framework category like "just" (or indeed "unjust"), we can accept the phrase "Western liberal societies", as used in my paper's title, and use it simply to pick out a set of states, political communities, politically organised nations, which *inter alia* allow the Catholic Church and its members the liberty of participating in public deliberation and choice, as one among many groups and individuals similarly participating in public decision-making. So my question, my title, comes to this: On what basis should we as Catholics participate in those public deliberations, and abide by or

---

[1] John Rawls, *Political Liberalism*, New York: Columbia University Press 1993 (paperback ed. 1996), pp. 61, 127, etc. Truth, he argues, should be replaced, as the criterion of right political action, by an idea of the "reasonable" which entails that many conceptions of public policy are "reasonable" although quite untrue.

reject their outcomes (social choices such as legislation, adjudication, and administrative practice)?

My reflections in response to this question have three main parts. The first concerns the faith which, by God's grace and our decisions, can shape and guide all our choices, including choices of the kind we are reflecting upon now (choices to participate in public debate, accept or reject its outcome, and so forth). The second concerns some relevant issues of cooperation, and the question when it is wrong, and when it can be right, to choose to do what will assist others in their wrongdoing. The third concerns the role of the Church acting (e.g. speaking) precisely as Church, that is through its pastors.

## II

A first condition for well-grounded participation as a Catholic in public policy deliberations and debates is that one be quite clear about the relations between faith and reason. There are many propositions of our faith which are not accessible to natural reason, i.e. to someone who is unaware of the particular set of historical realities which were the revelation culminating in the life and teaching of Christ. These propositions – e.g. that there are three persons in the one and only God – are proposed by the Church for our and everyone's acceptance on the basis of the Church's confidence that they are part of the revealed word of God; and that is the only basis on which we can accept them and propose them to others. But the Church also proposes for us to accept in faith a good number of propositions – e.g. that God exists, that each human being is a body animated and unified by an intellectual soul, or that it is always wrong to choose to kill an innocent human being – propositions which are indeed accessible to natural reason (reason unaided by revelation). Indeed, that there are such propositions (including those three) is itself a proposition of faith. And of natural reason!

If we are clear about these different types of relationship between the faith and natural reason, we can avoid some mistakes common outside and inside the Church. Outside the Church, it is widely assumed and asserted that any proposition which the Catholic Church in fact proposes for acceptance is, by virtue of that fact, a "religious" (not a philosophical, scientific, or rationally grounded and compelling) proposition, and is a proposition which Catholics hold only as a matter of faith and therefore cannot be authentically willing to defend as a matter of natural reason. Inside the Church, there are a good many moral theologians who hold or presuppose the positions defended 20 years ago in Gerard Hughes SJ's little book *Authority in Morals: An Essay in Christian Ethics*,[2] in particular that revelation and its custodian the magisterium of the Catholic Church can never decisively settle an ethical question because to attribute to them that sort of authoritativeness would be to adopt an irrational fideism – irrational because one cannot reasonably decide to accept revelation in general, or reasonably interpret the sources of revelation in

[2] London: Heythrop Monographs 1978.

particular, without presupposing moral criteria which revelation and its sources, to be creditworthy and properly understood, must satisfy, criteria which must therefore be more ultimate than revelation, and be accessible to us independently of revelation.[3] (The independent criteria these theologians usually have in mind are the norms they shape and rationalise by whichever version of consequentialism or proportionalism they take from the surrounding philosophical or popular culture.)

But the Catholic faith is entirely coherent when it teaches both (i) that there are moral truths accessible prior to revelation, including truths which make it obligatory for us to search for the truth about God and to adhere to it when we judge that we have discovered it, and (ii) that these truths are clarified and decisively confirmed by the revelation which also makes accessible some moral truths which are not otherwise knowable with appropriate clarity and certitude (e.g. truths about mercy, or the impossibility of dissolving a valid and consummated marriage between Christians). It is utterly fallacious to argue, like Frs Fuchs, Hughes, and Sullivan, that because revelation alone, without moral presuppositions, cannot settle all questions, therefore revelation, even when rationally accepted on morally compelling grounds, cannot settle any.[4]

Distinctions of this kind, clarified long ago by St Thomas but already proposed in the tradition by St Paul and by Irenaeus, and reproposed by Vatican I and Vatican II, enable and entitle us as Catholics to participate in public policy deliberations on many matters without appealing to revelation or faith as the grounds for accepting and acting upon truths which are in fact part of revelation and the propositional content of the faith. These truths, for example about retributive justice, or killing, or enslavement, can be defended on the basis of arguments which are rationally accessible to people who, by ignorance or mistake, do not accept the revelation proposed by the Catholic Church. These arguments are rather confusingly called in the tradition principles of "natural law" or "natural reason", and could be called "public reasons", in a sense of that term more reasonable and durable than John Rawls' use of the phrase "public reason" to signify the propositions, true or false, in a truth-bracketing "overlapping public consensus", or Stephen Macedo's related use to signify those truths which are accessible without any complex argument.

The fact that we could apply the new and fashionable phrase "public reason" to the natural moral law and the natural or human rights defended by (amongst others) Catholics, taken with the fact that *those* public reasons are accessible to all independently of divine revelation, should not lead us to conclude that revelation itself is not a public reason. On the contrary, what in the Catholic tradition and the Second Vatican Council (*LG* 25) is called "public revelation" is truly accessible to all, just as Peter proclaimed in the middle of Jerusalem on the day of Pentecost,

[3] J. M. Finnis, *Moral Absolutes: Tradition, Revision, and Truth*, Washington: Catholic University of America Press 1991, pp. 92–3.
[4] See J. M. Finnis, 'Reflections on an Essay in Christian Ethics', 65 (1980) *The Clergy Review* 51–57, 87–93; Finnis, *Moral Absolutes: Tradition, Revision, and Truth*, pp. 92–93.

reminding his listeners that "Jesus of Nazareth was a man duly accredited [*apodedeigmenon*] to you from God; such were the miracles and wonders and signs which God did through him in your midst, as you yourselves know" (Acts 2:22), and as Paul proclaimed "in full view of the Areopagus" in Athens, informing his listeners that "the man whom God has appointed [to pronounce just judgment on the whole world] he has accredited to all [*pistin paraschôn pasin*], by raising him up from the dead" (Acts 17:31; cf. 2:32). Thousands of Peter's hearers were persuaded, rather few if any of Paul's in Athens. What is accessible as creditworthy to all may in fact be accessed and accepted by most, many, some, or few; the *de facto* variation is explained in part by what Elizabeth Anscombe once called[5] the endless twistiness of the human mind. But the *accessibility* to reason, and the credit-*worth*iness, of evidence and argument and other premises for reasonable judgment are all independent of the facts about actual acceptance.

Whatever the opinions of those around us, we ought to reject the reduction of Catholic faith to a private sentiment which happens to be shared with others. We ought to think of the truths of the faith as good and proper grounds for action, including one's activity as a voting citizen or a public official, even though they are grounds which many members of the political community do not accept and would denounce as improper. This does not amount to "imposing Catholicism"; one of the truths of the faith is that everyone – even those who unreasonably reject Catholicism in favour of some false religion or some false denial of every truth about God – everyone is entitled not to be coerced in relation to such beliefs so long as the actions which result from them respect (1) the rights of others (effectively safeguarded and peacefully harmonised), (2) the decent public peace which is an ordered living together in true justice, and (3) public morality duly preserved.[6]

Here it is helpful also to recall (as I have already) St Thomas' rejection, in principle, of paternalistic laws restricting the truly private activities of adults.[7] He himself did not consistently adhere to this rejection, so far as it bore on the practice of employing state power to punish departure from the Catholic faith. For his defence of the practice relied on the premise that heresy is not merely infectious and corrosive of the true faith of naive or wavering people (*ST* II-II q. 10 a. 7c & 10c), and therefore contrary to the common good – as other unbelief (e.g. of pagans) can be – but is also, unlike those other forms of unbelief, a *culpable* infidelity consisting of, or closely analogous to, a breach of promise (q. 10 a. 8c). This analogy was always unsound: the faith was usually adopted by proxy in infant baptism, and even when this subscription was made by explicit act on conversion at or above the age of reason, it was not accurately regarded as having the character of a commitment made to other people. Rather, as Aquinas

---

[5] G.E.M. Anscombe, 'War and Murder', in her *Collected Philosophical Papers* vol. 3, Blackwell: Oxford, 1981, pp. 51ff. at p. 60 (originally in Walter Stein (ed.), *Nuclear Weapons: A Catholic Response*, London and New York 1961).

[6] Vatican II, Declaration on Religious Freedom, *Dignitatis Humanae* (1965), secs. 2 and 7.

[7] See J. M. Finnis, *Aquinas: Moral, Political and Legal Theory*, Oxford: OUP 1998, ch. VII.

himself says elsewhere, the human good at stake in matters of faith, though it is a good which benefits not just one person but many, is not a good which consists in community but rather one which "pertains to each person alone as an individual [*ad unum aliquem pertinet secundum seipsum*]" (*ScG* III c. 80 n. 15 [2560]). And the "medicinal" (i.e. retributive, deterrent, and eliminative) punishment of heresy was too tenuously distinguishable from compulsion of belief, a compulsion which Aquinas (like the Church) always vigorously rejected. Aquinas tried to insist on the distinction (*IV Sent.* d. 13 q. 2 a. 3 ad 5), but slipped into saying – inconsistently also with his own account of the nature of the assent of faith (e.g. *ST* II-II q. 1 a. 2c; q. 10 a. 8c) – that the punishment of heretics was justifiable as a matter of "compelling them [back] to faith", "physically compelling them to carry out what they promised and to hold fast to what they once accepted" (*ibid.*).

The requirement that faith be voluntary and free from coercive pressures is an implication of the basic good of religion as a personal search for, appropriation of, and adherence in practice to the truth about God as one can grasp it. Taken with the truth that faith as act and disposition of acceptance pertains as such to the individual person and does not as such affect civil justice and peace, the requirement that that act be free yields the conclusion which, as I have already mentioned, was stated by Vatican II: provided public peace, public morality, and the harmonised rights of others are respected, all persons have a right, as against political authorities, to freedom from coercion in respect of all their expressions of religious belief. This right is not that mere tolerance of erroneous religious practices which Aquinas argued for (*ST* II-II q. 10 a. 11c).

We should not be nostalgic for, and do not need to defend, the paternalism defended by Plato and Aristotle, or the religious intolerance of the mediaeval and post-mediaeval Catholic (not to mention Protestant) states. Nor should we accept other package deals, in which Catholicism might be yoked to a restorationist politics of conservatism or a liberationist politics of socialism or state capitalism, or whatever. So far as anyone can see, the Catholic Church is still near the beginning of its long journey to the end of the ages; its Augustinian, mediaeval, and subsequent experiments with harnessing state power were no more than a passing phase in which faith and benevolence were harnessed together without sufficient attention to differentiations which the faith itself suggests and, when developed, ratifies. If we make and insist upon those differentiations, we can peacefully and without even implicit threat affirm, in our own reflections and when and as appropriate in public, that the centre of human history is the life and teachings of Jesus Christ, and that the truths which his Church conveys, even in periods when it is humanly speaking as decayed, confused, and weak as it at present is, are the true *centre* of the culture which can and should direct political deliberation in Western liberal as much as any other kind of political society. The disarray within the Roman Catholic Church is surely a substantial cause (as well as a consequence) of the disarray within these societies, even those societies which for many centuries have had no reason to think (or have made it their business not to think) of Catholics as other than virtual strangers.

If we look for the roots of the present disarray and demoralisation within the Church, we find I suggest two outstanding candidates: the muffling of the public, historical character of revelation by biblical scholars who have uncritically accepted some unsound tenets and presuppositions of secularised, Enlightenment philosophy; and the practical elimination of transcendent hope, the hope of heaven. I have said a little elsewhere about the first;[8] let me add just a word to what Germain Grisez's paper[9] says about the second.

The doctrine of hell was as emotionally repugnant to, say, St. Thomas More as it is to us.[10] But it is so clearly part of what has been revealed in the life and teaching of Jesus that its undermining in Christian consciousness had to await radical confusion about, or denial of, the true relations between revelation and reason. I have mentioned already some instances of such confusion or denial. But many people have been quite needlessly surprised at the impact of the loss of the fear of hell on the hope of heaven. Their surprise is needless because if X will happen, or not happen, regardless of anything one does, one cannot *intend* X. So, if one assumes that either everyone reaches heaven regardless, or heaven is mere myth, we know not which, then one cannot *intend* heaven. Hope, not as dream unconnected with practical deliberation and choice, but as standing intention of shaping one's choices and actions in the hope of being made fit for the integral human fulfilment – the life of heaven – on offer in the covenant, becomes *impossible*.[11] So it is practical reason's own logic that makes inevitable the shift from "Christianity" without fear of hell (and so with certitude of heaven) to Christianity without hope of heaven (and so with some perhaps grand, perhaps modest this-worldly hope) – the shift to secularism so widespread among so-called liberal Jews and Christians.

It is obviously a precondition of sustainable engagement in public policy debates that one keep bright one's hope, and keep clear and firm the presuppositions of that hope. The Council, rearticulating the Church's perennial faith, stated the content of that hope in a way that makes full sense of participation in the affairs of this world, great or small, even when that participation seems doomed to failure. For it recalled and restated the promise of the covenant in terms recalled here by Cardinal Winning and again by Germain Grisez: that if we act on the

---

[8] J.M. Finnis, *"Historical Consciousness" and Theological Foundations*, Etienne Gilson Lecture No. 15, Toronto: Pontifical Institute of Mediaeval Studies 1992.

[9] Chapter 10 in this volume.

[10] See Thomas More, *Dialogue of Comfort against Tribulation*, ed. Monica Stevens, London: Sheed & Ward, 1951, p. 249. Cf. More's last written prayers: "Give me thy grace, good Lord . . . /To walk the narrow way that leadeth to life;/ To bear the cross with Christ;/ To have the last thing in remembrance;/ To have ever afore mine eye my death that is ever at hand;/ To make death no stranger to me;/ *To foresee and consider the everlasting fire of hell*;/ To pray for pardon before the judge come . . ."; *Thomas More's Prayerbook*, New Haven: Yale University Press 1969, p. xxxvii.

[11] See the very important analysis of the proper integration of hope and fear in Christian life in Germain Grisez, *The Way of the Lord Jesus*, vol. 2, *Living a Christian Life*, Quincy, Illinois: Franciscan Press 1992, pp. 91–94; also Grisez, *The Way of the Lord Jesus*, vol. 3, *Difficult Moral Problems*, Quincy, Illinois: Franciscan Press, 1997, pp. 21–8.

Lord's command, we will somehow find again – but cleaned up and transformed – all the good fruits of our nature and our efforts, when Christ hands over to the Father the completed Kingdom of truth and life, holiness and grace, justice, love, and peace.[12]

## III

Our engagement in public deliberation will be greatly facilitated if we are clear in our own minds, and can make it clear to other people, that the purpose of moral reflection is not to identify certain persons and their acts as *culpable*. Its purpose is rather to settle, for one's own conscience, the question: What should I do? What may I do? What options may I adopt, and what options must I not adopt however attractive they otherwise are? This clarification is important for many reasons. Public debate is frequently distracted and rendered fruitless by the question whether conduct of type X is *as bad as* conduct of type Y – e.g. whether intending the death of innocents as part of a strategy of nuclear deterrence which includes (as all militarily coherent policies of nuclear deterrence do) the options of city swapping and final retaliation is *as bad as* killing them in an act of city swapping or final retaliation on the night. In truth, the only fruitful and interesting question is whether it can be reasonable (morally acceptable) to form the intention. The question how much worse it would be to carry it out is a question we simply need not engage with.

Similarly, the important question for deliberation is never whether it is with feelings of repugnance or with thoughts of "disapproval" that one is doing what one chooses to do. The question is always whether the option is choice-worthy, or is instead excluded from upright choice by its injustice, or by its opposition in some other way to the human goods (*bona humana*) to which St Thomas says one is directed in the first principles of one's practical thinking, the basic reasons for action which the encyclical *Veritatis Splendor* (1993) refers to frequently and calls fundamental human goods.[13]

As that encyclical makes very clear, it is only in this perspective, the perspective of the person deliberating towards action, that one can understand what human action actually is, for the purposes of moral judgment:

> The morality of the human act depends primarily and fundamentally on the "object" rationally [whether reasonably or unreasonably] chosen by the deliberate will... In order to be able to grasp the object of an act which specifies that act morally, it is therefore necessary to place oneself in the perspective of the acting person. The object of the act of willing is in fact a freely chosen kind of behaviour.... By the object of a given moral act, then, one cannot mean a process or an event of the merely physical order, to be assessed on the basis of

---

[12] Vatican II, Pastoral Constitution on the Church in the Modern World, *Gaudium et Spes*, sec. 39.

[13] See e.g. *Veritatis Splendor*, sec. 48.3; see also secs. 13.3, 67.2, 78.2, 79.2.

its ability to bring about a given state of affairs in the outside world. Rather, that object is the proximate end of a deliberate decision which determines the act of willing on the part of the acting person. (*VS* sec. 78)

This is well understood in our society to the extent that most people still easily grasp the distinction between giving painkillers to kill the patient and giving the same dose to kill pain. It seems to be poorly understood to the extent that people assert that getting a patient dead by omitting nutrition and hydration cannot be murder;[14] or to the extent that people think the fact that a bomb was aimed at a military target settles the question whether it was intended to kill non-combatants.

The question of cooperation in wrongdoing depends firstly on grasping firmly this understanding of the *object* of a human choice, and secondly on understanding that there are moral responsibilities which bear on what we foresee and cause even though those effects are not within the object or any other part of the intention with which one is choosing and acting. Formal cooperation is defined in terms of object and intention, i.e. of the whole set of means and ends which one chooses and intends (including the ends which are means to yet further ends); material cooperation is defined in terms of foreseeable side-effects, i.e. effects not within one's intention (in that same sense of intention: the whole set of ends and means one chooses and intends). Joseph Boyle's paper takes us skilfully through all this. Let me use an example closer to my theme of Catholic participation in the deliberations of partially corrupt societies.

In *Evangelium Vitae* (1995) sec. 73 you find two statements: (i) it is never licit to vote for a law permitting abortion; (ii) a Catholic elected legislator whose absolute personal opposition to procured abortion is well known can, in a legislative vote decisive for the passage of a bill, licitly give his or her support to a bill for a law which permits abortion but less permissively than the existing law or than a bill which will otherwise be passed and become law. Are these two statements consistent? Someone may say that they are not, because the vote which the second statement declares licit is for a law permitting abortion even though the permission is less extensive than the existing or a likely alternative law; but the first statement precisely judges illicit any and every vote for a law permitting abortion.

But the objection is, I think, mistaken, and the two statements are consistent. The kinds of acts which are always, exceptionlessly illicit are, as *Veritatis Splendor* sec. 78 made clear, acts defined by their object. The always illicit vote is for a law *as permitting*, precisely *to* permit, abortion. This is always illicit, even if one is personally opposed to abortion and is voting for it only to keep one's seat and prevent euthanasia or genocide laws, or only to equalise the position of the poor and the rich. The kind of vote which the second statement judges can be licit has as its object not: *to permit* abortions now illegal, but rather: *to prohibit* abortions now legal or imminently likely otherwise to become legal. (Say: the existing law or the threatened alternative bill says abortion is lawful up to 24

14 See J.M. Finnis, '*Bland*. Crossing the Rubicon?', 109 (1993) *Law Quarterly Review* 329–337.

weeks, while the law or bill for which the Catholic legislator is voting says abortion is lawful up to 16 weeks.) Even though it is a vote for a law which does permit abortion, it is chosen by this legislator as a vote for a law which restricts abortion. That this restrictive law also permits abortion is only a side-effect – when we consider the act of voting in the perspective of the acting person – even though the side-effect of permission is as immediate as the object of restriction.

Sec. 73 of *Evangelium Vitae* concludes with the words: "This [second sort of vote] does not in fact represent an illicit cooperation with an unjust law, but rather a legitimate and proper attempt to limit its evil aspects." The wording is a little incautious, for the sentence is dealing with two things at once. It is implicitly saying *first* what I have been saying, that such a vote need not be *formal* cooperation in the wicked choice to permit abortion up to 16 weeks – sec. 74 will go on to say that formal cooperation in moral evil is never licit. But the sentence at the end of sec. 73 is also saying, secondly, that the legislator's non-formal but obviously real material cooperation in enacting the new law which does in fact permit abortion up to 16 weeks can be justifiable. The incautiousness in the wording is twofold. On the one hand, the sentence says, not *"can* be" (as I did) but *"does in fact* represent a legitimate and proper attempt" etc. The legitimacy of material cooperation depends upon many factors, not all of which are considered by the paragraph. "Does" should be read as meaning "can be, provided all relevant conditions are fulfilled". And on the other hand, the paragraph spoke of legislators who have made known their "absolute personal opposition to procured abortion". This phrase "personally opposed" has the bad side-effect of seeming, in isolation, to give some blessing to a certain type of Catholic politicians, who have defended their illicit formal cooperation in the enactment of permissive abortion laws and indeed of arrangements precisely to facilitate the procuring of abortion precisely by the slogan "I am *personally opposed* (or absolutely opposed) to abortion but I vote to permit or facilitate or arrange for it because, in a pluralist society or a liberal democracy, no-one is entitled to impose their religious beliefs or their private moral convictions on others in matters which go to the very heart of personal existence etc, etc." Of course, taken as a whole sec. 73 of *Evangelium Vitae* gives no support and no room to such politicians, but it would have been better, I think, not to use their slogan "personally opposed", where the word "personally" summons up a contrast actually quite foreign to the thought of EV 73 – the thought that there can be true moral judgments about justice which are only private, not valid public reasons for action. The true question is not whether upright Catholic legislators are personally opposed to abortion but whether they are publicly opposed to it and will never vote to permit it, i.e. to make it more permissible, and will always take every reasonable opportunity to vote for its restriction, including if possible the absolute prohibition of all intentional killing by abortion.

Is this sort of object-centred analysis of acts perhaps too psychologistic and indeed dualistic or Cartesian and incompatible with healthy Aristotelianism or Thomism for which John Haldane argues?[15] I think not. Neither *Veritatis Splendor*

---

[15] See chapter 6 of this volume.

nor *Evangelium Vitae*, nor my own restatements of their position, are psychologistic in a dualistic or any other objectionable way. When Professor Haldane, in the course of his address, waved his hand and shifted his weight from one foot to the other to illustrate what he called the bodily expression of the soul, we all understood the wave as precisely that: a manifestation of deliberate control of bodily functions at will, in this case to make a philosophical point. In the context his intentions were clear. Otherwise the shifting of weight might have been an animal reflex corresponding to nothing he wanted to show us about his soul, and his wave might have been a signal for a bomb to be thrown, or (in another forum) attracting the attention of the teller for the affirmative and thus the casting of a pro-abortion vote, or a cancellation of that vote and an expression of prompt repentance, or greeting a friend, or we know not what. As St Thomas so often says, one and the same type of behaviour (*actus in genere naturae*) can be one or more of many different types of morally significant human act (*actus in genere moris*),[16] and the moral judgment one should make about such acts, when deliberating about choosing them, will depend in the first instance on one's object in doing it (the act's object), and then on one's further intentions in doing it (the act's end or intention), and then on the circumstances including the side-effects of doing it (the effects *praeter intentionem*). The envisaged outer act is assessed as the carrying out of one's inner act of intending and choosing and setting oneself to do what one chose, and as a manifestation (expression) of one's virtuous or negligent and vicious dispositions in relation to foreseeable side-effects.

With a care and precision new in the tradition, volume 3 of Germain Grisez's *The Way of the Lord Jesus* traces out and articulates the various sorts of possible bad side-effects of material cooperation[17] (they are also, as he points out, bad side-effects of formal cooperation, but that is not the present issue). These bad side-effects include the basic or primary bad effect of contributing to another's wrongdoing, a wrongdoing which necessarily has bad effects; and then a whole raft of secondary bad side-effects of the cooperation. There are (1) the bad effects of one's very accepting of the primary or basic bad effects – the effects on one's feelings and dispositions of, say, voting for a law which does in fact permit abortion up to 16 weeks in concert with people who think abortion should be freely available and are voting for 16 weeks only because they can't get something more permissive; (2) the occasion this cooperation offers for the grave sin of for-mally cooperating in some other morally bad project of those whose collaboration one needed to enact the restriction to 16 weeks; (3) the comfort likely to be drawn by the principal wrongdoer from one's cooperation, understood by the wrongdoer as endorsement of the wrongdoing, and similarly the scandal to third parties who understand one's cooperation in the same way, the resentment of victims of the

---

[16] J.M. Finnis, 'Object and Intention in Moral Judgments according to St Thomas Aquinas', 55 (1991) *The Thomist* 1–27; slightly revised version in J. Follon and J. McEvoy (eds.), *Finalité et Intentionnalité: Doctrine Thomiste et Perspectives Modernes*, Bibliothèque Philosophique de Louvain No. 35, Paris: J. Vrin, 1992, pp. 127–148.
[17] See Grisez, *Difficult Moral Questions*, pp. 879–82.

wrongdoing, and other forms of disharmony between the cooperator and them, and the impairing of one's witness to the moral truth, say about killing the innocent. It is about the fairness of accepting all these types of bad side-effect that one must judge when one deliberates whether to vote for the 16-week law to save the 16–24 week unborn babies.

All the bad side-effects which I just listed as that third set are of particular importance in reflecting on the engagement of the Church itself, through its leaders and representatives, notably the bishops. For the mission of the Church is precisely to bear witness to the truth, particularly the moral truths at stake in Jesus' summons to repent and live a life worthy of the Lord. It is one thing for a legislator to vote for the law, quite another thing for Catholic bishops to be heard as saying that such a law is acceptable.

## IV

So I reach my last theme, the role of the Church acting (e.g. speaking) precisely as Church, that is through its pastors, in a modern liberal society. My remarks about the meaning of "liberal" left unstated one of the primary characteristics of these societies as we actually know them. I made some remarks about the loss of practical hope among Christians, and in doing so I was identifying, implicitly, the third of the three varieties of practical atheism which Plato long ago analysed in his last work, *Laws*.[18] That third sort of practical atheism or (as we now say) secularism Plato saw as the assumption that God is easily satisfied with human conduct or easily appeased and bought off. The other two sorts are at least as pervasive: that there is no God, or any god there may be is unconcerned with human affairs. *Veritatis Splendor* takes up this whole theme in sec. 88:

> The separation [between faith and morality] represents one of the most acute pastoral concerns of the Church amid today's growing secularism, wherein many, indeed too many, people think and live "as if God did not exist". We are speaking of a mentality which affects, often in a profound, extensive, and all embracing way, even the attitudes and behaviour of Christians, whose faith is weakened and loses its character as a new and original criterion for thinking and acting in personal, family and social life.... It is urgent, then, that Christians should rediscover the newness of the faith and its power to judge a prevalent and all-intrusive culture.

As the Council made clear, in line with the whole tradition, pre-eminent among all the principal responsibilities of the successors of Peter and Paul and the other apostles is to announce and confirm that faith.[19] If those who have that

---

[18] See Plato, *Laws* X 885b, 888c, 901d, 902e-903a, 908b-d, 909a-b. Plato usually speaks of "gods" or "the gods", but when getting to the heart of the matter switches to talk of God or "the god" (see 902e, 903d, 910b).

[19] Vatican II, Decree on Bishops, *Christus Dominus* (1965), sec. 12.

responsibility, and those whose duty it is to assist them, do not carefully assess and constantly reassess and vigorously respond to the "profound, extensive, and all embracing" inroads of secularism in the Church's seminaries, teacher training colleges, and schools (and universities), and its bookshops, publishing houses, and newspapers and if pastors fall silent about heaven and hell and therefore also about other unpopular teachings, and about the public good reasons for accepting the revelation in Jesus Christ then no-one should be surprised to find the Church ceasing to be even an interesting participant in the secular debate, and faltering in its own primary and irreplaceable purpose of leading people to salvation.

It is not, it seems to me, the responsibility of the Church itself, the bishop as such, to make the kind of assessment of complex contingent facts that is necessary to reach a deliberative judgment about, say, a social welfare policy or a strategy of nuclear deterrence. It is the Church's, a bishop's, role to teach in season and out all the moral principles and norms which any such policy must meet if it is to be morally acceptable to Catholics or anyone of good will. So ecclesiastical teaching on morals, and ecclesiastical participation in public deliberations, should in relation to many matters be framed strictly hypothetically. To give an example: *If* a policy of nuclear deterrence involves the intention to destroy non-combatants then it is immoral and may not in any circumstances be approved or formally cooperated in, whatever the consequences; and cannot be saved from that conclusory judgment by facts such as that the intention is conditional, or is formed with good motives, or has been and seems likely to be successful in facing down the enemy and avoiding war. Does the deterrence policy involve that intention? That question should, I believe, be left to the judgment of those whose responsibility it is to decide whether or not to participate in making and carrying out the strategy or policy, a responsibility about whose gravity and urgency the Church should not fall silent. The attempts of the US bishops, extended over years and conducted in the full blaze and buzz of secular publicity, to reach a non-hypothetical judgment about nuclear deterrence were skewed from the start by their committee's own resolution, made privately in advance, that their contribution to the public debate would not condemn their country's deterrent, and were then waylaid by the willingness of public officials to contrive artful formulae to disguise the facts about national policy's intentions from the bishops' not too probing inquiries.[20]

Secular liberal societies and their public officials as such have a horizon of concern which (like the horizon of every secularism and every consequentialism)[21] is arbitrarily limited by emotional interests. In that horizon the Church and the collectivity of its members appear as walk-on bit players to be managed in the interests of whatever short-term goals are felt currently to be pressing. The horizon of the Church and of each of its faithful members is, as I have tried to suggest, far

[20] See J Finnis, J Boyle & G Grisez, *Nuclear Deterrence, Morality, and Realism*, Oxford: OUP 1987, pp. 23–24, 36–37, and especially 160–161.
[21] See Finnis, *Moral Absolutes*, pp. 16–20.

different. The transformation of this world into the new heavens and new earth will not be accomplished by the success of any human project or calculus, yet every reasonable human undertaking, every act of love of neighbour as oneself, will be taken up as material usable by God in the building up of that new world, discontinuous but in that mysterious way also continuous with this one. Philosophy even unaided by revelation can discern that kingdom of ends from afar off, as an ideal, the only acceptable ideal of practical reason, the only principle capable of integrating the basic reasons for action. Reason's own trajectory, which every worthwhile public or private debate seeks to trace and track, is headed towards that same end. If we undertake the demanding disciplines of reasoning, private or public, we should do so in that confidence.

# 17

# Bioethics and public policy: Catholic participation in the American debate

ROBERT P. GEORGE WITH WILLIAM L. SAUNDERS

MY ASSIGNED TOPIC is "Contributing to public policy debates on bioethical issues: the American Catholic experience". I accepted Luke Gormally's invitation to address this topic with a certain trepidation. Its proper exploration requires historical and sociological, rather than philosophical, analysis, and I claim no expertise as an historian or sociologist. Still, the topic deeply interests me. My impression has been that the American Catholic experience of contributing to major public policy debates about bioethical issues has been one marked by many disappointments and failures.[1] Luke's kind invitation provided an opportunity to test this impression and, upon confirming it, to attempt to understand the factors that account for these disappointments and failures.

Let us take note of some recent developments and work backwards in time. This procedure has the advantage of enabling us to begin with a bit of good news. In June of 1997, the Supreme Court of the United States handed down two unanimous decisions rejecting constitutional challenges to state laws prohibiting people from assisting others in committing suicide. In *State of Washington v. Glucksberg* and *Vacco v. Quill*, not a single justice was prepared to endorse the proposition that the Constitution of the United States implicitly contains a general "right-to-die" analogous to the "right-to-abortion" the Court claimed to discover in the Constitution in the 1973 case of *Roe v. Wade*. It is important to note, however, that the Court has by no means ensured that the prohibition of assisting in suicide will remain in place in the American states. The practical effect of its decisions is to return the issue of assisted suicide to the individual states where it will be fought out in referenda and legislative contests.[2]

And here there is some rather alarming news: Polling data in many states show that substantial majorities favour changes in the laws to permit physicians

---

[1] In saying that the American Catholic experience of contributing to public policy debates over bioethical issues has been marked by many disappointments and failures, I do not wish to obscure the fact that the lives of many unborn children and other vulnerable persons have been saved by the Church's witness to the core bioethical principle of respect for human life, nor to minimize the assistance the Church has provided through her concrete programmes to pregnant women and others in need.

[2] For analysis of the Supreme Court's decisions in the assisted suicide cases, see Robert P. George's contribution to the 'Symposium on the Supreme Court's 1996–97 Term' in *First Things*, October 1997.

274

to assist in the suicides of terminally ill patients. Even worse, it appears that throughout the country support for physician assisted suicide among self-identified Roman Catholics closely parallels, and sometimes even exceeds, that of the population generally. Nevertheless, referenda in the States of Washington, Michigan, and California prove that effective public education campaigns – campaigns in which the Catholic Church has played critically important roles – can reverse a voting population's initial support for assisted suicide.[3]

The Church's ability to contribute effectively to the resistance to physician assisted suicide in the United States is significantly enhanced by the fact that America's cultural elites – leading journalists, academics, television and film personalities, professionals and their associations, etc. – have not (yet) united in the cause of assisted suicide as they have in the cause of, say, abortion. Indeed, in asking the Supreme Court to deny the existence of a fundamental constitutional 'right-to-die', the United States Catholic Conference found itself in the company of many individuals and groups – including the Solicitor General of the United States, on behalf of the Clinton administration, and the American Medical Association – with whom the Conference has been in conflict over abortion and other bioethical issues. I do not mean to disparage in any way the Church's contribution to the political struggle against assisted suicide, much less her powerful witness in the cause of human life, when I observe that the Court's unwillingness to invent a right to physician assisted suicide probably had more to do with the AMA's opposition, than with that of the USCC.

Furthermore, I am personally pessimistic about the prospects that the AMA and other elite institutions will maintain their opposition to physician assisted suicide and euthanasia over the long term. Indeed, I will be surprised if, a decade from now, America's cultural elites are not firmly united in support of these practices. The logic of a commitment to an unqualified right to abortion-on-demand virtually compels such an outcome – a fact that has not been lost on scholar-activists such as Professor Ronald Dworkin, not to mention jurists such as Ninth Circuit Court of Appeals Judge Stephen Reinhardt (whose invalidation of a state law prohibiting assisting in suicide was overturned by the Supreme Court in the *Glucksberg* case). Reinhardt pressed the logic of the Supreme Court's abortion holdings[4] relentlessly in seeking to induce the justices to create a right to physician assisted suicide. If I am correct, then the true struggle over assisted suicide and euthanasia – a struggle in which the Church will once again find

[3] Oregon, the one state – thus far – to have legalized physician assisted suicide, did so by a very narrow margin (51% to 49%) in a referendum in 1994. In the autumn of 1997, however, Oregon voters, by a much larger margin, declined to reverse course and re-establish the legal prohibition of assisted suicide. It is worth observing that Oregon is the most highly secularized state in the union, having the nation's highest percentage of unbelievers and 'unchurched' persons. (Its history, incidentally, is marked by notable instances of antireligious and, particularly, anti-Catholic prejudice. Such prejudice has plainly been a feature of the campaign to establish and maintain legalized assisted suicide in Oregon.)

[4] "At the heart of [constitutionally protected] liberty is the right to define one's own concept of existence, of meaning, of the universe, and of the mystery of human life." (*Planned Parenthood v. Casey*, 112 S.Ct 2791, 2807 (1992).)

herself in opposition to the most powerful constituencies and interests in American society – is yet to come.

On the issue of abortion, there have also been important recent developments. Bernard Nathanson, a former abortionist and founder of the National Abortion Rights Action League, who defected to the pro-life cause some years ago, was baptized and received into the Roman Catholic Church by John Cardinal O'Connor in New York's St. Patrick's Cathedral. Dr. Nathanson said that it was above all the quiet, persistent, loving witness of pro-life activists that brought him to faith in Jesus Christ.[5] (In my view, continuing co-operation between Catholics and evangelical Protestants in the pro-life movement in the United States is a 'sign of the times' pointing, perhaps, toward a fulfilment of the hope for Christian unity expressed by the Holy Father in *Ut Unum Sint*.)

In another important development in the struggle over abortion, the United States Congress has for a second time voted to ban dilation and extraction, better known as "partial birth", abortions. Apparently because of the graphically barbaric nature of this procedure, public support for such a ban is particularly high. However, the President of the United States vetoed the ban the first time it was enacted – claiming, utterly implausibly, that partial birth abortions are sometimes necessary to protect the health and preserve the future fertility of pregnant women – and has now vetoed it again.[6] Although this veto was overridden in the House of Representatives, as was the first veto, it was probably sustained again in the Senate, where ten of the thirty-three votes needed to prevent an override of the veto were provided by self-identified Catholics.[7]

The night before the President's first veto, hundreds of Roman Catholics gathered in the pouring rain outside the White House in a silent, candlelight vigil to pray that Clinton would reconsider his announced opposition to banning partial birth abortions. Present were several American cardinals. The American hierarchy had placed a very high priority on banning partial birth abortions as

---

[5] See the concluding chapter of Bernard N. Nathanson, *The Hand of God*, Chicago: Regnery 1996.

[6] Clinton's original veto was denounced by the U.S. Catholic bishops as "shameful". Adding to the shame, Clinton arranged to veto the bill in the highly publicized presence of a group of women (and their families) who allegedly had undergone partial birth abortions for health reasons. (It later became clear that the procedures performed on at least some of the women were not, in fact, partial birth abortions.) Clinton went out of his way in public remarks to point out that some of these women were "personally pro-life" Roman Catholics; he did not mention the religious affiliations of the others.

[7] To their shame, the following self-identified Catholic members of the United States Senate could not bring themselves to vote for a ban even on the graphically barbarous procedure known as partial birth abortion: Christopher Dodd (Democrat, Connecticut); Tom Harkin (Dem., Iowa); John Kerry (Dem., Massachussets); Carol Moseley-Braun (Dem., Illinois); Jack Reed (Dem., Rhode Island); Richard Durbin (Dem., Illinois); Edward Kennedy (Dem., Massachussets); Barbara Mikulski (Dem., Maryland); Patty Murray (Dem., Washington); and Susan Collins (Republican, Maine). At least four Catholic members of the Senate who usually support abortion drew the line at partial birth abortion and supported the legislation prohibiting it: Joseph Biden (Dem., Delaware); Tom Daschle (Dem., S. Dakota); Daniel Patrick Moynihan (Dem., New York); and Mary Landrieu (Dem., Louisiana).

a modest first step in the direction of bringing the unborn within the protection of American law. A few weeks after the veto, *all* of the active American cardinals came to Washington to urge Congress to override the veto. This was the first – and only – time in the history of the United States that all of the nation's active cardinals have appeared together to speak out on a matter of public policy. Yet their witness appears to have had no impact on President Clinton (who, as it happens, as a Georgetown University graduate is the first president ever to hold an earned degree from a Catholic institution of higher learning) or on those Catholic members of Congress who supported the president. Indeed, Clinton went so far as to refuse the cardinals the courtesy of an invitation to the White House. It is conceivable that he and his advisors believed – perhaps rightly – that he had more to gain politically from publicly snubbing the American Catholic leadership than he had to lose.

However that may be, Clinton and the Catholic members of the House and Senate who acted to protect partial birth abortion received valuable "cover" for their deeds from a politically prominent Catholic clergyman whose actions had long served the pro-abortion cause. At a critical moment, Fr. Robert Drinan published articles in *The New York Times* and *The National Catholic Reporter* supporting Clinton's decision to veto the ban on partial birth abortions and urging members of Congress to sustain that veto. Drinan is a Jesuit priest, a law professor at Georgetown,[8] and a former member of Congress. He gained wide public recognition in the early 1970s as an outspoken Democratic member of the House Judiciary Committee which recommended the impeachment of President Richard Nixon. What received less attention at the time was the fact that he was one of the first notable Catholic politicians in the country to begin opposing pro-life initiatives and voting in favour of legalized abortion and its public funding.[9] This happened at a time when even Senator Edward Kennedy, brother of the late president, scion of the most celebrated Roman Catholic family in the country, and since the mid-1970s one of the nation's most aggressively pro-abortion politicians, was professing implacable opposition to legal abortion and a desire for America to "fulfil its responsibility to its children from the very moment of conception".[10]

Unfortunately, Drinan did worse than set a bad example for Catholic politicians – particularly political liberals who were coming under increasing pressure to cast pro-abortion votes. He enabled them to rationalize support for pro-abortion legislative initiatives, and justify their votes to others, on the ground that they were doing nothing that a Catholic priest in good standing was not able and willing to do. Moreover, Drinan provided a much imitated model for Catholic politicians

[8] Drinan is an acknowledged leader in the field of international human rights. This renders his failure to work to protect the human rights of the unborn even more inexplicable and tragic.

[9] If, as he said, Drinan believed there was a right to abortion under the Constitution (per *Roe v. Wade*), and if, as he also asserted, he subscribed to the Church's view on the grave injustice of abortion, it is impossible to understand why he consistently opposed efforts to amend the Constitution to protect the unborn.

[10] Letter from Edward M. Kennedy, member of the United States Senate, to Thomas E. Dennelly of Great Neck, New York, August 3, 1971.

who wished to support the pro-abortion movement while claiming to be faithful to Catholic moral teaching. When a constituent would write to his office expressing pro-life views, Drinan would respond with a letter giving assurances of his full agreement with the Church's teaching that abortion is gravely wrong. The letter would reveal nothing of Drinan's consistent support for pro-abortion legislative initiatives and opposition to pro-life initiatives. Drinan's legislative record on the subject was mentioned only when he replied to constituents whose letters to his office expressed pro-abortion sentiments.[11] What Drinan was developing in practice was the 'personally opposed but pro-choice' position which was later to be defended formally in a famous speech by New York Governor Mario Cuomo at Notre Dame University.[12]

Drinan became a recognized leader of the 'pro-choice' forces. For instance, a fund-raising letter from the National Abortion Rights Action League in 1980 identified Drinan as a friend of the movement whose re-election to the House of Representatives was critical to the 'pro-choice' cause. He left Congress in 1980 only after the Holy See issued a general order requiring all priests to abstain from seeking or holding political office. He went on to become president of Americans for Democratic Action, a leading liberal advocacy group. In that connection, he sent out a fund-raising letter urging the moral necessity of electing candidates to Congress who favoured legal abortion and its public funding.[13]

[11] On Drinan's letters to constituents regarding abortion, see 'Father Robert Drinan Under Siege', by Mary Meehan in *Our Sunday Visitor*, September 9, 1996, pp. 8, 9. Defenders of Drinan may assert that he was simply adding "nuances" to letters to different constituents as all politicians do. If, however, he were forced to stoop to such misleading actions by virtue of serving in elective office, that simply underscores the wisdom of the Holy See in requiring all priests to withdraw from political office. In fact, Drinan's Jesuit superiors had discouraged him from being involved in elective office from the beginning. The sad story of the effort to evade their wishes is detailed in 'The Strange Political Career of Father Drinan', *The Catholic World Report*, July 1996, which is based on material from the archives of the New England Province of the Society of Jesus.

[12] Support of the 'prochoice' position necessitates willing that only certain persons – the unborn – be denied the protection of the law and subjected to the risk of lethal violence, while all other persons continue to be protected by the law from this threat. See Robert P George, 'Conscience and the Public Person', in Russell E Smith (ed.) *Catholic Conscience: Foundation and Formation* Braintree, Mass.: Pope John XXIII Medical-Moral Research & Education Center 1991, pp. 217–231.

*Evangelium Vitae*, following centuries of Catholic teaching, emphasizes that this position violates elementary principles of justice and the common good, which require the protection of the innocent.

"The legal toleration of abortion . . . can in no way claim to be based on respect for the conscience of others, precisely because society has the right and the duty to protect itself against the abuses which can occur in the name of conscience and under the pretext of freedom." (para. 71)
"In the case of an intrinsically unjust law, such as a law permitting abortion . . . , it is . . . never licit to . . . vote for it." (para. 73)

[13] On Drinan's pro-abortion activities as a Congressman and later as President of Americans for Democratic Action, see 'The Strange Political Career of Father Drinan', *Catholic World Report*, July 1996, p. 38.

Drinan continued this line of argument in his articles supporting Clinton's veto of the ban on partial birth abortions. He claimed that the ban "would allow federal power to intrude into the practice of medicine". Further, he argued that banning these abortions would "detract from the urgent need to decrease abortions". Repeating the pro-abortion line on which Clinton had relied in justifying his veto, Drinan suggested that partial birth abortions are rarely performed in the United States and then only when necessary to save women's lives or prevent grave injury.

This time, however, Drinan's efforts landed him in trouble, forcing him in the end into a humiliating retreat. First, a coalition of physicians, including former U.S. Surgeon General C. Everett Koop (who is not a Catholic), blasted apart the claim that partial birth abortions are sometimes therapeutically indicated. Shortly thereafter, a leading lobbyist for the abortion movement publicly admitted lying about this and other issues pertaining to partial birth abortion, including its frequency. At the same time, Drinan finally began to feel some heat from ecclesiastical sources. *The Pilot*, Boston's archdiocesan newspaper, published an editorial denouncing Drinan's defence of partial birth abortion as "shocking, schizophrenic, and even scandalous". New York's John Cardinal O'Connor, writing in his own archdiocesan newspaper, dramatically called Drinan to account:

> You could have raised your formidable voice for life; you have raised it for death.... Hardly the role of a lawmaker. Surely, not the role of a priest.

James Cardinal Hickey, Archbishop of Washington, D.C., where Drinan resides and teaches, demanded that Drinan "clarify" his position since his published comments had, the Cardinal's spokesman said, "caused public confusion about Church teaching on abortion". Not long thereafter, Drinan issued a statement "withdrawing" what he had said in *The New York Times* and *The National Catholic Reporter*. After noting that he had relied on what turned out to be false information concerning "the true nature and widespread use of partial-birth abortion". Drinan reaffirmed his "total support" for the Church's "firm condemnation of abortion". I shall quote in full the concluding paragraph of his statement:

> I do not believe that every moral evil should be outlawed. I do, however, see abortion – particularly partial birth abortion – as a grave evil and can understand why Church leaders are urging lawmakers to ban it. I do not want anything to impede that effort. On the contrary, I join that effort and stand ready to promote laws and public policies that aim to protect vulnerable human life from conception until natural death. I support the Catholic bishops in their efforts to exercise moral leadership in the fight against abortion.[14]

Quite a satisfactory statement, I think. It would be interesting, and, indeed, instructive, to know what went on behind the scenes to produce it. The sad truth, however, is that it came more than twenty-five years too late. For, by 1997, Drinan's efforts, his bad example, and the profound scandal he had

---

[14] For an account of the episode, see 'Father Drinan Retracts Controversial Remarks, says he was wrong on partial-birth abortion', *Catholic Standard*, May 15, 1997.

given, beginning in the early 1970s, had done immeasurable damage to the pro-life cause. The Church's failure to find a way effectively to meet the challenge presented by a notable priest's public activities and advocacy on behalf of abortion is among the most disappointing chapters in the story of the Church's participation in public policy debates on bioethical issues in the United States.

In the early 1970s, while Fr. Drinan was doing grave mischief in Congress, a prominent Catholic layman was doing similar harm in the far less public setting of the Supreme Court. Although it is difficult to obtain perfectly reliable information about the justices' deliberations, by all accounts Associate Justice William J. Brennan, who recently died at the age of 91, was a key player in creating a constitutional right to abortion in *Roe v. Wade*. Not only was Brennan a Catholic, he was appointed to the Court in the 1950s by President Eisenhower *precisely because he was a Catholic* – he filled the so-called 'Catholic seat' on the Court. For most of his tenure on the Court, he was its only Catholic member. Yet, Brennan consistently worked to manufacture constitutional rights to activities condemned by the Church on moral grounds: pornography, contraception, sodomy, and abortion. Like Drinan, he claimed to be a faithful Catholic, fully supportive of the Church's moral teaching. Nevertheless, he repeatedly acted to undermine principles of public morality that the Church teaches are central to justice and the common good. Each time, he would rationalize his actions by claiming that his judicial decisions reflected, not his own political views, but the constitutional principles he was sworn as a federal judge to uphold. However, his extreme view of individual liberty (on issues such as abortion) is simply not compelled by the Constitution itself.[15] In addition, one cannot help but wonder why someone who "defined" the Constitution as the protection of "the dignity" and "fundamental rights" of "the human being",[16] and who used that understanding of the Constitution to protect the poor, prisoners, the mentally retarded, and others, could not find within that same document protection for the dignity and fundamental rights of the vulnerable and defenceless unborn. After the opinion in *Roe*, which Brennan formally joined, was handed down, Catholics – including Catholic politicians – who wished publicly to join the elite consensus supporting abortion, while claiming to be faithful to the Church's moral teaching, could point to another prominent person – in this case the nation's highest ranking Catholic jurist – as a model.

It was even more difficult for the Catholic hierarchy to deal with Brennan and other Catholic laymen than it was to deal with Drinan. Public criticism of them, and *a fortiori* public action against them, was all but ruled out because of the likelihood that it would backfire. Anti-Catholicism remained, and remains, a fact of American life – especially among American elites.[17] Powerful individuals

---

[15] The idea that the Supreme Court's decision creating a right to abortion in *Roe v. Wade* was compelled by the Constitution itself, and was not a matter of the court imposing the independent moral and political preferences of a majority of its members, is hardly plausible.

[16] See 'William Brennan: A Legacy of Liberty' by Nat Hentoff in *The Washington Post*, July 29, 1997.

[17] For a valuable historical account of the prevalence of anti-Catholicism among America's liberal elite, see John T. McGreevy, 'Thinking on One's Own: Catholicism in the American Intellectual Imagination, 1928–1960', 84/i (1997) *The Journal of American History*, pp. 97–131.

and interests who remain contemptuous and suspicious of the Church, particularly for her moral teachings, are always ready to make a hero of any Catholic public figure who defies the bishops. This is particularly true when they can depict the bishops as intervening in political affairs and attempting to tell Catholics how to vote.[18] Many American Catholics have themselves internalized a (mis)conception of the constitutional "separation of church and state" according to which religion, and religious authorities, should have nothing to say about the conduct of public life. Non-Catholics and Catholics alike seem to believe that full Catholic participation in public affairs is conditioned upon the bargain struck by John F. Kennedy – the first (and, so far, only) Roman Catholic president – when he spoke to a group of Protestant ministers in Houston during his campaign for the presidency in 1960:[19]

> I believe in an America where the separation of church and state is absolute – where no Catholic prelate would tell the President (should he be a Catholic) how to act and no Protestant minister would tell his parishioners for whom to vote – where no church or church school is granted any public funds or political preference...where no public official either requests or accepts instructions on public policy from the Pope, the National Council of Churches or any other ecclesiastical source – where no religious body seeks to impose its will directly or indirectly upon the general populace or the public acts of its officials.[20]

[18] Where a bishop has dared to act against, or even publicly to criticize, a Catholic politician for his or her pro-abortion record, the elite media has quickly depicted the politician in question as a martyr for freedom and the bishop as a modern day Torquemada. This is certainly true of *The New York Times'* coverage of Cardinal O'Connor's criticism of New York Congresswoman Geraldine Ferraro when she was the Democratic candidate for Vice-President of the United States in 1980. Of course, the *Times* sang a different tune a generation earlier when a Catholic bishop in New Orleans excommunicated a prominent politician who was taking a position contrary to the Church's moral teaching by actively opposing racial integration in Louisiana's parochial schools.

[19] Remarks of Senator John F. Kennedy on Church and State, delivered to Greater Houston Ministerial Association, Houston, Texas, September 12, 1960.

[20] Kennedy apparently endorsed the extreme version of church-state separation embraced by the Supreme Court in the 1947 case of *Everson v. Illinois*, and defended by American liberals ever since. Historical scholarship makes clear that this conception of the separation of church and state was alien to the thinking of those who framed and ratified the First Amendment to the U.S. Constitution which forbids Congress from making any law "respecting an establishment of religion or prohibiting the free exercise thereof". See Gerard V. Bradley, *Church-State Relationships in America*, Greenwood Press 1987. As I have already suggested, Kennedy's speech contributed massively to the tragic illusion that faith and politics are utterly separate spheres, hermetically sealed off from each other. For people in the grip of this illusion, any involvement of overtly religious people, and *a fortiori* of religious leaders, in politics is viewed with suspicion. A striking exception for American liberals is the involvement of clerics, particularly black Protestant ministers such as Martin Luther King and Jesse Jackson, in the political campaign for civil rights. It is interesting to note that even the prohibition on tax-exempt religious (and other) organizations (e.g., churches) from engaging in political activity is not a result of "the constitutional separation of church and state", but of a politically motivated change in the tax laws in 1954, reversing nearly 200 years of accepted practice. See "What if churches could be more politically active?", *Our Sunday Visitor*, August 17, 1997 (discussing recent research).

Kennedy went on to say that "Whatever issue may come before me as President … on birth control, divorce, censorship, gambling, or any other subject – I will make my decision in accordance with … what my conscience tells me to be in the national interest, and without regard to outside religious pressure or dictate. And no power or threat of punishment could cause me to do otherwise." Thus, at least as this speech was interpreted, Kennedy embraced the enduring, popular misconception that the Catholic Church seeks to "impose" its views on (rather than reason with) Americans, and declared his independence from any such interference with his conscience, which was itself apparently free to disregard Church teachings. He gave no positive account of how his Catholic faith would help make him a good president; rather, he accepted the view that religion should be separated from public life.

Kennedy effectively declared his Catholic faith to be irrelevant to his public life. For this and other reasons, few today cling to the old image of John F. Kennedy as a model Catholic. Still, he was a very public Catholic whose campaign and election largely set the terms of the American electorate's understanding of the relationship of politics and religion – at least as far as Roman Catholicism was concerned. And these terms – though they have been altered a bit in recent years and certainly are subject to further alteration – are realities with which faithful American Catholics and their ecclesiastical leaders have had to deal. And they make the job of bringing Catholic witness to bear in public debates over bioethical issues very difficult indeed – especially where the Church finds itself in sharp opposition to elite opinion.

With these facts in mind, let us examine the efforts of the United States Catholic Conference to influence these debates. Its approach to public policy matters has developed over the years, and we can understand its efforts best, I think, by dividing our analysis into certain periods, as follows: first, let us examine the period from the Second Vatican Council up to the preparation of the bishops' pastoral letter on nuclear war; second, let us look at the period from 1983 through 1987 when the nuclear pastoral was issued and the late Joseph Cardinal Bernardin of Chicago developed his widely publicized idea of a "seamless garment" or a "consistent ethic of life"; and third, let us focus on the period from 1988 to Fr. Drinan's retraction, which takes us up to the present moment. After reviewing the development of the USCC's approach, I shall conclude by raising the question whether the bishops have recognized, and fully taken the measure of, the central problems they confront.

Preliminarily, let me make two points. First, the American Catholic experience of participating in public policy debates on bioethical issues cannot be accurately recounted if we focus on bioethical issues in isolation from other public policy debates. So it will be necessary for us to consider how the USCC has addressed a broad range of issues of public policy. Second, in undertaking this analysis, I have relied in large part on collections of official documents which the USCC itself publishes. Unfortunately, these publications are not entirely up-to-date.[21] Nevertheless, I think we can reach some fairly secure conclusions.

The United States Catholic Conference was 'born' in 1966, in the exhilarating wake of Vatican II.[22] As the Popes and Fathers of the Council saw things, the Holy Spirit was moving in the Church to effect a much needed renewal. As the secular media saw things, however, the Catholic Church was preparing to accommodate itself to, if not fully to embrace, the 'new morality' which was fast entrenching itself among Western elites. More than a few Catholics shared the secular media's view, or, at least, hoped that it would prove to be correct. In many countries, including the United States, change and the demand for novelty, even if heretical, exploded and overwhelmed some of the Church's pastors.

Within four years of the creation of the USCC, the American bishops, in their pastoral letter *Christians in Our Time*, acknowledged candidly that the period since the Council had been one of "extraordinary testing for the Church".

> Most of us expected a gradual, orderly process of change and renewal.... Instead, we have seen dissension, controversy, and turmoil.... The problems are real, profound, and vitally crucial. They must be viewed with grave concern.[23]

This, by the way, was three years before *Roe v. Wade* and the flight from the pro-life cause by many Catholic liberals and liberal Catholic politicians.

The demands for change within the Church and within the larger society – the coinciding of what was misleadingly called 'the spirit of Vatican II' with the 'liberationist spirit of 1968' (the latter of which was expressing itself in widespread political unrest, the expansion of the drug culture, and a leap forward in the sexual revolution) – confronted the bishops with a nearly impossible array of problems to which they felt called to respond. And respond they did. In the ten years preceding the opening of Vatican II (1951–1961), the American bishops issued roughly three pastoral letters or statements per year. In the decade following the conclusion of the Council (1966–1976), they issued approximately seven per year.

---

[21] These collections, published jointly by the National Conference of Catholic Bishops and United States Catholic Conference, under the title *Pastoral Letters of the United States Catholic Bishops*, are currently in five volumes. Volume I covers the years 1792–1940, Volume II covers 1941–1961, Volume III covers 1962–1974, Volume IV covers 1975–1983, and Volume V covers 1983–1988. Hereinafter, individual volumes will be cited as "*Pastoral Letters*, Volume – ".

[22] Following Vatican II, the bishops of the United States were organised into two bodies – the United States Catholic Conference (USCC) and the National Conference of Catholic Bishops (NCCB). The former replaced the National Catholic Welfare Conference as the body which dealt with public policy issues. As originally envisioned, the NCCB was formed to deal with internal church matters. Subsequently, this line of demarcation has blurred. For convenience we shall use "the United States Catholic Conference", "the Conference", and "the USCC" to refer to either or both.

[23] *Pastoral Letters*, Volume III at p. 251.

Here is a listing of some of the topics of pastorals issued by the U.S. bishops within ten years of the Council (many of which have been revisited in subsequent pastorals): "the government and birth control"; "peace and Vietnam"; "penance"; "race relations and poverty"; "war in the middle east"; "clerical celibacy"; "the Church in our day"; "the national race crisis"; "human life in our day"; "farm labor"; "abortion"; "poverty"; "ecumenism"; "conscientious objection"; "parental rights and the free exercise of religion"; "Christian concern for the environment"; "population and the American future"; "Mary – woman of faith"; "human rights in Chile and Brazil"; "the world food crisis"; "Catholic charismatic renewal"; "Panama-U.S. relations"; "toward a U.S. domestic food policy"; "the introduction of the family viewing period during prime time"; "hand-gun violence"; "the United Nations and the Republic of South Africa"; "the Eucharist and the hungers of the human family"; "Catholic-Jewish relations"; and "society and the aged".[24]

During this period, the United States experienced the Vietnam War, the struggle for civil rights for African Americans, the flowering of the drug culture, and the brunt of the sexual revolution. Then, in 1973, came *Roe v. Wade*, which, though accurately described by dissenting Justice Byron White as nothing more than "an exercise of raw judicial power", was widely understood to commit the nation to a regime of abortion-on-demand as a matter of constitutional principle. (As discussed above, it seems that Catholic jurist William Brennan played a key role in creating this 'right'.) The Supreme Court's declaration that abortion – which had been restricted in varying but significant ways in all fifty states – was a federal *constitutional right*, gave many politicians, including Catholic politicians, an excuse for unburdening themselves of the pro-life political cause which, even in the early 1970s, was unpopular with elites. Before *Roe v. Wade*, Teddy Kennedy, as we have seen, had taken the position that "the legalization of abortion on demand is not in accordance with the value which our civilization places on human life".[25] In the aftermath of *Roe*, he and many other Catholic politicians revised their positions to bring them into conformity with the allegedly authoritative constitutional ruling of the Supreme Court on the subject. By the time Kennedy challenged President Jimmy Carter, a self-described 'born again Christian' and a sort of 'centrist' on the abortion question, for the Democratic Party's nomination for the presidency in 1976, the most visible Catholic public figure in America was an unabashed political champion of the most extreme wing of the pro-abortion movement.[26]

[24] See, generally, *Pastoral Letters*, Volumes III and IV.
[25] Letter of Edward M. Kennedy, member of the United States Senate, to Thomas E. Dennelly of Great Neck, New York, August 3, 1971.
[26] Kennedy's current, permissive, views on abortion are, of course, well-documented. One personal account – in which the author recounts that, following *Roe*, "Kennedy...stated to me publicly that he no longer knows when human life begins" – can be found in Letter from Joseph J. Reilly, Chairman, Massachusetts Citizens for Life, to *The Lawrence Eagle-Tribune*, February 19, 1980.

To their credit, the U.S. bishops responded vigorously to the challenge of *Roe*, issuing three statements in less than a year denouncing the judicial imposition of the abortion license and calling for a constitutional amendment to protect unborn human beings.[27] In 1975, they developed a sophisticated "Pastoral Plan for Pro-Life Activities", in which emphasis was placed on educating and equipping people at the parish and diocesan levels to defend the right to life.[28] In several documents issued in this period, they linked abortion, the quintessential 'bioethical' issue, to others, particularly euthanasia and poverty.[29] Nevertheless, supporters of abortion, including influential figures within the print and broadcast media, depicted the bishops, and the Church as a whole, as being solely concerned with the issue of abortion, and of struggling to impose their allegedly purely 'religious' view of the matter on Catholics and non-Catholics alike.

The bishops responded in their 1976 statement, *Political Responsibility: Reflections in an Election Year*.[30] They began in something of a defensive mode by asserting that their speaking out on political topics posed no threat to the domestic political order. Then, echoing the words of John F. Kennedy in Houston that "I believe in an America...where there is no Catholic vote, no anti-Catholic vote, no bloc voting of any kind", the bishops declared that they did "not seek the formation of a voting bloc". At least partially, in my judgment, to blunt the claim that the Catholic Church is concerned about abortion and nothing else, the document went on to draw together USCC positions on *eight* issue "clusters": abortion, the economy, education, food policy, housing, human rights/U.S. foreign policy, the mass media, and military expenditures. This combination of defensiveness and eagerness to show that they were not preoccupied with abortion would continue to mark USCC statements to the present.

The USCC's approach in this period was subjected to respectful but powerful criticism by J. Brian Benestad.[31] While acknowledging many strengths of the bishops' statements, Benestad noted several problems:

1. Instead of being integrated into education and evangelization, the pursuit of social justice became a separate, parallel concern of the bishops.
2. By proposing particular policy initiatives, the bishops failed to communicate the richness of Catholic social teaching as a whole.
3. The bishops' teachings failed adequately to instruct and involve the laity in ways envisioned by the Second Vatican Council.
4. Apart from abortion, the bishops permitted secular liberalism to set their agenda.

[27] See *Pastoral Letters*, Volume III, pp. 235, 236.
[28] *Pastoral Letters*, Volume IV at p. 81.
[29] See, e.g. 'Statement on Abortion' and 'Statement in Protest of U.S. Government Programs Against the Right to Life' in *Pastoral Letters*, Volume III.
[30] *Pastoral Letters*, Volume IV at p. 129.
[31] J. Brian Benestad, *The Pursuit of a Just Social Order: Policy Statements of the U.S. Catholic Bishops, 1966–80*, Ethics & Public Policy Center 1982.

5. Contrary to the Church's teaching on subsidiarity, the bishops seemed to embrace the liberal political view that there was a federal governmental solution to every social problem.

Although Benestad has been accused of exaggerating the extent and seriousness of these problems, it cannot reasonably be denied that problems existed. A review of the documents confirms that the bishops seem to be taking something of a 'scattershot' approach to issues, to be responding too much to the left-liberal agenda of secular elites, and to be emphasizing governmental and, indeed, *federal* governmental solutions where more creative reflection would have suggested local governmental, and even non-governmental, approaches. Dealing with a very wide array of social problems, and attempting to resolve questions on which faithful Catholics might differ (both in their assessment of relevant social facts and in their prudential judgments as how best to address the problems), the bishops set themselves up for respectful disagreement by manifestly faithful Catholics on issues of social fact and prudential judgment on which the bishops could claim no special expertise or teaching authority. This was to be exploited aggressively by manifestly less faithful Catholics – particularly pro-abortion politicians – who sought to justify their dissent from the bishops' authoritative teachings on the right to life by depicting those teachings as matters of prudence on the order of the bishops' recommendations on, say, taxation and housing policy.

Let us next turn to the crucial period from 1983 to 1987. The key figure in our story now becomes the late Joseph Cardinal Bernardin of Chicago. Bernardin, who had been general secretary of the conference from 1968 through 1972 and its president from 1974 through 1977, was thoroughly familiar with its operations. He agreed with critics such as Benestad that Catholic teaching as a coherent whole had not been adequately communicated in previous pastoral letters and statements. He was aware that the bishops' approach had been too 'scattershot'. When, in January of 1981, he was appointed chairman of an *ad hoc* committee to draft a pastoral letter on the arms race, he sought to avoid replicating these problems. As Bernardin saw it, the goal of the pastoral was to "present a theory which is in conformity with the totality of the Church's moral teaching".[32]

Bernardin designed a "consultation" process with "experts" and laity far more extensive than the USCC had previously undertaken. Partially due to this consultation, and partially due to the fact that the first draft was leaked to the press, "it would be difficult to find a document more widely researched and discussed during its formation, from the very beginning".[33]

The pastoral went through three drafts, numerous meetings and consultations, and scores of amendments. *The Challenge of Peace*, as it was called, was finally issued in May of 1983. It was controversial from the outset. While some objections were spurious (such as the demand – this time heard more often from political conservatives than from liberals – that "religion be kept out of politics"), I believe

---

[32] Quoted in *Pastoral Letters*, Volume IV at p. 302.
[33] *Pastoral Letters*, Volume IV, p. 301.

there is at least one valid objection, an objection that may justly be made to many of the USCC's documents. Although the bishops "set forth...the principles of Catholic teaching on war", including, quite rightly, the Church's strict teaching regarding the absolute immunity of non-combatants from direct attack, they went on to make "a series of judgments, based on these principles, about concrete policies".[34] Many of these judgments involved assessments of fact and prudential judgments on which reasonable people and faithful Catholics can, and do, legitimately disagree. This was a recipe for confusing the faithful about what teaching of the bishops is binding in conscience and what is not. And, as I have already suggested, this confusion is bound to be – and, undeniably, has been – promoted and exploited by people who, in varying degrees of bad faith, have sought to rationalize their support for abortion and their efforts in its cause.

Cardinal Bernardin's famous initiative for a "seamless garment" or "consistent ethic of life" appears to have grown out of his experience with *The Challenge of Peace*. A few months after that document was issued, the Cardinal used the occasion of a lecture at Fordham University in New York to announce the "seamless garment" initiative.[35] It was to have important ramifications for the development of a Catholic bioethic in America.

At that time, the pro-life movement was in the doldrums. Efforts to reverse or even substantially modify *Roe v. Wade* had failed. Commitment to the pro-life cause had steadily eroded among Catholic elites, and many Catholics in the pro-life movement had grown disheartened. Among 'progressive' Catholics, many of those who remained formally pro-life came to view abortion as a side issue – an issue, indeed, inferior in importance to others. In this atmosphere, Cardinal Bernardin's effort may be seen in the most positive light as trying to unite Catholics of all stripes in a revivified effort to protect human life from the range of contemporary threats to it.

During his lecture at Fordham, the Cardinal noted that *The Challenge of Peace* provides a "starting point" for shaping a consistent ethic of life inasmuch as it

> links the questions of abortion and nuclear war.... No other major institution presently holds these two positions in the way the Catholic bishops have joined them. This is both a responsibility and an opportunity.[36]

He went on to argue that "the long term ecclesiological significance of the pastoral rests with the lessons it offers about the Church's capacity for dialogue with the world in a way which helps to shape public policy on key issues". In proposing the "seamless garment" initiative, his purpose, he said, was to "argue that success

---

[34] The quotation appears in the pastoral, published by the NCCB as *The Challenge of Peace – God's Promise and Our Response*, at p. iii.

[35] This and subsequent speeches by Bernardin were collected as part of a symposium, drawing together scholarly commentators on the "seamless garment", at Loyola University of Chicago in November 1987, and published in Joseph Cardinal Bernardin (et al.) *Consistent Ethic of Life* edited by Thomas G Fuechtmann, Kansas City, Mo.: Sheed & Ward 1988 (hereinafter, *Consistent Ethic*).

[36] The Fordham speech appears in *Consistent Ethic* at p. 1.

on any one of the issues threatening life requires concern for the broader attitudes in society about respect for human life''.

There is not a great deal to disagree with in what Cardinal Bernardin said thus far. But then he made the intellectual move which would bedevil the seamless garment initiative, and, eventually, rend the garment.

> The issue of consistency [of application of moral principle] is tested . . . when we examine the relationship between the "right to life" and the "quality of life" issues. . . . Those who defend the right to life of the weakest among us must be equally visible in support of the quality of life of the powerless among us. . . . Such a quality of life posture translates into specific political and economic positions on tax policy, employment generation, welfare policy, nutrition and feeding programs, and health care.

Bernardin's analysis here has been subjected to searching criticism by John Finnis.[37] As Finnis observed, it is at best tendentious to assert that people active in the pro-life cause must be "equally visible" in other good causes. Moreover, the Cardinal's suggestion that a sound "quality of life posture translates into *specific* political and economic positions" is ambiguous to the point of being misleading. On a great many political and economic issues, choice is between, or among, not (or not only) good and bad policy options, but (also) between, or among, a range of choices all of which are consistent with a morally proper 'posture'. And even with respect to certain issues that do admit of a uniquely 'best' policy option, the identification of that option may depend upon empirical and prudential judgments that are reasonably in dispute among people who share a sound 'posture'.

Questions of tax and welfare policy in the United States are good examples of political and economic issues of the sort I have in mind. Unlike the question whether abortion ought generally to be permitted by law or forbidden, the question whether the income tax should be replaced or supplemented by a national sales tax, or whether welfare responsibilities ought to be shifted from the federal government to the states, requires many judgments of fact and prudence. In a very general sense, perhaps, we could say that a proper concern for justice and the common good must be 'translated' into a fair programme of tax or welfare reform, but it will hardly do to suggest that such a concern translates into *"specific* political and economic positions" in these areas. But the intellectual weaknesses of Bernardin's initiative are less important to the story of Catholic participation in public policy debates in the United States than are its actual political consequences.

Let me state clearly that I do not believe that the purpose of Cardinal Bernardin's seamless garment initiative was to provide "cover" to Catholic politicians (and others) who wished to advance the pro-abortion agenda while claiming

[37] See J. M. Finnis, 'The Consistent Ethic – A Philosophical Critique', in *Consistent Ethic* at p. 140.

to be faithful (or, at least, friendly) to Catholic social teaching generally.[38] Unfortunately, however, a side effect of the initiative was that it provided precisely such cover. The best example of someone seizing it is that of Mario Cuomo, the very publicly Catholic politician who served two terms as Governor of New York.

On September 13, 1984, barely one year after Cardinal Bernardin had announced his seamless garment project, Cuomo delivered his famous speech on abortion at the University of Notre Dame.[39] At the time, Cuomo was the leader of the liberal wing of the Democratic party and a much touted presidential possibility. The central point of his speech was to claim that while he "personally" accepted, and lived by, the Church's teaching on abortion, he considered it wrong to deny his fellow citizens, including many who did not accept the teaching authority of the Catholic Church, the choice as to whether to have an abortion.

Noting that the Church does not insist that every immoral action be prohibited by law,[40] Cuomo depicted the question of abortion's legal treatment as a matter of prudence akin to the range of questions with which the seamless garment was concerned. It was a question on which, he suggested, reasonable people, including reasonable Catholics, could disagree. According to Cuomo, what made a politician truly pro-life, and truly someone who was prepared to act in the spirit of the Catholic teaching, was not his opposition to legal abortion or its public funding, though Cuomo acknowledged the bishops' clear teaching on those issues, it was, rather, the politician's stance on the whole range of sanctity and quality of life issues. And here, he implied, liberal Democrats such as himself, who shared the bishops' stated positions on capital punishment, welfare, housing, taxation, defence spending, international human rights policy, etc., had records far superior to those of pro-life conservatives whose

---

[38] Bernardin spoke publicly against such an interpretation of the "seamless garment":

> I know that some people on the left, if I may use that term, have used the consistent ethic to give the impression that the abortion issue is not all that important any more, that you should be against abortion in a general way but that there are more important issues, so don't hold anybody's feet to the fire just on abortion. That is a misuse of the consistent ethic, and I deplore it. (Interviewed in *National Catholic Register*, June 12, 1988 (hereinafter, 'Bernardin Interview').)

[39] Published as 'Religious Belief and Public Morality: A Catholic Governor's Perspective' in 1 (1987) *Notre Dame Journal of Law, Ethics & Public Policy* 13 (hereinafter, 'Religious Belief').
[40] Cuomo observed that the Church in antebellum America did not insist that slavery be abolished, nor does the Church insist that contraception and divorce be made illegal. He suggested that similarly the Church ought not to insist that abortion be legally prohibited. Of course, abortion is unlike contraception and divorce in a crucial respect: namely, its legal permission is incompatible with the moral right of its victims to the equal protection of the laws. In this same respect, it is like slavery, whose legal permission, the Church now plainly teaches, is never consistent with the requirements of justice. Surely Cuomo agrees that the Church's failure to teach this principle in the context of the debate over slavery in 19th century America was regrettable and certainly ought not to be emulated in the case of abortion.

only specific areas of policy agreement with the bishops had to do with abortion and related issues.[41]

Cuomo prides himself on being something of an intellectual. And there is no denying that he is a bright fellow. He must know, then, that, at its root, this is utter nonsense. He must be aware that the Church's teaching on abortion truly does 'translate' straightforwardly into a specific public policy – the unborn, like the rest of us, are to be afforded the equal protection of the laws; abortion is to be generally prohibited and never publicly promoted – in a way that her teachings regarding care for the poor or the requirement of fairness in distributing tax liability, for example, simply do not.[42] But the fact is that Cuomo brilliantly exploited Bernardin's seamless garment teaching, and the USCC's practice of adopting specific positions on a wide range of policy questions, to undermine the bishops' efforts to give the right to life the priority it deserves in a society in which more than one million unborn human beings are destroyed by abortion every year.[43]

Cuomo's Notre Dame speech provided a virtual playbook for pro-abortion Catholic politicians who wished to claim that their public support for 'the right to choose' abortion was not inconsistent with their personal moral opposition to deliberate feticide. It taught liberal politicians of every religious persuasion how to explain to Catholic constituents that their differences with the bishops over the particular issue of abortion are overshadowed by their broad agreement with the bishops across the wide range of 'quality of life' issues. It relieved much of the tension – internal as well as external – experienced by public men and women – Catholic and non-Catholic alike who wanted to be 'pro-life' and 'pro-choice' at the same time.

By 1986, pro-life Democrats were an endangered species and pro-life liberals were virtually extinct. It was in November of this year that the USCC issued

[41] For example, because abortion "involves life and death", Cuomo said, it "will always be a central concern of Catholics. But so will nuclear weapons, and hunger and homelessness and joblessness, all the forces diminishing human life and threatening to destroy it. The 'seamless garment' that Cardinal Bernardin has spoken of is a challenge to all Catholics in public office..." He then concluded: "We cannot justify our aspiration to goodness simply on the basis of the vigour of our demand for an elusive and questionable civil law declaring what we already know, that abortion is wrong." ('Religious Belief', pp. 28–29)

[42] *Evangelium Vitae* declares (para. 90):

Although laws are not the only means of protecting human life, nevertheless, they do play a very important and sometimes decisive role in influencing patterns of thought and behaviour. I repeat once more that a law which violates an innocent person's natural right to life is unjust and, as such, is not valid as a law. For this reason I urgently appeal once more to all political leaders not to pass laws which, by disregarding the dignity of the person, undermine the very fabric of society.

[43] The futility of the approach publicly advocated by Cuomo, Drinan, and others – allow abortion to be legal (and even pay for it with public funds) and "evangelize" against it – is shown by the fact that, as Professor Mary Ann Glendon of Harvard Law School has demonstrated, the United States now has the most radically permissive abortion laws in the democratic world and one of the highest rates of abortion. Indeed, despite the tireless efforts of pro-life counsellors, abortion is among the most frequently performed surgical procedure in the United States.

what is probably its most famous pastoral, *Economic Justice for All*.[44] However it might have been intended by the bishops, for liberal politicians it was an early Christmas present. Although the pastoral began by denying that it was "a blueprint for the American economy",[45] it undercut that claim by offering specific prescriptions on a host of issues. Again, though the bishops state that "we do not claim to make these prudential judgments with the same kind of authority that marks our declarations of principle", they "feel obliged to teach by example how Christians can undertake concrete analysis and make specific judgments on moral issues".[46] But why, if their prudential judgments are no more binding on the faithful than are mine or yours, do the bishops "feel obliged" to offer them? Is prudential political judgment of this sort not precisely the business of the laity? Is the failure to leave it to the laity not confusing and ultimately undermining of the bishops' proclamations of principle and their public witness on specific moral evils such as legal abortion? "We look for a fruitful exchange among differing viewpoints", the bishops say. "[T]ogether we will test our views by the Gospel and the Church's teaching . . . "[47]

The bishops apparently failed to see how their general approach and specific statements such as those I just quoted would be exploited by the enemies of their pro-life witness. What should they have done? More to the point: What should they do?

The bishops should say what they can say as a matter of moral principle consistent with their authority and responsibility to preach the Gospel.[48] Beyond that, politics should be left to the laity. That, as I understand it, is the teaching of Vatican II. It is what the American bishops themselves seemed to recognize in their 1980 pastoral, *Called and Gifted: The American Catholic Laity*, in which they wrote that "it is [the laity] who engage directly in . . . relating

---

[44] Published as *Economic Justice for All: Pastoral Letter on Catholic Social Teaching and the U.S. Economy* by the National Conference of Catholic Bishops in November 1986 (hereinafter, *Economic Justice*). It was developed pursuant to the most extensive consultation process yet. Though it is clear that the bishops hoped that such wide consultation with nonclerics would give the document's conclusions greater persuasiveness, such consultation does not alleviate the basic problem of bishops – however well-informed – speaking on matters of prudential political judgment which should properly be left to the laity.

[45] *Economic Justice* at p. ix.

[46] *Economic Justice* at p. xii.

[47] *Economic Justice* at p. xiii.

[48] Although the bishops should certainly communicate the riches of Catholic social teaching to their flock, and while they should insist that Catholic laity who are grappling with difficult practical matters seek genuinely to advance the common good, the bishops should consider the benefits in social justice which society reaps through the proper catechesis of their flock. Much recent research demonstrates that religious practice (including regular church attendance) is one of the most important factors in reducing nearly every major social pathology in America, from drug abuse to out-of-wedlock births to crime to suicide. It is demonstrably beneficial in helping individuals to escape poverty. And it strengthens the family bond, greatly reducing the divorce and illegitimacy rates. Much of this research is summarized and discussed by Patrick Fagan in 'Why Religion Matters: The Impact of Religious Practice on Social Stability', published by the Heritage Foundation in *Backgrounder*, no. 1064 (January 25, 1996).

Christian values...to complex questions".[49] Yet, in continuing to speak out on matters on which they can claim no special expertise or authority, the bishops diminish their public standing and, unintentionally, risk impeding potentially valuable lay initiatives. So, though there are faithful, pro-life Catholics who deeply disagree with me about this, I believe that the bishops should desist from pronouncing specific prescriptions on matters that are subject to honestly disputed questions of fact and prudential judgments. (This extends, by the way, to questions of *strategy* disputed among committed pro-life activists, such as whether to move forward in Congress with a partial-birth abortion ban before attempting to ban late-term abortions, or whether the goal of pro-life political action should be a Human Life Bill invoking Congress's power under section five of the 14th Amendment as opposed to a constitutional amendment to overturn *Roe v. Wade*.)

In the first two years after the publication of *Economic Justice for All*, the USCC issued statements on topics ranging from "biblical fundamentalism" to "the Ku Klux Klan", and from "principles for legal immigration policy" to "food, agriculture, and rural concerns".[50] As the foreword to one volume of the USCC's pastoral letters put it: "There is scarcely a serious international or domestic problem involving the United States during these years that the National Conference of Catholic Bishops and the United States Catholic Conference have not touched with a thoughtful statement."[51] Certainly, some – perhaps many – of the USCC's statements qualify as "thoughtful". But, thoughtfully or not, the USCC is talking too much, and the consequences of this excessive talking are part of the disappointing story of Catholic efforts to influence public policy regarding bioethical issues in the United States.

All this talk – all this taking of positions on specific policy proposals about which faithful Catholics (together with other men and women of goodwill) reasonably disagree – creates the image of the Catholic Church and its leadership as an *interest group*. This is the perception of the media, of politicians, and of many of the Catholic faithful themselves. In my view, the linking of its pro-life witness with advocacy on a wide range of 'quality of life' issues has failed to accomplish the Church's goals in any area. It has not produced particularly valuable initiatives in areas such as tax and welfare, and it has arguably put the Church on the wrong side of several important debates. And who can blame politicians and others for perceiving, and treating, the Church much like any other interest group? The USCC's own documents report that it had over fifty Congressional "legislative priorities" for 1991–92. And in teaching on such a bewildering variety of subjects, the USCC is in danger of "failing to see the forest for the trees". For instance, in testimony to the Democratic and Republican platform committees in 1988, the USCC mentions civil rights protection against every form of invidious discrimination and denial of liberty except that practised against

---

[49] *Pastoral Letters*, Volume IV at p. 420.
[50] See *Pastoral Letters*, Volume V.
[51] See *Pastoral Letters*, Volume V at p. 1.

people of faith![52] The Holy Father travels the world stressing the importance of religious freedom, what he calls the "first freedom" – yet, the USCC forgets to mention it.

Let me tell a related story. According to USCC materials,

> On March 22, 1988, the United States Congress voted to override President Reagan's veto of the Civil Rights Restoration Act. Almost angrily, Msgr. Daniel Hoye, then general secretary of the United States Catholic Conference declared that the President had vetoed one of the most important pieces of civil rights legislation in many years. Once the veto was overridden, Msgr. Hoye issued a *Statement on Civil Rights* [on behalf of the USCC]...[53]

Now, having served as a member of the United States Commission on Civil Rights, I can assure you that the intelligent assessment of the desirability of enacting any proposed piece of contemporary civil rights legislation requires prudential judgments of precisely the sort *lay people* are called to make in light of an evaluation of the complex facts of race relations in the United States. Calling something a "civil rights bill" or a "civil rights restoration act" is no guarantee of its soundness or justice. In fact, it will rarely make sense for the USCC to claim that *Catholic moral teaching* requires a particular judgment on a proposed piece of contemporary civil rights legislation. The question, mind you, is not whether racial discrimination is good or bad, or whether it should be permitted or forbidden. It is, rather, whether a particular policy (say, 'affirmative action') constitutes racial discrimination, or, even more frequently, what is the best way, among a range of possible ways (all of which have drawbacks as well as advantages), to prevent racial discrimination or ameliorate its effects. When the bishops insist on weighing in with an opinion on issues of this sort, their views in Washington (and beyond) will "receive mostly a politically partisan reaction" (as did the one in question). And the reason for this, I would dare to suggest, is that the USCC's statement is in truth, however inadvertently, a politically partisan statement.

There are signs that the USCC is becoming aware of these problems. For instance in marking the 10th anniversary of its pastoral on economic justice, the USCC issued a one-page document called *Economic Justice for All: A Catholic Framework for Economic Life*. It is obviously much shorter than was the 185-page *Economic Justice* pastoral. It is also much better. It lists ten principles which it "urge[s] Catholics to use ... as principles for reflection, criteria for judgment, and directions for action". It does not advocate specific fiscal, monetary, or tax policies.

In addition to talking too much about too many issues, the USCC's efforts to advance an effective Catholic bioethic in the United States have been hampered, as I have already suggested, by a certain defensiveness in engaging the opposition

---

[52] See *Pastoral Letters*, Volume V at p. 647.
[53] *Pastoral Letters*, Volume V at p. 304.

over the question of abortion. This criticism must, however, be tempered in two ways. First, people in the Pro-life Office of the USCC have been courageous to the point of heroism in their defence of the right to life. Nothing in my remarks should be taken to imply anything negative about these Evangelists of Life. Second, I must applaud the specific courageous acts of the USCC in criticizing the Supreme Court for its abominable abortion rulings. It has been in the great tradition of St. Ambrose, who defied and called to public penance the Emperor Theodosius after he had ordered the massacre of innocent civilians, that the USCC has denounced the immoral and unconstitutional acts of judges who abuse their authority.

Having said that, I must return to the defensiveness with which the Conference has often engaged the opposition in the debate over abortion. I fear that the factors which account for the temptation to go overboard in linking the Church's pro-life witness to other issues also accounts for this defensiveness. The bishops and their staff must be brought to see that no matter how reasonable the terms in which they couch their pro-life witness, no matter how extensively they link abortion to other issues, no matter how careful they are to avoid sounding as though stopping abortion is the only thing they care about, American cultural elites, for whom the ready availability of abortion is critical as a matter of self-interest as well as ideology, will viciously attack them. A tenor of defensiveness will not facilitate 'dialogue' with these people. It will be taken by them, rather, as a sign of weakness or irresolution.

Furthermore, in constructing, as the Holy Father calls us to do, a new "culture of life", the USCC should be clear-headed about who are our friends and who are our enemies. As pleasant as it is to enjoy terms of cordiality with well-to-do, influential people who 'happen' to be 'prochoice', our true friends are the ones we have encountered in the trenches of the pro-life movement – evangelical Protestant Christians, black and white. Instead of disavowing any attempt to form a voting bloc, we lay Catholics, inspired by the witness of our bishops, should be joining with our evangelical brethren in a voting bloc *for* life. The bishops, and the priests who preach with their authority, should, moreover, instruct the faithful that every single one of them is called by the Holy Father in *Evangelium Vitae* to be involved at some level in building the culture of life.[54] The indispensable first step in building that new culture is to oppose abortion, euthanasia, and all unjust killing. Teachers of the faith should make it clear that never may a faithful Catholic support a candidate even in part because he is pro-choice; only in the most extraordinary circumstances could it ever be legitimate to support a pro-abortion candidate over a reasonable pro-life candidate who presents himself as an alternative.[55] The urgent priority

---

[54] "Everyone has an obligation to be at the service of life." (*Evangelium Vitae*, para. 79) Throughout Chapter Four of the encyclical, the Holy Father discusses the wide range of activities to which individuals are called in building the "culture of life".

[55] See the Pastoral Statement of John J. Myers, Bishop of Peoria, *The Obligations of Catholics and the Rights of Unborn Children*, 20/5 (1990) *Origins* 65, 67–72, esp. sec. V.

of the pro-life cause demands at least this much, and our pastors should be prepared to say so.[56]

Now, a moment ago I praised the heroic efforts of the USCC's Pro-life Office. That Office has been very effective in promoting Catholic values in public policy debates in Washington concerning abortion and other bioethical issues. It has consistently made the case for desirable legislation and often played a central role in preventing bad legislation from being enacted. It is a sophisticated Catholic voice in media debates. And the Office also works vigorously to assist pro-life leaders at the diocesan and parish levels. Yet, if you ask people in the Pro-life Office why, in light of the continuation of abortion-on-demand in America, the bishops have not issued a pastoral letter on abortion recently, they will tell you, I am sure, that Catholics already know very well the Church's teaching on this issue. And, of course, they are right. The real question is why so many Catholics disobey it. The abortion rate among self-identified Catholics appears to be equal to (or greater than!) that of the general population. And Catholic politicians are at least as likely to be pro-abortion as pro-life in their public advocacy and action. Why are Catholics not living as "signs of contradiction" to the "culture of death"?

If lay Catholics could be energized on the issue of abortion, if they could be inspired to make it a *primary* factor in their political considerations, then we could truly begin rolling back the abortion license in the United States. Bill Clinton, or some future president, would then find it politically disastrous to veto a ban on partial birth abortion. And, even if he were prepared to fly a kamikaze mission in the cause of 'abortion rights', the Congress would immediately override his veto. The question is: What stands in the way of energizing and inspiring lay Catholics in the cause of human life?

When he retired as president of the USCC in 1977, Cardinal Bernardin identified three "continuing, long-term problems" for the Catholic Church in America: (1) the difficulty many Catholics have in accepting the teaching authority of the Church; (2) the legality of abortion-on-demand; and (3) the refusal to accept the Vatican's position on the question of ordaining women to the priesthood.[57] As the third is simply an example of the first, we could say he identified two problems – abortion and disobedience to the teaching authority of the Church. Further, if I am correct in suggesting that the consequences of a unified, energized Catholic witness on abortion would be the rolling back of the abortion license, there is, at bottom, one "continuing, long-term problem" – refusal to accept the teaching of the magisterium.

In my judgment, the single factor most responsible for undermining the laity's understanding of, and willingness to be guided by, the teaching authority of the

[56] Cf. *Evangelium Vitae*, para. 72:

Disregard for the right to life, precisely because it leads to the killing of the person whom society exists to serve, is what most directly conflicts with the possibility of achieving the common good.

Cardinal Bernardin, whose "consistent ethic" has often been misused to just such a purpose, said, "I don't see how you can subscribe to the consistent ethic and then vote for someone who feels that abortion is a 'basic right' of the individual." (*Bernardin Interview*, p. 7)

[57] *Pastoral Letters*, Volume IV at p. 40.

Church is the scandalous defiance of this authority by theologians, especially priest-theologians and members of women's religious orders. Above all, the suggestion – sometimes formal, often merely implicit – that theologians represent a parallel, or even superior, magisterium has had a devastating effect on the faith of many lay Catholics. If there are two, equally valid sources of authoritative teaching, and these sources disagree, then the individual believer is free to choose between them. The public dissent of theologians becomes a licence for the very practical dissent of ordinary Catholics on issues ranging from contraception and in vitro fertilization, to divorce and remarriage, and, of course, abortion.

Commenting with approval on the strategy of dissident theologian Hans Küng, the American pro-abortion, feminist theologian Rosemary Radford Reuther explained in 1981 that

> A new consensus could only come about if this traditional power [i.e., the authority of the magisterium] could be deposed and the Church restructured on conciliar democratic lines accountable to the people. Then the theological consensus in the academy could serve as a guide for the pastoral teaching of the Church. This is really what Küng is calling for: *that the academy replace the hierarchy as the teaching magisterium of the Church.* This cannot be accomplished by the academy itself. It entails the equivalent of the French Revolution in the Church, the deposing of a monarchical for a democratic constitution of the Church ... In the immediate future we cannot hope for a new consensus that will overcome the theological split between the academy and the hierarchy. Rather the best we can hope for is the defence of pluralism .... Pluralism can be defended only by making sure that this hierarchical power structure is not strong enough to repress successfully the independent institutional bases of conciliar and liberation theology.[58]

And so we find as recently as June 8, 1997, the Catholic Theological Society of America voting overwhelmingly to urge not that the magisterium reverse its teaching regarding the reservation of the ordained priesthood to males – liberal theologians do not expect that to happen any time soon – but that discussion of the question be continued despite the Holy Father's teaching *in Ordinatio Sacerdotalis* that the matter is settled and that discussion of the possibility of ordaining women harms the Church and should cease. So, the laity must choose whom to believe, the Pope or the theologians. The call by the CTSA to keep the issue open for discussion in defiance of the Pope's solemn teaching is precisely the sort of thing Reuther had in mind in calling for "pluralism" as the strategy best suited to the period prior to the one in which a French-style revolution can be made to destroy the teaching authority of the magisterium and replace it with a new "magisterium" of the theologians. Does anyone doubt that the real goal of those CTSA theologians who voted with the majority is to reverse the magisterium's teaching regarding the reservation of the priesthood to males? Does anyone doubt that these theologians, in their hearts, simply do not believe that

[58] Quoted in 'Bishops and Bishop-Bashers', *The Catholic World Report*, June 1997, p. 36.

the magisterium possesses authority superior to their own to settle issues such as women's ordination?

Theological dissent and defiance of this sort is largely, though, of course, not exclusively, to blame for the fact that many – perhaps most – American Catholics today embrace secular liberal understandings of marriage and sexual morality. The U. S. bishops' efforts to reinforce an authentically Christian understanding of these matters among the faithful in documents such as *Human Life in Our Day* (1968), *To Live in Christ Jesus* (1976), and *Statement concerning Human Sexuality* (1977)[59] have been constantly undercut by the scandal of theological dissent. Sometimes, as in the famous press conference of July 30, 1968 at which Charles Curran and eighty-six other theologians issued a statement dissenting from Pope Paul VI's teaching in *Humanae Vitae*, theologians' attempts to undermine authoritative teachings of the magisterium are explicit, public, and orchestrated. More often, however, their efforts are informal, subtle, and dispersed. And the consequences extend beyond questions of sex, marriage, and the sanctity of human life. Many of us were shocked – though perhaps we should not have been – by recent polling data revealing that significant numbers of self-identified (and in many cases active) American Catholics reject the Church's teachings on such matters as the bodily resurrection of our Lord and his real presence in the Eucharist. Dissenting theologians have won the hearts and minds of many, many American Catholics. It is only a bit of an exaggeration to say that heresy is so widespread that it threatens to become the norm. It is almost as if, to paraphrase St. Jerome, "the whole world groaned *again* to find itself Arian".

In responding to this challenge, the bishops should, I believe, follow the Pope's lead in *Evangelium Vitae* by formally and publicly identifying abortion, euthanasia, and other threats to life as issues of the highest priority for faithful Catholics.[60] The Church's firm, constant, and in my judgment – and, apparently, the Pope's – *infallibly proposed*[61] teachings on these matters should be resoundingly reaffirmed,

---

[59] See *Pastoral Letters*, Volumes III and IV.

[60] In this regard, I am pleased to note that the teaching of *Evangelium Vitae* – particularly the need to resist the "culture of death" (especially abortion and euthanasia) and the centrality of the family in building the "culture of life" – is featured in the recent USCC statement, 'Faithful for Life: A Moral Reflection'.

[61] See *Evangelium Vitae:*

[B]y the authority which Christ conferred upon Peter and his Successors, and in communion with the Bishops of the Catholic Church, I confirm that the direct and voluntary killing of an innocent human being is always gravely immoral. (para. 57)

[B]y the authority which Christ conferred upon Peter and his Successors, in communion with the Bishops . . . , I declare that direct abortion, that is, abortion willed as an end or as a means, always constitutes a grave moral disorder, since it is the deliberate killing of an innocent human being . . . . No circumstance, no purpose, no law whatsoever can ever make licit an act which is intrinsically illicit, since it is contrary to the Law of God which is written in every human heart, knowable by reason itself, and proclaimed by the Church. (para. 62)

[I]n harmony with the Magisterium of my Predecessors and in communion with the Bishops of the Catholic Church, I confirm that euthanasia is a grave violation of the law of God, since it is the deliberate and morally unacceptable killing of a human person. (para. 65)

and it should be made clear by individual bishops throughout the land that public dissent from these teachings by anyone speaking with their authority or as a Catholic theologian or teacher in their dioceses will not be tolerated.[62]

Perhaps most importantly of all, the bishops should firmly implement *Ex corde Ecclesiae*, the constitution for Catholic colleges and universities which John Paul II has given as a gift to the Church. As the bishops recognized in their 1980 pastoral, *Catholic Higher Education and the Pastoral Mission of the Church*,[63] it is crucial for Catholic colleges and universities to maintain their Catholic identity. In the cases of most major Catholic institutions, that identity has been seriously compromised by, among other things, the presence (often as teachers) of theologians who publicly dissent from the Church's firm and constant teachings on a variety of moral and doctrinal questions. As *Ex corde Ecclesiae* makes clear, it is the diocesan bishop's responsibility to ensure that Catholic institutions in his diocese retain their Catholic character and enrich, rather than undermine, the faith of Catholic students. The occasion of implementing *Ex corde Ecclesiae* provides an excellent opportunity for the bishops to restate the Catholic vision of education, a vision which inspires young people to lead lives of fruitful and faithful service to Christ and his Church. The juridically firm implementation of *Ex corde Ecclesiae* is critical, for, to a very large extent, it is on Catholic campuses that the future of the Church in America, and of a Catholic bioethic, will be decided. Let us be under no illusions: much of this ground is currently under enemy occupation.

Now, what can the bishops do about Catholic public officials who publicly support such evils as abortion and euthanasia? What can be done about Catholics in the legislative, executive, and judicial branches of government whose public advocacy and action in support of these evils gives scandal to the faithful and undermines the Church's witness for life? In most cases, it would likely be a mistake for bishops to excommunicate individual office holders or formally deny them access to the Eucharist pursuant to provisions of canon law authorizing such a denial to those who persist in manifest, grave sin. The reason is that such action by the bishops would often backfire by enabling the media to depict the anti-life politician as a 'martyr for freedom' in the way I have already indicated. There are two things I would suggest as alternatives. First, bishops should not hesitate publicly to criticize the anti-life activities of specific politicians, nor should they refrain from pointing out the inconsistency of these activities with any profession of Christian faith. Second, I would urge bishops to revive the ancient and honourable practice of shunning. Individual bishops should refuse to share the head table at any Catholic event (not just those sponsored by the NCCB) with anti-life politicians (including jurists), or the dais at events at Catholic

---

[62] "We [bishops] are also entrusted with the task of ensuring that the doctrine which is once again being set forth in this Encyclical is faithfully handed on in its integrity. We must use appropriate means to defend the faithful from all teaching which is contrary to it. We need to make sure that in theological faculties, seminaries and Catholic institutions sound doctrine is taught, explained and more fully investigated." (*Evangelium Vitae*, para. 82)

[63] *Pastoral Letters*, Volume IV at p. 401.

colleges and universities or other institutions. They should refuse to be photo-graphed with such people or permit themselves to be used by them to any political advantage. They should ensure that such persons are never honoured by Catholic institutions in their dioceses or given the podium in any context other than one designed to highlight the disgracefulness of their support for the "culture of death". The shunning of anti-life politicians would vividly remind ordinary lay Catholics of the seriousness of the church's teachings regarding the sanctity of human life and would send the clear message that Catholics (and other Christians) who serve the "culture of death" are tragically weakening their relationship with Christ and alienating themselves from the community of Christian faith.

## Afterword

After this paper was presented in the summer of 1997, the USCC issued *Living the Gospel of Life: A Challenge to American Catholics* (December, 1998). That statement powerfully criticises the abuse of the "seamless garment" metaphor to, in the words of Fr Richard John Neuhaus, "relativise the enormity of taking innocent human life by making it one item on a long list of concerns". The statement properly recognises the principle of respect for the right to life of the unborn as the foundation of a sound Catholic bioethic in America. One hopes that the Bishops will spread its mesage widely and reiterate it ceaselessly, calling upon all Catholics, but particularly Catholic political officials, to inform their con-sciences in the light of its teaching.

# 18

# The prolife cause in Great Britain: reflections on success and failure, on the Church's record and the present challenge[1]

## J. J. SCARISBRICK

FROM A BRITISH prolife point of view, the last three decades have produced much to be proud of – not least the development of what is probably the most comprehensive prolife pregnancy care service in the world and the establishment twenty years ago of the Linacre Centre, which has done much to guide and encourage the prolife movement as a whole, as well as making a major contribution to bioethical debate in this country and beyond. But the last thirty years have also brought much pain and shame for anyone who is British and a Catholic. In 1967 our Parliament passed a very permissive Abortion Act which has now claimed nearly five million victims as well as greatly encouraging the spread of abortionism through much of Western Europe and the English-speaking world. In 1990 our Parliament extended that Act to allow selective pregnancy reduction and abortion, in some circumstances, up to birth. Meanwhile, of course, the various new techniques of assisted conception, especially IVF, had been developing fast, and it was English doctors who produced the first IVF baby in 1978. Predictably, the committee set up by the Government to advise on regulation of the new reproductive technology and chaired by Lady Warnock gave virtually unqualified approval to the generation of human beings in the laboratory and their cultivation *in vitro* up to fourteen days. The Warnock Committee reported in 1984. In the following years the Government went through the motions of extensive public consultation but, as far as one could judge, paid little attention to the carefully reasoned prolife responses to the Warnock proposals, and in 1990 forced through Parliament the Human Fertilisation and Embryology Act which established not only the IVF industry in this country but also, for the first time in our history, the principle that human beings could be used as subjects in destructive experimentation and even specifically manufactured for that purpose. As well as this, the Act permitted the casual throwing away of surplus embryos and freezing of "spares", and set up a token Authority to oversee the inspection of IVF units, etc. which, while having the outward appearance of an effective gamekeeper, has in fact exercised minimal restraint and is not responsible to Parliament.

---

[1] I gratefully acknowledge the help I have received in preparing this paper from my colleague Peter Garrett, National Research Officer of LIFE.

Between 1991 and 1994 some 300,000 human beings were generated in IVF clinics around the country. Of these only 7000 have been born live. Most of the rest were either immediately thrown away or died in the womb; 25,000 more were killed in laboratory experimentation. The remainder have been stored in refrigerators. 7000 of these were thrown away in August 1996 because they had been abandoned by their parents, or so we were told, and had therefore come to the end of the storage period allowed by the 1990 Act. Many of those remaining in the freezers will be found to have been killed if they are ever unfrozen. Thousands more "orphaned" or abandoned embryos have been "culled" regularly since August 1996. And to all this destruction of embryonic human beings we must add the widespread, but unrecorded, devastation caused by abortifacients masquerading as postcoital or "emergency" contraception, which, of course, prevent implantation in the womb and thus procure the death of the young embryo. Alas, this is not the end of the catalogue of wrongdoing. The authorities have approved fetal tissue and organ transplanting (but not fetal oocyte harvesting) and surrogacy. In 1981 an English Court ruled that a regime deliberately and knowingly intended to cause the death of a newborn Down's syndrome baby was merely a "holding operation" and lawful.[2] In February 1993 the Law Lords ruled that since doctors certified that a PVS patient's life was worthless, it was in his best interests to be put to death by starvation and dehydration.[3] In February 1997, we heard of the first successful cloning of an adult mammal, a sheep, in Scotland, a feat previously declared to be impossible. However politicians may try to lull us, we can be sure that human cloning using the new techniques of enucleation and electrical stimulation cannot be far away. Nor, for that matter, is the artificial human womb.

I know, of course, that Britain does not have a monopoly of the wrongdoing I have just listed and that yet worse things have been happening elsewhere – and probably still are. I must also acknowledge that the voluntary euthanasia and assisted suicide lobby suffered a surprising setback in February 1994 when the House of Lords Select Committee on Medical Ethics rejected the call to legalise active euthanasia; and there was a much more surprising and complete rebuff at the conference of the British Medical Association in June 1997. The former surely owed a good deal to the magisterial submission by the Linacre Centre;[4] the latter to the hard work of the organisation Alert and people like Dr Keown who have done so much to expose the truth about what has really been happening in Holland.

---

[2] This was the ground on which a Dr Leonard Arthur, a pediatrician in Derby City Hospital, was acquitted of murder of a Down's syndrome infant who had been given a lethal dose of the drug DF118 explicitly and solely for the purpose of preventing him from seeking food. Prompted by LIFE, the police recovered the child's corpse and soon after arrested Dr Arthur. He was charged with murder (subsequently attempted murder) but acquitted.

[3] See John Keown's contribution (chapter 15) to the present volume.

[4] Reprinted in Luke Gormally (ed) *Euthanasia, Clinical Practice and the Law* London: The Linacre Centre 1994, pp. 111–165.

To have been English, Catholic and actively prolife during the last thirty years has been a fairly bewildering, as well as deeply painful, experience. I say this for three particular reasons. First, following the disastrous inaction of the Hierarchy in 1967–68, Catholic bodies which could and should have played important – even decisive – roles proved to be ineffectual.[5] It was not until 1980 that the Hierarchy produced any comprehensive statement on prolife issues[6] and, although individual bishops have been very supportive, there has never been any collective, organised commitment of the Catholic community to the prolife cause by its leaders – though I must quickly add that recently Britain's two Cardinals have been speaking out and acting admirably, and I do not forget the magnificent leadership which Rome has always supplied.

Nonetheless the British prolife movement has been essentially a lay movement largely left to its own devices, often hampered by interventions from one or two disloyal theologians and some of the Catholic media, an enemy within that has been hard to bear. That enemy has not been as damaging, however, as have many non-Catholic religious leaders, especially in the upper house of Parliament. Michael Ramsey, the then archbishop of Canterbury, for example, played a significant part in securing the passage of the 1967 Act through the Lords, together with the Methodist leader, Lord Soper. The then archbishop of York, John Habgood, did much to persuade Parliament to accept IVF and embryo abuse, and hence to pass the 1990 Human Fertilisation and Embryology Act. And so on. Several other Anglican bishops in the Lords have been committed pro-abortionists. Only a handful have been prolife. Most have ducked the issue and absented themselves from crucial debates.

Secondly, what began in 1967 as a single issue (abortion) quickly escalated into a maze of often highly complex issues. The target has been moving and changing so fast that it has often been difficult to keep pace. And as we face the frightening new worlds opened up by the Human Genome Project and hitherto undreamt-of power to control and manipulate human life, it is clear that the challenge is going to become even more intense.

---

[5] The story of the English Hierarchy's conduct during this critical period deserves detailed study. Briefly, the bishops accepted the advice of some "leading politicians" that to have spoken out while the future Abortion Act was being debated would have done more harm than good. As well as this, there was widespread belief that this private member's measure would never reach the Statute Book. Later, Cardinal Heenan conceded that he and his brother bishops had seriously misjudged the situation. It was a measure of him that he should have made this public confession. But this is not the end of the story. The Act received the royal assent on 27 October 1967 but did not come into force for six months (i.e. 27 April 1968). On that very day the bishops were at their annual Low Week meeting. Nothing had been done in the meantime to mobilise Catholic bodies – like doctors and nurses – and prepare them for the impending battle. Now, on 27 April 1968, when there was nothing to lose and perhaps much to gain by speaking out, the bishops were silent once again. Cardinal Heenan never subsequently adverted to this second, more serious, failure.

[6] *Abortion and the Right to Live*. A Joint Statement of the Catholic Archbishops of Great Britain. London: Catholic Truth Society 1980.

Thirdly, in trying to engage our opponents in rational debate we have continually found ourselves wading after them through a marshland of muddle-headedness, slogan-mongering, ignorance, incoherence, fudge, misunderstanding, sentimentality, evasion – and sometimes what can only be described as downright dishonesty. A few quick examples of what I mean. How does one cope with an apparent inability to grasp that sedating a newborn disabled child so that he does not seek food and hence dies of starvation is not allowing that child to die but causing him to do so? How does one cope with the repeated assertion that, by devising ever more efficient methods of screening for abnormalities before birth and then killing those suffering from them, we are actually *conquering* those diseases ? That is to stand truth on its head. But it has seemingly duped politicians and the media. Equally dishonest is what we have mockingly called the ''New Biology'', invented by the contraception lobby, which alleges that fertilisation and conception are not, after all, the same event and that conception and pregnancy do not begin until implantation, several days after fertilisation. This is unblushing manipulation of the truth. I could produce a long list of similar offences – but that would not be very helpful. However, I cannot resist one final, glaring example of what I mean. It comes from the (alas) widely influential Warnock Report. Having trumpeted its determination to engage in rigorous moral reasoning, that Report eventually braces itself to confront what is the crucial question, namely, the moral status of the human embryo. Is it or is it not truly human? When do life and personhood begin? Having raised these questions it promptly ducks them. ''Instead of trying to answer these questions directly'', it explains, ''we have therefore gone straight to the question of how it is right to treat that human embryo''.[7]

To that we will reply: of course you did! But what you did is intellectually contemptible (like much of your Report). How can you know how to treat something until you know what that something is, i.e. what its moral status is? Without a blush you have moved to a second question which can be answered only after the first one is answered, and this you have declined to do.

We prolifers have, of course, had to battle constantly with those who claim that the human embryo and, up to a certain time, the child in the womb, is not fully human – is human but not yet hominised or humanised, human but not yet a person (because not yet self-conscious or decision-making, etc.), is not yet a person because not yet recognised as one, is not yet a ''person in being'', and so on. Our opponents have produced all manner of theories about when a ''not yet'' human achieves full membership of the human family – at the appearance of the primitive streak, about day 40 or later. For that former Archbishop of

---

[7] *Report of the Committee of Inquiry into Human Fertilisation and Embryology* (the ''Warnock Report'') London: HMSO 1984, para 11.9. Notice the impertinent ''therefore''. This is presumably justified by the previous sentence, which asserts that answers to questions about when life or personhood begin are ''complex amalgams of factual and moral judgements''. But should a distinguished Committee of Inquiry, charged with ''consideration of social, ethical and legal implications'' of the new reproductive technology, have been frightened of ''complex amalgams of factual and moral judgements''? Was it not precisely their duty to confront such complexity squarely and honestly, not to run away from it?

York, John Habgood, becoming human is a process, like becoming middle-aged, not an event, so we will never know when it begins![8] And inevitably dissident Catholic theologians have confused discussion with irrelevant and/or ill-informed objections based on the phenomenon of twinning and the question of delayed animation (ensoulment).

It is not necessary for me to comment on these views. They have all been comprehensively refuted – not least by some contributors to this volume.[9] However, I would like to pursue them from another direction and to speak briefly about what, in my view, has been a useful clarification and therefore contribution to the bioethical debate which we have made.

Suppose our opponents are right after all. Suppose that fully personal, individual human life does not begin until 14, 40, 72 days or whatever after fertilisation, or that ensoulment does not occur until then. Alternatively, suppose that personhood is achieved only when others recognise it. Suppose that becoming a person is indeed a process with no precise beginning. Suppose any or all of what our opponents say is true. All abortion, all embryo abuse remain absolutely wrong. Our opponents will have gained nothing.

This is because of the following principle: to prevent a being from becoming that which, by virtue of its own inner dynamism, it is capable of becoming is to do it harm, i.e. wrong – and it is no defence to say that it was not yet doing or being that which it was capable of eventually doing or being when the offence was committed. Thus to castrate an infant is to do it a serious injustice; and it is no defence that the victim was not yet sexually mature. Castration then is as wrong as castration twenty years later. Similarly, to borrow an example supplied by Luke Gormally, intentionally to cause a newborn child's mental or physical growth to be severely stunted by the use of drugs would clearly be gravely wrong, because gravely harmful. How much more so is killing a being who, though allegedly not yet fully human, would have become so, by virtue of its own inner dynamism, if allowed to develop naturally! To prevent that which is on its way to becoming a full human being (and hence enjoying the fundamental right to life) from actually becoming a full human being endowed with that right to life, is morally indistinguishable from denying the right to life of an achieved human person.

Thus we do not say: let us give early human life the benefit of the doubt and play safe by treating life from conception onwards as though it was fully

[8] The Archbishop made the mistake of believing that a process cannot have a beginning. Clearly it can. A cricket match is a "process" but begins precisely when the umpire calls "Play", whereupon what were previously two teams "fuse" and a unique new match begins. Similarly, every human life is a process, a continuous "becoming", but has an exact starting-point, namely, the fusion of sperm and ovum.

[9] See, for example, Teresa Iglesias, *IVF and Justice*, London: The Linacre Centre for Health Care Ethics 1990, esp. pp. 59ff.; Anthony Fisher, OP, 'Individuogenesis and a recent book by Fr. Norman Ford', 7 (1991) *Anthropotes* 199ff.; Germain Grisez, 'When do people begin?', in Stephen J Heaney (ed) *Abortion: a new generation of Catholic responses* Braintree: Mass.: The Pope John XXIII Medical-Moral Research and Education Center 1992, pp. 1–28.

human. We say: even if it is not yet fully human we are still absolutely forbidden to kill or abuse it. That which will in time become fully human deserves the same respect and protection now as one who has already passed the critical threshold. The "not yet" argument does not work. It never works.

The virtue of this line of reasoning, it seems to me, is that it leaves our opponents stranded. It is not just that they are wrong (which they are); even if they are right they are still in the wrong. To change the metaphor, their every attempt to get off the hook has been frustrated.

Not surprisingly, the leading pro-abortion apologists have recently shifted their positions significantly. Two rather new sets of ideas are currently being peddled. The first is very crude. It runs thus. Whether the child is human or a person, or whatever, is irrelevant. In the real world abortion is inevitable, like prostitution. Women have always sought it and always will. Since there is no possibility of abolishing it, society should at least control it, undesirable though it is.

The quick reply to that, of course, is: even if we allow your premiss we deny your conclusion. You might just as well say that because there have probably always been rape, sexual abuse of children and mugging, and doubtless always will be, we should legalise these things and make them available on the National Health Service.

The second line of attack is much more sophisticated. It was launched years ago in the USA[10] but made little impact on this side of the Atlantic until very recently when Eileen McDonagh's *Breaking the Abortion Deadlock* was published here – to the exultant applause of the militant feminists. Its argument can be summarised as follows: the unborn child (always, of course, called "the fetus") is "the direct cause of pregnancy and, if it makes a woman pregnant without her consent, it severely violates her bodily integrity and liberty". No one can be coerced into being the Good Samaritan or even coerced into giving a pint of blood to a close relative. The fetus so "massively intrudes on a woman's body and expropriates her liberty" that a woman cannot be required or coerced into being a Good Samaritan to it, i.e. continuing with a pregnancy she does not want. She has a right of self-defence and this justifies the use of deadly force against the intruder. Thus we should no longer talk of a woman's "right to choose" but of her right to give or refuse her consent to pregnancy.[11]

This argument, we are told, completely side-steps the "clash of absolutes" which hitherto produced stalemate between the prolife and prochoice camps and provides an unanswerable justification of abortionism. But does it?

[10] In 1971 Judith J. Thomson published 'A Defence of Abortion' in 1 (1971) *Philosophy and Public Affairs* 47ff., which, using a far-fetched analogy of a person waking one morning to find himself involuntarily keeping alive a famous violinist whose kidneys had failed, argued that just as that man could not be required to sustain the violinist, so no woman could be forced to use her organs to keep her unborn child alive. The "unplugging the violinist" argument was given a big boost when Thomson's article was reprinted in J. Feinberg (ed), *The Problem of Abortion*, Belmont, California: Wadsworth Publishing Company 1973.
[11] Eileen McDonagh, *Breaking the Abortion Deadlock*, New York & Oxford: Oxford University Press 1996, esp. pp. 6ff.

A crucial defect in the argument lies in the first words I have just quoted, viz. "the fetus is the direct cause of pregnancy". This cannot be true. It may be possible to describe the child in the womb as part of the material cause of pregnancy. But it cannot be the instrumental or "efficient" cause. And that is the cause which matters. It is the parents of the child, those who engaged in the sexual act which resulted in the conception, who are the efficient cause of pregnancy. That is where moral responsibility for the pregnancy lies. They deliberately engaged in an activity which they knew could result in pregnancy, even if they did not want or will it. McDonagh's case falls to the ground, therefore. What she has shown is that a woman should not engage in sexual activity unless she is prepared to accept the possibility of pregnancy and also be prepared to consent to it – which is very different from what she thought (or hoped) she was proving!

Over the years our opponents have abandoned one position after another. The author of the 1967 Act, David Steel, claimed that "proof" of the unborn child's disposability was, absurdly, its dependence. We never hear that now – and only the English courts still dare to describe the child as part of the mother, which was basic abortionist dogma at one time.[12] No one seriously advances the "population explosion" argument any longer. That cunning invention, "the pre-embryo", has vanished from our vocabulary. The smart talk about difficulties posed by twinning and ensoulment has been exposed for what it was. And so on. And now a momentous thing has happened. Our opponents have implicitly admitted that they cannot sustain their case or refute ours concerning the personhood of the preborn human being. The reason why McDonagh's book has been so gratefully received by them is precisely that it seemed to give them complete protection even when they had conceded, as they had to, that the victim, the child, is indeed a person and hence the moral equal of the mother. This was an enormous relief to the abortionists. As we have seen, however, in reality they were clutching at straws.

We should not be surprised at the intellectual muddle, incoherence and occasional downright dishonesty which we have encountered. These things are inevitable when one sets out to defend the indefensible and to defy truth. But we prolifers can still be proud of and must proclaim the following fact: we have, I believe, won all the arguments. Our opponents have been in continuous retreat, continually shifting their ground, darting from one makeshift dugout to another. I also know only too well that we have not yet won back the hearts and minds of many of our fellow-citizens. So, though we have won all the arguments, we have not yet won the debate.

---

[12] Despite all the evidence to the contrary, the English courts still hold that an unborn child is not a "person in being" and becomes one only when born and breathing independently of the mother. It is not a "third person" and cannot be made a ward of court. As late as November 1994 the Court of Appeal ruled that the child in the womb is part of the mother. This "unity of persons" doctrine, it should be noted, confers some protection on the unborn child against injury in utero (which would not otherwise be available), since an attack on the child constitutes an attack on the mother, a legal person of whom the child is an integral part.

To do this requires heroic prophecy. Constant, heroic prophecy. We have learned that we must do more than simply refute our opponents: we have to take the initiative, challenge the World head-on.

In a powerful passage in *Evangelium Vitae* Pope John Paul points to the glaring contradiction between modern society's commitment (and especially young people's commitment) to human rights and the wanton denial to a whole section of the human family, the preborn, of the fundamental right to life.[13] We are confronted again and again by other, similar, double standards: the failure, for instance, to see that the grounds for opposing racism, sexism, ageism, sizeism, etc. are yet more urgent reasons for rejecting abortionism; the failure of defenders of foxes, whales and rainforests and indeed, all ecologists, to see that *a fortiori* they should be prolifers; the failure to perceive the contradiction between providing parking spaces, ramps, loos, and all the rest of it for the born disabled (and going to great lengths to protect them) and the ever more ruthless campaign to seek out and destroy special-needs children in the womb; the failure of the militant feminists to see that they are making exactly that egocentric claim to power, privilege and domination which they rightly denounce in others and that, in their aggressive abortionism, they are promoting the very thing which feminism has rightly protested against and fought, namely, violence.

Our society is in a terrible muddle. It cannot live with the moral schizophrenia it has inflicted on itself. There must be a resolution, a catharsis. In its heart it yearns for this, I believe.

We have to continue to proclaim, day in and day out, that abortion, of its nature, *per se*, is a violation of women. For the womb, which in pregnancy becomes the wondrous, sophisticated sanctuary for new, innocent life, protecting and nourishing it and providing the ideal environment for it to flourish – for this to be forcibly entered by a third party intent on killing and turned into the site of violent, bloody shattering of all that has been taking place there, is an ontological enormity, a gross assault on and inversion of the natural order.

Every abortion violates a woman's integrity and personhood (and that is why post-abortion trauma is the fearful distress that we increasingly know it to be). It follows, therefore, that it is we prolifers who are the authentic feminists. It is we who truly uphold the dignity of women against the violence of abortion, the womb-abuse of surrogacy, and the exploitation of women by the sex industry and the hedonistic machoism which it and abortion so vigorously promote.

It is especially important that we prolifers should claim this "moral high ground" because too often in the past the pro-choice lobby, perhaps with good reason, has been able to portray us as almost exclusively concerned with the child, while they guarded the status of women. This is a false polarisation. It is we, and only we, who give due respect to the rights and dignity of both mother and child.

It is also we who have emerged as the authentic democrats affirming the fundamental moral equality of all human beings. We are the people who have

---

[13] *Evangelium Vitae*, section 18.

seen a great light – the light of what a truly just society would be and therefore what our society ought to be. Insofar as it submits to the culture of death, the World is engulfed in a darkness; for the culture of death breeds guilt, shame, self-disgust and tears. Every abortion, like every mercy-killing, however cleverly disguised as compassion, involves a turning away from a fellow-human by others, a humiliating rejection and isolation of another, a betrayal of another person – in the case of abortion, two others – followed by destruction. The culture of death preys on ignorance and defeatism. It does not want people to see the unborn child through the "window on the womb" provided by the ultrasound scanner or to know how abortions are done. It does not want to hear about the hospice movement and recent progress in palliative care and symptom-control of the dying. It does not rejoice in Zoë's Place in the LIFE Health Centre in Liverpool, the first baby hospice in the world. It does not want such good news. Its message is that we cannot overcome; we must run away. Above all, it preys on fear: fear of not being able to cope, fear of what partners, parents, grandparents, friends and neighbours will say, fear of disability, fear of being a burden, fear of pain, fear of death. It preys on these things and in turn feeds them. It corrupts and diminishes. But we, we are the people of life and hope and courage.

We must tell the world that our opponents have corrupted obstetrics and strive to corrupt pediatrics and geriatrics.[14] Direct and deliberate killing of patients is the antithesis of good medicine, just as the relentless search for prenatal genetic and other abnormalities in order to kill the people suffering from them is a disincentive to seeking their cure. It is bad for medicine. And it revives and legitimises ancient phobias and prejudices concerning physical and mental abnormality, phobias and prejudices which we had striven to put behind us because they are unworthy of us.

We live amidst destruction of human life without parallel in our history. The abortoirs, IVF laboratories and deep-freezers have trivialised human life and sexuality. Our opponents are the enemies of awe, reverence and wonder in the face of newly-begotten life and, at the other end of the human earthly pilgrimage, the mystery of death, which are among the richest experiences of the human spirit. They preach a sinister eugenics and consumerism. Their autonomism atomises society. It produces a nihilistic self-love which leaves human beings increasingly unloved and unlovable.

No doubt many parents of IVF children are good and loving ones, but children are not objects to be manufactured by white-coated technicians carrying out impersonal, technical procedures in laboratories. In the face of, say, a Diane Blood, the English woman who sought to be inseminated by sperm taken from her dead husband, we have to say that children are not prizes or trophies, nor are they to be used as a means of coping with bereavement or as memorials to dead husbands.

IVF can produce children with three, four, or, (if there are two gamete-donors, a surrogate mother and two commissioning parents) even five parents. The

---

[14] This sad "de-professionalising" of the medical profession is explored by Luke Gormally elsewhere in this volume (chapter 12).

designer-baby is no longer a piece of science fiction. But a society which treats procreation thus is a sick society – its disease consumerism. It is abusing children – even as the media and the sex industry are abusing the young by destroying, or trying to destroy, adolescence and, from all directions, seeking to destroy the innocence of childhood.

Modern communications and information technology have given us a sense of "the global village" and the unity of the human family that was impossible for previous generations. Natural and manmade disasters, human rights abuses, out-rages like the Tianaman Square massacre – wherever they occur – immediately involve us, stir our consciences, demand response. In upholding the utmost respect for all human life we prolifers are promoting the unity and solidarity of the human race, things which all people of goodwill instinctively recognise as intrinsic goods. We are promoting them "vertically" – from fertilisation to natural death – as well as "horizontally"; and in affirming the duty of society to protect the small, the young and vulnerable against predators and abusers, we are promoting that justice and peace which all people of goodwill crave.

*    *    *

No impartial observer could claim that the so-called sexual revolution unleashed in the 1960s has delivered the following things which it confidently promised: more stable marriage, happier (because wanted) children and more harmonious families, a healthier population, etc. What has happened to marriage, like the six-fold rise in illegitimacy rates, is only too well known. Sexually transmitted diseases have reached epidemic proportions in many of our cities. Post-abortion trauma is now a major women's disease. Female and male infertility are increasing alarmingly. There is more domestic violence, especially against women, more child abuse, especially sexual. "Planned", wanted children are more vulnerable to parental neglect and assault, we are told. Our streets are more dangerous than they have been for a 100 years – and our cites are witnessing for the first time all-female teenage gangs and gang-warfare. All these are direct or indirect consequences of the sexual revolution. It has not worked. It never could or will work.

We have had, and still have, enormously important good news for our fellow-citizens. It goes thus. We do not need your condoms and pills and all those nasty bits of plastic and copper and those chemicals with which our bodies (especially women's bodies) are being so incessantly assaulted. We have a better way, a more human and empowering way – and one which is body-friendly, natural and green – of ordering our fertility. We do not need (in the sense of want or require) abortion. Or at any rate the people directly involved assure us they do not. For here is an extraordinary thing. We are constantly told by the pro-abortion lobby that women do not want abortion. Doctors who do abortions, except for a few brutalised perverts, assure us they do not like doing them. Nurses tell us they do not like assisting at them. We can be sure that the children involved like them even less. So, all the people directly involved say they do not want them. So why is there so much of them? The answer, apparently, is that all those involved believe there is no alternative. That being so, what we really need and want is the loving pregnancy care service which organisations like LIFE provide.

Similarly, we do not need euthanasia. We need more hospices. We do not need doctors to starve to death special-needs children. Come to Zoë's Place, our baby hospice, and there you will see the response of love to the mystery of suffering and experience the joy of being among totally innocent human beings already talking to the angels.

We do not need IVF. This is not just because it is very inefficient (it has about an 85 per cent failure rate and is crushingly expensive). Much female infertility is caused by blocked fallopian tubes, tubal occlusion, and much of this is "triggered" by abortion, especially when there is chlamydia, a very widespread but little-known sexually transmitted disease. So there would be much less need for IVF if we had much less abortion. There would be no need for IVF if abortion had not reduced to a trickle the number of children available for adoption by childless couples. I wish I could also add that we do not need IVF because we have succeeded in developing the prolife alternative to it, which we call NEST (Natural Egg Sonographic Transfer) at the LIFE Health Centre. Alas, not yet. But we have had fourteen natural pregnancies out of just over a hundred patients treated, which is a higher success rate than many IVF units achieve.

As Pope John Paul has powerfully pleaded, the prolife cause is the supreme, the defining issue of our times. We are indeed in the midst of a worldwide, titanic struggle between the Gospel of Life and the Culture of Death. That is why Cardinal Bernardin's famous call for consistency across a wide range of contemporary issues (the "seamless garment" argument) still leaves the prolife cause, in its strictest sense, at the centre of our concerns. It is also why we English prolifers were disappointed by our bishops' statement *The Common Good* which was produced before the last General Election to guide Catholic voters.[15] Though the right to life came first in its list of concerns, the prolife cause itself did not come first in its thinking. It was treated simply as one of many issues facing today's society – alongside poverty, trade union rights, threats to the environments and the like. The bishops failed to see that there is a hierarchy of causes and that ours is at its pinnacle, transcending, and more urgent than, all others. They made matters worse by suggesting that, provided a candidate was more right than wrong on the broad sweep of issues, one could vote for him or her regardless (the assumption being that all these issues were more or less equal) and that 'single-issue' politics was, as a matter of principle, always ill-judged – a verdict on political tactics which is surely beyond bishops' competence or duty to deliver.[16]

Fortunately *The Common Good* did not stifle a brave initiative, namely, the launch of the Pro-life Alliance, the first expressly prolife political party in the

---

[15] The Bishops' Conference of England & Wales, *The Common Good and the Catholic Church's Social Teaching* [issued 21 October 1996] Manchester: Gabriel Communications 1996.

[16] Here is a striking example of bishops straying into discussion of political tactics which elsewhere in this volume both John Finnis (chapter 16) and Robert George (chapter 17) criticise.

world. This new party did not expect to secure many votes at the General Election, let alone any seats in Parliament. Rather, it was an act of witness – and one which was more than justified by the media attention it received. Its Manifesto is a glorious proclamation of the prolife vision: it says what *The Common Good* should have said and would have delighted Cardinal Bernardin. We must hope that the PLA can grow in strength and perhaps encourage imitators elsewhere. Even as modern abortionism, alas, came out of Great Britain, so may the ultimate political response to it have its birthplace in this country.

There are two profoundly important things which we Catholics can see more clearly than can most others. On the one hand, is the enormity of what is happening in our midst. Every abortion is an affront to God our Father who lovingly shapes and knits together, as the Psalmist (and the prophet Job) tells us, every human being in the secrecy and safety of the womb. Every act of euthanasia is an affront to God the Creator. Every contracepting act and every generation of a human being outside the human body is an abuse of the power of procreation generously bestowed by God on His creatures. Every one of those acts is also an affront to the second person of the Trinity who, by deigning to take on and thereby to elevate our human nature radically united Himself with the human race. Every human body has been ransomed by Him at a great price. Whatever we do or allow to be done to the least of His brothers and sisters we do or allow to be done to Him. And every one of these destructive acts is also an affront to the Holy Spirit, since the divine plan is that every human body shall become His temple. And since for nine months Mary's womb was the sanctuary of the Word Incarnate, a sacred vessel, Temple and Ark of the Covenant, the womb – every woman's womb – has been sanctified. Every violation of the womb is therefore a sacrilege, a profanation.[17]

All this enables us to begin to discern the full enormity of the man-made catastrophe which surrounds us. We may almost feel overwhelmed by it. But over and against all this we have to cry out: be not afraid. Our society is stricken with a profound and growing unease, a deep sense of moral crisis which will not go away. Our society, in its heart, is pining, thirsting for the Gospel of Life. And this has so much to offer it. We have won the argument. Truth and justice are on our side. Because there is a light which enlightens all men and women coming into the world and because we live in the age of Resurrection, truth and justice must somehow prevail.

---

[17] These last ideas are derived from John Saward's *Redeemer in the Womb* San Francisco: Ignatius 1993. Dónal O'Mathúna, 'Abortion and the "Image of God"', in John Kilner, Nigel M de S Cameron and David Schiedermayer (eds) *Bioethics and the Future of Medicine* Grand Rapids, Mi.: Eerdmans & Carlisle: Paternoster Press 1995, esp. pp. 206–9, reveals the richness of the Hebrew words translated as "weave" in Psalm 139:13, "knit" in Job 10:11 and "in secret" in Psalm 139:15 – the latter carrying strong overtones of the child being hidden in the safety of the womb (as in a lair) by a protecting God.

# Disputed
questions

# 19

# Is it reasonable to use the UK protocol for the clinical diagnosis of 'brain stem death' as a basis for diagnosing death?[1]

D. ALAN SHEWMON

## 1. Introduction[2]

### Statement of the problem

PROBABLY SOME of you chose to attend this session expecting to hear the standard debate over US "whole-brain" vs. UK "brain-stem" criteria for diagnosing death. As nicely summarized by Pallis and Harley,[3] the essential points of this disagreement are twofold:

(1) What is "the critical system of the body's critical system"? (That is, what part of the brain is to the brain as the brain is to the body?) – and

---

[1] **Editorial note.** At the Conference Professor Shewmon's paper was paired with a paper by Professor Richard Frackowiak (Professor of Cognitive Neurology, University of London) defending the use of the standard UK protocol for diagnosis of 'brain stem death' as a basis for diagnosing death. Because of pressure of other work Professor Frackowiak was unable to prepare a manuscript for this volume. However, he is happy for his position to be described as substantially the one presented by Dr Christopher Pallis in a number of publications, and most readily accessible in his *ABC of Brainstem Death* [1st edition 1983; now available in a 2nd edition in Pallis and Harley 1996]. Dr Pallis's defence of current practice has been the dominantly influential one in UK medical circles. Those familiar with that defence will not find it difficult to recognise the radical character of the critique Professor Shewmon presents of UK practice (along with all 'brain death' protocols for diagnosis of death). In assessing Shewmon's paper it is clearly important to distinguish two issues: (i) whether Shewmon's critique shows the falsity of the standard claim that clinical diagnosis of 'brain stem death' establishes the death of the patient; and (ii) whether Shewmon is correct in thinking that, though UK practice is indefensible and for that reason should be abandoned, its abandonment need not significantly reduce the availability of viable vital organs for transplantation. Shewmon thinks this because he believes that a variation on the 'non-heartbeating donor' approach to transplantation could be morally acceptable. The present paper did not offer him an opportunity to answer the fairly formidable moral objections that approach seems to invite. If those objections cannot be answered then acceptance of Shewmon's critique of 'brain death' protocols for diagnosis of death would significantly affect the availability of vital organs for transplantation.

[2] The full details of the references given in the footnotes to this paper are provided at the end of the paper.

[3] Pallis and Harley 1996, p. 6.

(2) Can physicians identify the death of the brainstem by exclusively clinical (non-instrumental) methods?

Well, I hate to disappoint anyone who has come to hear that debate, because I will not be arguing the US side of it. Rather, my message is much more radical: to challenge certain fundamental assumptions common to both sides, specifically that:

(1) the body's "critical system" is the brain, and that
(2) the body even *has* a localized "critical system".


## *Background*

First some background. As a neurologist in a major academic transplant center, I have extensive clinical experience with "brain death". And as a convert from atheism to Catholicism, I have a particular interest in the relationships among brain, mind, body and soul.

In the early and mid-1980s I was a strong proponent of the notion that human death was essentially neurological in nature, that death of the entire brain was death of the person, and that the most convincing rationale for that equivalence also implied that "neocortical death" was equally death.[4] This opinion evolved to a modified version of "whole-brain death", which I presented in 1989 at the Pontifical Academy of Sciences.[5] Since then, I have come to reject all brain-based formulations of death.[6] Thus, I am thoroughly conversant first-hand with the arguments on all sides of the debate.

Most people think that "brain death" is a settled issue. Although this may have seemed true around the turn of the decade, it no longer is the case. An increasing number of experts have begun to re-examine critically and to reject various key underlying assumptions.[7]

Of particular interest is the recent public debate in Germany over incorporating "brain death" into statutory law.[8] A surprising number of intellectuals have argued against it, not the least among them the Archbishop of Cologne, Joachim Cardinal Meisner, who stated officially that "the identification of brain death with death of the person is from a Christian point of view no longer justifiable".[9] Moreover, the Pontifical Academy for Life has been asked to restudy the topic in light of

---

[4] Shewmon, 1985.
[5] Shewmon, 1992.
[6] Shewmon, 1997.
[7] Botkin and Post, 1992; Byrne and Nilges, 1993; Danish Council of Ethics, 1989; Danish Council of Ethics, 1991; Evans, 1994; Halevy and Brody, 1993; Jones, 1995; Rodriguez del Pozo, 1993; Truog, 1997; Veatch, 1993; Youngner, 1992; Youngner, 1996.
[8] Klein, 1995; Klein, 1996; Schmidt-Jortzig and von Klaeden, 1997; Stapenhorst, 1996; Thomas, 1994.
[9] Meisner, 1996; Meisner, 1997.

new information since the 1989 Working Group of the Pontifical Academy of Sciences, and I am privileged to serve on a Task Force to that end.

My position against "brain death" *must not* be misconstrued as necessarily anti-transplantation. The equating of "brain death" with death was quite unnecessary even for the utilitarian purposes which historically inspired it. Through a variation on the "non-heart-beating donor" approach,[10] it is possible to remove vital organs from a patient just disconnected from extraordinary means of support but not yet dead, in such a way that death is neither caused nor even hastened. (I.e., organs are not touched until after final, though not yet irreversible, cessation of heartbeat and circulation; the heart is still resuscitatable, but resuscitation prior to its excision for transplantation would constitute an extraordinary means appropriately forgone along with the ventilator. Excision of what would otherwise be a permanently non-beating heart in no way alters the circulation-less body's physiology during the remaining few minutes of the dying process. Informed consent is of course assumed.) Thus, transplantation techniques *could* be modified to fall under the moral rubric of donation *inter vivos* rather than of the Fifth Commandment.[11] This approach to transplantation deserves further research into means of improving outcomes as well as intense study by expert moralists, few of whom (as far as I can tell) are even aware of it.

Moreover, the requirement of donor "brain death" may have paradoxically *hindered* rather than facilitated the transplantation enterprise. There is good reason to believe that a significant factor contributing to the low rate of signing of organ donor cards is a widespread instinctive suspicion that "brain-dead" donors are really still alive (though fatally injured)[12] and that historically the "brain-death" concept was manufactured through "conceptual gerry-mandering"[13] for purely utilitarian purposes.

## 2. Concept of death

Let us turn, then, to the key ontological question: Is a dead brain equatable with a dead person?

One must distinguish three levels of consideration, which are unfortunately often confused:[14]

(1) the *definition* of death – an essentially philosophical matter;
(2) the *anatomical criterion* which instantiates this definition – a hybrid philoso-phical/medical matter; and

---

[10] Arnold *et al.*, 1995.
[11] Shewmon, 1997.
[12] Halevy and Brody, 1993; Shewmon, 1992; Shewmon, 1997; Tomlinson, 1990; Truog, 1997; Youngner, 1990; Youngner, 1994; Youngner *et al.*, 1985; Youngner *et al.*, 1989.
[13] Youngner, 1992.
[14] Bernat, 1994: pp. 113–143.

(3) the *clinical signs or tests* to determine the occurrence of that anatomical criterion in concrete cases – a purely medical matter.

The US vs. UK debate is at the second and third levels, whereas I shall be focusing here on the first and second. After all, what good are valid diagnostic criteria for an invalid concept?

Three distinct concepts of death run throughout the "brain-death" literature:[15]

(1) *Sociological: loss of conferred membership in human society* – an arbitrary, culturally relative, social construct, which presently happens to be brain-based. Clearly this is incompatible with the Judeo-Christian view of human life and death.

(2) *Psychological: loss of essential human properties or personhood,* independent of the vital status of the body. It is species-specific and applies to many cognitively disabled human beings apart from the "brain-dead". It reduces personhood to consciousness, in turn reduced to a material product or epiphenomenon of brain electrochemical activity. It is also clearly inimical to the Judeo-Christian world-view.

(3) *Biological: loss of integrative unity of the body.* This is species non-specific and corresponds to the ordinary understanding of "death". It is harmonious with the Judeo-Christian heritage and underlies the mainstream theory of "brain death".

Philosophically, the principle of unity of any living thing is its *substantial form or soul.* In humans this has a spiritual dimension, so that the principle of personhood is one and the same with the principle of substantial unity of the body. This Aristotelian-Thomistic view contrasts markedly with the Platonic-Cartesian view, which equates the soul with the conscious mind and the body with an organic machine.

The formulation of the soul as substantial form of the body was even dogmatically defined in 1312 by the Catholic Church's Magisterium at the Council of Vienna:

[W]hoever shall obstinately presume in turn to assert, define, or hold that the rational or intellective soul is not the form of the human body in itself and essentially must be regarded as a heretic.[16]

This teaching has been reinforced in more recent Magisterial pronouncements[17] and particularly by Pope John Paul II in his address to the 1989 Working Group of the Pontifical Academy of Sciences:

[Death] occurs when the spiritual principle which ensures the unity of the individual can no longer exercise its functions in and upon the organism, whose elements, left to themselves, disintegrate.[18]

---

[15] Shewmon, 1997.
[16] Denzinger, 1957: 481.
[17] Pius X, 1914; Pius XI, 1923; Pius XII, 1930.
[18] John Paul II, 1990.

318

The same concept has been expressed in the secular arena, merely minus the word "soul". For example:

> We define death as the permanent cessation of functioning of the organism as a whole... [that is] the spontaneous and innate activities carried out by the integration of all or most subsystems... and at least limited response to the environment.[19]

This view of the nature of human life carries two immediate consequences:

(1) if there is a live human body, there is *ipso facto* a live human person, and
(2) unconsciousness *per se*, even if irreversible, is ontologically a cognitive disability, not death.

A brain lesion can paralyze the intellectual and volitional faculties of the soul – can prevent their activation or realization – without necessarily causing the soul to cease informing the body as its living principle.

## *1995 UK Concept of Death*

In this light let us examine the definition of death officially endorsed in 1995 by the Conference of Medical Royal Colleges[20] and elaborated on in Pallis and Harley's *ABC of Brainstem Death*:[21]

> We consider human death to be a state in which there is irreversible loss of the capacity for consciousness combined with irreversible loss of the capacity to breathe spontaneously (and hence to maintain a spontaneous heart beat). Alone, neither would be sufficient. Both are essentially brainstem functions... The concept is, admittedly, a hybrid one, expressing philosophical, cultural, and physiological concerns. The loss of the capacity for consciousness can be thought of as a reformulation (in terms of modern neurophysiology) of the older cultural concept of the departure of the 'conscious soul' from the body. In the same perspective, irreversible apnoea can also be thought of as the permanent loss of 'the breath of life'.

This statement is remarkable for at least eight reasons.

*First*, apneic coma as a *concept of death* is completely idiosyncratic, pulled out of philosophical thin air.

*Second*, the UK seems unable to make up its mind about fundamental concepts. In 1976, the Conference described the significance of a dead brain stem as essentially *prognostic*.[22] Three years later, it *equated* this with death, offering no reason except that it was a "point of no return" in the process of dying (an *implicit*

[19] Bernat *et al.*, 1981: p. 390.
[20] Working Group, 1995.
[21] 1996: p. 3.
[22] Conference of Medical Royal Colleges, 1976.

integrative-unity rationale).[23] The new *explicit* concept of apneic unconsciousness is therefore completely unrelated to the earlier explanations. Moreover, Pallis and Harley continue to emphasize imminent cardiac arrest as somehow of validating significance,[24] but that has no logical relationship with the new concept, which is merely a variation on the unacceptable loss-of-personhood rationale.

*Third*, there is no reason why the new concept should require the *entire* brain stem to be dead or *all* brain-stem reflexes to be absent, most of which have no bearing on either consciousness or breathing. Therefore, the UK is in the strange position of having a clinical diagnostic algorithm relevant to an earlier *implicit* concept of death but completely *irrelevant* to the present *explicit* concept of death.

*Fourth*, the new concept is not *uniquely* fulfilled by death of the brain stem. A patient in permanent vegetative state with diaphragmatic paralysis would meet the definition yet possess a perfectly intact brain stem.

*Fifth*, selective brain-stem destruction does not constitute loss of the "capacity for consciousness" any more than destruction of an electrical outlet constitutes loss of a lamp's capacity for illumination. Patients comatose from pure brain-stem lesions have been restored to consciousness by electrical stimulation of the reticular formation above the lesion.[25] If "brain-stem death" is death, therefore, such patients would have to be classified as "conscious corpses"!

*Sixth*, the "capacity to breathe spontaneously" is *not* a prerequisite for maintain[ing] a spontaneous heart beat," as implied by Pallis and Harley. Ventilator-dependent patients maintain spontaneous heart beats perfectly well.

*Seventh*, the reference to "the conscious soul departing" from the body is a Cartesian caricature of the true philosophical principle, disdainfully dismissed as an "older cultural" concept of death.

*Eighth*, the phrase "breath of life" is poetry, not physiology.

In summary, the *concept* of death officially endorsed in the UK is quite unrelated to the standard use of the word, rests on flimsy philosophical ground, is incompatible with the Judeo-Christian tradition and the Catholic Magisterium, and ironically even lacks any coherent relationship with the clinical entity of "brain-stem death," of which it is supposed to be the rationale.


## 3. Anatomical criterion for death

Let us, then, accept loss of somatic integrative unity as the concept of death and examine the empirical evidence whether destruction of the entire brain instantiates this concept. If not, then *a fortiori* neither does destruction of only the brain stem.

[23] Conference of Medical Royal Colleges, 1979.
[24] 1996: pp. 28–33.
[25] Hassler, 1977.

*Invariably imminent cardiac arrest*

One important line of evidence has to do with the supposed inability of the "brain-dead" body to maintain stable cardiovascular function in the absence of the co-ordinating influence of the brain (specifically of the brain stem), suggesting that such a body is no longer really a true body but merely a disunited collection of organs. As Pallis wrote in 1983 and has been repeating ever since:

> Asystole invariably develops [within a few days]...The reasons why the heart stops within a short while...are complex but the empirical fact is established beyond all doubt.[26]

Similarly, the 1981 US President's Commission stated:

> Even with extraordinary medical care, these [somatic] functions cannot be sustained indefinitely – typically, no longer than several days.[27]

I could spend the next hour reciting similar quotations.

Such assertions reduce to the following implicit syllogism:

- All bodies without integrative unity necessarily deteriorate inexorably to imminent cardiovascular collapse despite all therapeutic measures.
- All "brain-dead" bodies necessarily deteriorate inexorably to imminent cardio-vascular collapse despite all therapeutic measures.
- Therefore, all "brain-dead" bodies lack integrative unity.

This would be a good argument...if only the facts were correct and the logic valid. Re-expressed symbolically, it runs:

- All X have property Y.
- All Z have property Y.
- Therefore, all Z are X.

But the illogic matters little anyway, for the minor premise is not even true. The correct syllogism really is:

- All X have property Y
- Not all Z have property Y.
- Therefore, at least some Z are not X.

*Prolonged survivals in "brain death"*

Over 126 "brain-death" cases with survival exceeding one week have been published in the medical literature, many involving children or pregnant women whose support was maintained either on account of parental insistence or to

[26] Pallis, 1983: pp. 33–36.
[27] President's Commission, 1981: p. 33.

save the fetus. Four more have come to my attention through other neurologists and two through personal experience. Ten additional cases have been reported in the news media. Most of these cases involved "whole-brain death", often confirmed by absent brain waves or intracranial blood flow; the rest fulfilled UK brain-stem criteria.

Fifty-two cases had sufficient information for statistical analysis, which I am presently submitting for publication.[28] In 35 cases treatment was continued until spontaneous cardiac arrest, and in 17 it was withdrawn. More than half the cases (27/52 = 52%) survived longer than one month, and a third (16/52 = 31%) longer than two months. Seven (13%) survived longer than 6 months and four (8%) longer than one year, the record being 14 years!

Given that most of these cases are public domain, it is difficult to understand how Pallis and Harley, as recently as 1996, could claim with a straight face:

> What was clearly established in the early 1980s was that *no patient* in apnoeic coma declared brain dead according to the very stringent criteria of the United Kingdom code . . . *had ever failed to develop asystole within a relatively short time.* That fundamental insight remains *as valid today as it was 20 years ago* – and not only in the United Kingdom but *throughout the world.* (emphasis added)[29]

A prime example, it would seem, of filtering the facts to fit the theory.

Had support been continued in the treatment-withdrawal subgroup, those survival durations would have increased by unknown amounts. Such uncertainty can be taken into account statistically, resulting in a single so-called Kaplan-Meier curve representing *probability* of survival as a function of time after brain death – a more faithful indicator of the "brain-dead" body's intrinsic survival *capacity*. The curve for these cases is bimodal, with a rapid initial drop-off followed by a second phase of relative stability, the transition occurring around 1–2 years out from "brain death".

An important determinant of survival capacity is age. The longest survivors (2.7, 5.1 and 14.1 years) were all young children, and all 9 survivors beyond 4 months were below 18 years old. Conversely, all 16 patients over age 30 survived less than 2.25 months. This age-effect can be demonstrated with statistical rigor by comparing the survival curves of various age brackets, verifying that young adults and children had relatively long survivals, the elderly had shorter survivals, and middle-aged adults had intermediate survivals.

Another key determinant of survival capacity is the *cause* of "brain death". Etiologies were divided into two categories: primary brain pathology (such as spontaneous intracranial haemorrhage or gunshot wound to the head) and diffuse or multisystem damage (such as cardiac arrest or motor vehicle accident). That the latter should impair survival more than the former makes intuitive sense and is verified statistically by comparing the respective survival curves.

---

[28] Shewmon, 1998.
[29] Pallis and Harley, 1996 (Preface to the second edition).

322

These data teach us several lessons:

(1) "Brain death" does *not* necessarily lead to imminent cardiac arrest.
(2) The heterogeneity of survival duration is largely explainable by non-brain factors. Moreover, the *process* of brain damage *leading up to* "brain death" frequently induces secondary damage to heart and lungs. Therefore, the tendency to early cardiac arrest in the majority of patients is attributable more to *somatic* factors than to mere absence of brain activity *per se*.
(3) The first few weeks are especially precarious. But those who make it through tend to stabilize, no longer requiring sophisticated technological support. Some have even been discharged home on a ventilator. Although a materialist-reductionist might try to argue that these are not human *persons*, no one can seriously claim that they are not living human *organisms*, living human *beings*.

Let me introduce you to TK, the record survivor. At age 4 he contracted meningitis, causing such intracranial pressure that even his skull bones split. Multiple brain-wave tests have been flat, and no spontaneous respirations or brain-stem reflexes have been observed over the subsequent 14 years. Physicians suggested discontinuing support, but his mother would not hear of it.

His early course was very rocky, but eventually he was transferred home, where he remains on a ventilator, assimilates food placed in his stomach by tube, urinates spontaneously, and requires little more than nursing care. While "brain dead" he has grown, overcome infections and healed wounds.

TK's mother gave me permission to examine him and to document everything photographically. I was satisfied that he had no brain-stem function. The skin of his face and upper torso did, however, become mottled in response to my pinching parts of his body, associated with a rise in heart rate and blood pressure. This spinally mediated stress response could not be elicited from the face, sensory input from which is normally processed in the brain stem, which in him is missing.

Further confirming the diagnosis, evoked potentials showed no cortical or brain stem responses, a magnetic resonance angiogram showed no intracranial blood flow, and an MRI scan revealed that the entire brain, including the brain stem, had been replaced by ghost-like tissues and disorganized proteinaceous fluids.

TK has much to teach about the necessity of the brain for somatic integrative unity. There is no question that he became "brain dead" at age 4; neither is there any question that he is still alive at age 18.

*Litany of integrative functions*

Another common argument for equating "brain death" with death is to recite a litany of brain-mediated integrative functions and exclaim, "How can a 'brain-dead' body possibly be a unified organism without all these?" Take, for example, the following statement by Bernat:

> [I]t is primarily the brain that is responsible for the functioning of the organism as a whole: the integration of organ and tissue subsystems by neural and neuroendocrine control of temperature, fluids and electrolytes, nutrition, breathing, circulation, appropriate responses to danger, among others. The cardiac arrest patient with whole brain destruction is simply a preparation of unintegrated individual subsystems, since the organism as a whole has ceased functioning.[30]

But mere function-listing of this sort is not a very scientific approach to an essentially empirical question. To determine whether a given body has integrative unity (hence, *is* a body as opposed to a collectivity of organs), one must first *define the term* and then examine that body for *properties relevant to the definition.* Surprisingly, despite the vastness of the "brain-death" literature and the import of the question, this has never been done. I therefore propose the following two operational definitions or criteria:

> **Criterion 1.** "Integrative unity" is present *if there exists at least one emergent property at the level of the organism as a whole.* A property of a composite is defined as "emergent" (or "gestalt") if it is not localizable to, or predicable of, any constituent part or subset of parts and derives strictly from the mutual interaction of the parts.

Healthy living organisms typically possess many such properties, whereas a sick organism might possess fewer. But only one suffices for it to *be* an organism, for if the property is truly at the level of the whole, there must be a whole of which it is predicated.

The second operational criterion is a corollary:

> **Criterion 2.** Any body requiring *less* technological assistance to maintain its vital functions than some other body that is nevertheless a living whole must possess at least as much integration and hence also be a living whole.

Clearly many "brain-dead" bodies in intensive care units require less technological support than many other extremely sick or dying patients in those same units, who are nevertheless still alive. *Ergo,* those "brain-dead" patients, with even *more* integration, must also be alive.

But let us return to the litany of integrative functions in light of Criterion 1. On closer inspection[31] one discovers that, surprisingly,

- most *brain-mediated* integrative functions are not *somatically integrating,* and conversely,
- most *somatically integrating* functions are not *brain-mediated.*

Moreover, some key "integrative functions", if understood as *brain-mediated,* are not *somatically integrating,* and if understood as *somatically integrating,* are not *brain-mediated.*

[30] Bernat 1984: p. 48.
[31] As elaborated elsewhere in Shewmon, 1997.

Take, for example, breathing and nutrition, cited by Bernat in the quotation above. If "breathing" is understood as moving air in and out of the lungs, it is a function of the diaphragm co-ordinated by the brain stem. If, however, it is understood as "respiration," in the technical sense of exchange of oxygen and carbon dioxide (more relevant to integrative unity), then it is a chemical function of the mitochondria in every cell of the body. (In fact, the final series of macro-molecules involved in the generation of energy from oxidative burning of chemical fuel is known as the "respiratory chain".)

Similarly, if "nutrition" is understood as eating, it is a function of the mouth and pharynx co-ordinated by the brain. If, however, it is understood as the break-down and assimilation of nutrients for energy and bodily structure (the only sense relevant to somatic integration), then it is both a function of the gastrointestinal tract and a chemical function of every cell throughout the body.

Here is another irony. Although neurologists often cite the supposed immi-nence of cardiovascular collapse to justify equating "brain death" with death, the American Academy of Neurology's recent diagnostic guideline states that *"normal* blood pressure *without* pharmacologic support" is explicitly "compatible with the diagnosis of brain death" (emphasis added).[32] Moreover, heart transplant surgeons agree that "most donors can be withdrawn successfully from [pharma-cologic] support with vigorous volume resuscitation",[33] and that cardiovascular *stability* is a relative *requirement* for heart donation candidacy.[34] In other words, the very feature intended to assure us that heart donors are dead is itself a contra-indication to heart donation; and conversely, the best hearts for transplantation come from donors with intrinsic somatic integration not deriving from the brain.

Further, although the mainstream *rationale* for equating "brain death" with death (at least in the US) is the loss of integrative unity,[35] the official *diagnostic criteria* (1) do not require *absence* of a single somatically integrative brain function, and (2) explicitly allow *preservation* of some somatically integrative functions (for example, hypothalamic/posterior pituitary function, cardiovascular stability, and autonomic and endocrine stress responses to skin incision).[36]

Further still, there is an impressive parallel litany of non-brain-mediated somatically integrative functions, most (if not all) of which are gestalt properties fulfilling Operational Criterion 1.[37] These include:

- homeostasis of a limitless variety of physiological parameters and chemical substances;
- assimilation of nutrients;
- elimination, detoxification and recycling of cellular wastes;
- energy balance;

---

[32] American Academy of Neurology – Quality Standards Subcommittee, 1995.
[33] Darby *et al.*, 1989.
[34] Darby *et al.*, 1989; Guerriero, 1996.
[35] President's Commission, 1981.
[36] American Academy of Neurology, 1995.
[37] Shewmon, 1998; Shewmon, 2000.

- maintenance of body temperature (albeit subnormal);
- wound healing;
- fighting of infections and foreign bodies;
- development of a febrile response to infection (albeit rarely);
- cardiovascular and hormonal stress responses to incision for organ retrieval;
- successful gestation of a fetus, as in 11 women of the 52 prolonged survivors;
- sexual maturation, as in two children of the 52;
- and proportional growth, as in three children of the 52.

In addition to fulfilling Operational Criterion 1, the following also fulfil Criterion 2:

- recovery and stabilization following cardiac arrest and other complications (at least in some cases);
- spontaneous improvement in general health, such as loss of the need for pressor drugs to counteract hypotension, return of gastrointestinal motility (allowing tube feedings), etc.;
- ability to maintain fluid and electrolyte balance with rare or no serum monitoring and rare or no adjustment of fluid volume and composition;
- and the overall ability to survive with little medical intervention outside a hospital (as in 7 of the 52 cases).

Why should all these non-brain-mediated functions be selectively ignored, when they are more truly somatically integrating than the brain-mediated ones?

Far from constituting a "central integrator", without which the body reduces to a mere bag of organs, the brain serves as modulator, fine-tuner, optimizer, enhancer, and protector of an implicitly *already existing, intrinsically mediated* somatic unity. Integrative unity is *not* a top-down imposition from a "central integrator" on an otherwise unintegrated collection of organs. (If it were, even the healthy body would lack *true* unity, but would rather consist of a brain carried around and kept alive by dictatorially micromanaged body parts.) Rather, it is a *non-localized, emergent (gestalt) property* deriving from the mutual interaction among all the parts of the body.

### Brain-body disconnection and brain destruction – somatic equivalence

If the foregoing considerations have been insufficiently convincing that a "brain-dead" body is a living human organism, there is a final trump card that seems to me definitive. It is explained somewhat in a recent article[38] and extensively in a manuscript just submitted for publication.[39] In broad strokes the argument runs as follows.

If the body's integrative unity depended on brain functioning, then the body should fall apart just as surely from functional disconnection from the brain as

[38] Shewmon, 1997.
[39] Shewmon, 1999.

from destruction of the brain. Now the brain exerts its co-ordinating role over the body through basically three anatomical pathways: the spinal cord, the vagus nerve, and the pituitary gland. "Brain death" with relatively intact pituitary function (as is often the case) should therefore have the same effect on somatic physiology as high cervical cord transaction plus pharmacologic ablation of the vagus nerve. Or for a more striking analogy, one could suppose that the spinal injury victim was an endocrinology patient with chronic hypopituitarism, stable on hormonal replacement therapy. Thus, the somatic pathophysiology of high spinal cord transection can be made *identical* to that of "brain death" (the *only* difference being that in spinal injury consciousness is preserved but in "brain death" it is not – a difference irrelevant to the question at hand, namely whether brain function is necessary for the body's integrative unity).

The tendency to acute cardiovascular instability, the hypothermia and other symptoms of "spinal shock", the subsequent stabilization of those who survive the acute period, and the eventual return of autonomous spinal cord function – all these characterize both conditions equally. In fact, one can take a typical book chapter on the intensive care of "brain-dead" organ donors and a typical chapter on the intensive care of high spinal cord injury victims and transform the one into the other merely by switching the terms "brain death" and "spinal cord injury".

Now if everyone recognizes that the body of the high cervical cord transection victim is alive despite its lack of regulation by the brain, why should not the same be said of a "brain-dead" body, which is in an identical physiological state (again, the issue of consciousness aside)? The prevailing interpretive double standard is intellectually schizophrenic and should be rejected.

## 4. What *is* death if not "brain death"?

But if "brain death" is not death, what is? We orient once again to the three conceptual levels: definition, anatomical criterion, and clinical tests.

Now, the basic *definition* remains precisely what we have been discussing all along: the loss of integrative unity of the body.

The *anatomical criterion*, however, shifts from a single locus (the brain) to the entire body and consists in a critical degree of molecular-level damage (not yet grossly detectable) throughout the body, beyond a thermodynamical "point of no return". The body's intrinsic tendency to active, anti-entropic self-development and self-maintenance (the essence of "life") is irretrievably lost, so that physico-chemical processes now follow the path of increasing entropy characteristic of inanimate things (i.e., decay). This does *not* require supracritical damage of every single cell in the body, but rather supracritical damage of enough cells of enough different types that the body as a whole loses its intrinsic ability to counteract entropy (and thus, in principle, would continue to "dis-integrate" even if hypothetically forcibly perfused mechanically by oxygenated blood).

The *clinical tests* correspondingly shift from those implying loss of brain function to those implying thermodynamically supracritical microstructural damage diffusely throughout the body. Now a *sine qua non* of the opposition to entropy is energy, generated by chemical respiration, and a *sine qua non* of somatic integration is the circulation of blood, by means of which the body parts mutually interact. A clinical test for the "point of no return" is therefore sustained cessation of circulation of oxygenated blood. The critical duration of cessation depends greatly on body temperature; under ordinary circumstances (i.e., normal temperature), an educated guess is that 20 to 30 minutes probably suffice to surpass the "point of no return".

Although "circulatory-respiratory" sounds similar to the old-fashioned phrase "cardio-pulmonary", they are not synonymous. Neither spontaneous heartbeat nor breathing through the lungs is essential for life (as cardiopulmonary bypass machines effectively prove), but circulation and chemical respiration *are*. Thus, the proposal of a circulatory-respiratory standard represents, far from a reactionary regression, actually a conceptual advance, bringing our criterion and tests for death more in line with the basic concept.

## 5. Conclusion

In summary, the notion of "brain death" as bodily death turns out to be logically and physiologically incoherent. Historically, the introducers of "brain death" intended a radical redefinition of death in terms of loss of personhood by virtue of permanent unconsciousness, for the purely utilitarian purposes of turning off ventilators and organ transplantation.[40] Ironically, a redefinition of death was completely unnecessary for either purpose.

But – one might legitimately ask – even if 'brain death' *is* a legal fiction, it has produced much good and no apparent harm. To eliminate it at this point would entail a major medical, legal, and social upheaval. Why not just let it be? I see five reasons.

*First* many professionals involved in transplantation do not really believe that "brain-dead" donors are dead.[41] Thus, consciences may be compromised by a subliminal sense of participation in utilitarian killing. Moreover, the widespread perception that society approves the killing of certain moribund patients for a good enough cause (or that it approves legally defining some powerless live human beings as "non-persons", if so doing sufficiently benefits those empowered to selectively define themselves as "persons") – all made morally palatable through the guise of a legal fiction of "death" – such a perception may be contributing to the general erosion of respect for the sanctity of life.[42] The evisceration of

---

[40] Shewmon, 1997.
[41] Castelnuovo-Tedesco, 1971; Shewmon, 1992; Shewmon, 1997; Tomlinson, 1990; Youngner, 1994; Youngner *et al.*, 1985.
[42] John Paul II, 1995: 15.

live patients with destroyed brains could thereby be causing much more harm to doctors, nurses and society than to the organ donors themselves.

*Second*, the mainstream physiological rationale for "brain death" has become increasingly implausible. But as "brain death" is falsely regarded as a bioethical sacred cow that must be preserved at all costs, theorists have been turning increasingly to the only remaining coherent rationale, namely loss of personhood in the materialistic-reductionistic sense. Consequently, "brain-death" praxis is beginning to evolve in a direction consistent with *that* notion and *inconsistent* with the sanctity of human life. For example, proposals to use *live* anencephalic infants or patients in a "persistent vegetative state" as organ sources, unthinkable only a few years ago, are now taken seriously among the intelligentsia and in the medical literatures.[43]

*Third*, the notion of "brain death" has inspired the invention of its supposed mirror image, so-called "brain life", as a justification for abortion and human embryo experimentation.[44] Although the "brain life" idea is contradicted by considerations of integrative unity, it *does* logically follow from the reductionistic consciousness-personhood approach, which is gradually becoming the unspoken but *de facto* rationale for "brain death".

*Fourth* there is a serious issue of informed consent.[45] Most signers of organ donor cards and families authorizing donation have very little understanding of "brain death" and what actually happens in operating rooms. When they read the phrase "after my death", many imagine a pulseless corpse and might be horrified to learn that it really means "after I become comatose and apneic but all my other organs are working fine," and that "I will be eviscerated while still pink and warm, with my heart still spontaneously beating and blood circulating." Moreover, no one is informed that the rationale for equating "brain death" with death remains controversial and that empirical evidence has been accumulating that casts serious doubt on the mainstream rationale. Thus, information highly relevant for the potential donor's moral decision making is systematically withheld.

*Finally*, for the state to define someone as legally dead according to a criterion contrary to that person's deeply held convictions violates freedom of religion or other fundamental rights. (I am thinking particularly of orthodox Jews but also of anyone who rejects "brain death" even for non-religious reasons.) So far, only the state of New Jersey has shown itself sensitive to these rights by introducing into its "brain-death" statute a "conscience clause" exempting those who want their own deaths diagnosed the traditional way.[46] This has given rise to the bizarre anomaly whereby one patient with a destroyed brain could be legally

---

[43] Council on Ethical and Judicial Affairs, 1995; Gianelli, 1994; Halevy and Brody, 1993; Ivan, 1990; Kaufman, 1996 (pp. 819–20); Oski *et al.*, 1987; Payne *et al.*, 1996; Powner *et al.*, 1996; Schneider, 1996; Singer, 1994 (pp. 38–56).

[44] Beller and Reeve, 1989; Jones, 1989; Sass, 1989.

[45] cf. Evans, 1993.

[46] Olick, 1991; Veatch, 1993.

dead while another patient in exactly the same condition could be legally alive – or whereby a patient could be legally dead in New York, driven across the bridge to New Jersey, and suddenly become legally alive. Only a circulatory-respiratory statutory definition has the potential for universal acceptance, without compromising any rights of those who believe that death is brain-based (their ventilators could still be discontinued and they could still donate organs through a non-heart-beating donor protocol).

These, then, are my reasons for challenging "brain-death" dogma. And I am convinced that its replacement by something scientifically more credible would promote not only the sanctity of life, but ironically perhaps even transplantation as well.

## References

American Academy of Neurology – Quality Standards Subcommittee (1995) Practice parameters for determining brain death in adults (Summary statement). *Neurology*, **45**, 1012–4.

Arnold RM, Youngner SJ, Schapiro R, Spicer CM (1995) *Procuring organs for transplant: the debate over non-heart-beating cadaver protocols*. Baltimore: The Johns Hopkins University Press.

Beller FK, Reeve J (1989) Brain life and brain death–the anencephalic as an explanatory example. A contribution to transplantation. *Journal of Medicine and Philosophy*, **14**, 5–23.

Bernat JL (1984) The definition, criterion, and statute of death. *Seminars in Neurology*, **4**, 45–51.

Bernat JL (1994) *Ethical Issues in Neurology*. Boston: Butterworth-Heinemann.

Bernat JL, Culver CM, Gert B (1981) On the definition and criterion of death. *Annals of Internal Medicine*, **94**, 389–94.

Botkin JR, Post SG (1992) Confusion in the determination of death: distinguishing philosophy from physiology. *Perspectives in Biology and Medicine*, **36**, 129–38.

Byrne PA, Nilges RG (1993) The brain stem in brain death: a critical review. *Issues in Law and Medicine*, **9**, 3–21.

Castelnuovo-Tedesco P (1971) Cardiac surgeons look at transplantation – interviews with Drs. Cleveland, Cooley, DeBakey, Hallman and Rochelle. *Seminars in Psychiatry*, **3**, 5–16.

Conference of Medical Royal Colleges and their Faculties in the United Kingdom (1976) Diagnosis of brain death. *Lancet*, **2**, 1069–70.

Conference of Medical Royal Colleges and their Faculties in the United Kingdom (1979) Diagnosis of death. *Lancet*, **1**, 261–2.

Council on Ethical and Judicial Affairs AMA (1995) The use of anencephalic neonates as organ donors. *Journal of the American Medical Association*, **273**, 1614–8.

Danish Council of Ethics (1989) Death Criteria. First Annual Report, 1988. Denmark: The Danish Council of Ethics.

Danish Council of Ethics (1991) 3rd Year of the Danish Council of Ethics: Annual Report for 1990. Denmark: The Danish Council of Ethics.

Darby JM, Stein K, Grenvik A, Stuart SA (1989) Approach to management of the heart-beating 'brain dead' organ donor. *Journal of the American Medical Association*, **261**, 2222–8.

Denzinger H (1957) *The Sources of Catholic Dogma [Enchiridion Symbolorum].* Translated by Deferrari, Roy J. St. Louis, MO: B. Herder Book Co.

Evans DW (1993) Brain stem death – a deception. *Philosophy Today,* **12,** 1–2.

Evans M (1994) Against brainstem death. In: R. Gillon (Ed) *Principles Of Health Care Ethics.* Chichester: John Wiley & Sons, Ltd., pp. 1041–51.

Gianelli DM (1994) AMA organ donor opinion sparks ethics debate. Should anencephalic infants be 'living donors'? In: *American Medical News,* pp. 1, 13–4.

Guerriero WG (1996) Organ transplantation. In: *Neurotrauma.* Edited by R. K. Narayan, J. E. Wilberger, Jr. and J. T. Povlishock. New York: McGraw-Hill, pp. 835–40.

Halevy A, Brody B (1993) Brain death: reconciling definitions, criteria, and tests. *Annals of Internal Medicine,* **119,** 519–25.

Hassler R (1977) Basal ganglia systems regulating mental activity. *International Journal of Neurology,* **12,** 53–72.

Ivan LP (1990) The persistent vegetative state. *Transplantation Proceedings,* **22,** 993–4.

John Paul II, Pope (1990) Determining the moment of death. Address of Pope John Paul II to participants in a congress on the determination of the moment of death (December 14, 1989). *The Pope Speaks,* **35,** 207–11.

John Paul II, Pope (1995) *Evangelium Vitae (The Gospel of Life).* Boston, MA: St. Paul Books and Media.

Jones DA (1995) Nagging doubts about brain-death. *Catholic Medical Quarterly,* **47,** 6–16.

Jones DG (1989) Brain birth and personal identity. *Journal of Medical Ethics,* **15,** 173–8, 185.

Kaufman HH (1996) Brain death following head injury. In: *Neurotrauma.* Edited by R. K. Narayan, J. E. Wilberger, Jr. and J. T. Povlishock. New York: McGraw-Hill, pp. 819–33.

Klein M (1995) Hirntod: Vollständiger und irreversibler Verlust aller Hirnfunktionen? [Brain death: Irreversible loss of all brain functions?]. *Ethik in der Medizin,* 6–15.

Klein M (1996) Es gab keine Debatte darüber, was wir unter Tod verstehen wollen. Warum der Hirntod nicht mit dem Tod identisch ist und trotzdem Organe entnommen werden können. [There was no disagreement over how we should understand death. Why brain death is not identical to death and why it is permissible to remove organs anyway.] In: *Frankfurter Rundschau.* Frankfurt, November 7, 1996 (Nr.260), p. 12.

Meisner JK (1996) Erklärung des Erzbischofs von Koln zum beabsichtigten Transplantationsgesetz [Declaration of the Archbishop of Cologne concerning the proposed transplantation law.] Koln, Germany: Presseamt des Erzbistums Koln, p. 1.

Meisner JK (1997) Wann trennen sich Seele und Leib? [When do the body and soul separate?] In: *Frankfurter Allgemeine Zeitung.* Frankfurt, January 25, 1997 (Nr.21), p.14.

Olick RS (1991) Brain death, religious freedom, and public policy: New Jersey's landmark legislative initiative. *Kennedy Institute of Ethics Journal,* **1,** 275–92.

Oski FA, Fost NC, Freeman JM, Seidel HM, Joffe A (1987) Ethical dilemma: should organs be taken from this patient? [edited discussion]. *Contemporary Pediatrics,* **4,** 110–7.

Pallis C (1983) Whole-brain death reconsidered – physiological facts and philosophy. *Journal of Medical Ethics,* **9,** 32–7.

Pallis C, Harley DH (1996) *ABC of Brainstem Death.* London: BMJ Publishing Group.

Payne K, Taylor RM, Stocking C, Sachs G (1996) Physicians' attitudes about the care of patients in the persistent vegetative state. *Annals of Internal Medicine,* **125,** 104–10.

Pius X, Pope (1914) Doctoris Angelici. *Acta Apostolicae Sedis,* **6,** 336–41.

Pius XI, Pope (1923) Studiorum Ducem. *Acta Apostolicae Sedis,* **15,** 309–26.

Pius XII, Pope (1950) Humani generis. *Acta Apostolicae Sedis,* **42,** 561–78.

Powner DJ, Ackerman BM, Grenvik A (1996) Medical diagnosis of death in adults: historical contributions to current controversies. *Lancet,* **348,** 1219–23.

President's Commission for the Study of Ethical Problems in Medicine and Biomedical and Behavioral Research (1981) *Defining Death: Medical, Legal, and Ethical Issues in the Determination of Death*. Washington, DC: U.S. Government Printing Office.

Rodriguez del Pozo P (1993) La muerte cerebral: diagnostico o pronostico? *JANO*, **44**, 85–92.

Sass HM (1989) Brain life and brain death: a proposal for a normative agreement. *Journal of Medicine and Philosophy*, **14**, 45–59.

Schmidt-Jortzig E, von Klaeden E (1997) Leichen bekommen kein Fieber. Die Fragwürdigkeit des Hirntod-Kriteriums. [Corpses do not develop fever. The legitimacy of brain-death criteria.] In: *Frankfurter Allgemeine Zeitung*. Frankfurt, May 13 1997 (Nr. 109), p. 15.

Schneider S (1996) Traditional transplant standards don't apply to anencephalic organ donation. In: *American Medical News*, February 19, 1996, p. 21.

Shewmon DA (1985) The metaphysics of brain death, persistent vegetative state, and dementia. *The Thomist*, **49**, 24–80.

Shewmon DA (1992) "Brain death": a valid theme with invalid variations, blurred by semantic ambiguity. In: R. J. White, H. Angstwurm and I. Carrasco de Paula (Eds) *Working Group on the Determination of Brain Death and its Relationship to Human Death. 10–14 December, 1989. (Scripta Varia 83)*. Vatican City: Pontifical Academy of Sciences, pp. 23–51.

Shewmon DA (1997) Recovery from "brain death": A neurologist's *Apologia. Linacre Quarterly*, **64**, 30–96.

Shewmon DA (1998) Chronic "brain death": meta-analysis and conceptual consequences. *Neurology*, **51**, 1538–45.

Shewmon DA (1999) Spinal shock and 'brain death': somatic pathophysiological equivalence and implications for the integrative-unity rationale. *Spinal Cord*, **37**, 313–24.

Shewmon DA (2000) The brain and somatic integration: insights into the standard biological rationale for equating 'brain death' with death. *Journal of Medicine and Philosophy*, **24** [in press].

Singer P (1994) *Rethinking Life & Death. The Collapse of Our Traditional Ethics*. New York, NY: St. Martin's Press.

Stapenhorst K (1996) Über die biologisch-naturwissenschaft unzulässige Gleichsetzung von Hirntod und Individualtod und ihre Folgen fur die Medizin. [The biological and scientific difference between brain death and human death and the ethical consequences for the physician]. *Ethik in der Medizin*, **8**, 79–89.

Thomas H (1994) Sind Hirntote Lebende ohne Hirnfunktionen oder Tote mit erhaltenen Korperfunktionen? [Are the brain dead alive but without brain functions, or are they dead but still in possession of body functions?]. *Ethik in der Medizin*, **6**, 189–207.

Tomlinson T (1990) Misunderstanding death on a respirator. *Bioethics*, **4**, 253–64.

Truog RD (1997) Is it time to abandon brain death? *Hastings Center Report*, **27**(1), 29–37.

Veatch RM (1993) The impending collapse of the whole-brain definition of death [published erratum appears in *Hastings Center Report* (1993) **23**(6):4]. *Hastings Center Report*, **23**(4), 18–24.

Working Group of the Royal College of Physicians (1995) Criteria for the diagnosis of brain stem death. Review by a Working Group convened by the Royal College of Physicians and endorsed by the Conference of Medical Royal Colleges and their Faculties in the United Kingdom. *Journal of the Royal College of Physicians of London*, **29**, 381–2.

Youngner SJ (1990) Organ retrieval: can we ignore the dark side? *Transplantation Proceedings*, **22**, 1014–15.

Youngner SJ (1992) Defining death. A superficial and fragile consensus. *Archives of Neurology*, **49**, 570–2.

Youngner SJ (1994) Brain death and organ transplantation: confusion and its consequences. *Minerva Anestesiologica*, **60**, 611–3.

Youngner SJ (1996) Brain death: another layer of confusion. *Center Views* [Center for Biomedical Ethics, Case Western Reserve University School of Medicine], **10**, 1, 4–5.

Younger SJ, Allen M, Bartlett ET, Cascorbi ELF, Hau T, Jackson DL *et al.* (1985) Psychosocial and ethical implications of organ retrieval. *New England Journal of Medicine*, **313**, 321–4.

Younger SJ, Landefeld CS, Coulton CI, Juknialis BW, Leary M (1989) 'Brain death' and organ retrieval. A cross-sectional survey of knowledge and concepts among health professionals. *Journal of the American Medical Association*, **261**, 2205–10.

# 20

# Can a patient's refusal of life-prolonging treatment be morally upright when it is motivated neither by the belief that the treatment would be clearly futile nor by the belief that the consequences of treatment would be unduly burdensome?

BERNADETTE TOBIN

THE FOLLOWING discussion has two parts. In the first section, I set out several principles from the Catholic tradition of moral theologising which form the background to the question and say something about how these principles inform our thinking about medical treatment. In the second section, I argue that though the concepts of futile and burdensome treatment encapsulate the reasons for legitimate refusal of life-prolonging treatment, they do not capture what is deepest in the tradition's teaching about the responsibility to take care of one's life.

I

There are several ideas in the Catholic tradition which form the background for this discussion: (a) the idea that decisions about one's own health care are the responsibility of each individual person, (b) the idea that though one is obliged to take good care of one's health, one is not obliged to undergo futile or overly-burdensome treatment, and (c) the idea that suicide is always wrong. I shall say a little about each.

(a) Human flourishing is not primarily a matter of chance. By our choices and the settled character-traits which we acquire through our habits of choice, we make a significant contribution to our own flourishing or diminishment. This is what it means to call human beings 'self-determining' creatures. We have the capacity substantially to form our own characters, to make something of ourselves. Choices and decisions about one's own health, like all choices and decisions, are the responsibility of the person whose flourishing is at stake. This responsibility for making decisions about one's health includes a responsibility to decide which medical treatments to undergo.[1] Given that this self-determining capacity can be used for good or ill, the challenge for human beings is to make wise (or 'morally upright') choices.

Which choices are wise and which are not? Within the Catholic tradition there are various ways of answering this question: however, it can readily be seen that the pursuit of health is an aspect of human flourishing. In the tradition the pursuit of one's own health is taken to be not so much a right as a responsibility. (It is a matter of debate within the tradition whether the protection of one's life ought to be thought of as a *part* of the responsibility to take care of one's health, or whether care of one's health ought to be thought of as a *part* of the protection of one's life, or whether these two responsibilities are *independent* of each other. I shall assume that taking good care of one's life is a part of what it is to look after one's health.)

However health is only one of the goals worthy of pursuit in life. Friendship, knowledge, aesthetic experience, recreation, religious experience, the prospering of one's community: these are some of the other goals that are worthy of choice and pursuit in life, goals (or 'goods') which may compete with the pursuit of the goal of health. The (Aristotelian) idea that these goals cannot be added together to form a single composite goal for an individual person (and, *a fortiori*, a single composite goal for a group of people) forms part of the tradition's thinking.

(b) The tradition recognises that there are limits to the pursuit of health. With respect to undergoing medical treatment in the care of one's health, a distinction is made between the taking of 'ordinary' and of 'extraordinary' means: one is obliged to take ordinary means but not obliged to take extraordinary means. The concept of 'extraordinary means' is generally explained in terms of treatment which is either futile or overly-burdensome.

The idea that a treatment would be futile is in principle clear enough.[2] To call a treatment futile is to say that it has little or no chance of protecting or promoting a

[1] In what follows I shall set aside questions about decision-making on behalf of people who cannot make decisions for themselves. Decision-making in these circumstances ought to be understood as the responsibility of the (senior) doctor who must make (or, better, faces the challenge of making) decisions about what is in the patient's best interests. He or she thus ought to consult the family and 'significant other(s)' in order to ensure that his or her judgement properly takes into account (a) any information about what the patient would have wanted (if anything *is* genuinely known about that), (b) any signs as to what the patient in fact wants now, (c) the capacity of the family/significant other(s) to look after the patient and (d) the views of the family/significant other(s) regarding the appropriateness of the proposed care. There are many issues which bear on this topic. Two stand out: First, the doctor's decision-making responsibility is widely misunderstood to be a matter of 'whatever the family wants': at the very best this is an exaggerated way of restating the importance of consulting them to see what they know about what the patient might have wanted and of taking into consideration their capacity to look after the patient should that need arise. Secondly there are often sub-stantial pressures on doctors to do the wrong thing: to overtreat or to undertreat the patient for the sake of the family/significant other(s).
[2] Clear enough, that is, if one assumes that the responsibility to take proper care of one's life is a part of the responsibility to take care of one's health. It is more difficult if one has a different sense of the relatonship between 'life' and 'health'.

person's health, whether that be curing someone's illness, stabilising him in a reasonable condition all things considered, modifying his handicap, relieving him of the symptoms of his disease, etc.

Two points about the idea that treatment may be futile should be noted. First, the idea that a *treatment* may be judged futile is sometimes confused with the quite different idea that a *life* may legitimately be judged futile or not worth living. Sometimes it may be difficult to discern which idea is at work in someone's thinking. But the tradition challenges us to make that distinction: only medical treatments, not human lives themselves, may legitimately be judged futile. Secondly, a distinction is made between the idea that a treatment is futile (that it is unlikely to restore a person to some semblance of health) and the idea that a treatment may prolong life: a treatment which prolongs life may indeed be futile in the sense that it offers insufficient hope of restoring or maintaining a condition which, for a particular patient in his or her particular circumstances, could genuinely be called 'health'.

That said, it may often be difficult to decide whether, in specific circumstances, a particular treatment will be futile for an individual patient.

The idea that a treatment would be overly-burdensome is more complex.[3] Three features of the concept of burdensomeness should be noted. First, just as the concept of futility may be misapplied to the value of a *life* rather than to the value of a *treatment*, so the concept of burdensomeness may be similarly misapplied: in the tradition it is medical treatment and not the so-called 'quality' of a life which may legitimately be judged overly-burdensome. I take it that in the mind of a young man with AIDS Dementia Complex who refuses to enter hospital to have his condition treated because of what he anticipates as the loneliness and boredom of life in hospital, it is medical treatment and not his life itself which he finds overly-burdensome.

Secondly, a patient may judge that a treatment would be too burdensome relative either to the goal of health or to some other goal. Some treatments for cancer offer patients who are dying the prospect of another few months of life but only at the cost of the patient's being much more sickly in the last (slightly longer) stage of life than he or she otherwise would be in the last (slightly shorter) stage of life. A refusal of such treatment may invoke the goal of health: relative to

---

[3] "The more difficult factors to assess in judging whether treatment is obligatory concern what is traditionally called the burdensome character of treatment. In judging how burdensome treatment is, consideration is to be given (a) to the degree of risk, cost and physical and psychological hardship involved relative to this particular patient, his overall condition and its potential for improvement, his resources and sensibilities, and (b) to this particular doctor (or medical team), his time, effort and other obligations. A patient is entitled (though not obliged) to refuse treatment on the ground that, considering all the above factors, it is too costly and/or physically or psychologically burdensome to him or to his dependants or to those in attendance on him, even in circumstances in which he expects the consequences of his refusal to be fatal or drastic for him. The burden of treatment can depend . . . on a patient's overall condition and its potential for improvement, his resources and sensibility; as these vary from patient to patient so may and should the assessment of burden." Luke Gormally (ed), *Euthanasia, Clinical Practice and the Law* London: The Linacre Centre 1994, p. 63.

that goal, the treatment may be judged too burdensome. And someone in the same kind of circumstances who wishes to devote his remaining energies to preparing himself spiritually for death rather than to undergoing treatment which may marginally prolong his life may judge further treatment overly-burdensome relative to the good of his spiritual life.

Thirdly, the burden of treatment may fall not only on the patient but also on others: primarily those providing the treatment (the doctor or nurse, the patient's family, significant others) but also the community which is providing the resources for that treatment.[4] A patient may recognise that (for instance) his treatment for an advanced cancer has become too burdensome not so much for himself as for his family (in that, say, his wife must interrupt the care of their children to bring him down from the country to the city, stay overnight in the city, and return with him the next day) and he may refuse further treatment for the sake of his family.

Of course, all such judgements are fallible. A person who refuses treatment because of the pain and discomfort it brings may be giving up too soon. Because the sufferings associated with illness, especially the illness that precedes dying, are both particular to the individual and inherently mysterious, it will be hard to know whether this is so in a particular case. None the less, since we recognise the phenomenon of people (often, ourselves) giving up too soon in other arenas of life, presumably it can also happen when a person is faced with arduous medical treatment. In addition, the giving up may be motivated by a misunderstanding of the likely efficacy of further treatment or by a fear (or indeed the realisation) of being a burden on others, or by a feeling (particularly in an older person) that one has 'used up' one's entitlement to medical treatment and care (a very different kind of refusal from one motivated by a generous sense of the burdens one's treatment imposes on others). Often it may be difficult to discern the person's attitude to his own life: but suicide by omission may be an accurate description of what he or she proposes. Which leads us to the third critical idea in the tradition which forms the context for this discussion.

(c) In the Catholic tradition suicide is taken to be wrong itself. For Catholics, as for other Christians, life is a gift from God in respect of which human beings are challenged to be good and faithful stewards. The Declaration on Euthanasia of 1980 put it this way:

> Intentionally causing one's own death, or suicide, is equally as wrong as murder; such an action on the part of a person is to be considered as a rejection of God's sovereignty and loving plan. Furthermore, suicide is also often a refusal of love for self, the denial of the natural instinct to live, a flight from

---

[4] "But normally one is held to use only ordinary means – according to circumstances of persons, places, time and culture – that is to say, means that do not involve any grave burden for oneself *or another.*" Pope Pius XII, 'The Prolongation of Life', (November 24, 1957), reprinted in Kevin O'Rourke and Philip Boyle (eds) *Medical Ethics, Sources of Catholic Teachings* St Louis, Mo: Catholic Health Association of the United States 1989 (emphasis added).

the duties of justice and charity owed to one's neighbour, to various communities or to the whole society – although, as is generally recognized, at times there are psychological factors present that can diminish responsibility or even completely remove it.[5]

Just as killing of another (whether euthanasia or not) can be brought about by either an act or an omission, so too can suicide. The refusal of life-prolonging treatment with the objective in mind of bringing about one's own death, in order to bring about one's own death, is suicide by omission. Some faithful Catholics who accept the prohibition on suicide sometimes think that suicide must involve some 'positive' action (such as the taking of a lethal dose of medications) and fail to see that a refusal of life-prolonging treatment might be motivated by a suicidal intent. On the other hand, one of the most difficult sets of circumstances, for doctors in Australian Catholic hospitals at least, is the circumstance in which they fear that they may be assisting a person to commit suicide. For some of these doctors, the fear is merely that they will be doing something illegal. But for others, the fear goes beyond that: they fear they may be assisting someone to do something which he or she ought not to do.

Of course, someone suffering from a clinical depression, or from some other mental illness as a result of which he refuses treatment, is hardly responsible for the choices he makes. Rather, those looking after him are faced with the challenge of recognising the signs of clinical depression or mental illness and of responding to that. The possibility that depression is the motivating factor behind a refusal of life-prolonging treatment must always be considered (particularly since some psychiatrists think that the incidence of clinical depression in the general community is much higher than is generally recognised). However we should resist the temptation to label someone as depressed or insane merely *because* he refuses life-prolonging treatment. That would be unfaithful not only to the needs of very many people who are dying; it would be unfaithful to a tradition which recognises that life-prolonging treatment may sometimes legitimately be refused.

2

It seems, then, that the concepts of futile and burdensome treatment do indeed encapsulate the reasons for legitimate refusals of life-prolonging treatment, that a refusal of life-prolonging treatment will not be legitimate unless it invokes either the notion of the futility of life-prolonging treatment or the notion of its burdensomeness. However I now want to suggest that, though that may be the case, these two concepts do not convey what is deepest in the tradition's discussion of one's responsibilities to take care of one's life, that these two concepts do not convey what is at the heart of the tradition's teaching on these matters.

[5] Sacred Congregation for the Doctrine of the Faith: *Declaration on Euthanasia*, St Paul's Publications, 1980 (Australian edition) p. 7.

To explain, I shall sketch a scenario which is very different from the kind of case which involves a refusal of medical treatment. Though this scenario involves nothing which could plausibly be called a 'refusal', nor even a 'forgoing', of medical treatment, it none the less throws light on what is at the heart of the tradition's teaching about the legitimacy of refusals of futile or burdensome treatment.

A professor of classical history has spent a part of every year of his professional life working with a group of archaeologists and students in the exploration of an archaeological site in an underdeveloped country a long way from his home. This has been a central part of his academic responsibilities: it has informed his teaching and through it he has introduced his students to the study of archaeology. Over the years his responsibility for the 'dig' has increased, and in the last ten years he has been the expedition leader. Some years ago he discovered that he suffered from a life-threatening heart condition. It was thought that only a heart transplant would save his life. However, after the initial acute phase of treatment, which he accepted without reservation and indeed with gratitude to those whose care of him had saved his life, his health improved to such an extent that his name was removed from the heart transplant list on the grounds that his heart condition was not grave enough to warrant a transplant. In fact his health could be maintained by drug therapy. When in the following year the time came for him to lead the annual archaeological expedition, he was in good health. However he knew that, were his health suddenly to deteriorate, he might need intensive treatment of a kind which would not be available in the circumstances in which he would be living for the next six weeks. With the blessing of his wife and his now grown up children, he decided once again to return to the archaeological dig. Whilst there he contracted a virus, as a result of which he died from complications of his heart condition.

This man proposed to do something which would put his life at substantial risk. But, in spite of his readiness to take that risk with his life in pursuit of his vocation, he did not have the attitude to his life which the tradition condemns in its prohibitions on suicide and euthanasia.

This raises the question: what *is* the attitude to life which the tradition condemns in its prohibition on suicide and euthanasia? For the Catholic tradition maintains that there is something deeply wrong with suicide *even when* no one (else) is harmed by it and *even when* it is not the expression of a vice (that is to say, even when it does not involve a 'flight from the duties of justice and charity owed to one's neighbour, to various communities or to the whole society' and when it is not a 'refusal of love for self, the denial of the natural instinct to live'. What *is* the character of that wrongness?

Here I think we need to draw on ideas from outside the Catholic Christian tradition. In his book *Good and Evil: An Absolute Conception*, the philosopher Raimond Gaita reminds us that Socrates thought that suicide was a kind of ingratitude, and that Kant rebuked those who would commit suicide in the disdainful spirit of 'leaving the world as though it were a smoke filled room'.[6]

[6] Raimond Gaita, *Good and Evil, An Absolute Conception* London: Macmillan 1991.

What Socrates and Kant offer us are ways of conceiving the *value* of human life. They suggest that it is something that we ought not *throw away*, that taking one's own life, or asking someone else to do so or to help one to do so, is somehow *unworthy* of a human being, that (to put the point in the positive) human life is a *gift* in response to which we are *called* to live *properly* or *worthily*, even in the most extreme circumstances of suffering and despair. (In fact it might be said that Gaita's book is an exploration of the idea that we can speak of human life as a gift without thereby being committed to the thought that it must be *God's* gift: but that is more contentious!)

It seems to me that we do not condemn the archaeologist because, though he was prepared to put his life at real risk, he did not have the attitude to life which is condemned in the Catholic tradition's prohibition on suicide and euthanasia. Rather, the fact that he was prepared to take a risk with his life and health in the pursuit of his archaeological work reveals that he *did* have a sense of his life as a vocation, that he recognised that there is *more* to living human life properly or worthily than simply protecting life and health at all costs, more to living human life properly or worthily than merely prolonging it.

What has this to do with the topic of legitimate refusals of life-prolonging treatment? It shows, I suggest, that there is something deeper to be appreciated in the tradition's teaching on these matters than is conveyed by the idea that futile or overly-burdensome treatment may legitimately be refused. This deeper idea (about the *kind* of value which human life has) gives meaning and point to the principle that there are limits to the obligation to preserve one's life and health. If we are to understand the obligation to take proper care of our lives and health in a way which is faithful not just to the complexities of human life but also to the depths of despair to which we are tempted, we need a sense of what gives meaning to the thought that sometimes life-prolonging medical treatment may be forgone. What gives it its meaning is the idea that human life is not something merely to be enjoyed or endured and then to be disposed of when it is no longer enjoyable or endurable. Rather, each of us has to discover in our own circumstances how to be true to the challenge of living it *worthily*. That is to say, each of us needs a sense of what Aristotle called 'what's worth what'.

To conclude: The thought that there is something *ignoble* about suicide and euthanasia is what gives point to the tradition's prohibitions on suicide and euthanasia. The thought that the *kind* of value human life has is such that it ought to be lived *worthily* is what gives point to the tradition's teaching that there are limits to the obligation merely to preserve our lives. I suggest that this is the *truth* that our tradition expresses when it says that futile or overly-burdensome treatment may legitimately be refused.

# 21

# Are there any circumstances in which it would be morally admirable for a woman to seek to have an orphan embryo implanted in her womb?

## I.

### MARY GEACH

I ASSUME IN this paper that an embryo is a human being from the first moment of conception, as from then on it is an individual member of our species. I do not need to argue this assumption, which is largely made by men of good will, since if it is false, my side of the argument is even stronger.

The question of whether it is ever admirable to 'adopt' an orphan embryo has arisen because of the plight of embryos generated *in vitro*. Most of those not inserted in wombs shortly after generation, and which are stored in a frozen condition for possible future use, are destined to be destroyed. This horrible and bizarre situation is seen as calling for the indecent solution which has been proposed: that women should submit to technological impregnation, and should bear in their wombs children which are not their own.

Those who *feel* the indecency of this suggestion, but nevertheless are ready to make it, do in some cases excuse themselves on the ground that what we have to deal with here is a moral mess. Morally indecent situations can call for ugly and indecent solutions: solutions like war, and prisons, and body searches. That, I take it, is how people think. Thus the miasma of evil which surrounds reproductive technology has obscured the intrinsic moral evil of the suggestion being made.

Let us briefly clear away this miasma by considering the plight of the embryo which is begotten in a normal fashion, but whose mother's endometrium is unfit for implantation. Such embryos have at least as much right to life as embryos in freezers. Now, it is possible, by a technique called embryo flushing, to remove an embryo in the pre-implantation stage, to freeze him, and to look about for a surrogate mother. Would it be all right to do *that*, in the case of a woman incapable of bearing?

We can now see that the moral question about making some women pregnant with other women's children, does not only arise because of evil choices which have already been made.

If it is all right to 'adopt' an embryo, it follows that the act of admission, whereby a woman allows herself to be made pregnant with a child not her own, is not an intrinsically evil kind of act. But if it is not an intrinsically evil kind of act, it is hard to see that there is anything intrinsically wrong with surrogate motherhood. If we can dissociate surrogacy from IVF, then why should there be any objection to it? If it is not wrong to impregnate women with children not their own, then we can have a nice Catholic reproductive technology, with some women bearing other women's children. Technological advance will thus increase the number of the sexes: there will be fathers, and mothers, and bearers. The bearer, it may be added, is likely to have a powerful influence on development, and can fairly be regarded as a third parent.

It used to be the case that a good woman only allowed herself to be made pregnant by an act which was generative, and was an expression of her permanent, intimate, and sexually exclusive relationship with the father of the child. Her act said "I am yours", and what she gave was her womb, her blood, her whole body. But now we see that she can give herself in another way; a way which expresses a relation to the father and mother which is non-unitive and non-generative. Her womb is a valuable resource, which she makes available as a wet-nurse makes her breasts available to the babe she suckles.

Those who believe in embryo adoption have compared it to suckling an unwanted child. If the two actions – of receiving an embryo into one's womb, and of accepting a babe as a nursling – are indeed similar in all but degree (of risk, commitment, wear and tear on the body, etc.), then I suppose it would be reasonable to ask payment for performing this service. A wet-nurse used to be paid, and it was fair enough that she should be: she was fulfilling an important, and in some cases necessary, function, and could quite reasonably expect payment for fulfilling it.

So a rich and fertile woman might pay for lots of surrogate mothers, and have twelve children a year, like a male polygamist, but all without sin, if there is nothing sinful in making a woman pregnant with children not her own. Of course, one should not do this if one is capable of bearing one's own children, but now the excuse of incapacity may make one the mother of hundreds. Wonderful!

By this point, everyone will have drawn the line. Perhaps this last greedy use of resources is what you object to. But what is a woman to do? Avoid intercourse just because someone is pregnant with her baby? Practise NFP? Leave her embryos to perish? If you think it permissible to pay a woman for this service, these problems will arise.

So perhaps you think it impermissible to *pay* a woman for such a service. You have a problem now about the old wet-nurses. Was it impermissible to pay them? If it is all right to make this considerable self-sacrifice on another woman's behalf, why is it wrong to be paid for it?

Well, you may say, it is not right to do this on another woman's behalf. Only orphan embryos should be adopted: embryos whose mothers have died or do not want them. Others should be left to die. Why?

Some think that only married women should 'adopt' embryos. This shows that embryo adoption is not seen as being like ordinary adoption. An old bachelor would not be obliged to leave a baby to die because his menage was an unsuitable one for child-rearing. If we observe this restriction, and if the woman with the bad womb and the good ovaries should not *employ* other women, she might still hand her babies on for 'embryo adoption', and still be the mother of hundreds. And all begotten in marriage!

What I have said so far brings out the moral difficulties that arise from supposing that a woman may allow herself to be made pregnant with a child not her own. These may best be seen by considering the question: in what ways, and to what extent, is 'embryo adoption' like nursing another woman's child at the breast?

Nowadays, we look back with some distaste at a social system in which a lady never fed her own child, but clearly a busy or sick or dry woman might have reason for employing another woman to feed her baby, and there was nothing wrong with this. So if you object to the idea of the hired surrogate mother you must see that there is a morally relevant difference between nursing and gestating. What is this difference?

The difference is that the act of admission, whereby one allows oneself to be made pregnant, is usually the female part of the act of generation. The act of accepting a child for nursing never is. The act of generation is normally *the* human act through which a woman is made pregnant, *the* human act through which she is made liable to give birth. By this act she is not merely committed to pregnancy; by this act she is made pregnant, as no subsequent choice on her part is usually needed if her pregnancy and giving birth are to occur. This fact about the marriage act is obviously important to it as a marriage act; but it is a fact which also holds of technological impregnation, whether with semen or with an already-existing embryo.

Bodily sins against chastity are objectionable because in committing them one performs acts which are like enough to marriage acts to carry some of the psychological significance of marriage acts, but are, in one way or another, not marriage acts. By acting unchastely, one dissociates the parts of the marriage act from one another, thus destroying in oneself the full sense of the significance of man in all his psychophysical unity. For the importance of this topic derives from the fact that human beings are rational animals: not spiritual beings attached to animals, but animals whose life is spiritual. The life begun through human procreation is this spiritual life of an animal. One's sense of this is kept intact if one's act of generation is not resolved into its component elements, but is itself one act, the animal and the rational being the same, defined by the conjoint end, which is to perform a unitive act of procreative kind. In this joint act, there is a part played by the man, and a part played by the woman, and it is important, and not a mere mechanical detail, that those parts are different: that the man's act involves producing seed, and the woman's does not. So we need to think here about what a *woman* does in the marriage act; what is the woman's act of generation?

An act of admission whereby one allows oneself to be made pregnant is profoundly like such an act of generation. This similarity is more profound than the similarity of a woman's perverse sexual act to the female act of generation. A woman could perform a complete marriage act without having any of those motions of the flesh some of which usually occur and make the act more efficacious and pleasurable. But a complete marriage act is *always* an act of admission which is of a kind to make one pregnant: nor would it be a true marriage act if one was unaware of this fact. It is this which gives it a large part of its significance as an act of self-giving. To separate it from the other parts of a marriage act would be to destroy in oneself that same reproductive integrity which is destroyed by unchaste actions.

Those who see chastity as being simply a matter of temperance, and the regulation of sexual passion, should consider what the norm is, about which the passion is to be regulated. It is not a mere sense of moderation that rules out sodomy and adultery; consideration of this fact should make one realise that temperance is only part of chastity: reproductive integrity is the profounder element. This integrity does not simply consist in the right direction of one's passions and sensations. A very important part of it has to do with what one allows other people to do to one. This is especially important for women, since the marriage act is, on the woman's side, an act of admission.

Chastity has to do with the correct treatment of libidinous passion in oneself and others. However, the virtue of chastity is not the only part of reproductive integrity, which we will see if we consider what the objection is to unchaste actions. The fundamental objection is that in performing them one is using a central part of one's psyche out of context, and in such a way as to deprive it of its significance, which derives from the totality of the act to which that part of one's psyche is directed, and of the relationship which the act signifies. So the question about the woman who allows herself to be made pregnant by technology is whether she is doing this: is dis-integrating the marriage act by using a part of it out of context.

The marriage act is, in this field, the central one to be considered; just as in studying disease we need to know about healthy functioning, so in studying the general topic of reproductive integrity, we need to know about the marriage act. Both in sexual behaviour, and in reproductive medicine, the impermissible act is the one that distorts or replaces some aspect of the marriage act, leaving out the central core of self-giving to the other through an act of generative kind. Thus we have the principle that the unitive and procreative aspects of the marriage act are inseparable. This principle affects both sexual conduct, and reproductive medicine. However, it does not cover the whole field. Consider the objection to solitary vice in women. This is neither unitive nor procreative in kind, but involves a use of something usually connected with the marriage act. There is no general objection, I may say, to doing things to one's body in order to enjoy the resulting subjective sensations. I don't suppose that any of you ever told your children not to turn round and round to make themselves dizzy, on the ground that this was a sinful use of the body as a mere instrument of subjective gratification. No, what is objectionable about solitary vice has specifically to do with using one part of the marriage act out of context.

Thus it is the marriage act as a whole which should not be dismembered, and the principle about not separating the unitive and the procreative, on the ground of their joint significance, is only a part of this more general principle. But, as I have said, the fact that one is laying oneself open to an impregnating intromission is a vital part of the self-giving involved in the woman's part of the marriage act. This self-giving is not just a self-giving to the possible child, but to the father, since it would be his child that she would be bearing.

The man gives up a part of himself in the marriage act, committing the fruit of the act to the womb of the woman; the woman's complementary act of self-giving is to lay herself open, to surrender her body to an impregnating kind of act whose consequence is to occupy and use her whole body. This mutual self-giving is important to the marriage act as unitive and generative. The sensations and motions of the flesh which are usually associated with the marriage act in women are the material component of an act whose form, whose spiritual component, is a giving up of the whole body. (That is why it is appropriate to women's libidinous feeling and sensitivity that it should be so generalised in the body.)

Now if these sensations are ones which it is wrong to excite by acts of solitary vice, how much worse must it be to isolate the spiritual component of the marriage act, the giving up of the body to the impregnator, dissociating oneself from the parents of the child, and substituting for the relation to the father a mere arrangement with a technician. What is being asked of women is that they take a vital part of the marriage act, and perform it without the father. If solitary vice is objectionable as a part of the marriage act taken out of context, much more so is this giving up of one's body to an impregnating intromission.[1]

If one performs an act of admission, which is of a kind to make one pregnant, it should be an act of generative kind, expressive of a pre-existing, permanent, sexually exclusive relationship with the father of one's child. To lay one's womb open to an impregnating intromission which is not performed by the father, and is not generative, and is not expressive of a pre-existing, sexually exclusive personal relationship, would be seriously to damage one's ability to give oneself in marriage, and one's sense of oneself as a psychophysical unity, and one's understanding of the human animal as an image of the creator.

That the only way to save certain people is morally impermissible should not be regarded as surprising. That those who have been acting very evilly should be in a

---

[1] We should note also, that the dissociation of the woman from the parents of the child masks, without removing, the indecency of her relationship to *them*. If one has an embryo implanted in one, a woman becomes something like the father of one's child, as one is made pregnant with her baby. One's quasi-sexual relationship with them increases, as I have said, the number of the sexes. This is the objection to bearing a child for another woman, not merely that it is exploitative. Taking away any suggestion that one is being *used* by the other woman does not alter the indecency of one's relationship to her, that one has allowed oneself to be impregnated with her child, by an act which, on one's own side at least, is importantly similar to the wife's part in the marriage act, in that it is an act of admission which is of kind to make one pregnant.

situation which allows no morally acceptable solution is not surprising at all. Nor is it wrong to exalt reproductive integrity in a way which allows death. Death is what follows the assault on marriage that is involved in unchastity, and death doubled and redoubled has followed that involved in IVF. If women assail their own reproductive integrity by allowing themselves to be made pregnant by mechanical means, death will follow as it always does when men destroy the sense of human dignity.

HELEN WATT

IVF AND OTHER forms of non-sexual conception are, I will assume in this paper, morally wrong. Surrogate motherhood, or pregnancy on behalf of others, is also, I believe, a fragmentation of maternity which has to be excluded. Pregnancy, unlike breast-feeding where the baby is readily transferable from woman to woman, is specifically *maternal* support – it makes a woman a *mother*. In this respect, pregnancy is unique among forms of child nurture. Bringing up a child is normally shared, at least to some extent, with the father and with others, whereas one needs a clinical procedure to be pregnant with another woman's baby. Ideally, pregnancy should have, I want to argue, a particular symbolic content which has to do both with past and future – both with genetic and with social motherhood.

It is therefore wrong to plan in advance of conception (or, if one is not the genetic mother, in advance of gestation) to bear a child who will be brought up by others. A genetic mother may plan to bear and then give up for adoption a child who already exists, but may not conceive a child intentionally whom she does not intend to carry, give birth to and bring up herself.

However, once a child has been conceived, at least *one* break in the continuum 'conception–gestation–birth–child-rearing' is sometimes morally justified. This is the break between prenatal and postnatal nurture – between looking after the child before and after he or she is born. Normal postnatal adoption is far from ideal; however, it is sometimes a good response to the non-ideal situation of existing parents and children.

One reason *why* adoption is not ideal lies in the way in which pregnancy and birth lack the *social significance* they should have. Normally, pregnancy and birth should be a *public sign* both of the child's *destiny* and of the child's *origin*: a sign that the child has come to be through (or partly through) the union of those who will look after him or her. Through pregnancy and birth, the child is publicly established as the child of one woman and, by means of her commitment to her husband, as her husband's child as well. In the case of adoption, pregnancy and birth retain their significance, or some of their significance, with regard to the child's origin, while losing their significance with regard to the child's being looked after by the woman who gives birth. Not surprisingly, adopted children do experience certain identity problems, so that, for example, they will often develop a strong desire to meet their birth parents. It is clearly better if children are not put in such a situation that they must come to terms with their relinquishment – however reluctant – by one or more than one parent.

What I want to argue is that just as the significance of pregnancy and birth with regard to future care need not be present in the case of adoption after birth, the significance of pregnancy and birth with regard to origin need not be present in the case of adoption of an embryo. In the case of embryo adoption, birth does have its normal significance with regard to the child's future care, but lacks its normal significance with regard to his or her origin in an act of marital union. While embryo adoption does, it is true, fragment the maternal role to some extent, it does not create any *more* breaks in this role than does adoption after birth.

Here I would, however, concede that prenatal adoption is less easy to defend than adoption after birth, in that it should not be chosen by the genetic mother if she can bear the child herself. Unless she is literally incapable of bearing the child – because, for example, she has had a hysterectomy – she will normally have a moral obligation to carry him or her to term. In contrast, there are many factors besides sheer incapacity which excuse a birth mother from her *prima facie* obligation to bring her child up. There is therefore *some* sense in which the significance of pregnancy and birth with regard to origin is more important than its significance with regard to future care. Why this is so I am not sure. Pregnancy is, of course, a limited commitment compared to that of bringing up a child; however, there seems to be more to the distinction than this. Perhaps it is more important during than after pregnancy to encourage maternal commitment, since the woman who has gone through nine months with her child is unlikely to relinquish him or her on trivial grounds. Perhaps a mother is best prepared for her postnatal role in which she is hard to replace by a period during which she is even harder to replace as the mother of her child.

In most cases, the genetic mother of the 'surplus' frozen embryo is able to bear the child herself, but is unwilling to do so. There would therefore be serious problems in approaching such a mother for permission to do what she should do herself – gestate her own genetic child. However, if an embryo had already been abandoned by the mother and/or if she had died, disappeared, or was unable to gestate, the embryo could, I want to argue, be gestated by a woman who planned to raise it as her own.

Embryo adoption is not, like surrogate motherhood, the *temporary* assumption of maternal care, but the assumption of *total* maternal responsibility for an orphaned or abandoned child. While maternal care in the case of the orphan embryo has not yet been divided in the sense of being split between two women, it has already been truncated. Embryo adoption does not, therefore, constitute wrongful disruption or distortion of family relationships, given the fact that links with the original mother and father have already been severed, and given the fact that the child will both be gestated and reared by the woman who has it transferred to her womb.

Is the act of embryo transfer by a doctor in any way perverse? Dr Geach has argued that a woman should only allow herself to be made pregnant through normal marital relations. It is, she says, morally wrong to make one's womb available to the child of strangers, and to make one's body available to a technical act of impregnation. Dr Geach has argued that such a procedure shares the fault of IVF and unchaste acts in destroying reproductive integrity. What is normally the result of the marital act is now the result of a technical procedure. Not only is pregnancy normally the result of the marital act, but part of the essence of the marital act is that it is the kind of act which makes a woman pregnant. In having intercourse of the right kind, a woman makes herself available, as far as she can be, to gestate a child as well as to conceive one. For this reason, a woman should not displace the role of the marital act by allowing herself to be made pregnant in other ways.

To this I would respond that the term 'allowing oneself to be made pregnant' covers two quite different intentions, which affect in different ways the morality of what is being done. The first intention is the intention to allow a child *to come to be* – to be created – inside one's body. Such an intention can exist in combination either with the intention to have intercourse or with the intention to have artificial insemination. Intercourse and AID or AIH are different ways of achieving the result that a child is created inside the body of a woman. For this reason, artificial insemination can be seen as wrongfully displacing the marital act: substituting a technical act for the role of husband and wife in causing their child to be conceived.

Quite different from the intention to have a child *come to be* inside one's body is the intention to have a child *put* inside one's body. This intention is present in the case of embryo transfer, but not in the case of intercourse or AID (leaving aside exotic beliefs about the presence of a child within the sperm). Certainly, embryo transfer, intercourse and AID all have in common the fact that a woman allows herself to be made pregnant. However, this description is, I believe, too vague to be helpful, since it covers two kinds of intention which are significantly different.

It might be responded that intercourse causes not only conception but implantation in the womb. Intercourse may not, like embryo transfer, put a child within one's body; however, it does cause the movement of any child conceived from one part of the body to another. Does not embryo transfer do the same? If so, does not embryo transfer displace intercourse in causing implantation, even if it does not displace intercourse in causing conception?

There is no doubt that intercourse of the right kind can, when conditions are right, directly cause conception. 'Openness to life' in having sex means openness to the life-*causing* aspect of sex – openness to conception being directly caused, and not just preceded, by intercourse. Is uterine gestation also directly caused by intercourse, or is intercourse not rather an event which normally precedes it? Surely, what intercourse directly causes is the union of sperm and ovum, not uterine gestation of the embryo so created. While the embryo's creation within the mother's body is, indeed, caused, at least partly, by intercourse, any subsequent positioning of the embryo, and any actual implantation of the embryo, is brought about in other ways. For the embryo to travel down the fallopian tube and implant in the womb, it needs nothing further from its father, but simply the assistance of its mother. The journey of the embryo is, after all, in a different direction, as well as involving a different subject, from the earlier journey of the sperm. It is the mother and embryo, not the father and mother, who cause the embryo to implant.

It is therefore not the case that uterine pregnancy – that is, pregnancy after implantation – is directly caused by intercourse. If this is so, should it still be said that intercourse must *always precede* uterine pregnancy? What I want to argue is that whereas ideally intercourse *should* precede uterine pregnancy, the only *absolute* moral requirement is that intercourse precede – and indeed, directly cause – *in vivo* conception.

The fact that conception and implantation are separate events immediately raises the question of what a woman's duties are after non-marital conception. Take the case of a woman who has conceived as a result of an extramarital affair. Should such a woman not then make her womb available to her child? What if she chose to expel the child before implantation by means of embryo flushing? Even if she had no intention to kill the child, or to invade its body in a way she knew would do it harm, embryo flushing would be a wrongful denial of normal uterine support. Of course, it is not ideal that uterine pregnancy will not now result from a marital act; however, once the child exists the mother has a duty to support it. For the mother, her pregnancy will sadly not be a sign of marital union – nor, perhaps, of future care of the child who will be born. Nonetheless, despite the fact that the symbolism of pregnancy will be in her case impoverished, such a woman has a right and duty to make her womb available to her child.

So much for a woman who can expect to give birth in the normal course of events. What if she needs an intervention by a doctor to help her reach that point? For example, what if the pregnancy develops in the fallopian tube, and the tube is then removed? The woman, now no longer pregnant, is offered a new technique to transfer the embryo to her womb. The woman's new, uterine pregnancy will be preceded not by a marital act, but by a purely technical procedure. Nonetheless, if this procedure carries no great risk or burden for herself, she surely has, not just a right but an obligation to accept it.

Here an analogy might be drawn between implantation and giving birth. In having intercourse 'open to life', a woman normally makes herself available not merely to conceive, if she is fertile at the time, but to give birth to any child she *does* conceive. However, it is only conception, as something directly caused by intercourse, to which a woman must make herself available in order to be open to life. Ideally, giving birth should be the end result of a series of natural events begun by an act of marital union. However, some women do not give birth themselves at the end of this series of events, but need Caesarian sections. Just as a Caesarian section is a non-ideal, but sometimes permissible way of *completing* a pregnancy, so embryo transfer is a non-ideal, but sometimes permissible way of *beginning* a pregnancy.

Even if a woman was originally made pregnant with an ectopic embryo after IVF, there would be no objection, I would argue, to a doctor reinserting the embryo in such a way as to allow the mother to bring it to term. It is not only good for the health of the child that it be placed in the mother's uterus, but good for the mother's own reproductive health. Once a woman has become a mother – genetic and/or gestational – it is in her health interests that her child be safely delivered. The situation in which a woman and her embryo are geographically apart is surely unhealthy both for mother and child. If so, then it seems *prima facie* that an IVF embryo still in the petri dish should be transferred to the genetic mother, for the sake of the welfare of both parties.

Again, it is not ideal that pregnancy result from this kind of intervention. Over and above the disvalue attached to *any* bypassing of normal bodily functions, there is the disvalue attached to the loss of the symbolism pregnancy should carry. However, given the fact that the child has already been conceived in a non-marital way, we need to make the best of a bad deal. To return to the case of the IVF embryo who begins by implanting in the tube, even if this embryo was conceived from a donor ovum, and even if the woman who has the embryo reinserted does not now plan to raise it, her uterine pregnancy is surely basic care for the child she has already been gestating.

It may be objected that in all these cases, the woman to whose body the embryo is transferred is already the mother of that embryo. In having the embryo transferred to her womb, after IVF and/or ectopic pregnancy, the woman is not *becoming a mother* by the act of embryo transfer. A genetic or gestational mother – or even a woman who *has been* a gestational mother – is already a mother, with maternal rights and obligations. Such a woman may become (or become again) a *gestational* mother by means of embryo transfer; however, she is already a mother of *some* kind to the embryo transferred. In this respect she clearly differs from the woman who adopts an orphan embryo, without a pre-existing maternal obligation to nurture that embryo. The adoptive mother will not *go on* acting as a mother to the embryo transferred to her womb; rather, she will *become* a mother by having the embryo transferred and/or by consenting to the transfer.

It is true that there is an additional disvalue attached to the fact that such a woman becomes a mother by means of, or in connection with, a clinical procedure. There are, for one thing, no health interests of the woman to justify the clinical bypass of normal bodily functions. The bypass does not, in this case, help the woman to complete a reproductive project already begun. Once she has had the child transferred to her womb, it will be in her health interests to support it; however, before she has had the child transferred, she has no such health interests. All this is certainly true.

However, here again I want to return to the question of postnatal adoption. Is postnatal adoption the ideal way of becoming a mother or father? Should people ideally become parents through signing forms, filling in questionnaires, or smuggling orphans out of Romania? Ideally, they should not. Adoption of this kind, too, is an imperfect response to the needs of existing children after the death, relinquishment or, sometimes, abandonment of those who had first claim.

What kind of mother should one *not* become except by sexual means in a marital context? Clearly, there is no objection to becoming a *social* mother by non-sexual means, or adoption would be ruled out entirely. Nor, it would appear, is there any objection to becoming a *gestational* mother by such means, if those who are not now gestational mothers – for example, genetic IVF mothers – may have embryos transferred. While ideally genetic, gestational and social motherhood would, of course, be combined, it is only *genetic* motherhood one should *never* seek to achieve by a purely technical procedure.

In supporting the adoption of embryos in principle, I do not wish to minimize the practical problems it would raise. There would be a very real danger of encouraging the view that IVF was morally permissible and/or that there were couples available to take on all future 'spare' embryos. The couple who wanted to adopt an orphan embryo would have to explain their position very clearly both to their friends and family and to the IVF practitioner. In so doing, they might be more convincing if they were not infertile themselves, but already had children of their own. A single woman should not adopt an embryo, as it would be hard to establish *her* good faith, and as she would be, to the eyes of casual observers, just another single parent.

It should be remembered that gestating frozen embryos carries risks for the woman; for example, the risk of ectopic pregnancy may be higher than normal. Moreover, it would be important not to let more embryos be thawed than were transferred to her body, since this would not only cause the death of the embryos *not* transferred, but would confirm the clinic in the view that embryos were expendable.

Despite all these caveats, there might be some cases in which adopting orphan embryos would be morally praiseworthy. Indeed, I can even imagine cases in which it might be morally obligatory, because one was morally responsible for the embryo's being conceived. The woman who commissions the production of embryos from her husband's sperm and another woman's ova bears considerable responsibility for the fate of any embryos left on ice. If the ovum donor is unwilling or unable to gestate, a woman who regrets the commission might rightly consider she herself has a duty to gestate, in groups of two or three, all remaining frozen embryos.

Pregnancy is, eventually at least, a public sign – a social event. There is, however, a sense in which pregnancy is also a period of family privacy – of *exclusive* relationships – following on from a similarly exclusive act of procreation. This exclusivity – greater than that involved in subsequent 'parenting' – is a sign that the relationship of parents to their children is in some way unique. Through pregnancy, parents are given a chance to bond with the child before his or her more public life; a life in which he or she will sometimes be cared for by others, just as the parents will sometimes care for other people's children. It is important for a child to know that he or she was born from his or her social parents, and for a pregnant woman and her husband to know that she is carrying *their child*. However, there is a very real sense in which the woman who adopts an orphan embryo is carrying a child who *is* now her child and her husband's. If this is so, would not the exclusivity of pregnancy be sufficiently maintained, at least in the case of a child who already exists? To return one final time to the case of postnatal adoption, are there reasons of so much greater force against the transfer of maternal roles before a birth has taken place?

# 22

# Is the 'medical management' of ectopic pregnancy by the administration of methotrexate morally acceptable?

## I.

### CHRISTOPHER KACZOR

I BELIEVE THE answer to this question must be a qualified "no." Pope John Paul II in *Evangelium Vitae* wrote: "Therefore, by the authority which Christ conferred upon Peter and his Successors, and in communion with the Bishops of the Catholic Church, *I confirm that the direct and voluntary killing of an innocent human being is always gravely immoral.*"[1] John Paul later applies this principle specifically to the case of abortion: "[B]y the authority which Christ conferred upon Peter and his Successors, in communion with the Bishops – who on various occasions have condemned abortion and who in the aforementioned consultation, albeit dispersed throughout the world, have shown unanimous agreement concerning this doctrine – *I declare that direct abortion, that is, abortion willed as an end or as a means, always constitutes a grave moral disorder*, since it is the deliberate killing of an innocent human being."[2] He continues: "This evaluation of the morality of abortion is to be applied also to the recent forms of intervention on human embryos...."[3] Arguably these moral principles are infallibly taught in accord with the teaching of *Lumen Gentium* as cited in the notes that follow the proclamations. Although I believe that such teachings are also philosophically defensible, today I will not defend these principles but instead will presuppose that a Catholic answer to the questions raised by ectopic pregnancy must be in accord with these principles.[4] My remarks then will presuppose both that intentionally killing, mutilating, or risking the injury of an innocent person is morally wrong and that human life from the moment of conception should be given the respect accorded to an innocent person.

The application of these norms to concrete cases is in many ways difficult. The word "direct" in the quotation from *Evangelium Vitae* refers to the intention of an

[1] John Paul II, *Evangelium Vitae*, 57, emphasis in the original.
[2] John Paul II, *Evangelium Vitae*, 62, emphasis in the original.
[3] John Paul II, *Evangelium Vitae*, 62.
[4] I assume throughout that the human conceptus implanted in the fallopian tube should receive the respect due innocent human life.

agent and is used in this context in contrast to the "indirect" or the foreseen effects of an agent's act. Hence, one's account of intention determines whether or not a given act resulting in death should be accounted as "direct" or "indirect" killing. In addition, even if one does not intend an evil effect, nevertheless even permitting or allowing an evil effect can, at least at times, be morally wrong.

The first question at hand is the following. Is the use of methotrexate to treat ectopic pregnancy direct or intentional killing? Methotrexate is one non-surgical method of managing ectopic pregnancy. It is also used to treat forms of cancer and arthritis. The drug acts in the case of ectopic pregnancy by inhibiting cellular reproduction in the recently conceived.[5] The drug thus simultaneously injures the conceptus and relieves the possible danger to the mother. Is the negative effect of embryonic death intended or not?

One account of intention, arguably put forward by Aquinas and clearly put forward by later writers in the Catholic tradition, holds that not only the immediate effect desired but also all concomitant effects are intended by the agent. On this 'broad' account of intention, the good desired effects and evil undesired effects, in so far as they are chronologically simultaneous and are always or often connected, are all considered intended. If one goes jogging, one intends all that is necessarily connected with and/or chronologically simultaneous with jogging, i.e., perspiring, increasing one's heart rate, wearing out one's running shoes, becoming more healthy, etc. If one adopts this 'broad' account of intention, then even though the *death* of the human conceptus caused by the administration of methotrexate is not desired as effecting the end of preserving the life of the mother, the death is nevertheless intended. Given this broad account of intention, the use of methotrexate to treat ectopic pregnancy is intentional or "direct" killing of an innocent person. Hence, it is "gravely immoral."

The other account of intention held by a number of authors in the Catholic tradition has been called the 'narrow' account of intention. On the 'narrow' account of intention, one advocated by Germain Grisez and John Finnis among others, only what is one's goal and what is chosen precisely as contributing to the achievement of one's goal is properly said to be intended. When one jogs with a view to becoming healthy, becoming healthy as a result of jogging and all that contributes in the activity of jogging to becoming healthy, such as a rise in heart-rate, are properly intended by the agent. Other aspects of the act, say wearing out one's running shoes, are not intended, even though these effects may be necessarily connected and chronologically simultaneous with running.

If one adopts a narrow account of intention, then the death of the human conceptus in the use of methotrexate to treat ectopic pregnancy would not be intended. The *death* as such contributes nothing to the restoration of health in the mother. The cessation of growth and a change in the location of the human conceptus alone are intended. If the narrow account of intention is true, then in

---

[5] Jean DeBlois CSJ, 'Ectopic Pregnancy' in Jean DeBlois CSJ (ed) *A Primer for Health Care Ethics: Essays for a Pluralistic Society* Washington, D.C.: Georgetown University Press 1996, p. 209.

using methotrexate to treat ectopic pregnancy, one does not intentionally or "directly" kill an innocent person.

One does however strictly intend to inhibit the cellular reproduction of the newly conceived and its necessary supporting organ the trophoblast. This intended effect, without further addition, constitutes a serious injury to the health of the fetus. Intending to inflict serious injury on the health of another, except, according to some writers, by those responsible for the common good, is forbidden as a form of mutilation (on the reasons why mutilation is wrong, one may want to look at St Thomas Aquinas, *Summa theologiae* 2a 2ae q.65 art. 1). Hence, although one does not on the narrow account strictly intend to *kill* with the use of methotrexate, one does strictly intend to *mutilate*. Mutilation, like the intentional killing of the innocent, is an intrinsically evil act. Hence, the use of methotrexate is not licit, even if one adopts a narrow account of intention.

Nor can one invoke in this instance the 'principle of totality', as we could for example in the removal of a cancerous organ. For the mother and conceived child are not one being, or one totality, but two. The use of methotrexate is aimed at affecting the newly conceived and not at affecting merely a part of the woman's body, as is the case in the removal of a gravid cancerous uterus. The conceived human person does not belong to the mother nor is the 'value' of the embryo contingent upon its contribution to the mother's health as are the organs of the mother's body.

Hence, given a broad account of intention, the use of methotrexate is illicit under the description of the intentional killing of the innocent. Given a narrow account of intention, the use of methotrexate to treat ectopic pregnancy is illicit under the description of mutilation of the conceptus.

There is, however, one kind of case described as "ectopic pregnancy" in the literature in which the use of methotrexate *per se* is not morally objectionable. These are cases of what is called "persistent ectopic pregnancy."[6] Sometimes, although the human conceptus is no longer present, the trophoblast (the layer of tissue which normally nourishes the newly conceived) continues to develop. This continued growth can lead to hemorrhaging, just as in the case of the growth of the human embryo in the tube. Use of methotrexate in cases of "persistent ectopic pregnancy" would be neither intentional killing nor intentional mutilation, and hence would be, other things being equal, licit.

It is far from clear however that other things are indeed equal. Counterfactually let us suppose that the use of methotrexate in order to effect the human conceptus was neither intentional killing nor intentional mutilation. This alone could not allow one to conclude that the use of methotrexate is licit. It would seem clear that on either account of intention, an agent ought to avoid foreseen evil effects, if this can be reasonably done. Thomas's account of self-defense as offered in *Summa theologiae* 2a 2ae, question 64, article 7 is helpful

---

[6] Hans-Göran Hagström MD, Mats Hahlin MD, Barbro Bennegard-Éden MD, Peter Sjöblom PhD, Jande Thorburn MD, and Bo Lindblom MD, 'Prediction of Persistent Ectopic Pregnancy after Salpingostomy' 84 (1994) *Obstetrics and Gynecology*, pp. 798–802.

here. "[I]t can happen that some act proceeding from a good intention, be rendered illicit, if it is not proportioned to the end ( *proportionatus fini* ). Therefore," Thomas writes, "if someone for the sake of defending his life uses *more force than is necessary* it will be illicit." If one can defend one's life from attack by fleeing rather than fighting, one ought to flee. If one has to fight, one ought to use lighter force rather than deadly force if both will secure self-defense.

The treatment of ectopic pregnancy by methotrexate may be such a case of using deadly force when lighter force can achieve the same end. Methotrexate can be used only in early ectopic pregnancy before rupture or other serious damage to the fallopian tube. At this stage of ectopic pregnancy, there are other options available that will both secure the protection of the mother's health and preserve the mother's fertility in the affected fallopian tube.

There are three such options. The first option is known as salpingostomy, that is, the surgical removal of the embryo alone leaving the tube intact. If one adopts a narrow account of intention, salpingostomy, that is the opening of the tube and the "gentle" removal of the conceptus,[7] may be seen as licit. The death itself contributes nothing to the goal of preserving the mother's life, but only the alteration in the location of the human embryo. In fact, salpingostomy will often, *but not necessarily*, bring about the death of the conceptus. In the majority of cases the newly conceived does die. Still, there is one documented case of a salpingostomy resulting in the live birth of a healthy baby boy.[8] Advances in microsurgery could make salpingostomy an even more attractive option for preserving the newly conceived life while also retaining the functional capacity of the fallopian tube.

The second option is the removal of the segment of the tube containing the pregnancy with subsequent anastomosis or reconnection of the two sections of the tube. This technique, a form of the longstandingly approved "salpingectomy," that is, the removal of the entire tube along with the human embryo, is fully licit on either a wide or a narrow account of intention. The death of the embryo is not, in these cases, a means or an end to preserving the mother's life. At the same time, this form of salpingectomy preserves the mother's fertility.

Nor can we assume in an attempt at a *reductio ad absurdum*, following James Keenan, that even salpingectomy fails to fit the Principle of Double Effect paradigm of the removal of a cancerous gravid uterus. On this view, if we applied traditional Catholic teaching to the question of ectopic pregnancy, we would be forced to simply stand by and hope that the conceptus spontaneously aborted, knowingly doing nothing to prevent the likely death of the mother. Hence, traditional principles cannot be applied to this case.

Although it is true that in the case of ectopic pregnancy the presence of the embryo is not 'accidental' to the excision of the tube, i.e., "the embryo's removal is intrinsic to the order of activity; the only part of the tube to be removed is that in

---

[7] Jean DeBlois CSJ, 'Ectopic Pregnancy' in *op. cit.*, p. 209.
[8] C J Wallace MD, 'Transplantation of Ectopic Pregnancy from Fallopian Tube to Cavity of Uterus', 24 (1917) *Surgery, Gynecology, and Obstetrics* pp. 578–579.

which the embryo adheres'', it does not follow that salpingectomy is illicit according to traditional principles. Indeed, the two cases are not perfectly analogous. In one case the womb is removed because of cancer and in the other case the tube is removed because of the embryo. However, in both cases – and here the analogy between the cancerous uterus case and the ectopic pregnancy case holds – though the causes are different the result is the same – a pathological organ. The tube is a damaged one, one that threatens the life of the mother now through uncontrolled bleeding and threatens in the future through increased likelihood of recurring ectopic pregnancy. Even if the embryo were dead, the tube would often still need to be removed. The presence of the embryo is in this way, the relevant way, directly analogous to the presence of the fetus in the case of the cancerous uterus.

Finally, there is the "milking" or "squeezing" technique. Medical doctors Diamond and DeCherney describe this technique as follows: "In this procedure, the tube is grasped just proximal to the site of dilation and then compressed, advancing toward the infundibular aspect of the tube. In this manner, the products of conception are excluded from the fimbria."[9] Like the salpingectomy, the "milking" technique avoids the intentional bringing about of the evil effect on either a broad or a narrow account of intention. This "squeezing" technique leaves open the possibility of the pregnancy proceeding in a normal way. Most often the newly conceived dies, but implantation in the uterus is not a possibility which can be altogether excluded.

This "milking" technique when compared with the use of methotrexate is better not only for the newly conceived but also for the mother. The milking technique avoids the side effects associated with the use of methotrexate while also being effective in preserving both maternal health and respect for the human conceptus. A study by Capi and Sherman concludes: "[T]he postoperative results [of the milking technique] are remarkably good, even when compared with the more popular salpingostomy. When tissue is handled gently and vigorous 'milking' efforts are avoided, this procedure is not only harmless but may technically prove to be the simplest and the most beneficial in terms of subsequent fertility."[10] Although other studies suggest an increase in the rate of future ectopic pregnancies as a result of this technique,[11] this option at present seems like the most promising way of treating ectopic pregnancy detected at an early stage.

Although the use of methotrexate is advantageous in not being a surgical intervention, the use of such a powerful drug may be in the end even more disadvantageous than surgery. Methotrexate, as is well known, has many side

---

[9] Diamond and DeCherney, 'Surgical Management of Ectopic Pregnancy' in 30 (1987) *Clinical Obstetrics and Gynecology* p. 205.

[10] Capi and Sherman, 'Tubal Abortion and Infundibular Ectopic Pregnancy' in 30 (1987) *Clinical Obstetrics and Gynecology* p. 162.

[11] Some studies report an increase in the rate of future extrauterine pregnancies (Oelsner, 'Ectopic Pregnancy in the Remaining Tube and the Management of the Patient with Multiple Ectopic Pregnancies' 30 (1987) *Clinical Obstetrics and Gynecology* pp. 225–229, at 226) others do not (Capi and Sherman, *op. cit.*, p. 162).

effects avoided by the other options about which we have spoken. The reported side-effects of methotrexate in the treatment of ectopic pregnancy include upset stomach, nausea, vomiting, sleeplessness, hot flushes, sores in the mouth, abdominal pain, loss of appetite, diarrhea, dizziness, mood alterations, decrease in red blood cell count requiring blood transfusion, and, rarely, lung and liver damage. Of course, the side effects vary from person to person and some side effects may be decreased or eliminated with the use of other drugs. Still, these side effects of methotrexate have resulted in hospital stays, documented in one study, of between 8 and 25 days.[12] These powerful side-effects have caused some medical doctors to question the usefulness of methotrexate in treating ectopic pregnancy: "At this point in time, chemotherapy [by means of methotrexate] offers a viable alternative to surgery in a small select number of cases as mentioned above. Its routine use is not yet justified, however, where conservative surgery [i.e., salpingostomy] has proven efficacy."[13] Louis Weinstein, in the *American Journal of Gynecology*, wrote: "Simply stated, the use of a potent antineoplastic, anti-metabolite drug, methotrexate, for treatment of an ectopic pregnancy is inappropriate and potentially dangerous."[14]

In conclusion, the use of methotrexate to treat ectopic pregnancy is not morally justified. If the broad account of intention is adopted, then its use is morally excluded under the description of intentionally killing an innocent person. If the narrow account of intention is adopted, then its use is morally excluded under the description of intentionally mutilating an innocent person. Finally, even if the use of methotrexate is not illicit as intentional killing or mutilating, it is disproportionate to its end. Given the other options of treatment available, options less harmful to both mother and child, the use of methotrexate brings about foreseen evil effects that one could have and should have avoided.

---

[12] Steven J Ory MD, Alelei L Villanueva MD, Peter K Sand MD, and Ralph K Tumura MD, 'Conservative Treatment of Ectopic Pregnancy with Methotrexate' *American Journal of Obstetrics and Gynecology* (June 1986) pp. 1299–1306, at 1304.
[13] Bruce S Shapiro MD, 'The Nonsurgical Management of Ectopic Pregnancy' 30 (1987) *Clinical Obstetrics and Gynecology* pp. 230–235, at 232.
[14] Quoted in Steven J Ory MD et al., *op. cit.*, p. 1304.

## 2.

## GERALD GLEESON

DR CHRISTOPHER KACZOR'S argument that methotrexate ought not be used in the treatment of an ectopic pregnancy is a powerful one. Given that methotrexate (MTX) prevents the continued development of the embryo, it is not difficult to see why one would conclude that its use constitutes a direct killing of the embryo in the interests of the mother's health and future fertility. Nonetheless, many people do not think that "directly killing or harming the embryo" is always the appropriate description for this use of MTX. They regard an ectopic pregnancy as a pathological situation which threatens the lives of both mother and embryo, and they simply look to whatever surgical or chemical intervention is indicated as the most effective and least invasive way of resolving this situation, while doing minimal harm to the mother's future reproductive capacity.

In this response I explore points of unresolved tension in Catholic moral theology which might provide a basis for justifying the latter view. I will consider three issues of method in moral theology which are relevant to this and to other difficult moral questions, such as the early induction of a fetus which is unable to live independently, methods of fertility testing for males, ways of assisting human conception, the withdrawal of nutrition and hydration, the use of condoms to prevent transmission of HIV, and so on. The resolution of all these disputed questions turns on crucial judgments about the correct description of an agent's moral object, of what an agent is actually doing, and about what constitutes an "intrinsically disordered" kind of action. The three issues I will consider are: (a) the relationship between moral principles and particular cases; (b) the characterisation of the moral object in direct killing; and (c) the principle of double effect.

In the course of my discussion it will become clear why I am considering the justification of the use of MTX only in those cases in which it is morally certain that the life of the embryo cannot be saved. I agree, of course, that to the extent to which it is possible, without endangering a mother's health or life, either to wait or to intervene in order to give a developing embryo a chance of survival one should do so (e.g. by using the squeezing technique mentioned by Dr Kaczor). As early diagnosis and micro-surgery techniques advance further, we may expect the possibilities for saving embryos which have not implanted correctly to increase markedly. Accordingly, I will argue that the most decisive consideration with respect to the moral evaluation of MTX is not so much the physical effect of the drug, but whether, in the circumstances of its proposed use, there is an obligation to give the embryo an opportunity to continue to develop.

## I. The relationship between principles and cases

The straightforward moral objection to the use of MTX is that it involves an assault on the developing embryo, since it inhibits DNA synthesis, and the development of the trophoblastic cells, as the embryo embeds itself in the tissue of the mother's fallopian tube. The central moral question, therefore, is whether this use of MTX involves "direct killing" of the developing embryo. The relevant magisterial teaching was most recently affirmed in *Evangelium Vitae* s.57: "the direct and voluntary killing of an innocent human being is always gravely immoral". Although the application of this teaching to the present issue may seem obvious enough, the first question I wish to raise concerns the explanatory relationship between principles and prudential judgments about particular cases. Do principles explain prudential judgments, or do prudential judgments about what ought be done in particular cases shed light on the meaning of the principles?

Along with many Catholic moralists, I am inclined to the latter view. Principles articulate and summarise the practical wisdom exhibited in particular judgments, they manifest the congruency of moral rationale between like cases.[15] Abortion and euthanasia both involve "direct killing of the innocent", but we do not, I suggest, deduce that abortion and euthanasia are wrong because they involve direct killing of the innocent. Rather, understanding why abortion and euthanasia are wrong, along with understanding why some killings in warfare or self-defence may not be wrong, contributes to our understanding of what the direct killing of the innocent consists in. This is why the authoritative teaching in *Evangelium Vitae* does not, without further inquiry, settle such complex moral issues as the treatment of an ectopic pregnancy or the early induction of a fetus whose condition is incompatible with independent life. The key terms such as 'direct', 'voluntary' and 'innocent' are the subject of legitimate theological and philosophical debate, and this as part of a wider debate about the correct way to describe and evaluate human actions.

The treatment of ectopic pregnancy raises 'borderline issues' about what constitutes a 'direct' killing. Moreover, right reasoning and prudential judgment on such issues involves evaluation: in concluding that a particular killing is 'direct', we are thereby judging it to be wrong. This does not mean that 'direct killing' cannot, for the most part, be identified in a non-evaluative or descriptive way, viz. as killing the innocent. There is not usually any doubt about whether a voluntary action is a killing, or about whether the victim is innocent. However, the existence of borderline cases in which the descriptive explication of a moral category needs further refinement suggests that such moral categories cannot be reduced to wholly descriptive categories.[16]

That the concept of 'direct killing' is ultimately a moral category is, I think, reflected in *Evangelium Vitae* s.55, where it is said that in legitimate self defence "the fatal outcome is attributable to the aggressor whose action brought it about". Pope John Paul II seems to be suggesting that the direct responsibility for a lethal defensive act lies with the aggressor; it is this moral consideration

15 See for example: James F. Keenan, 'The Function of the Principle of Double Effect', 54 (1993) *Theological Studies*, pp. 294–315, and Jean Porter, *Moral Action and Christian Ethics* Cambridge: Cambridge University Press 1995, pp. 1–40.
16 See J. M. Brennan, *The Open Texture of Moral Concepts* New York: Barnes and Noble 1977.

which makes the lethal act of the defender an 'indirect' killing (even when, presumably, the chosen defensive act will certainly be lethal, will be, with respect to its causality, a 'direct' killing).[17]

## 2. How is direct killing to be understood?

This brings me to my second question, namely about the correct description of human actions. As *Veritatis Splendor* s.78 reminds us, in the Catholic tradition moral description and evaluation go hand in hand, and centre on the identification of the 'moral object' of one's activity. Yet the concept of the moral object is 'essentially contested' in that it is the focus for continuing debates between rival ethical theories within Catholic moral theology. The Church does not endorse any one ethical theory (*Veritatis Splendor* s.29), though it does direct us to the thought of St Thomas. But, since moral action shares in the mystery of the human person, it may be supposed that absolute clarity about an agent's moral object will not always be attainable. The moral object (and hence the evaluation) of some kinds of action might always remain 'essentially contested'.

For Catholic theologians the priority of the 'moral object', after the mind of St Thomas, requires that direct killing be identified and understood from the viewpoint of the acting subject, that is, in terms of the agent's intended purpose, not in terms of the physical causality of an action. The 'object' is the 'subject matter' of an action as revealed in the purposeful reasoning by which the agent gives intelligibility to what he or she actually does. For this reason, Thomas distinguishes between the agent's "inner object" (the object of reason accepted and intended by the will) and the "external action" in which that object is realised. Inner object and external object are related as form and matter, as the *materia circa quam* and the *materia ex qua* which together constitute a particular moral act.

Accordingly, the different ways in which human actions are described may be located on a spectrum between the poles of formal and material description (as "inner" object and as "external realisation" respectively). Some action descriptions are ambiguous between these two modes of description, e.g. 'direct killing' is ambiguous between directly causing death and directly intended to cause death. I believe that the tension between material and formal action descriptions is central to the moral debate about the use of MTX to resolve an ectopic pregnancy, and to the other vexed moral issues noted above.

Viewed in its physical causality, MTX is about as 'directly lethal' to the embryo as any intervention could be. But, viewed in its moral intelligibility, many people regard the use of MTX not as a killing, but as a minimally invasive intervention to counter a life-threatening pathology in a situation where the embryo cannot be saved. Are people entitled to invoke this description despite the evidence as to

---

[17] But cf. Thomas A. Cavanaugh, 'Aquinas's Account of Double Effect', 61 (1997) *The Thomist*, pp. 107–121, who argues that Thomas did not permit certainly lethal defensive actions.

how MTX works? Or: Is the way in which MTX is lethal to the embryo sufficient to establish that its use must involve the evil of direct killing? In order to answer these questions, we need to address the more general question about the relationship between, on the one hand, the meaning and intention an agent gives to his or her action and, on the other hand, the external actions the agent performs. Is an agent's moral object ultimately determined by the external action performed, or is the agent's formal intention able to determine, and finally re-shape, the meaning of his or her external actions? This issue is at the heart of some current debates in Catholic moral theology, and two approaches to it can be identified.

## (a) The primacy of the intentional

On the one side are those authors who question the derivation of the moral object from the external action. James F. Keenan, for example, argues that for St Thomas actions are defined in terms of agency, such that "the object" of one's action is the "proximate content of one's intention rather than the physical action" one performs. The object of one's intention is prior to and able to inform one's external action.[18] "One is hard pressed to find anywhere in Thomas's writings an explicit derivation of an 'object' from an exterior act."[19] For this reason, Keenan argues, it is easier to identify wrong or disordered intentions than it is to identify precisely which external actions are the embodiment of disordered objects and intentions. For example: whereas the intention to exercise dominion over a child as a commodity, and the intention to subordinate the conception of a child to the prowess of technology, are clearly disordered intentions, Keenan says it is less obvious which particular procedures to achieve conception must constitute wrong actions because they embody these disordered intentions.[20] Likewise, we may ask whether the use of MTX to resolve an ectopic pregnancy must embody the disordered intention to kill an embryo in order to save the mother's life.

Of course, every action has many descriptions. The challenge for those who give primacy to intention is to explain how intention governs the correct description of action. The most noteworthy response to this challenge is that of Germain Grisez, who accounts for the content of an intention in terms of a theory of practical reasoning with respect to basic goods. He argues that the primacy of the agent's intention requires us to describe the agent's external action under the precise description it has as intended by the agent as a means to achieving the good end-state which is the agent's goal. In this vein, Grisez

[18] James F. Keenan, 'Moral Horizons in Health Care: Reproductive Technologies and Catholic Identity', in K. Wm. Wildes (ed.) *Infertility: A Crossroad of Faith, Medicine, and Technology* Dordrecht: Kluwer Academic 1997, pp. 53–71, at 55.
[19] James F. Keenan, *Goodness and Rightness in Thomas Aquinas's Summa Theologiae* Washington, DC: Georgetown University Press 1992, p. 81.
[20] Keenan, 'Moral Horizons', pp. 55, 64.

supposes that a woman could simply want the end-state of not being pregnant and, without in any way desiring or intending the death of the fetus, have an abortion, where this is understood and formally chosen not as an act of killing, but as an act of ending the state of pregnancy.[21] Grisez believes such an abortion would be wrong because unjust; nonetheless, he does not think the woman would be guilty of directly intending to kill the fetus, for "someone might choose to abort without choosing to kill". Likewise, it has been suggested that a doctor crushing a baby's head to resolve a situation in which prolonged labour is life-threatening to mother and child, may be choosing merely to "re-size" the baby's head, but not to kill it, since "re-sizing" is all that is strictly required as a means to ending labour.[22] On Grisez's account, the death of the fetus in these examples would be "indirect" with respect to the agent's formally intended end, and hence the actions would not be direct killings.

The explanation of the 'direct' and 'indirect' distinction which is central to Grisez's theory has been strongly criticised.[23] Two criticisms are relevant to my discussion. First, Grisez's focus on the selective description of actions in formally intended terms has the paradoxical consequence that an agent's chosen actions do not have moral meaning in themselves, but only insofar as they are associated with the attitude of the agent's will towards an end or good.[24] Secondly, Grisez's account of intention focuses on the psychology of the agent, on the agent's stated understanding of what he or she is doing. This approach allows an agent to over-ride what may be, from the moral viewpoint, the more accurate description of an action chosen as a means, when in reality it is a mark of moral maturity and virtue to recognise with lucidity what one is actually doing in pursuit of one's ends.

*Pace* Grisez, the distinction between 'direct' and 'indirect' killing is ultimately a moral distinction. That in the mind of a particular agent a death causing action is only 'indirectly' related to the goal sought, is not enough to establish that morally the action is an 'indirect' killing. As much as a person might truthfully say, "I only intended to end this pregnancy, I didn't intend the fetus to die", in some cases it will be a ground for moral criticism that the person supposed he was entitled to describe his action in this narrow way. A critic could rightly object, "You may not say, 'I'm just ending a pregnancy', for in these circumstances ending a pregnancy is (directly) killing a fetus." It follows that although moral action must be understood "from the perspective of the acting subject", moral action and evaluation is rightly understood, not from the perspective of just any subject, but only from the perspective of the virtuous subject, the *phronimos* or person of

[21] Germain Grisez, *The Way of the Lord Jesus, Vol II. Living a Christian Life* Quincy, IL: Fransciscan Press, 1993, p. 500.
[22] See Joseph M. Boyle, 'Double Effect and a Certain Type of Embryotomy', 44 (1977) *Irish Theological Quarterly*, pp. 303–318. For a critique of this view, see Kevin Flannery, 'What is Included in a Means to an End?', 74 (1993) *Gregorianum*, pp. 499–513.
[23] See Flannery, 'What is Included', and, most recently, Jean Porter, ' "Direct" and "Indirect" in Grisez's Moral Theory', 57 (1996) *Theological Studies*, pp. 611–632.
[24] I owe this point to Stephen J. Jensen, 'A Defense of Physicalism', 61 (1997) *The Thomist*, pp. 377–404, at 399.

practical wisdom. The moral judgment on what one is actually doing and (formally intending) is, for St Thomas, a matter of 'right reasoning' (*recta ratio*) by which the acting subject aspires to that 'objective' judgment on action which the person of practical wisdom would make.[25]

The distinction between one's rightly intended object and the various intentional features of one's action is normally clear-cut: the doctor removing a cancerous uterus may truly say, "The death of the fetus is not my intention, it is neither my goal nor a means to it". But on some occasions, only right reasoning and prudential judgment can determine whether circumstances and features of an action truly belong to an agent's object or whether they are indeed incidental, and 'outside' the intention. At all times, of course, the side-effects and incidental effects of one's action remain intentional in the broad sense, and so morally relevant, precisely because they need to be acknowledged and evaluated in relation to the agent's formal purpose.

In short, I am arguing that, *pace* Grisez, it is not possible to develop a morally neutral, or pre-moral, account of what is or is not formally and directly intended by an agent. There is often a tension between the intended subject matter of one's action and its external realisation, between the formal intentionality embodied in an action, what is "strictly required" (in Grisez's sense) for the achievement of one's purpose, and the many other descriptions of an action under which it is knowingly and intentionally undertaken. That the resolution of this tension is the work of prudence and right reasoning is confirmed by consideration of an alternative approach to the determination of the moral object.

### (b) The primacy of the physical

On the other side of the debate over the meaning of the moral object are those who argue that we cannot always "confine the agent's actual [i.e. formal] intention to what is strictly required" (in Grisez's sense).[26] For how, it might be asked, can an agent's intentions be characterised other than in terms of a description of the very actions he or she chooses to perform?[27] That an agent knowingly and voluntarily does what is certain to be lethal is surely strong evidence that the agent is intending to kill. Some effects of what one does are simply "too close" to the realisation of one's formal intention to be merely incidental effects. In self-defence, for example, the degree of force necessary in the circumstances and the foreseen death of the assailant may not be distinguishable effects of the same act. This is the thought which underlies William E. May's argument against the use of both MTX and salpingostomy (surgical removal of the embryo) in treating the ectopic pregnancy:

---

[25] See my study, 'A Living Catholic Conscience' in Richard Lennan (ed.) *Redefining the Church* Sydney: E J Dwyer, 1995, pp. 103–128.
[26] Suzanne Uniacke, *Permissible Killing – The self-defence justification of homicide* Cambridge: Cambridge University Press, 1994, p. 109.
[27] See Jensen, 'A Defense of Physicalism', pp. 394–404.

the death dealing effects of these treatments, he argues, are so immediate and so closely connected with the good effect of ending the ectopic pregnancy that they must constitute 'intentional' and 'direct' killing as a means to one's end.[28]

Despite its appeal to commonsense, emphasis on the physical nature of the actions one performs is also problematic. Firstly, it is out of keeping with the spirit of St Thomas's approach, in which "the notion of object is a primary notion: it is not derived from the external act or from the end; rather it gives meaning to both".[29] Knowing an agent's immediate purpose is often essential to knowing what an agent is doing, particularly when an action has several effects, only some of which are intended. In any case, appeal to the physical effects of an action as determinative of an agent's moral object is often inconclusive precisely because the physical facts are open to various interpretations. Where William E. May thinks it quite evident that salpingostomy involves direct killing, other moralists such as Albert S. Moraczewski conclude that salpingostomy "is the removal of damaged tissue and detachment of the trophoblast (of the embryo) from the abnormal site. The specific focus of the surgical action is the removal of damaged tubal tissue and damaging trophoblastic tissue, not the destruction or death of the embryo".[30] Similarly, Moraczewski's reading of the scientific evidence is that MTX does not directly kill the embryo by destroying the trophoblast; it rather stops the DNA synthesis by which the trophoblast grows and implants in the tissue of the fallopian tube.[31] On Moraczewski's interpretation, the physical action of stopping protein synthesis is distinct from the physical action of attacking the trophoblast/embryo. For many, of course, this is a distinction without a difference.

If neither Grisez's 'intentionalist' account of the object in terms of the agent's attitude to good end-states, nor May's 'physicalist' account of the object in terms of natural causality are satisfactory, we have reason to conclude that right reasoning and prudential judgment cannot be reduced either to abstract intentions or to physical causality. The tension between an agent's intended meaning and his or her external action is fundamental, and while often resolved without difficulty, this tension can sometimes only be resolved by prudential judgment. Grisez has suggested that Thomas's account of inner and external action is 'incoherent'.[32] I am suggesting that Thomas's account provides the flexibility needed for understanding how the same external action may embody diverse moral objects. This flexibility provides the necessary scope for those moral

---

[28] William E. May, 'The Management of Ectopic Pregnancies: A Moral Analysis', in Peter J. Cataldo & Albert S. Moraczewski (eds.) *The Fetal Tissue Issue – Medical and Ethical Issues* Braintree, MA: The Pope John Center, 1994, pp. 121–147.

[29] Keenan, *Goodness and Rightness*, p. 81.

[30] Albert S. Moraczewski, 'Managing Tubal Pregnancies: Part I', 21 (June 1996) *Ethics and Medics*, p. 4.

[31] Albert S. Moraczewski, 'Managing Tubal Pregnancies: Part II', 21 (August 1996) *Ethics and Medics*, pp. 3–4.

[32] Germain Grisez, *The Way of the Lord Jesus, Vol I. Christian Moral Principles* Chicago: Franscis- can Herald Press 1983, p. 247.

judgments by which a virtuous agent makes the final determination as to what he or she is doing.

In terms of the form/matter analogy favoured by Thomas, "the matter" of an external action will be such as to exclude some formal meanings or intentions, while also being able to accept a wider range of formal meanings than may be conventionally recognised. Thus, the physical effect of MTX is such that its use could not embody an agent's intention to treat a mother without lessening the embryo's chance of survival. If used at a time when the embryo ought be given a chance to continue its development, the use of MTX could not but constitute a pre-emptive intervention, which would be unjustified because lethal to the embryo. But in circumstances in which the judgment is rightly made that nothing can be done to save the embryo, and that an intervention to protect the mother from the invasive action of implantation is necessary, the use of MTX might embody the prudential judgment that it is the minimally invasive treatment, clinically indicated with respect to effectiveness and side-effects.

In other words, attention to the details of what one is actually choosing to do, viz. about how MTX works, is necessary, but not sufficient for moral evaluation. What matters most in the Thomistic perspective is the evaluation of the agent's object or intention. Should the agent be attempting to save the embryo or should the agent be attempting to care for the mother, knowing that the embryo cannot be saved? This is the primary issue which establishes the "trajectory" of the agent's purpose, for which the agent then seeks a "trajectory of realisation" in appropriate external actions.[33] Neither MTX nor salpingostomy could be a suitable realisation of the former object, but given the primacy of intention their physical causality (or "matter") does not of itself rule out MTX or salpingostomy as suitable realisations of the latter object. This proposal is thoroughly Thomistic insofar as the primary concern is whether the practical reasoning embodied in the choice to use MTX involves any injustice to the developing embryo.

## 3. The principle of double effect (PDE)

This proposal is reinforced by consideration of my third question, namely about the use of double effect reasoning in relation to the treatment of ectopic pregnancies. Double effect is usually regarded as the only acceptable way of justifying interventions to resolve an ectopic pregnancy. But is treatment of an ectopic pregnancy really congruous with such paradigm cases of double effect as removing a cancerous uterus while a woman is pregnant? Whereas a cancerous uterus would need to be removed whether a woman was pregnant or not, in the case of the ectopic pregnancy, "we are cutting the tube [e.g. in salpingostomy] only because the embryo is there...the embryo's removal is intrinsic to the object of the activity: the only part of the tube to be removed is that in which

---

[33] The metaphor of trajectory is used by Keenan, *Goodness and Rightness*, p. 78.

the embryo adheres".[34] William E. May concludes from this fact that salpingostomy is not permissible. James Keenan, on the other hand, seeks a justification for salpingostomy by analogy with other cases of defensive activity which occasion harm. "To confirm that ending an ectopic pregnancy is morally right, we can look for congruency with other internally-certain cases that belong to a rubric other than double-effect."[35]

So the final question I wish to consider is whether there can be a justification for defensive actions which cause harm, other than in terms of double effect. I have space here for just two points. First, I would again draw attention to James Keenan's landmark study of the function of the PDE, in which he contrasts two styles of moral reasoning: the 'geometrical' method of justification by appeal to principles such as the PDE which are 'extrinsic' to individual cases, and the 'taxonomic' method of prudential justification (or casuistry) which seeks to shed light on the inherent moral rightness of a kind of action by considering its congruency of rationale with like cases.[36] Keenan argues that it is a mistake to think the PDE functions as a justification, let alone as the only form of justification when causing harm, and his study should dissuade us from thinking that the only way in which harmful effects can be justified is by forcing them to fit within a double effect framework.

Secondly, I note that, once again, what is at stake is the correct identification of the agent's moral object. The manualists who developed the PDE used physicalist descriptions of human actions and so found ways of identifying "the action in itself" as good or morally neutral. But once we retrieve Thomas's understanding of action as intentional, the first condition of the PDE must be taken to refer to properly moral actions: one's action in itself must be morally upright. The PDE is relevant on those occasions in which one's upright action has a side-effect which is no part of the agent's intended course of action. The paradigm cases for PDE are those in which one is doing something one would or could rightly be doing anyway, such that the bad side-effects are merely permitted: e.g. when excising a cancerous uterus or a haemorrhaging fallopian tube, one does what one would need to do irrespective of whether a woman is pregnant. So the PDE holds that when, in the course of acting rightly, one foresees bad side-effects, these need to be acknowledged and a judgment made about whether one has a proportionate reason to continue with one's upright action. When a pregnant woman is diagnosed with cancer of the uterus, PDE reasoning helps us determine whether and when it would be right to remove her uterus, given the foreseen effect of surgery on the life of the fetus.

But is PDE-reasoning the key to the prior question of whether hysterectomy is an appropriate treatment for a woman with cancer of the uterus? I believe not – because what is at stake here is a judgment about the most effective way of

[34] Keenan, 'The Function of the Principle of Double Effect', p. 309.
[35] Keenan, 'The Function of the Principle of Double Effect', p. 314.
[36] Keenan, 'The Function of the Principle of Double Effect', 54 (1993) *Theological Studies*, pp. 294–315.

treating an illness in view of the good of the whole person. To be sure, the intervention will have good and bad effects which need to be considered, but one's "act in itself" is neither "morally indifferent" nor can it be characterised in isolation from those good and bad effects. It is a "direct" response to a threatening illness, and the "means" one has to employ involve an evil (e.g. hysterectomy) which is "not arbitrarily chosen, but . . . dictated by the evil that one is resisting"?[37] There is no need to re-configure one's intervention in terms of double effect in order to determine that it is morally upright.

It is at this point that the correct characterisation of practical reasoning becomes crucial. As noted above, Grisez does this in terms of one's attitude towards good end-states, rather than in terms of the concrete actions one performs.[38] This enables him to re-configure some cases in which an action causing evil seems to be directly intended as cases in which the evil caused is only indirectly intended. But given the doubts about whether Grisez's account of direct and indirect intention stands up, and given that at times his account seems to require a tendentious re-description of what one is actually doing, I believe we have an incentive to explore an alternative account which acknowledges that in some circumstances one may have to cause evil when defending goods from attack.

If we are to eschew the re-description of actions, we need to find a way of explaining what occurs when an action that would normally be the embodiment of a wrong intention becomes the realisation of an upright intention. I suggest that in circumstances of "defensive action", we think of a moral action which is generically (and normally) bad, having its moral species altered to become specifically good.[39] Paradigm cases of this transformation of a generically bad kind of action to a specifically good kind of action include interventions usually justified in terms of totality and live organ donation.[40] I am proposing that, in those cases in which treatment of an ectopic pregnancy has its sole meaning as a defence against life-threatening pathology, it is more closely analogous to cases of direct intervention (e.g treatment of cancer) than it is to cases of double effect.

I am thus contrasting two kinds of evil effects: those which are truly 'outside' one's moral object and course of action, and those which are inevitably a part of

---

[37] William Daniel, 'Double Effect and Resisting Evil', 56 (1979) *The Australasian Catholic Record*, p. 382.

[38] See Grisez, *The Way of the Lord Jesus*, Vol. II, p. 542, footnote 143. For the contrast between choice of end-states and actions, see Jensen, 'A Defense of Physicalism', p. 399.

[39] See Brian Byron, 'The Catholic Tradition of Intrinsic Morality', in 29 (1995) *Compass Theology Review*, pp. 41–45. Byron notes one manualist in support of this terminology: Aertnys-C. Damen CSSR, *Theologia moralis, Secundum doctrinam S. Alfonsi De Liguorio Doctoris Ecclesiae*, Editio XVII (J. Visser CSSR) Turin: Marietti 1956.

[40] St Thomas held that the species of generically bad actions could be altered by the command of God. As Patrick Lee argues, this did not involve God authorising an intrinsically evil action. In terms of the account I am suggesting, the moral species of the action is altered such that an external action (e.g. Abraham killing Isaac) becomes the realisation of an upright moral object (viz. obedience to God). See Patrick Lee, 'Permanence of the Ten Commandments: St Thomas and his modern commentators', 42 (1981) *Theological Studies*, pp. 422–443.

one's moral object and course of action. PDE-reasoning is appropriate with respect to the former (e.g. the death of the fetus following life-saving hysterectomy), but it is not appropriate with respect to the latter (e.g. to life-saving hysterectomy in itself). PDE-reasoning does not exhibit the agent's moral rationale for life-saving surgery, or for self-defence, or for 'defensive' situations more generally, where the agent's moral object is ordered precisely by the intention to combat evil. In these defensive situations one would not be acting at all but for the presence of the evil 'threat' and, typically, the bad effects one foresees are part and parcel of one's defensive action (e.g. defending myself by the use of force which harms my assailant; excising healthy tissue to prevent the spread of cancer, and so on). In these cases, the good and bad effects of one's action are often such closely linked results of one's action that it is implausible to speak merely of 'permitting' the evil effects one causes.

With respect to the agent's moral object, what is crucial to the justification of defensive actions which involve causing harm is whether the agent's purpose and object are rightly ordered. Assuming one's immediate purpose really is good, how is the rightness of the actions one chooses as a means to be determined? How can I determine that I am not, albeit in response to evil, myself "doing evil that good may come"? Sometimes there is an option available which is clearly upright or morally neutral (e.g. I might simply be free to avoid visiting a place where the risk of infection was high). But in other cases, "evil is already at work" and one's "freedom of choice is restricted. [One] can act or not act. But if [one] does act there is likely to be only one course open."[41]

I recognise the force of the objection that, even when the range of options is restricted, the only way of ensuring that one's response to evil does not involve doing evil will be to ensure that one is not intending evil as an end or a means. But this returns us to the problematic issue at the heart of this whole discussion, as to what it is to intend evil in the morally objectionable sense. I am recommending that we recognise that not all cases in which one causes harm in the course of doing good should be assimilated to the kind of intention involved in the PDE. The PDE rationale is not the key to questions of legitimate material cooperation,[42] nor to those 'defensive actions' in which consideration of both the evil to be repelled and the harm one causes in repelling it, enter essentially into the formation of the agent's moral object in itself. In these cases, we require another way of understanding the causation of evil in the pursuit of an upright moral object in response to threatening evil. The key to this understanding is prudence and right reasoning as to the moral meaning and object which ought be ascribed to one's action, despite its causation of evil.

If this defensive model is applied to the case of the ectopic pregnancy, the reasoning might run as follows: We should not think of the embryo as an aggressor, for the embryo is as much a victim of the pathological situation as is

[41] Daniel, 'Double Effect', p. 383.
[42] James F. Keenan and Thomas R. Kopfenstelner, 'The Principle of Cooperation', 76/4 (1995) *Health Progress*, pp. 23–27, at 26.

the mother. The threat ultimately derives from the pathological condition of the mother's fallopian tube. The end is to protect a mother from the grave threat to her life and reproductive health posed by the fact that the embryo has implanted where it has. Prudential judgment about the necessary and appropriate means to this end determines what needs to be done, viz. to halt the destructive process of implantation in the least invasive way. In cases where nothing can be done to help the embryo to survive, the only way in which harm can be minimised is with respect to the mother. Whether the intervention should be surgical or chemical depends on a clinical judgment as to effectiveness and side-effects. The foreseen death of the embryo is not part of what is being sought, it is outside the agent's intention and does not render the action one of intentional killing.

Like St Thomas, this approach emphasises first, the agent's intended end, and then the necessity and appropriateness of the means chosen to realise that end. In using MTX or salpingostomy to resolve an ectopic pregnancy, it need not be the case that one intends to kill the embryo: that is to say, one's intervention does not arise from an intention to kill, and what one chooses to do is not chosen because it is lethal to the embryo. It is chosen in circumstances in which there is a necessity to act, and on the assumption that the intervention is, from the clinical evidence, a more effective and less harmful option than the alternatives. This is not strictly speaking an act of self-defence against the embryo, but it is a defensive act in which the evil results of the defensive measures one needs to take are intentionally accepted. William Daniel suggests that the traditional distinction between 'directly' and 'indirectly' bringing about evil may correspond to the difference between the 'exploitative' and the 'defensive' use of evil means. The 'direct' intending of evil would imply the attacking of a value, the 'indirect' occasioning of evil would arise when the agent is resisting a disvalue.[43]

\*       \*       \*

My argument for the use of MTX in treating some ectopic pregnancies is tentative, since I agree that the more obvious interpretation of this treatment is that it involves the choice to directly harm the embryo. Nonetheless, I have drawn attention to three topics of continuing debate in Catholic moral theology which raise doubts about whether this judgment applies to every use of MTX. On the account proposed here, the crucial issue for moral judgment is whether circumstances are such as to require the embryo to be given a chance to develop further. The use of MTX at a time when one should still be trying to save the embryo would indeed constitute an unjustified, pre-emptive intervention. It is less clear, however, that the use of MTX in circumstances in which the embryo cannot be saved should be regarded morally as a direct killing. In these circumstances, the agent's moral object would be governed by considerations of effectiveness and side-effects in meeting a grave, life-threatening pathology, rather than by the physical effect of MTX on the doomed embryo.

[43] Daniel, 'Double Effect', p. 387.

# Contributors

JORGE V ARREGUI obtained his first degree in philosophy at the University of Navarre in 1980, for which he wrote a dissertation on "Practical Reason in Aquinas". He subsequently obtained a PhD from the same university for a thesis on "Meaning and action in Wittgenstein's thought". He was awarded an MPhil degree by the University of Glasgow for a dissertation on "Hutcheson's Theory of Taste". He has been Lecturer in Philosophical Anthropology in the University of Navarre and since 1996 Reader in Philosophy at the University of Malaga. His particular interests are in: philosophical anthropology; Wittgenstein's philosophy of mind; and hermeneutics and aesthetics, in particular British aesthetics of the Enlightenment period. He has published forty papers in Spanish and international journals of philosophy and the following books: *Accion y sentido en Wittgenstein* (Pamplona 1984); *El horror de morir* (Barcelona 1991); *Filosofía del hombre* (Madrid 1991); and *Inventar la sexualidad* (Madrid 1996). He is the translator into Spanish of works by the Earl of Shaftesbury, Hutcheson, Thomas Reid and Professor Peter Geach.

MICHAEL BANNER studied law and then philosophy and theology at Balliol College, Oxford. He wrote a doctorate, which was subsequently published, on *The Justification of Science and the Rationality of Religious Belief* (Oxford University Press 1990). He was Bampton Research Fellow at St Peter's College, Oxford, 1985–88, during which time he was ordained deacon and priest in the Church of England. In 1988 he became Dean and Director of Studies in Philosophy and Theology at Peterhouse, Cambridge. He moved to King's College, London, in 1994 to take up the F D Maurice Chair of Moral and Social Theology. He was Chairman of a Government enquiry into the ethics of emerging technologies in the breeding of farm animals and is currently a member of the Royal Commission on Environmental Pollution. He is also a member of the Church of England's Doctrine Commission and of its Board for Social Responsibility. He has written on the nature of Christian ethics and on its relevance to a number of contemporary issues; some of his papers on these topics are collected in a forthcoming volume *Christian Ethics and Contemporary Moral Problems* (Cambridge University Press).

JOSEPH M BOYLE is Professor of Philosophy and Principal of St Michael's College, University of Toronto. He is also a member of the University's Center for Bioethics. He obtained his doctorate at Georgetown University. He is a past president of the American Catholic Philosophical Association. He is the co-author of four books:

*Free Choice: A Self-Referential Argument* (with Germain Grisez and Olaf Tollefsen) 1976; *Life and Death with Liberty and Justice* (with Germain Grisez) 1979; *Catholic Sexual Ethics: A Summary, Explanation and Defense* (with Ronald Lawler OFMCap and William E May) 1985; 2nd edition 1996; and *Nuclear Deterrence, Morality and Realism* (with John Finnis and Germain Grisez) 1987. He has published numerous articles on moral theory, natural law, free choice and intention, bioethics and international ethics. He is co-editor of the journal *Christian Bioethics*.

CARDINAL CAHAL B DALY is Archbishop Emeritus of the Metropolitan See of Armagh and Primate Emeritus of All Ireland. He was ordained a priest in 1941, and after postgraduate studies in both theology and philosophy, he taught Scholastic Philosophy at Queen's University, Belfast, for 21 years, as a Lecturer (1946–63) and a Reader (1963–67). He was ordained Bishop of Ardagh and Clonmacnois in July 1967, and was transferred to the See of Down and Connor in 1982. He became Archbishop of Armagh and Primate of All Ireland on 6 November 1990, retiring on his 79th birthday on 1 October 1996. He was created a Cardinal by Pope John Paul II on 28 June 1991. Cardinal Daly has been a leading figure in the Church both nationally and internationally, and has played an important role in the search for peace in Ireland. Among his many publications are: *Morals, Law and Life* (1962); *Natural Law Morality Today* (1965); *Morals and Law* (1993); *Tertullian the Puritan and his Influence* (1993); and *Moral Philosophy in Britain from Bradley to Wittgenstein* (1996).

JOHN FINNIS has been a Fellow of University College, Oxford since 1966, and has been Professor of Law and Legal Philosophy in the University of Oxford since 1989. He has also been Biolchini Professor of Law at the University of Notre Dame since 1995, where he teaches in the first semester. He is a Fellow of the British Academy and a barrister of Grays Inn. He was one of the first two lay members of the International Theological Commission (1986–91) and was a consultor to the Pontifical Commission 'Iustitia et Pax' (1977–89) and subsequently a member of the Commission (1990–95). He was Governor of Plater College (1972–92), and is a Governor of The Linacre Centre, having been Vice-Chairman of its Board during the period 1986–96. Among his contributions to jurisprudence, moral philosophy, political theory and moral theology are: *Natural Law and Natural Rights* (Oxford 1980), *Fundamentals of Ethics* (Oxford 1983), *Nuclear Deterrence, Morality and Realism* (with Joseph Boyle and Germain Grisez; Oxford 1987), *Moral Absolutes* (Catholic University of America Press 1991), and *Aquinas: Moral, Political and Legal Theory* (Oxford 1998).

FR ANTHONY FISHER OP lectures in ethics and moral theology in the Australian Catholic University, Melbourne, and is Episcopal Vicar for Health Care in the Archdiocese of Melbourne. He is a Research Associate of the Plunkett Centre for Ethics in Health Care, Sydney, and a member of several Catholic hospital ethics committees. He is Chaplain to the Parliament of Victoria and a member of the Infertility Treatment Authority (the body which regulates artificial reproductive technology and embryo research in Victoria). He has published books and articles in theology, ethics and healthcare issues, and is currently writing a book on justice in the allocation of healthcare resources based on his Oxford University doctoral thesis. He is a member of the Drafting Group for the forthcoming code of ethical standards for Australian Catholic health and aged care providers.

MARY GEACH studied philosophy and psychology at Somerville College, Oxford, and completed her doctorate (on the topic of the soul) at New Hall, Cambridge in 1981. She has taught philosophy at the College of St Thomas, St Paul, Minnesota, and Morley College, London, ethics at the Institute of Advanced Nursing Studies of the Royal College of Nursing, and Christian Ethics at Westminster College, Oxford. In recent years she has been homeschooling her children. She has published papers on 'Death and dreaming', 'The effects of principles and actions', 'The ethical root of language', and 'Marriage: arguing to a first principle in sexual ethics'.

ROBERT P GEORGE is the Cyrus Hall McCormick Professor of Jurisprudence at Princeton University where he teaches in the areas of philosophy of law, constitutional interpretation and civil liberties. He holds graduate degrees in law and theology from Harvard University, and a doctorate in the philosophy of law from Oxford University. He is the author of *Making Men Moral: Civil Liberties and Public Morality* (Oxford University Press 1993) and *In Defense of Natural Law* (Oxford University Press 1999). His articles and reviews have appeared in *The Harvard Law Review*, *The Yale Law Journal*, *The Columbia Law Review*, *The University of Chicago Law Review*, *The Review of Politics*, *The Review of Metaphysics*, *Law and Philosophy*, and *The American Journal of Jurisprudence*. He is general editor of *New Forum Books*, a Princeton University series of books on law, culture, and politics. He recently completed a six-year term as a presidential appointee to the United States Commission on Civil Rights. He is a former Judicial Fellow at the Supreme Court of the United States, where he received the 1990 Justice Tom C. Clark Award. In 1994 he served as Counsel of Record to Mother Teresa of Calcutta on her brief to the Supreme Court of the United States asking the Court to reverse *Roe v. Wade* and declare "the unalienable rights of the unborn child".

GREGORY YURI GLAZOV was born in Moscow from which his family emigrated to Canada when he was ten. After a first degree in Classics and Biology at Dalhousie University, he went on a Rhodes Scholarship to Oxford University in 1986 where he studied at the Oriental Institute. He obtained an MPhil in 1989 for a thesis entitled *A Classification of Speech Organ Imagery in Biblical and Intertestamental Literature*. In 1993 he was awarded a doctorate for a thesis on *The 'Bridling of the tongue' and the 'Opening of the Mouth' in Biblical Prophecy*. He is Lecturer in Hebrew (Exeter College, Oxford), Tutor in Old Testament Studies (St Benet's Hall, Oxford), and Tutor in Theology (Plater College, Oxford). He has published a number of papers and a revised version of his doctoral dissertation is due for publication in 1999.

FR GERALD GLEESON is a priest of the Archdiocese of Sydney who teaches philosophy and Christian Ethics at the Catholic Institute of Sydney. He is also a Research Associate at the Plunkett Centre for Ethics in Health Care. He is a graduate of the Catholic Institute of Sydney and the University of Cambridge, and he completed his doctoral studies in philosophy at the Catholic University of Leuven (Belgium) in 1989. More recently his research has focused on fundamental philosophical themes in Catholic moral theology, and on the revival of an ethics of practical wisdom. He is the author of the chapter entitled 'Seeking understanding – on the role of philosophy in Catholic theology', in Richard Lennan (ed) *An Introduction to Catholic Theology* (New York: Paulist Press 1998). He has published in *Pacifica*, *The Australasian Catholic Record*, the *Faith and Culture* series, and *The Irish Theological Quarterly*, and in popular magazines and newspapers.

LUKE GORMALLY has been Director of The Linacre Centre for Healthcare Ethics since 1981, having previously been Research Officer at the Centre from its establishment in 1977. He has been a member of The Catholic Bishops' Joint Bioethics Committee since 1984, and was elected a Corresponding Member of the Pontifical Academy for Life in 1996. He was a founder member of both the ecumenical umbrella group HOPE (Healthcare OPposed to Euthanasia) and of the Human Values in Healthcare Forum. Among his recent publications, he has edited and contributed to *The Dependent Elderly: Autonomy, Justice and Quality of Care* (Cambridge University Press 1992), *Euthanasia, Clinical Practice and the Law* (The Linacre Centre 1994), and *Moral Truth and Moral Tradition. Essays in honour of Peter Geach and Elizabeth Anscombe* (Dublin: Four Courts Press 1994).

GERMAIN GRISEZ has been The Reverend Harry J Flynn Professor of Christian Ethics at Mount St Mary's College, Emmitsburg, Maryland, since 1978. He previously taught philosophy at Georgetown University, Washington, DC, and at the University of Regina, Saskatchewan. Since 1978 his major concern has been to reshape Catholic moral theology in the light of the call for its renewal by the Second Vatican Council. To this end he embarked on writing a major 4-volume work under the general title *The Way of the Lord Jesus*. So far three volumes of this work have appeared: *Volume I: Christian Moral Principles* (1983); *Volume II: Living a Christian Life* (1993); *Volume III: Difficult Moral Questions* (1997). Among his many other publications are: *Contraception and the Natural Law* (1965), *Abortion: The Myths, the Realities and the Arguments* (1970), *Beyond the New Morality: the Responsibilities of Freedom* (with Russell Shaw; 1974), *Beyond the New Theism: A Philosophy of Religion* (1975), *Free Choice: A Self-Referential Argument* (with Joseph Boyle and Olaf Tollefsen; 1976), *Life and Death with Liberty and Justice: A Contribution to the Euthanasia Debate* (with Joseph Boyle; 1979), and *Nuclear Deterrence, Morality and Realism* (with John Finnis and Joseph Boyle; 1987).

JOHN HALDANE is Professor of Philosophy and Director of the Centre for Philosophy and Public Affairs in the University of St Andrews. He has published widely across the range of philosophy from metaphysics and the philosophy of mind to ethics, politics and aesthetics. He is co-author with J J C Smart of *Atheism and Theism* in Blackwell's 'Great Debates in Philosophy' Series, and a volume of his papers entitled *Faithful Reason* is due for publication in 1999 (from Routledge). Besides philosophy John Haldane writes on art, education and religion in both academic and journalistic publications. He also appears on radio and television. In 1996–98 he was a member of the Nuffield Council Working Party on Genetics and Mental Disorder.

FR DAVID ALBERT JONES OP is a Dominican Friar, sub-prior of Blackfriars, Oxford, who is reading for a doctorate on the theological meaning of death. He studied for his first degree at Sidney Sussex College, Cambridge, reading Part I Natural Sciences, and Part II Philosophy. He was clothed as a Dominican in 1988 and during subsequent studies obtained a BA and a Master of Studies in Theology from the University of Oxford. He was ordained priest on the Feast of Our Lady of Ransom 1994. From 1996–97 he was Catholic Chaplain to Leicester University and De Montfort University before returning to Oxford to commence doctoral studies. He has had a number of articles and short booklets published: *Can a Catholic believe in evolution?* (1991); 'Do whales have souls?' (1992); 'Nagging doubts about brain death' (1995); and *Christianity: An Introduction to the Catholic Faith* (1999).

CHRISTOPHER KACZOR is assistant professor of philosophy at Loyola Marymount University in Los Angeles. He received his AB from Boston College in 1992, a Master of Medieval Studies from the University of Notre Dame in 1994, and a PhD from the Joint Programme in Philosophy and Medieval Studies at the University of Notre Dame in 1996. He did postdoctoral research as an Alexander von Humbolt Federal Chancellor Fellow at the University of Cologne in 1996–97. He has published articles and reviews in *The Thomist, The Review of Metaphysics, Theological Studies, Studies in Christian Ethics,* and *Christian Bioethics*. He has edited a volume entitled *Proportionalism: For and Against* (Marquette University Press 1999), and is at work on a book about proportionalism.

JOHN KEOWN graduated in Law from the University of Cambridge, after which he obtained a doctorate from the University of Oxford for a thesis subsequently published as *Abortion, Doctors and the Law* (Cambridge University Press 1988). Having been called to the Bar in 1986 (and winning the Council of Legal Education's Ver Heyden Foundation Prize for Advocacy), he was appointed to a Lectureship in Law at the University of Leicester, where he specialised in the law and ethics of medicine. In 1990 he won Cambridge University's Ver Heyden de Lancey Prize in Medico-Legal Studies for a monograph on the legal status of the in vitro embryo. In 1993 he was appointed to a newly created University Lectureship in the Law and Ethics of Medicine in the Faculty of Law at the University of Cambridge and to a Fellowship of Queens' College. A collection of papers he edited on ethical, clinical and legal aspects of euthanasia, *Euthanasia Examined*, was published in 1995 (Cambridge University Press). He has published numerous papers and lectured widely on medico-legal topics. He has also served as a member of the Medical Ethics Committee of the British Medical Association.

FR BARTHOLOMEW KIELY SJ was born in Cork in 1942, and was educated there by the Irish Christian Brothers. In 1959 he entered the Society of Jesus. Early studies included a doctorate in biochemistry at St Louis University, Missouri. He was ordained priest in 1972. He then did further studies in psychology and moral theology at the Gregorian University in Rome. Since 1976 he has taught in the Institute of Psychology (of which he is now Director) at the Gregorian University, preparing young priests and religious for work in formation, and teaching some moral theology. His publications include *Psychology and Moral Theology: lines of convergence* (Gregorian University Press 1987) and 'The Impracticality of Proportionalism', 66 (1985) *Gregorianum* 655–86. He writes occasionaliy for *L'Osservatore Romano* and is a Consultor of the Congregation for the Doctrine of the Faith.

WILLIAM L SAUNDERS is a human rights lawyer in Washington, D.C. He is a graduate of the University of North Carolina and holds a law degree from Harvard University. He is a former Professor of Law at the Columbus School of Law of the Catholic University of America. He also practised law with the firm of Covington and Burling in Washington D.C. and worked for three years at the United States Commission on Civil Rights. He is a member of the Ramsey Colloquium of the Institute of Religion and Public Life in New York. He is currently working with the Family Research Council in Washington D.C. in the effort to expose and eradicate the persecution of Christians and other religious believers in China, Sudan, and elsewhere.

J J SCARISBRICK was educated at John Fisher School, Purley, and Christ's College, Cambridge, where he read History. After completing his PhD thesis, on John Fisher and his episcopal colleagues, he taught in the University of London, in Ghana and the USA, before being appointed Professor of History in the University of Warwick in 1969, a post he held for 25 years. His chief publications are *Henry VIII* (1968) and *The Reformation and the English People* (1984). In 1970 he co-founded LIFE, which has developed a pro-life educational and pregnancy care programme throughout the UK and fostered pro-life work in former Communist countries. In 1994 he helped to set up the LIFE Hospital Trust, which provides pro-life 'Well-Woman' care, especially infertility treatment, and runs the first baby hospice (Zoe's Place) in the world. His wife Nuala is also much involved in all this work. They have two daughters and (so far) seven grandchildren.

ALAN SHEWMON attended Medical School at New York University after first graduating from Harvard College as a music major. Following residencies in pediatrics and neurology, he joined the full-time faculty at UCLA Medical School in 1981, where he continues as Professor of Pediatric Neurology. He has pursued two parallel tracks in his career: clinical EEG/epilepsy and medical ethics. As

Director of the Pediatric Diagnostic Laboratory, he played a key role in innovative approaches to diagnostic evaluation and surgical treatment of epilepsy in young children, for which UCLA has become internationally renowned. He has written numerous articles and chapters on pediatric EEG and epilepsy, is frequently invited to speak at international meetings, and has been awarded various research grants. In tandem with this work he has pursued an intense interest in the mind-brain relationship and related philosophical and ethical issues. In consequence he has acquired an international reputation for his writings on brain death, vegetative state, anencephaly and euthanasia. He was a member of the 1989 Pontifical Academy of Sciences' Working Group on the Determination of Brain Death and its Relationship to Human Death. He is a Corresponding Member of the Pontifical Academy for Life.

BERNADETTE TOBIN is the Foundation Director of the Plunkett Centre for Ethics in Health Care and Senior Lecturer in Philosophy at Australian Catholic University. She has qualification in Philosophy from the University of Melbourne and a doctorate in the Philosophy of Education from the University of Cambridge. She has taught at the University of Melbourne and at Australian Catholic University in both Melbourne and Sydney. In 1990 she was the Inaugural Postdoctoral Research Fellow at Australian Catholic University (New South Wales). From 1991 to 1993 she was an Australian Research Council Postdoctoral Fellow. Her research project was on the development of a virtues-based approach to the ethics of health care. She is a member of the Australian Health Ethics Committee, a principal committee of Australia's National Health and Medical Research Council. She chaired its Transplant Ethics Working Party. She is the author of articles on moral development and moral education and on various aspects of the ethics of health care.

MICHAEL WALDSTEIN is founder-President of the International Theological Institute for Studies on Marriage and the Family at Gaming, Austria, a post he took up in 1996. He taught for the previous eight years at the University of Notre Dame (Indiana), initially as a Visiting Professor of Philosophy and finally as an Associate Professor of New Testament Studies. He has been a Research Fellow at the Catholic Theological Faculty of the University of Tubingen. A native of Salzburg, he studied at Thomas Aquinas College (California), the University of Dallas (doctoral thesis on the philosophical aesthetics of Hans Urs von Balthasar), the Pontifical Biblical Institute, Rome, and Harvard Divinity School (doctoral thesis on 'The Mission of Jesus in John'). Among numerous studies, he is the author of *The Apocryphon of John: A Curious Eddy in the Stream of Hellenistic Judaism,* and has translated works by Johannes Auer, Josef Ratzinger, and Hans Urs von Balthasar.

HELEN WATT is a Research Fellow at The Linacre Centre for Healthcare Ethics, a position she has held since 1992. From 1993 to 1996 she was also Senior Research Associate at Peterhouse, Cambridge. She holds a PhD in Philosophy from the University of Edinburgh for a thesis on 'The Origin of Persons', and an honours degree in Italian from the University of Western Australia. She is the author of *Life and Death in Healthcare Ethics: A Short Introduction* (Routledge, forthcoming). She was a member of the Working Party established by the Catholic Bishops' Joint Bioethics Committee which produced the Report *Genetic Intervention on Human Subjects* and she has published a number of papers on topics in bioethics.

CARDINAL THOMAS J WINNING is Archbishop of Glasgow and President of the Bishops' Conference of Scotland. After studies in philosophy and theology he was ordained to the priesthood in 1948, after which he completed doctoral studies in Canon Law in Rome. He was ordained Auxiliary Bishop of Glasgow in 1971, and was installed as Archbishop in 1974. He was created a Cardinal by Pope John Paul II in 1994. He is a member of the Pontifical Council for Promoting Christian Unity, and a member of the President's Committee of the Pontifical Council for the Family. He has been Chairman of the Catholic Bishops' Joint Bioethics Committee since it was established in 1983.

# Index of Names